JONATHAN BARDON was born in Dublin in 1941 and was educated at the High School Dublin, at Trinity College Dublin, and at Queen's University Belfast. He has lived in Belfast since 1963, teaching history at Orangefield Secondary School and at the College of Business Studies, now the Belfast Institute of Further and Higher Education, where he is a Faculty Adviser. He has scripted various schools broadcasts series, including the much-praised *Modern Irish History* for the BBC and *Understanding Northern Ireland* for UTV/Channel 4. He was chairman of the cross-curricular working groups on Education for Mutual Understanding and Cultural Heritage which reported in 1989, and currently he is chairman of the Community Relations Council.

His other publications include: *The Struggle for Ireland: 400–1450 AD* (1970); *Belfast: An Illustrated History* (1982); *Dublin: One Thousand Years of Wood Quay* (1984); *Belfast: 1000 Years* (1985); *If Ever You Go To Dublin Town: A Historic Guide to the City's Street Names* (with Carol Bardon) (1988); *Investigating Place Names in Ulster: A Teacher's Guide* (1991); and *A History of Ulster* (1992).

D1210224

A
Shorter Illustrated
HISTORY *of*
ULSTER

♦

JONATHAN BARDON

PICTURE RESEARCH BY
GERRY HEALEY

THE
BLACKSTAFF
PRESS

BELFAST

First published in 1996 by
The Blackstaff Press Limited
3 Galway Park, Dundonald, Belfast BT16 0AN, Northern Ireland
with the financial assistance of the
Cultural Traditions Programme
which aims to encourage acceptance and understanding
of cultural diversity.

This book is an abridged, illustrated and updated edition of
A History of Ulster first published in 1992.

Typeset by Techniset Typesetters, Newton-le Willows, Merseyside

Printed in England by Biddles Limited

A CIP catalogue record for this book
is available from the British Library

ISBN 0-85640-586-8

CONTENTS

PREFACE

'I ask you today as I bury my son, both of you to bury your pride.' Speaking to television reporters at St Colman's Cemetery in Lurgan, County Armagh, on Thursday 11 July 1996, Mick McGoldrick made his appeal to a divided Ulster. The previous Monday his son Michael had been found shot dead in his taxi at Aghagallon, the random victim of sectarian assassination. 'Please stop this,' he continued. 'Bury your pride with my boy.'

For five days Northern Ireland had been convulsed by disorder and destruction on a scale not witnessed in the region for more than a decade. The Portadown District Orange Lodge had insisted on its right to march from Drumcree church to the centre of the town by the route it had followed for 189 years, down the Garvaghy Road where the Catholic residents had declared their intention to oppose what they regarded as a triumphalist incursion. Ronnie Flanagan, the RUC deputy chief constable, observed: 'Garvaghy Road is a microcosm of the entire problem in Northern Ireland and it is not easily reconcilable.' So it proved.

When Sir Hugh Annesley, the RUC chief constable, announced his decision on Saturday 6 July that the Orangemen would not be allowed to march down the Garvaghy Road, loyalists all over Northern Ireland vented their anger by burning vehicles, erecting barricades, wrecking shops and confronting the police over the ensuing five days and nights. On 11 July Annesley reversed his decision to ban the procession. Now it was the turn of Catholics to express their outrage and take to the streets. By Monday 15 July the *Independent* was observing:

> It seems scarcely credible that a province which last year had the hope of a bright new future could so swiftly be transformed into a political wasteland, its economic prospects dashed, its image defaced, its communal relations in ruins. Even in Ireland the prospects have rarely seemed bleaker.

When first the Provisional IRA and then the Combined Loyalist Military Command announced their ceasefires in the autumn of 1994 the people of Northern Ireland were too unsure of the future to let themselves go in unrestrained celebration. Optimism grew, however, as Christmas approached. On a Saturday in December I joined a queue for a car park behind St Anne's Cathedral in Belfast. The city was enjoying an unprecedented boom as people from across the province were joined by scores of visitors: tour coaches from Mayo and Galway lined Fisherwick Place and parked vehicles bore registrations from as far away as Waterford and Kerry. Looking up, I saw a buzzard soaring overhead and for the next ten minutes and more I gazed as this creature, wild as the wind, banked over the great flat roof of Castle Court, glided towards the river and wheeled south to Donegall Square, quartering the city for prey. For the first time in twenty-five years helicopters were not hovering over Belfast and so this great bird was free to make the city its hunting ground.

The republican ceasefire lasted only for seventeen months, however, and the disturbances of the summer of 1996 would seem to encourage the gloomiest prognostications; on the other hand, the rapturous reception given to the American president, Bill Clinton, in November 1995 – when the people of Northern Ireland celebrated the ceasefires without reservation – demonstrated what might have been and still could be. Taken as a whole, the history of Ulster has been no more violent than that of most of the rest of Europe but for almost four centuries the province has been characterised by a deeply divided society. The origins of those divisions can be traced back to the turbulent events of the sixteenth and seventeenth centuries and perhaps even further back to the arrival of the first human beings in Ireland nine thousand years ago.

JONATHAN BARDON
AUGUST 1996
BELFAST

I

EARLY ULSTER

C. 7000 BC–AD 800

In 1888 Irish archaeologists learned that worked flints dating back to the middle Stone Age had been found in a field behind Mount Sandel, an imposing Gaelic fort later strengthened by the Normans. Here, on a high bluff overlooking the lower Bann just south of Coleraine, over a hundred flint axe heads were collected in the years that followed but as more than two dozen other Mesolithic sites had been located, Mount Sandel was not thought to have any special significance. Then more flint tools were ploughed to the surface in 1972 when land was being prepared for a new housing estate. The following year Peter Woodman and his team of archaeologists began what seemed a routine investigation only to discover – after the carbon-14 dating of charred hazelnut shells – that human beings had dwelt here between 7000 and 6500 BC. The generally accepted date of the arrival of people in Ireland had been put back by more than a thousand years.

Humans had been living in Australia for some forty thousand years before the very first people set foot in Ireland. Arctic conditions made the Irish landscape too inhospitable until around nine thousand years ago: twenty-five million years ago temperatures across the world began to fall; polar caps formed twelve million years later; and from then on glaciers and ice sheets waxed and waned while the northern hemisphere experienced a succession of periods of intense cold. Fifteen thousand years ago, when eastern Ulster lay under ice ninety feet thick, a long melt began.

The last great ice sheet tore and pulverised rock from the mountains of Ulster as it advanced south, and then as it retreated it dumped this rubble as huge mounds of boulder clay in serried ranks in their tens of thousands. The geographer and prehistorian E. Estyn Evans has likened these to 'a necklace of beads some thirty miles wide suspended between Donegal Bay and Strangford Lough'. These low, rounded hills, known as drumlins, formed a frontier which did much to shape the future history of Ulster. In the lowlands drumlins blocked surface drainage routes and became surrounded by soft-margined loughs and treacherous fens: densely overgrown with wolf-infested thickets and separated by standing water, these later created a division between the

Opposite:
Legananny portal tomb, County Down
LITTLE, BROWN AND COMPANY

Flint scales were probably
set in to wood to make a
fish spear
HMSO (DOE, NI)

northern province and the rest of Ireland. This barrier should not be overemphasised for it was never completely impenetrable; nevertheless, until the seventeenth century, easy access to Ulster from the south was only by the fords of Erne in the west and the Moyry Pass in the east – the gap that is the defile in the hills south of Slieve Gullion.

All the ice had disappeared by 11,000 BC and, as plants and animals once more invaded Ireland, bands of people began to migrate north from the Mediterranean region. Then a final and severe thousand-year cold snap, between 10,000 BC and 9000 BC, denuded the land of all but the hardiest plants such as mountain avens and purple saxifrage, which today hold out on the quartzite peak of Slieve League in County Donegal. Silt from this period from Drumurcher in County Monaghan has remains of beetles and arctic poppies, today strictly circumpolar in distribution. As the climate warmed thereafter, melting ice raised the sea level, but the land, relieved of its burden of ice, was rising even faster for a time. Land bridges connected Britain to the European mainland and Ireland to Britain. Archaeologists have yet to agree whether or not those glacial connections to Ireland had been swept away by the tides before human beings had reached Ireland. Even if the land bridges had been severed by 7000 BC, it was possible to travel by dry land far out west from Cumbria and beyond the Isle of Man before having to take to water and it was almost certainly from there that the first inhabitants of Mount Sandel came.

ULSTER IN THE STONE AND BRONZE AGE

For five seasons the site at Mount Sandel was meticulously excavated and its contents sieved, sifted and chemically analysed by specialists. Their findings cast a unique shaft of light back over nine millenniums on life in a Mesolithic camp in Ulster.

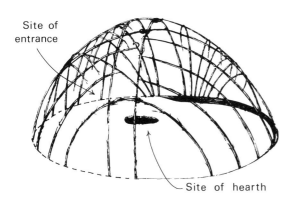

Site of
entrance

Site of hearth

Hypothetical
reconstruction of hut
framework during
construction
HMSO (DOE, NI)

The slope of post holes showed that saplings had been driven into the ground in a rough circle and bent over to form a domed roof by being lashed together. Lighter branches may have been interwoven to add strength and rigidity; then each hut – there were four built at different times – was covered with bark or deer hide, and reinforced against north winds with grass turfs lifted from inside. Around seven yards wide, each hut gave shelter to perhaps a dozen people gathered round a bowl-shaped hearth in the centre. Charred fragments showed that this camp was perfectly sited to provide a living all year round.

As the sea level was around fifteen feet lower than it is today, the falls and rapids by Mount Sandel must then have made a majestic sight; below them, in early summer, salmon waited in thousands for a flood to take them upstream to spawn, and sea bass foraged at high tide in pursuit of crab, flounder and smolt. Scale-shaped flints found in abundance almost certainly had been set into poles to harpoon these fish, together with myriads of eels dropping down from Lough Neagh in autumn. Autumn, too, was the season for gathering hazelnuts and these were supplemented by crab apples, goosegrass, vetches and seeds of water lilies – these last, prized by Elizabethans for cooling the passions, resemble popcorn when dropped into hot fat. In midwinter wild pigs, fattened on the abundant hazel mast, began their rutting, and male yearlings, driven out by mature boars, were vulnerable then to hunting parties armed with flint-tipped spears and arrows. This, too, was the time for trapping birds in the forest and overwintering wild fowl; the archaeologists found bone fragments of eagle, goshawk, capercaillie, red-throated diver, widgeon, teal and some song birds.

Flint had to be carried from as far away as the beaches of Portrush in County Antrim and was made to give service for as long as possible. At a tool-working area to the west of the hollow, flint cores were roughed out and fashioned into axes, picks and adzes, while the smaller blades struck from them were shaped into knives, arrowheads, hide scrapers, awls and harpoon flakes. One axe had traces of red ochre on its surface, which gives a hint that these people painted themselves on ceremonial occasions.

From about 6500 BC the rains became more persistent, the temperature range narrowed, and, at Mount Sandel, oak, alder and elm began to tower over the hazel. Pine woods survived only on the uplands and, thus deprived of its habitat, the capercaillie became extinct in Ireland around 4000 BC. While investigating a site at Ballynagilly, near Cookstown, County Tyrone, in 1969, Arthur ap Simon noticed a fall in pollen from broad-leaved trees beginning around 3500 BC. Pollen is remarkably resistant to decay and is therefore invaluable in helping to explain the distant past. Alan Smith followed with a meticulous study of a bog at Fallahogy in County Londonderry by combining pollen counts with radiocarbon datings; in particular, he traced a sudden drop in elm tree pollen from about 3200 BC and a rise in traces of plantain, dock and nettle. In short, he was uncovering irrefutable evidence of the dramatic impact of pioneering farmers on Ulster's landscape.

Some time during the first half of the fourth millennium BC intrepid family groups began to venture across the North Channel to Ulster with their domestic stock. A thirty-foot currach can take a couple of cows with their calves or, alternatively, half a dozen pigs or sheep – the perils of crossing the sea in frail craft with frightened and thirsty horned beasts, even when firmly trussed, can be imagined. If anything, the journey would have been longer than today, for investigations at Ringneill Quay at Strangford Lough (where the

Flint axe heads from Mount Sandel
HMSO (DEPARTMENT OF THE ENVIRONMENT, NORTHERN IRELAND)

earliest cattle, sheep and pig bones have been found in Ireland) show that the sea was then four yards higher than at present. On landing, the most urgent task was to find a stand of elm, the most reliable guide to good soil; as the men spread out through the wood girdling the trees with their stone axes, the women and children put up shelters and gathered leaves, twigs and fodder to carry the cattle through the first critical winter.

When the clearings lost their fertility, the farmers simply moved on to create new pastures. Flint was still highly prized but it shattered easily against tree trunks; much preferred for axes was porcellanite, formed sixty million years earlier when hot Antrim lavas poured over clays to bake and compress them into this hard china-like stone. Specialist factories emerged on Rathlin Island and at Tievebulliagh, County Antrim; the final polishing was painstakingly completed with sand and water on the seashore, notably at Whitepark Bay, and from there the axe heads were traded as far away as Dorset and Inverness.

It was at Ballynagilly that the oldest known Neolithic house in either Ireland or Britain was found. This rectangular dwelling, six and a half yards by seven yards, was made with radially split oak placed upright in trench foundations. Substantial posts evidently marked the position of thatched roof supports. Similar houses from the same period (about 3200 BC) have been found in central Europe, illustrating the steady movement of peoples westward, bringing with them knowledge of innovations such as cereal cultivation. Some corn was grown in Ulster, usually on light soils capable of being worked with a stone-headed mattock. Cattle predominated, however, as they do today. Protecting domestic stock from the predations of bear, wolf, lynx and fox was an unending task; animals brought into a stockade every night supplied manure for spreading on corn cultivation ridges. These Neolithic peoples made their own pottery and a distinctive Ulster pot shape emerged. At Goodland in County Antrim shards of at least 266 pots were found, thought to be offerings to spirits or gods.

Court cairns, the earliest megalithic monuments, were probably temples of a kind, where farming communities paid respect to departed ancestors and invoked magical help to ensure good harvests. It is likely that the dead were buried or burned elsewhere and their bones, together with other offerings, taken to the cairns at a later

Porcellanite axe heads from Tievebulliagh and Rathlin were exported widely.
MICHAEL GLEESON

Reconstruction of a house at Ballynagilly, County Tyrone
STEPHEN CONLIN

time. A court cairn at Audleystown in County Down contained the bones of thirty-four people in its two chambers. Portal tombs, or dolmens, were burial places and are the most splendid and striking reminders of Ulster's first farmers. Built of three or more great upright stones, with a huge capstone, the portal tomb is largely confined to the north.

Kilclooney portal tomb, County Donegal
PETER HARBISON

The drumlin belt seems to have cut the north off from the more sophisticated settlements in the Boyne valley, where immense and complex tumuli still remain as awesome monuments to Neolithic skill and organisation. It was on the edge of the great Newgrange tumulus by the River Boyne that hearths were found showing evidence of intense heat; dated around 2100 BC, the site gives one of the earliest signals that the skill of metalworking had arrived in Ireland.

Around 2000 BC Egypt's second golden age of the Middle Kingdom flourished, the Sumerians were building the great Ur ziggurat, the Chinese were cultivating tea, the Hittites were invading Anatolia, the Mycenaeans were moving into Greece, and the Minoan sea empire was approaching its zenith. Knossos in Crete had a population of some one hundred thousand, about the same as that for all Ireland. Technological advances, religious cults and artistic styles from these cradles of civilisation spread northwards and westwards. Steady immigration did not necessarily mean overwhelming invasions, however. A bronze axe head found at Culfeightrin, near Ballycastle in County

Axe head from
Culfeightrin, County
Antrim, fitting into a mould
found at Ballynahinch,
County Down
ULSTER MUSEUM

Right: Gold sun disc from
Tedavnet, County
Monaghan
NATIONAL MUSEUM OF
IRELAND

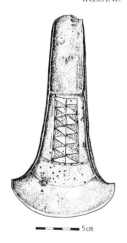

5 cm

Bronze axe head
from Rosslea,
County Fermanagh
JOURNAL OF THE ROYAL
SOCIETY OF ANTIQUARIES
OF IRELAND

Antrim, fits perfectly in a stone mould discovered at Ballynahinch, County Down, showing how the skills of metalworking could be taken quickly across the country by wandering craftsmen. The heavy weight of Irish axes indicates great abundance of copper, and enough tin – and sometimes arsenic and lead – could be found locally to mix with copper to make it into a stronger and more malleable bronze.

Wedge-shaped graves, round-bottomed pottery beakers, V-perforated buttons, and archers' wrist guards are all tell-tale characteristics of Bronze Age sites, but most evocative of a bygone culture shining across the centuries are the rich finds of gold. Amongst the earliest, made from thin hammered sheets of gold, are sun discs, such as the one discovered at Tedavnet in County Monaghan, and lanulae, half-moon-shaped neck ornaments with decoration similar to that found on ceremonial bronze axes unearthed at Scrabo in County Down and Ros-

slea in County Fermanagh. Later objects are so heavy they must have been used as a form of currency. It is likely that many of the beautiful and valuable ornaments found later were cast into the waters as offerings to spirits – religion had a central role in the lives of Ulster's prehistoric peoples.

On the southern slopes of the Sperrins an intriguing group of megalithic monuments was revealed when peat was carefully removed by archaeologists from 1945 onward. This elaborate complex of paired stone circles and alignments at Beaghmore, near Cookstown, seems to have been a ceremonial site where perhaps the aid of the gods was invoked to maintain fertility. Several of the stone circles appear to have been placed as pointers to the horizons which saw the rising and setting of the sun, the moon and major stars. Another place of ritual was the Giant's Ring near Belfast; we have only the barest hints of the ancient ceremonies performed in such places.

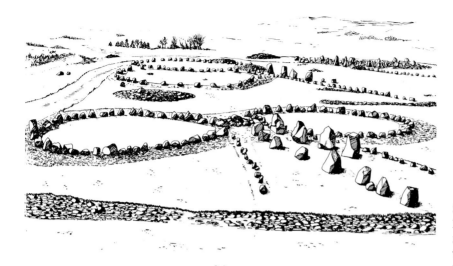

Stone circles and alignments,
Beaghmore, County Tyrone
HMSO (DEPARTMENT OF
THE ENVIRONMENT,
NORTHERN IRELAND)

Hill forts scattered across Ulster indicate an intensification of warfare during the late Bronze Age of the last millennium BC. Weapons became more sophisticated in their making, including socketed spear heads and axes cast from twin-valved moulds. At the same time an improvement in climate, which increased prosperity, helped to stimulate a remarkable flowering of artistic achievement in both bronze and gold. These include curling bronze horns, decorated bronze cauldrons and a hoard of gold from Broighter, County Londonderry, with a charming model boat, a cup, necklaces, and a torc with

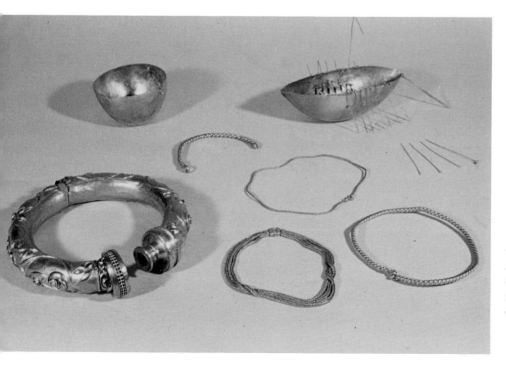

The Broighter hoard
of gold objects,
County Londonderry
NATIONAL MUSEUM
OF IRELAND

elaborate, swirling patterns – made when iron weapons were supplanting those cast from bronze, this neck ornament is a clear indication that the Celts had arrived in Ulster well before the start of the Christian era.

CELTS, ROMANS AND ULAIDH

The Celts were the first people north of the Alps to emerge into recorded history. Their distinctive culture evolved during the second millennium BC between Bohemia and the east bank of the Rhine and then radiated out from there. By 500 BC the Celts dominated northern Europe and, setting out from their hill forts, led by nobles on horseback or in chariots, they sacked Rome in 390 BC and looted the temple of the oracle at Delphi in 278 BC, crossing the Hellespont to settle Anatolia thereafter. The imaginative art of the Celts delighted in symbols and intricate patterns: the high form of this style, known as La Tène after a site in Switzerland, made its first appearance in Ireland in the decoration of scabbards found at Lisnacroghera and Toome in County Antrim.

The Bann disc, now the symbol of the Ulster Museum
ULSTER MUSEUM

Archaeological enquiry does not show evidence of formidable invasion; rather there was a steady infiltration from Britain and the European mainland over the centuries. The first Celtic speakers may have come as early as 1000 BC and in greater numbers from about 500 BC and, equipped with iron weapons and advancing on horseback, they brought the native people under subjugation. A constant blending of language, belief and tradition followed and the Gaelic civilisation which emerged in early Christian times – to survive independently longest in Ulster – evolved not just from the Celts but also from their predecessors to the earliest times.

By 133 BC the Roman conquest of Spain was complete and in 59 BC Julius Caesar began his conquest of Gaul. In 56 BC the Veneti were overwhelmed in Armorica and the Belgae were in retreat. The Celtic hegemony was collapsing before the might of Rome. In AD 82 Gnaeus Julius Agricola, gov-

Solid gold brooch from Loughan, County Londonderry
NATIONAL MUSEUM OF IRELAND

ernor of Britain, summoned his fleet into the Solway Firth to take aboard his waiting cohorts. Ulster was directly across the sea and this land he meant to conquer – a climax to a dazzling career the empire would not forget. Posted to Britain as military tribune twenty-one years before, Agricola had been in the thick of the desperate fighting with the Iceni and Brigantes during

Boudicca's uprising. Placed in command of the XX Legion, he directed the Irish Sea flotilla for a time; perhaps it had been then that the notion that Ireland was worthy of conquest had formed in his mind. Now in the fastnesses of Snowdonia he reduced the Ordovices to abject submission and then, pressing relentlessly northwards into Caledonia, he reached the base of the Highlands, harried the Inner Isles with his fleet and ordered the erection of a network of castella.

The Roman Empire knew little enough about this island of Hibernia on the northwestern edge of its world. It was not until the epic voyage of Pytheas from the Greek colony of Marseilles, who circumnavigated Britain about 300 BC, that Mediterranean traders were given Ireland's correct position; this explorer's account does not survive but it seems to have formed the basis of Ptolemy's map of Ireland prepared in the second century AD. Known only from a fifteenth-century copy, this map includes some identifiable names, such as Logia (the Lagan), Isamnion (Navan Fort) and Volunti (the Ulaidh, the people of Ulster). Even after Julius Caesar invaded Britain in 55 BC, the Greek geographer and historian Strabo was asserting that the Irish 'think it decent to eat up their dead parents', but Tacitus was a more acute observer, and his descriptions of the Britons and continental Celts dovetail remarkably well with early Irish law tracts and heroic tales.

Ptolemy's map of Ireland: a fifteenth-century copy
ROYAL IRISH ACADEMY

For information about the Celts of the British Isles, Tacitus relied on his father-in-law, Agricola; and it is from Tacitus that we learn that the invasion of Ireland was planned with a king in exile:

> Agricola received in friendly fashion an Irish petty king who had been driven out in a civil war, and kept him for use when opportunity offered. I have often heard him say that Ireland could be conquered and held by one legion and a modest force of auxiliary troops . . .

Some scholars have made a tentative suggestion that the Irish king was Tuathail Techtmar, forced to seek aid in Britain to recover his throne. However, Agricola's invasion was not to be: a legion of Germans stationed in Galloway mutinied and there was disturbing news of Pictish rebellion. The Emperor Domitian ordered his governor north, and later, after Agricola's recall, the

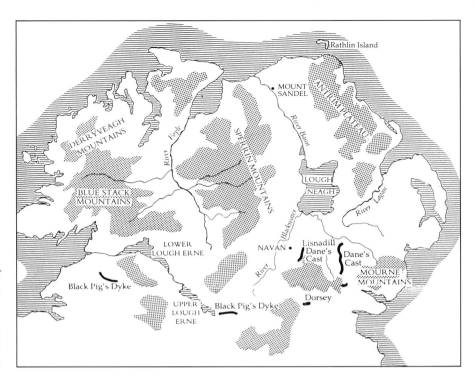

Physical features map of Ulster which includes Mount Sandel, Navan Fort and linear earthworks defending routeways through the drumlin belt

Romans retired behind Hadrian's wall. Ulster would not become part of the Roman Empire after all.

Ulster, too, has its defensive wall. Described on maps as the Dane's Cast, it begins in the east on the Down–Armagh border; the next section, known as the Dorsey, stands at Drummill Bridge in south Armagh; it continues into Monaghan, where it is known as the Black Pig's Dyke; and further short stretches extend through Cavan and Fermanagh to Donegal Bay. A tradition survives that it was ploughed up by the tusks of an enchanted black boar; archaeologists, however, have proved this great linear earthwork to have been a series of massive defences, not continuous, but guarding the routeways into Ulster between the bogs, loughs and drumlins. The Dorsey – from *doirse* meaning doors – is double-banked and double-ditched, being a full nine yards from the top of its largest rampart to the bottom of its parallel ditch. By matching oak tree rings Michael G.L. Baillie from Queen's University Belfast not only demonstrated that the timber for the palisade had been felled in 95 BC but also that the central post of a great ritual structure on Navan Fort had been cut down in the same year.

Reconstruction of the temple at Navan Fort
STEPHEN CONLIN

No one knows why a circular temple, forty-seven yards in diameter, was put up inside Navan Fort. It seems to have been built quickly and then the whole structure had been set on fire. Had this been a ritual to invoke the aid of the gods while Ulster was under attack? A huge circular hilltop enclosure, it is an

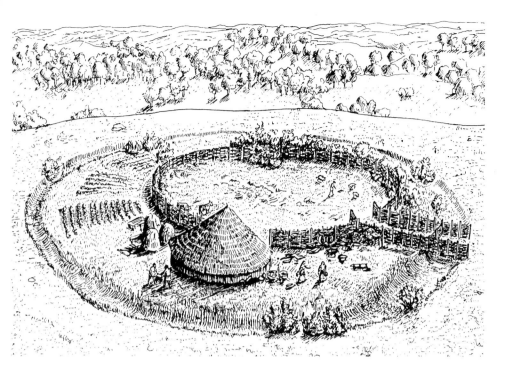

Reconstruction of a
settlement at Navan Fort
STEPHEN CONLIN

Iron Age site of European importance and its ancient name, Emain Macha, has an Indo-European foundation myth parallel to the story of Romulus and Remus. At a fair Crunniuc mac Agnomain boasted that his wife Macha could outrun a chariot. When she protested that she was about to give birth, Conor, King of Ulster, said that she must run. At the end of the race, beside the chariot, she gave birth to twins: Emain Macha means the Twins of Macha. At her delivery she screamed that any man who heard her would suffer the pains of birth for five days and four nights in their times of greatest difficulty.

This story is told in the *Táin Bó Cuailnge*, 'The Cattle Raid of Cooley': it tells how Queen Maeve of Connacht made war on King Conor of Ulster to win possession of the Brown Bull of Cuailnge and how – when the men of Ulster were struck down by their pangs in the time of great difficulty – the champion Cuchulain single-handedly held back the men of Connacht by the ford. The earliest versions of the *Táin* were written down in the monasteries of Bangor in County Down and Dromsnat in County Monaghan in the eighth century: this is the oldest vernacular epic in western European literature and it probably had a long oral existence before being committed to vellum. The *Táin* and other tales of the Ulster Cycle at their best possess arresting power, vividly graphic yet stylised, in which stark reality and magic intertwine and the principal characters are ordinary mortals able on occasion to act like gods. Such characteristics are displayed in an intense form in the sorrowful tale of Deirdre in 'The Exile of the Sons of Uisliu'. In this extract translated by Jeffrey Gantz the beautiful Deirdre, fostered by King Conor's command away from the eyes of other men, finds that as she reaches maturity romantic desire cannot be held back:

The Grianan of Aileach:
the great *dún* of the
Uí Néill dynasty,
Inishowen peninsula,
County Donegal
DEPARTMENT OF ARTS,
CULTURE AND THE
GAELTACHT, IRELAND

One day, in winter, Deirdre's foster-father was outside, in the snow, flaying a weaned calf for her. Deirdre saw a raven drinking the blood on the snow, and she said to Leborcham, 'I could love a man with those three colours: hair like a raven, cheeks like blood and body like snow.'

From these epic tales the historian gets a vivid picture of an aristocratic Iron Age society remarkably similar in many respects to Celtic Gaul described by Julius Caesar. It was a civilisation not touched by Roman conquest (though trading posts may have been established), major features of which survived in Ulster into the seventeenth century.

In the *Táin* the men of Ulster triumph in the end over the men of Connacht but, piecing together evidence from the annals, historians know that the province was on the defensive. The over-kingdom of the Ulaidh once encompassed all of Ireland north of a line extending from the River Drowes in the west to the River Boyne in the east. By the beginning of the eighth century the Ulaidh held sway over little more than the modern counties of Antrim and Down.

In wild country overlooking the marshland that separates the Inishowen peninsula from the rest of Donegal stands the Grianan of Aileach. This imposing circular hill fort, built massively of stone with inset stairways, wall passages and triple earthen bank defences, commands a wide view which includes Lough Foyle and much of mid-Ulster to the south-east and Lough Swilly, Muckish and the Derryveagh Mountains to the west. This for centuries was a principal stronghold of the northern Uí Néill, rulers who traced their descent from Niall of the Nine Hostages, who is usually credited with the conquest of most of Ulster.

The Uí Néill dynasty had emerged from their north Connacht homeland to thrust eastwards into Meath and northwards over the fords of Erne towards Inishowen. Having lost Donegal, the Ulaidh came under further assault: Navan Fort fell and the two sons of Niall of the Nine Hostages set up their own dynasties in the north-west, the Cenél Conaill and the Cenél Eóghain, *cenél* meaning a wide family group embracing all great noble families of royal blood. Most of Donegal became Tír Conaill, 'the land of Conaill', a name it kept until the seventeenth century; the other son gave his name first to Inishowen and then to Tír Eóghain, 'the land of Eóghan', an area of central Ulster conquered in later centuries, part of which is still known today as County Tyrone. The Uí Néill in turn exacted tribute from peoples in southern and central Ulster known as the Airgialla, meaning 'hostage-givers'.

Meanwhile, the Roman Empire, which had been so mighty in Agricola's time, was reeling under the attack of German-speaking peoples from central and northern Europe seeking new corn lands and pastures. Legion after legion was withdrawn from the outposts to defend Rome in the fourth and fifth centuries, leaving Roman Britain a prey to barbarian invaders. From the north came the Picts, from the east, along the Germanic North Sea Coast, came the English, and from the west came the Irish; some sought new kingdoms, some were content with loot – as torn pieces of decorated Roman silver found near Coleraine show – and others brought back slaves. One of these captives was Patrick – he was amongst those who saw to it that, as Roman Britain was falling apart, Roman civilisation most deeply affected Ireland.

'WE BEG YOU, HOLY BOY, TO COME AND WALK AMONG US ONCE AGAIN'

'I, Patrick, a sinner, the simplest of country men . . . was taken away into Ireland in captivity with ever so many thousands of people.' It is with these words of the Confession, later copied into the Book of Armagh, that written Irish history begins. For six years as a slave Patrick tended sheep 'near the western sea'; there in his extreme loneliness his faith was renewed so that 'the spirit seethed in me'. Then he walked two hundred miles to the east coast and, with the company of pirates, returned to his native Britain. There he had a vision in which a man brought him a letter and as he read he seemed to hear the voice of the Irish:

> 'We beg you, holy boy, to come and walk among us once again', and it completely broke my heart and I could read no more.

Resolved to return, he took holy orders and – in a mission clearly co-ordinated by a British Church not yet overwhelmed by the English – he began to preach the gospel to the Irish.

Christianity had already penetrated much of the south of Ireland as a result of regular trading contacts with the empire but Patrick is the only one to have left a written record and the authenticity of his words is still striking after more than one and a half thousand years. Most places traditionally associated with Patrick – Saul, Armagh, Downpatrick, Templepatrick, Lough Derg and Croagh Patrick, for example – are in the northern half of Ireland and it was probably in Ulster that he did most of his work, perhaps around the middle of the fifth century. Patrick's mission was undoubtedly sustained by a vigorously evangelical British Church and the new religion was particularly successful among the ruling class. There are no records of anyone being martyred by the Irish for acceptance of Christianity, which in turn adapted to the old beliefs and traditions that survived for centuries after Patrick's time.

The Tandragee idol, thought to be a representation of the Celtic god Nuadu; found near Newry and now held in Armagh Church of Ireland cathedral
PETER HARBISON

The Gaelic year began at *Samhain*, now Hallowe'en, a time when spirits flew free between the real world and the other world. *Imbolg* marked the start of the lambing season, and the feast of *Bealtaine*, at the start of May, was for the purification of cattle driven ceremonially between two fires. *Lughnasa* celebrated the corn harvest and paid homage to Lugh the Long-Handed, who had slain the evil Balor of the Baleful Eye. The greatest of the gods was Daghda, who had beaten off the monster Formorians when they had invaded Ireland in a magical mist. The Irish believed in the *sídhe*, the Tuatha Dé Danaann, who when conquered became invisible and lived in faery mounds. Their king, Lir, once had his palace at Finaghy in County Antrim and the story of his children – changed into swans by his third wife Aoife – is one of the most poignant in early western European literature. Some gods became Christianised, such as Brigantia who became Saint Brigid; her saint's day falls on *Imbolg*, 1 February. Places once important as ritual sites, such as Armagh, Tory Island and Derry, became significant centres of the Church in Ulster. Particularly favoured as locations for churches and monasteries were sacred oak groves. Derry, in Irish *doire*, means 'oak grove', and it was there that Colmcille founded his great monastery.

It was from Dál Riata, a sub-kingdom of the Ulaidh in the Glens of Antrim, that the Gaelic colonisation of Scotland began towards the end of the fifth century. For more than a hundred years territory on both sides of the North Channel formed one kingdom ruled by a dynasty tracing ancestry back from Fergus Mór mac Erc. By the middle of the sixth century Bruide, King of the Picts, threatened to overwhelm the Ulster interlopers and so Dál Riata turned to the northern Uí Néill for help. The pact was sealed at Druim Ceit at Mullagh near Derry in 575; Aedán mac Gabráin, King of Dál Riata, was able to free himself from the overlordship of the Ulaidh, extend his dominions, and raid islands as far apart as Man and the Orkneys. The man who negotiated this alliance was a Cenél Conaill prince and a renowned churchman, Colmcille.

Colmcille studied under Finnian at Movilla in County Down and at Clonard on the Boyne and returned to build his own monastic settlement at Derry. Just as their pagan ancestors had cast votive offerings into the water to appease the gods, so now Gaelic rulers gave generous grants of land to the Church; the high-born Colmcille could draw on impressive resources. The Dál Riata king granted Colmcille Iona, in Scotland, and for the next two centuries and longer the monastery there was to be the most famous centre of Christian learning in the Celtic world. From here missions were sent to preach to the Angles in Northumbria and to the Picts. At Iona the Annals of Ulster, the most ancient of Irish chronicles, were first compiled, and here some of the most beautiful manuscripts – including, perhaps, the Book of Kells – were executed. The Cathach, or Psalter, of Colmcille is the oldest parchment manuscript to have survived in all of western Europe; it may have been transcribed by Colmcille himself.

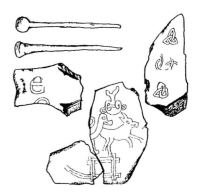

Local kings vied with one another to be patrons of monasteries and their founders became saints revered for centuries to come. Hundreds of monastic sites have been identified in Ulster but as most were built of wood, only traces survive. On Mahee Island in Strangford Lough, Nendrum monastery was surrounded by three concentric stone walls with a rectangular church, a graveyard and a sundial. In Donegal, at Fahan and Carndonagh in particular, finely carved stone cross slabs and pillar stones are decorated with elegant interlacing and bold figures similar to those on White Island on Lough Erne. Under the guidance of a 'senior', the novice learned to read and studied the Scriptures and the writings of the Fathers of the Church. The Psalms had to be memorised and copied onto slates – thirty slate tablets and several styles were found at Nendrum. A large monastery, such as Bangor or Derry, was the

Styles and stone tablets used by novices: Nendrum, County Down
BARBARA FAGAN

The Cathach: the Psalter of Colmcille, the oldest parchment manuscript to have survived in western Europe, thought to have been transcribed by Colmcille himself
ROYAL IRISH ACADEMY

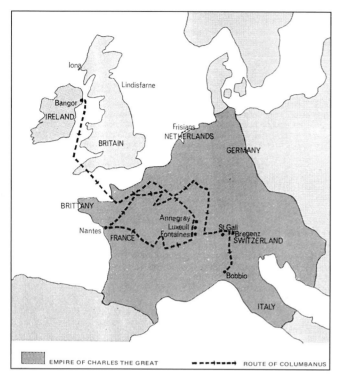

EMPIRE OF CHARLES THE GREAT ▪━▪━▪━▪ ROUTE OF COLUMBANUS

The journeys of
Saint Columbanus and
Saint Gall
BARBARA FAGAN

Saint Columbanus founding
a monastery: from his tomb
in Bobbio, Italy
BARBARA FAGAN

nearest equivalent early Christian Ulster had to a town; in such a community specialised arts, such as metalworking and manuscript illumination, could flourish. The development of a distinctive Irish script can be seen in a liturgical collection known as the Antiphonary of Bangor.

The Antiphonary is to be found not in Ulster but in Milan – evidence that the great Irish mission to the mainland of Europe had begun. Some Irish monks sought voluntary exile in far-off dangerous places and where better to go than the wreckage of the collapsed Roman Empire where Germanic rulers warred with each other? Towards the end of the sixth century monks from Bangor travelled nine hundred miles to the French Vosges Mountains, where their senior, Columbanus, founded three monasteries. Driven out by Theoderic of Burgundy, the Ulstermen struck overland to the Rhine, where they made their way upstream. When they reached Lake Constance they preached to the Germans, who had not heard the gospel before, and founded a monastery at Bregenz, now in the Austrian Vorarlberg. The restless Columbanus wished to press on, but Gall, one of the Bangor monks, stayed to become the local patron saint – a church, a town and a canton in Switzerland are called St Gallen to this day. Columbanus endured the perils of St Gotthard Pass to descend into northern Italy to found a monastery at Bobbio, where his tomb can still be seen.

Many others followed Columbanus and Gall to the European mainland. Later the Emperor Charlemagne delighted in the company of Irish scholars; for example, when there was an eclipse of the sun in 810 the astronomer Dungal of Bangor sent this explanation:

> If the moon comes afterwards, the sun blocks the sight of this heavenly body from human sight, by setting itself across it. In the event of an eclipse, nothing happens to the sun itself, it is simply hidden from our eyes.

Yet the society which produced such scholars was, by the standards of thriving urban centres in Charlemagne's empire, remarkably conservative and underdeveloped.

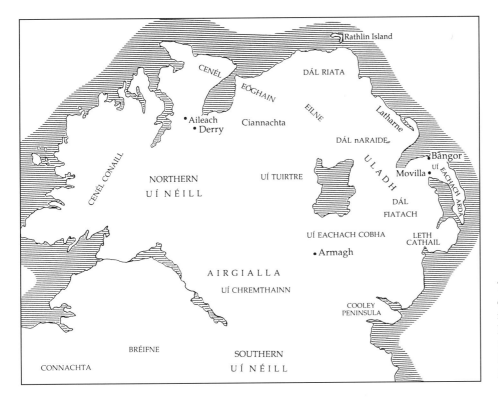

The north of Ireland
c. AD 800, showing
ruling families and the
kingdoms of the Ulaidh
(based on a map in
F.J. Byrne, *Irish Kings and
High-Kings*)

EARLY CHRISTIAN ULSTER SOCIETY

Congal One Eye, over-king of the Ulaidh, forged an alliance with Strathclyde
Britons and the men of Dál Riata in a bid to make himself king of all Ireland.
It was in vain; in 637 he was routed and slain at Moira by Donal mac Áedo,
the Uí Néill king. These events – which lost Dál Riata its control of its Scottish
possessions – are a reminder that no one in this period ever won complete
mastery over the whole island. Indeed the Uí Néill themselves never
conquered all of the province of Ulster.

The title *ard rí*, 'high king', had no political meaning until the eleventh
century; till then provincial- or over-kings held sway. The over-kingship of the
Ulaidh, for example, was drawn from one of their three strongest kingdoms:
Dál Fiatach, Dál nAraide, or Uí Eachach Cobha (which gives its name to
Lough Neagh and the Iveagh baronies). Beneath them in turn were numerous
petty kingdoms, or *tuatha* (a word of ancient origin which is related to the
English 'teutonic' and the German '*Deutsch*'). The Brehon laws stated that
when a king died all members of his *derbhfine* – descendants in the male line
of a common great-grandfather – were eligible for election to succeed him.
Succession disputes were endemic, which future invaders would successfully
exploit. The Gaelic ruling classes were rigidly class conscious and one of the
main functions of the *filí*, the hereditary professional poets, was to recite the
king's genealogy at his inauguration. The nobles distinguished themselves from
grád Fhéne, the commoners, by birth and by the number of their dependants,
or clients. A client such as the *bó-aire*, or farmer, paid rent in food, labour

service and free entertainment. Of the humblest tillers of the soil we know little but it is certain that slaves were integral to Gaelic society. Purchased as children from destitute parents or captured in war, slaves did much of the heavy farming work.

Ulster's landscape is thickly scattered with the remains of thousands of ring-forts, farmsteads surrounded by a circular bank and ditch. In rocky or mountainous areas, where the fort was known as a *caiseal*, the wall was made of stone and no ditch was dug. Where the ramparts were made of soil, the ring-fort was called a *ráth*, a common element in Ulster placenames, such as Rathcoole, 'Cumhal's fort'. The rath's enclosure was the *lios*, again a common prefix in northern placenames, as in Lisnaskea, 'fort of the whitethorns'. The ramparts may have done little more than prevent untended cattle from eating the thatch off houses. Oats, barley, rye and a little wheat were cultivated in small enclosed fields and reaped close to the ear in later summer. Small crops of onions, celery, leeks, carrots, parsnips and some peas and beans were grown in adjacent gardens, and it seems certain that the scale and variety of tillage was greatly extended by the monasteries. Domestic stock was the mainstay of the economy, however; cattle were driven to their summer pastures, known as *buailte*, generally to uplands or dried-out fen, but no hay was saved and the animals had to eke out the winter months on reserved pastures where the grass had withered naturally.

As cows gave no milk in winter, male yearlings were killed in autumn and the making of cheese and butter was vital to ensure a food supply during the short days. Artificial caves or souterrains, often connected to the ring-fort, seem to have been used for storing these *bánbíd*, or white foods, though some with double chambers, such as that running off the Shaneen Park rath on the slopes of the Cave Hill, may have served as a secret refuge in time of attack. Oats were eaten as porridge, and barley, when not eaten as bread, was malted and brewed into ale – wine was imported by the nobility but it was probably ale that inebriated an Airgialla king during a drinking bout in 1158, which led to his murder at the hands of his servant. The bounty of nature made a vital contribution to survival, though the nobility had hunted the wild boar to extinction by the twelfth century. Domesticated pigs fed on oak mast in the woods and good hazelnut crops were regularly recorded in the annals. The sea provided fish, seals, shellfish and duileasc, a seaweed still called dulse in Ulster today; freshwater fishing was jealously regulated; and a stranded whale could provide an unexpected feast – perhaps that is how a very large whale vertebra came to be incorporated in an early Christian pavement in Downpatrick.

A king or a noble, as a member of an élite military caste, usually lived apart from commoners in a ring-fort built for defence known as a *dún*, a word incorporated in many Ulster placenames, such as Dungiven, 'fort of the hide'. The *crannóg*, or lake dwelling, was preferred in some places to the *dún*: usually this was a strategically placed artificial island built up with logs, piles, woven brushwood and stones. The most striking example still to be seen is Lough-na-Cranagh on Fair Head in north Antrim. Monasteries, however, had become the most advanced places of economic activity by the end of the eighth century. The ruling classes made sure that they kept control of the monasteries; higher clergy married and passed on ecclesiastical offices to their children – Clann Sínaich was almost a dynasty which monopolised Church posts for generations at Armagh.

Armagh claimed the leading position in the Church in Ireland at the beginning of the ninth century – a claim laid out in the Book of Armagh which put forward the case that Patrick had made it the ecclesiastical capital. Under the patronage of the Uí Néill, Armagh flourished and became the largest urban centre in Ireland. As great centres of wealth, monasteries were vulnerable to attack and became embroiled in dynastic wars. In 793 Armagh was attacked by the Uí Chremthainn, an Airgialla people of Fermanagh, and in another raid in 996 the Airgialla drove off two thousand cows. Between those dates, however, Armagh had been the target of many more attacks by a new people to appear in Ulster – the Vikings.

White Island figures of churchmen, County Fermanagh, ninth or tenth century HMSO (DEPARTMENT OF THE ENVIRONMENT, NORTHERN IRELAND)

The building of
Noah's Ark from a
fourteenth-century
vellum manuscript
from the kingdom of
Lough Erne
NATIONAL LIBRARY
OF IRELAND

2

VIKING INVASION,
NORMAN CONQUEST
AND GAELIC RECOVERY
800–1485

At first nothing formidable stood in the way of the Northmen. Charlemagne had broken up the fleets of Frisian pirates in the North Sea, leaving the Vikings masters of the North Atlantic, and particularly in Ireland there could be no united opposition to the invaders while the country was split into so many warring kingdoms. Their longships were well suited to brave the hazards of the ocean; built of well-seasoned overlapping oak planks, and bound to the ribs with tough pine roots, their hulls could flex to the swell and, with their shallow draught, negotiate treacherous mud banks such as the Bann bar mouth. Iona, and Lambay Island, off the County Dublin coast, were attacked in 795 and Bangor and Down-patrick were plundered soon afterwards. The first raids were sporadic and not always successful; for the year 811 the Annals of Ulster have this terse entry: 'A slaughter of the heathens by the Ulaid.' Then in the next decade a sustained assault got under way. Bangor was pillaged in 823 and again the following year, as the author of *Cogadh Gaedhel re Gallaibh*, 'Wars of the Irish with the Foreigners', records:

> And they plundered Bangor of Ulad, and brake the shrine of Comgall, and killed its bishop, and its doctors and its clergy: they devastated, also, Movilla.

Ulster bore the brunt of this campaign as the Northmen moved from the coastal monasteries inland up the rivers, carrying their longships overland past rapids and falls to set up raiding fleets on Lough Erne and Lough Neagh. Their success is logged in the Annals of Ulster:

> 832: The first plundering of Armagh by the heathens three times in one month . . . 837: The churches of all Lough Erne, including Clones and Devenish, were destroyed by the heathens . . . 839: A raiding party of the foreigners were on

A longship from the town seal of Bergen, *c.* 1300
HISTORISK MUSEUM
UNIVERSITETET I BERGEN

Lough Neagh, and from there they plundered the states and churches of the north of Ireland . . .

Then, the *Cogadh* relates, 'there came great sea-cast floods of foreigners into Erinn' and Vikings overwintering on Lough Neagh were joined in 849 by 'seven score ships of adherents'. At this point, when all Ulster seemed about to be overwhelmed, the Vikings were checked; Danes made their first appearance only to fall foul of the Norse, who, with the help of the Ulaidh, routed them in a sea battle fought in Carlingford Lough. Then in 866 Áed Finnliath, King of the northern Uí Néill, cleared the Vikings from the province and defeated them on Lough Foyle, taking a prize of 'twelve score heads'.

The Northmen did not reappear in force in Ulster for many years to come and it was further south that they built their seaport towns. Only Larne in County Antrim seems to have any real permanence as a settlement and was still known as Ulfrek's fjord when the Normans arrived. There are very few placenames of Norse origin in Ulster – they are: Strangford, 'strong inlet'; the Skerries, referring to the shoals off Portrush; Carlingford, 'hag's fjord'; Olderfleet, a corruption of 'Ulfrek's fjord'; and when the Normans later conquered much of Antrim and Down they called the territory 'Ulster' from the Viking Uladztír, an adaptation of the Irish *tír* (land) and *Ulaidh*.

Viking warrior
BARBARA FAGAN

From about 860 the Annals of Ulster no longer refer to the Northmen as heathens, and Olaf, King of Dublin, was a Christian when he wed Áed Finnliath's daughter to seal his alliance with the northern Uí Néill. That did not prevent a new onslaught, however. By the beginning of the tenth century all the best land in Iceland had been portioned out and Vikings in Normandy and the English Danelaw had no wish to have their settlements ravaged by fresh attacks from their homeland. Thus Ireland became the victim of a concerted invasion and, according to the *Cogadh*, the country 'became filled with immense floods, and countless sea-vomitings of ships, and boats, and fleets'. It continues:

> Though numerous were the oft-victorious clans of the many-familied Erinn
> . . . yet not one of them was able to give relief, alleviation, or deliverance from
> that oppression and tyranny, from the numbers and multitudes, and the cruelty
> and the wrath of the brutal, ferocious, untamed, implacable hordes . . .

In this dire crisis Niall Glúndubh rallied all of the northern half of Ireland known as Leth Cuinn, 'Conn's half'. Son of Áed Finnliath, Niall was accepted as ruler of both the northern and southern Uí Néill, and in 917 he led a great host deep into Munster to do battle with the Vikings. Complete victory eluded him, however, and in 919 he was utterly routed and slain with twelve other kings on the outskirts of Dublin. Ulster itself now fell prey to invasion. In 921 the Northmen raided Tír Conaill, plundered Armagh again, and entered Lough Foyle with thirty-two ships, causing people to flee the adjacent countryside, 'except for a few who remained behind in it through sloth'.

It was in this period that monks took refuge in tall tapered round towers with conical caps; built of stone and mortar with narrow doors raised at least ten feet from the ground, they were designed to withstand fire and attack, and to serve as belfries in time of peace. Complete towers can still be seen at Devenish and Antrim, with others in various states of decay at Drumbo, Nendrum and Maghera in County Down; Clones and Iniskeen in County Monaghan; Drumlane in County Cavan; Armoy in County Antrim; and one on Tory Island in Donegal, uniquely made of round beach stones.

The Viking tide was turned by Muircertach, Niall Glúndubh's son and successor. In a vigorous campaigning career he beat the invaders at sea on Strangford Lough in 926, burned Dublin in 939, ravaged Norse settlements in the Scottish Isles with an Ulster fleet in 941 and died in combat in 943.

It was not a northern dynasty but a southern one, the Dál Cais, which came closest to dominating all of Ireland in the years that followed. In 1005 Brian Boru reached Armagh, recognised that city's claim to ecclesiastical primacy and ordered a scribe to write in the Book of Armagh the words *Imperator Scottorum,* 'Emperor of the Irish'. He had come north with a mighty army and, though he drew tribute from every other part of Ireland, the Ulster kings stood firm. It took a circuit of Ulster the following year and several more punitive expeditions before he could establish his claim to rule the whole island.

Antrim round tower
HMSO (DEPARTMENT OF THE ENVIRONMENT, NORTHERN IRELAND)

Brian's authority did not hold: Leinster and Dublin later refused tribute and called in allies from across the Viking world. On Good Friday, 1014, in perhaps the greatest battle fought in Ireland so far, the Leinster–Viking host was routed and driven into the sea at Clontarf near Dublin. At the close of the battle, with victory within his grasp, Brian himself was slain by King Brodar of Man. In the words of the Icelandic *Saga of Burnt Njal*:

> Brian fell, but kept his kingdom
> Ere he lost one drop of blood.

A nineteenth-century impression of Brian Boru being slain in his tent by Brodar, King of Man, after the Battle of Clontarf, 1014
LINEN HALL LIBRARY

Dermot MacMurrough, the Leinster king who brought the Normans from Wales to help him recover his kingdom
NATIONAL LIBRARY OF IRELAND

Brian Boru's body was taken to Armagh and there buried with great ceremony. Who now would be King of Ireland?

NORMAN INVASION

Clontarf brought neither peace nor unity to Ireland. Now that Brian Boru had ended the Uí Néill domination, any ruling family strong enough could make a bid to seize the high-kingship. To avoid protracted succession disputes, dynasties limited choice to descendants of a single grandfather. In this way many Gaelic surnames emerged with the prefixes Ó, meaning 'grandson of', and Mac, 'son of'. The O'Neills, for example, were descendants of Niall Glúndubh. Bloody contests between rivals continued to be frequent, however.

Over one and a half centuries the provincial kings allied and clashed with each other. Some came close to success, but all were high-kings 'with opposition', as the annalists put it. That opposition was often in Ulster, which, despite impressive fleets sent out by southern kings, presented a natural frontier and so was difficult to subjugate. Yet Ulster kings never had the strength to impose their will on the rest of Ireland, for they had not the wealth of Viking cities such as Limerick and Dublin to draw on. In addition, a powerful kingdom emerged in the eleventh century on the Ulster–Connacht borderlands: Bréifne, centred on the counties of Cavan and Leitrim and ruled by the O'Rourkes, effectively blocked expansion south from Tír Eóghain.

It was a dispute between Tiernan O'Rourke, the one-eyed King of Bréifne, and Dermot MacMurrough, King of Leinster, which set in motion the events leading to the Norman invasion of Ireland. One night in 1152 hooves thundered away from the Bréifne *dún* of Dromahaire as Dermot carried off Tiernan's wife, Dervorgilla, together with a great prey of cattle. This humiliation burned in Tiernan's memory and filled his heart with vengeful hatred to his dying day. He had to wait fourteen years to have his revenge, for MacMurrough had hitched his fortunes to the rising star of Muirchertach Mac Lochlainn, the sole Cenél Eóghain high-king of the period.

Rory O'Connor of Connacht challenged Muirchertach and the fighting between them was so fierce that, in the opinion of the annalist, 'Ireland was a trembling sod'. When Muirchertach was killed in 1166, Rory, now the

high-king, gave his blessing to a punitive expedition against Dermot long
planned by Tiernan. Leinster was devastated, but instead of making a glorious
last stand, Dermot sailed to Bristol and there he was advised to seek support
from Henry II, then busy suppressing a baronial revolt in his French
dominions. The King of Leinster had close ties with the Anglo-Norman
world: as a supporter of ecclesiastical reform, he was held in high esteem by
English bishops, and he had genuine claims on Henry's gratitude, for he had
championed his claim to the English throne during King Stephen's reign.
Beset by a kaleidoscope of troubles, Henry was not ready to help Dermot in
person but otherwise he gave him full support and permission to recruit
assistance. A momentous period in the history of Ireland was about to begin.

Henry II, the most powerful monarch in the western world, had brought
Norman sway to its zenith. A century before, William, Duke of Normandy, had
gripped the imagination of the people by his dramatic and sweeping conquest
of England. The genius of the Normans for organisation and strong government, and their skill in warfare, made them feared and respected
everywhere. Early in the twelfth century they conquered Sicily, extended their
dominions in France, and pushed northwards into Scotland and westwards to
Wales. It could only be a matter of time before they would come to Ireland.
In 1155, supported by John of Salisbury and other influential Churchmen keen
for ecclesiastical conformity in Ireland, Henry was granted Ireland by Pope
Adrian IV. John of Salisbury wrote later:

> The Pope granted and donated Ireland to the illustrious King of England,
> Henry, to be held by him and his successors . . . He did this in virtue of the
> long-established right, reputed to derive from the donation of Constantine,
> whereby all islands are considered to belong to the Roman Church.

This was the notorious bull *Laudabiliter*.

On a clear day Norman barons in south-west Wales could see the hills of
Ireland across the sea, seeming to beckon them on to further conquest. These
were the men who accepted Dermot's invitation to support him in return for
promises of land. To the greatest of them, Richard fitzGilbert de Clare, Lord of
Strigoil and better known as 'Strongbow', MacMurrough pledged the hand of
his daughter Aoife in marriage, and the kingdom of Leinster when Dermot
himself died.

The incursion was on a smaller scale than William the Conqueror's invasion
of England but the Norman achievement was striking, nevertheless. Between
1169 and 1171 the Viking cities of Waterford and Dublin – offering the
strongest resistance – had been taken, Rory O'Connor's army had been put to
flight and the kingdoms of Leinster and Meath had been overwhelmed. Then
the sudden death of Dermot in May 1171 left Strongbow master of Leinster.
Though the cares of his vast domains lay heavy on his shoulders, Henry could

Richard fitzGilbert de Clare,
Lord of Strigoil, better
known as 'Strongbow': from
his tomb, Christchurch
Catherdral, Dublin
LINEN HALL LIBRARY

not allow an independent Norman state to emerge across the Irish Sea: he would have to come in person.

In October 1171 Henry II landed at Waterford with a force so large no resistance was offered. The Church's continued zeal for ecclesiastical conformity gave Henry a unique opportunity to renew good relations with Rome by promising to introduce the desired reforms. All the Irish kings, except for the Cenél Eóghain and Cenél Conaill rulers, made submission. The Norman barons were confirmed in their conquests, except that Meath was granted to Hugh de Lacy as a counterweight to Strongbow. Dublin was made the capital of the lordship of Ireland and here the royal governors set up a central administration, an exchequer and new courts of justice. The high-king, Rory O'Connor, sued for peace and in 1175 Henry agreed to a status quo. In his absence, however, Henry could not control the martial ardour of his vassals.

In early February 1177 John de Courcy, a knight from Somerset, sallied out from Dublin with twenty-two mailed horsemen and some three hundred foot soldiers. The expedition marched through the plain of Muirhevna, over the Moyry Pass into Ulster, and then, turning east from Glen Righe, the invaders reached Lecale in fewer than four days. In front of Down, the capital of the kingdom of Dál Fiatach, the attack was prepared. 'John's followers were few in number,' the Norman chronicler Gerald of Wales recorded in his *History and Topography of Ireland*, 'but good brave men, the pick of the army.' The local ruler, Rory MacDonleavy, fled with all his people but, invoking his authority as over-king of the Ulaidh, he returned after a week with a great host. A fierce battle was fought on the open ground that slopes up south to Downpatrick from the River Quoile, as Gerald relates:

Hugh de Lacy, Lord of Meath, and father of the first Earl of Ulster
NATIONAL LIBRARY OF IRELAND

> They showered down a hail of arrows and spears at long range. Then they came to close quarters, lance encountered lance, sword met sword ... After an intense and for a long time indecisive struggle between these unevenly matched forces, John's courage at last won him the victory, and a great number of the enemy were killed along the sea shore where they had taken refuge ... For because the surface of the shore was soft and yielding, the weight of their bodies caused men to sink deep into it and blood pouring from their wounds remained on the surface of the slippery ground and easily came up to the knees and legs of their pursuers.

An even greater coalition, including the Cenél Eóghain king, Máel Sechlainn Mac Lochlainn, joined King Rory for a final assault to oust the Normans in a great assault on Down in June. Once again de Courcy triumphed and prized relics were seized, including the Bachall Íosa, the staff of Jesus, soon after presented to Christchurch Cathedral in Dublin. The

MacDonleavys were to fight de Courcy again but their kingdom was lost.

'In this island,' Gerald believed, 'as in every country, the people of the North are always more warlike and savage.' The Irish were not lacking in courage but they had as yet no answer to Norman military superiority. Unlike Irish noblemen, knights were protected by mail armour from head to toe and, seated on deep high-fronted saddles and with their feet secure in stirrups, they could charge their foe full tilt with lance under arm. De Courcy brought with him Flemish crossbowmen and Welsh longbowmen who could pour down a deadly rain of bolts and arrows long before the Irish could get within range to use their shortbows and hurl their lances. Gerald wrote that the Irish fought without armour, and he continued:

> They regard weapons as a burden, and they think it brave and honourable to fight unarmed . . . They are quicker and more expert than any other people in throwing, when everything fails, stones as missiles, and such stones do great damage to the enemy in an engagement.

Irish warriors, from Gerald of Wales
NATIONAL LIBRARY OF IRELAND

On several occasions the Irish did win battles, for in attempting to extend his conquest, the impetuous de Courcy took many risks. In 1178 Rory MacDonleavy and his allies from Oriel in central Ulster made an attack on the Normans camped in Glen Righe by the Newry river and, the Annals of Ulster record, 'defeat was inflicted upon the Foreigners and stark slaughter was put upon them'. Soon afterwards the Normans were overwhelmed in mid-Antrim: de Courcy escaped with only eleven knights, and Gerald tells us that

> he and this tiny number of followers fought their way through to his castle, despite the fact that they had to cover a distance of thirty miles, over which they continually had to defend themselves against a large force of the enemy, without their horses, which had all been lost, wearing their armour, on foot, and having nothing to eat for two days and nights. Truly an amazing achievement.

Perhaps the vital point in this narrative is that de Courcy had a castle as a refuge of last resort. Earthen mottes and stone castles were thrown up to form a network holding the conquered lands in subjection and giving access to the sea for trade, assistance, and – if necessary – escape.

Dromore motte and bailey, County Down
HMSO (DOE, NI)

The sea was the essential Norman lifeline, made more secure when de Courcy married Affreca, daughter of Gottred, King of Man, in 1180, which

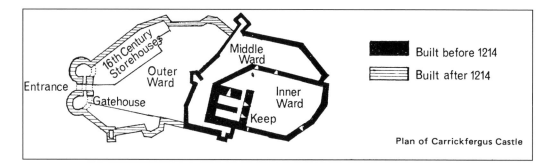

Plan of Carrickfergus Castle

Built before 1214
Built after 1214

Above: a plan of
Carrickfergus Castle,
County Antrim
Below: view of the castle
from the west
BARBARA FAGAN

gave him the use of a formidable fleet. Only the coastlands of Antrim and
Down were overrun: the frontiers of the conquest being guarded by mottes at
Antrim, Dromore and Magh Cobha at Ballyroney. A motte castle was a
fortification erected on top of an artificial mound; the steep-sided, roughly
circular mound was partly constructed with soil from its surrounding ditch but
raised higher by earth brought in from further afield. The typical Ulster motte

did not have a base court or bailey as was usual in England: an
exception was Dromore which housed a permanent garrison. In
1973 R.E. Glasscock identified 128 mottes in Ulster, most of them
concentrated in east Down and south Antrim, where the conquest
was most permanent. It was here, too, that de Courcy built the two
mightiest fortresses in his domain.

De Courcy began Carrickfergus, his most important castle, on a
tongue of rock jutting into Belfast Lough. Behind a surrounding
wall – now the inner curtain – masons erected a massive rectangular keep with walls nine feet thick and four storeys high,
rising ninety feet above the ground. On another defensible rock adjacent to
the sea, Dundrum Castle stood sentinel over the land approaches to Lecale.

Dundrum Castle,
County Down
LINEN HALL LIBRARY

The keep was a later addition but the great stone wall surrounding the summit was de Courcy's work. These mighty bastions signalled the determination of the newcomers to stay in Ulster, as well as being intimidating fortresses against which the Gaelic Irish seemed to have no answer.

For a quarter of a century John de Courcy ruled his Ulster lands with as much independence as a warlord. He minted his own halfpennies and farthings and administered his own justice with the assistance of his seneschal, chamberlain and constable. Information about his rule is pitifully fragmentary but the names of his principal barons appear in witness to his charters; they include Richard FitzRobert, William Savage, William Hacket, William Saracen, Richard de Dundonald, Walter de Logan and Henry de Coupland (who gave his family name to the Copeland Islands). Several of these surnames remain common in Antrim and Down, but it is clear that there was no extensive colonisation, the natives remaining to till the soil.

Eager to make amends for his initial slaughter and confiscation, de Courcy made generous grants to the Church. To atone for the burning of the abbey of Erenagh during his conquest, he founded the Cistercian abbey of Inch, just north of Downpatrick, and almost certainly the first building in Gothic style raised in Ireland. Other gifts to the Church included: the Benedictine Black Abbey in the Ards; White Abbey near Carrickfergus; Grey Abbey, a Cistercian monastery founded by his wife Affreca; and Down – in Irish Dún-da-lethglas – was renamed Downpatrick in honour of the patron saint and made an ecclesiastical centre.

In 1185 Henry II's son John, 'Lord of Ireland', named de Courcy his chief governor. In spite of an undistinguished term of office marked by inconclusive raids into Connacht, he seemed to keep the Crown's favour. Then, shortly after John became King of England in 1199, de Courcy's luck ran out – was it because he spoke out against John's ousting of Arthur of Brittany from the succession? Hugh de Lacy, younger son of the first Lord of Meath, was authorised to wage war on de Courcy. Now Norman fought Norman, and after campaigns stretching over five years, de Courcy was driven out of Ulster and in 1205 King John created Hugh Earl of Ulster. Eventually reconciled to the king as a humble knight, John de Courcy lived to assist in the subsequent downfall of his tormentor Hugh de Lacy.

KING JOHN IN ULSTER

William de Braose, Lord of Limerick, was King John's sworn enemy. Not only had he fallen behind in payments for his Irish lands but, worse still, his wife Matilda had denied the king her son as hostage, saying to the royal messenger: 'I will not deliver up my son to your lord, King John, for

King John hunting
BARBARA FAGAN

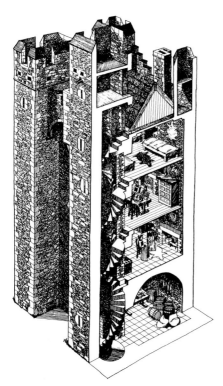

Jordan's Castle, Ardglass,
County Down
HMSO (DEPARTMENT OF
THE ENVIRONMENT,
NORTHERN IRELAND)

he basely murdered his nephew Arthur.' As John prepared a great expedition for Ireland to break the power of his overmighty subject, de Braose took refuge with his kinsman Hugh de Lacy.

On 20 June 1210 King John was in Waterford with the mightiest army yet seen in Ireland. Nine days later he was in Dublin, his force increased by feudal levies and by the army of Cathal Crobhdearg, King of Connacht. In desperation de Lacy levelled his castles at the approaches to Ulster and prepared an ambush in the Moyry Pass. By 9 July John was in Carlingford and then, using his great fleet, he transported his army over Carlingford Lough with a bridge made with boats and hundreds of pontoons brought from Dorset, Somerset and York. Then, while his men marched by the coast around the Mourne Mountains, John sailed to Ardglass and rested in Jordan de Saukeville's castle there. On seeing John's intimidating array of siege engines, the garrison of Dundrum fled, and later Carrickfergus Castle capitulated, after being besieged by land and sea.

De Braose and de Lacy escaped to France but Matilda and her infant son were captured at sea, cast into prison and there, by the king's orders, both starved to death. King John stayed at Carrickfergus for ten days making many payments, ordering repairs to the castle, arranging to have galleys built for Lough Neagh and receiving the homage of Áed O'Neill, King of Tír Eóghain. He returned to Downpatrick early in August, and then left for the Isle of Man and England. Perhaps no king had ever wielded such complete power over all Ireland and when in 1215 the English barons humiliated John at Runnymede, there was not a murmur of rebellion from his Norman vassals across the Irish Sea. John kept the earldom of Ulster for himself and the de Galloways and other Norman Scots were granted the Glens of Antrim as reward for their help in 1210.

John's successor, the boy-king Henry III, pardoned Hugh de Lacy but this was not enough: Hugh wanted the return of the earldom of Ulster and he meant to defy the king to seize it. De Lacy slipped back to Ireland in 1223, throwing the northern half of the country into turmoil. Though the mightiest baron in both England and Ireland, William the Marshal, led a host of colonists and Irish northwards against him, de Lacy got back his earldom in 1227 after fierce campaigning. It was de Lacy rather than de Courcy who was responsible for the conquest and colonisation of the northern coastland called Twescard, from the Irish *tuaisceart* meaning 'north'. Centred on Coleraine and the lower Bush valley, it had become one of the most prosperous parts of the earldom when de Lacy died in 1243. The earldom passed back to the English Crown (probably a condition of de Lacy's pardon) but it was to be a troublesome inheritance.

By the middle of the thirteenth century Gaelic Ulster had become the most extensive independent region in Ireland, the Normans penetrating more deeply into the other three provinces. Yet the two great Gaelic power blocs of the north, the Cenél Eóghain and the Cenél Conaill, fell more and more on the defensive. Brian O'Neill, King of Tír Eóghain, felt that decisive action was needed to halt the steady erosion of his territory. He had himself proclaimed 'King of the Gael of Erin' in 1258 and in 1260 joined forces with men of Connacht to make an assault on the earldom of Ulster: Brian, however, was defeated and slain near Downpatrick by a levy of the town and a force led by Sir Roger des Auters. Brian's head was sent to England, an indication of how serious a threat this O'Neill–O'Connor coalition was seen to be.

In 1264 Walter de Burgo, Lord of Connacht, was granted the earldom of Ulster by Edward, created Lord of Ireland by his father Henry III. With a great sweep of territory curving round from Connacht to Twescard, the new Earl of Ulster would – it was hoped – keep the Gaels of the north from threatening the outlying manors of the lordship of Ireland. Walter skilfully exploited the complex dynastic rivalries of Gaelic Ulster to his advantage, allying himself with the O'Neills against the O'Donnells of Tír Conaill.

Norman castles built in stone before c.1320

R.E. GLASSCOCK

Richard de Burgo, his son and successor, popularly known as the Red Earl, ruled with a firm hand and pushed his territory deeper into Ulster. By the first years of the fourteenth century he had seized much of the Inishowen peninsula and built the great castle of Northburgh (now called Greencastle) to command the narrows at the entrance to Lough Foyle. One of the most powerful nobles in the land, the Red Earl created an impressive network of marriage alliances: his son John married a granddaughter of Edward I and his four daughters married well – Matilda to the Earl of Gloucester, Catherine to the Earl of Desmond, Joan to the Earl of Kildare and Elizabeth to the Earl of

Carrick. The Earl of Carrick was none other than Robert Bruce: this marriage was to pull de Burgo's loyalties in conflicting directions in an episode which would herald the ultimate collapse of the earldom of Ulster.

The earldom of Ulster was a disturbed region at the furthest limits of the Irish lordship and it was often on a war footing. Knights were obliged to give military service, constables maintained castle defences, and able-bodied men of the towns and manors had to assemble in arms in times of danger. Mottes on the frontiers were often manned by full-time garrisons; the 1211–12 Pipe Rolls shows forty men at Antrim, thirty at Dromore and ten at Magh Cobha. The earldom was divided into five bailiwicks, or counties, each the responsibility of a seneschal or sheriff who was usually one of the earl's barons. The four great baronial families were, in effect, the principal landlords: the Savages, with manors mainly in Twescard; the Bissets in the Antrim Glens; the de Logans in the Six Mile Water valley; and the de Mandevilles with manors in north Antrim, Donegore, Comber, Killyleagh, Groomsport and Castle Ward. These vassals held great manors from the earl, valued in knight's fees; that is, land for which rent was due sufficient to maintain the service of a knight. Of lesser men we know almost nothing. Some tenants paid peppercorn rent only – literally in the case of the tenants of Frenestoun (Ballyfrenis in the parish of Donaghadee, County Down), who paid a pound of pepper.

At a time when the population of western Europe was rising, many settlers were attracted to Ireland, but for most the marchland of the earldom would

have been too inhospitable. The great majority in the earldom were Irish and for the most part it was they who farmed the land. Much of the rent was paid in corn, and landholders could increase their income by imposing charges in kind for the use of their mills. Cattle remained at the centre of the farming economy, though the FitzWarins complained of the loss of two thousand hogs and goats from their Twescard demesne during a conflict with the de Mandevilles.

Most Irish provincial towns were founded by the Normans and, while this is not true of Ulster, around fifteen have been identified on or close to the coast-

Greencastle, at the mouth of Carlingford Lough, County Down
HMSO (DOE, NI)

lines of Antrim and Down. Carrickfergus, the capital of the earldom, was the largest town, with a representative on the Dublin guild of merchants and direct trading links with France. Coleraine vied with Downpatrick as the second town in importance, and others mentioned in an inquisition of 1333 include

Limavady, Newtownards, Larne, Bushmills, Portrush, Greencastle, Dundonald, Holywood, Carnmoney and Belfast. Belfast (known as Le Ford) can have been little more than a village, like several of these boroughs: it had a castle, a parish church at Shankill, a chapel (on the site of the present St George's church in High Street), and a watermill at Millfield worth 6s. 8d. a year. Antrim was the only inland town of any size.

The earldom of Ulster was far from the centres of prosperity in the south-east and may not have accounted for more than one fiftieth of Ireland's overseas trade. Here at the frayed fringe of the Irish lordship and with a sparse settler population, the earldom was fatally vulnerable as a great Scots army prepared an assault on Ulster.

'WASTING AND RAVAGING': THE BRUCE INVASION

Transported by the notorious pirate Thomas Dun, a formidable Scots expeditionary force disembarked near Larne on 26 May 1315 with no less a mission than the complete conquest of Ireland: according to the annals this 'warlike slaughtering army caused the whole of Ireland to tremble, both Gael and Gall'. His triumph the previous year at Bannockburn notwithstanding, Robert Bruce had yet to force recognition that he was the rightful King of Scotland from Edward II of England. At the very least, this campaign in Ireland would strike at the heart of the English colony there, divert the English on the borders, and reward Edward Bruce, who had succeeded as Earl of Carrick, his steadfast brother and acknowledged heir. Bruce knew Ulster; he had taken refuge there in 1294 and 1306, and he had married Elizabeth, daughter of Richard de Burgo. Domnal O'Neill, King of Tír Eóghain, had pledged his support and made conquest seem possible: Edward Bruce could become King of Ireland and it was to him that King Robert entrusted this enterprise.

So unexpected was this Scots incursion that Edmund Butler, the newly appointed royal governor, was in Munster, and de Burgo was attending to his extensive possessions in Connacht. Both lords hastened northward to meet Edward Bruce and, the Annals of Connacht record,

Robert Bruce,
King of Scotland; portrait
by de Witte

> the Galls spared not saint or shrine, however sacred, nor churchmen or laymen or sanctuary, but went wasting and ravaging across Ireland from the Shannon in the south to Coleraine and Inishowen in the north.

Having plundered as far south as County Louth, Bruce pulled back with the Red Earl in pursuit. De Burgo advanced down the right bank of the lower

Bann only to find that the Scots

> threw down the bridge at Coleraine to hinder the Earl; and he followed them up and encamped opposite Edward and the Ulstermen on the river at Coleraine and between them they left neither wood nor lea nor corn nor crop nor stead nor barn, but fired and burnt them all.

Then the Scots crossed the Bann in Dun's fleet, driving de Burgo towards the heart of his earldom to make a last stand by the Kellswater at Connor in Antrim. There on 10 September 1315 the Scots spearmen completely over-whelmed the earl's feudal army and, as the annals record, 'Richard de Burgo, Earl of Ulster, was a wanderer up and down Ireland all this year, with nor power or lordship'. Only Carrickfergus Castle continued to hold out.

After the Battle of Connor as many survivors of the earl's broken army as could make it to Carrickfergus took refuge there. Ships carrying grain to the defenders were scattered by a storm and so those within the castle would have to survive on what lay within the storehouses. Lacking heavy siege engines, the Scots settled down to starve the garrison into submission, while the main body of their army prepared to conquer the rest of Ireland. It was not until Easter 1316 that an attempt was made to bring relief and it came to grief when an expedition from Drogheda was overwhelmed in a fierce skirmish in the streets of Carrickfergus. The garrison was reduced to chewing hides. During a parley in June, thirty Scots were seized and held prisoners in the dungeons; according to the Laud Annals, eight of these men were later killed and eaten by the defenders. Finally, after a year's siege, in September 1316 Carrickfergus surrendered.

In May 1316 Edward had had himself crowned King of Ireland at Dundalk and at the end of the year King Robert joined him with reinforcements. Together the brothers swept all before them, burning and plundering as far south as Limerick but, while they continued to win battles, they were losing the war. A terrible famine was sweeping Europe and, unable to live off the country despite their victories, the Scots were forced by hunger back into Ulster. The Laud Annals assert that Bruce's men 'were so destroyed with hunger that they raised the bodies of the dead from the cemeteries . . . and their women devoured their own children from hunger'.

Robert Bruce returned to Scotland in May 1317 and for a year neither Edward nor his opponents could get to grips with each other while the famine continued to rage. In a final attempt Bruce invaded south once more through the Moyry Pass only to meet an English army at the hill of Faughart near Dundalk. In the words of the Annals of Connacht:

> Edward Bruce, he who was the common ruin of the Galls and Gaels of Ireland, was by the Galls of Ireland killed at Dundalk by dint of fierce fighting . . . never was there a better deed done for the Irish than this . . . for in this Bruce's time,

for three years and a half, falsehood and famine and homicide filled the country, and undoubtedly men ate each other in Ireland.

It was the Irish lordship which suffered most from the devastation inflicted by the Bruce invasion. With the aid of his own Irish mercenary army, after Faughart the Red Earl rapidly recovered his ravaged lands in Ulster but the future of the colony in the north looked uncertain when he died in 1326. His fourteen-year-old grandson William, known as the Brown Earl, who succeeded, quarrelled with his relatives and vassals and, on 6 June 1333, he was killed at Belfast by a party of de Logans and de Mandevilles.

The Brown Earl's heir was his two-year-old daughter Elizabeth, taken by her mother Matilda to England, never to return. It was a disaster from which the earldom would not recover. Immediately following the murder, de Burgo lands west of the River Bann were lost and the process of attrition continued. The de Burgos of Connacht threw off their alliance to the King of England and, known thereafter as the Burkes, became thoroughly Irish. Other lords of Norman origin, who for generations had intermarried with the Irish, adopted Gaelic speech and customs and, showing scant regard for weakening royal authority, ruled great tracts of the Irish countryside as independent warlords. It was to no avail that the 1366 statute of Kilkenny 'ordained and established that no alliance by marriage, gossipred, fostering of children, concubinage or sexual liaison or in any other manner be made henceforth between English and Irish on one side or the other'.

In more senses than one the climate of the times accelerated the decline of the English colony in the fourteenth century. A steady deterioration of the weather across the northern hemisphere – causing the Norse to abandon Greenland, for example – brought a succession of harvest failures in its wake. The colonists, depending more heavily on corn and sheep than the Gaelic Irish, suffered most and, in addition, were scourged by a succession of plagues in the fourteenth and fifteenth centuries. The Black Death, making its first appearance during the summer of 1348, reaped its terrible harvest in the foul, congested streets of Dublin, Drogheda and Kilkenny and other English-held towns, rather than in the countryside where the Gaelic Irish predominated. Six further outbreaks before the fourteenth century closed probably reduced the population of the colony by 40 or 50 per cent. Also, the sharp population fall in England made more land available and many colonists left Ireland for good and, in particular, abandoned the troubled marchland of the earldom of Ulster. The Gaelic Irish in the north were given an unrivalled opportunity to recover and extend their lands.

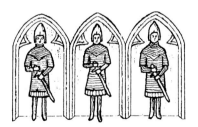

Gallowglasses carved on Roscommon Abbey
BARBARA FAGAN

The ability of the Gaelic lords of Ulster to strike at the Irish lordship was strengthened by their employment of mercenaries from the Highlands and Islands of Scotland; these were *galloglaigh*, meaning 'foreign warriors', anglicised as gallowglasses. The gallowglasses wore mail and fought in traditional Viking style, wielding a battle axe, 'moche like the axe of the Towre', as Sir Anthony St Leger described it. St Leger, who faced gallowglasses in battle in the sixteenth century, believed that 'these sorte of men be those that doo not lightly abandon the fielde, but byde the brunt to the deathe'. The Mac-Sweenys, the leading gallowglass clan, acquired land in Tír Conaill and divided into three families: MacSweeny na Doe (*na d'Tuath*, 'of the Tribes') in the Rosses and around Creeslough; MacSweeny Fanad, to the west of Lough Swilly; and MacSweeny Banagh in the vicinity of Slieve League. MacCabes, MacRorys, MacDougalls and MacSheehys came from the Hebrides to Ulster to fight there and further south; none of these, however, were as formidable as the MacDonnells, who, ensconced in the lands about Ballygawley, became a powerful arm of the O'Neills of Tír Eóghain.

'THE LAND OF THE SAVAGE IRISH WHERE KING O'NEILL REIGNED SUPREME'

Richard II responded to the desperate appeal of colonists, who declared that they were 'not able to . . . find or think of other remedy except the coming of the king, our lord, in his own person'. In an attempt to arrest the contraction of his Irish lordship, Richard landed at Waterford in October 1394 with the greatest army Ireland had yet seen and, after hard winter campaigning, he brought the Leinster Irish to heel; as a result, the chronicler Froissart records, 'the Irishmen advised themselves and came to obeissance'. Niall Mór O'Neill agreed to pay tribute to Richard's cousin, Roger de Mortimer, Earl of March, who had inherited the title to the earldom of Ulster, which had passed down to the de Mortimers from Lionel of Clarence, husband of Elizabeth, the de Burgo heiress.

Revised map of Ptolemy, 1513, showing Ireland with Saint Patrick's Purgatory prominently displayed

De Mortimer raided Ulster in a futile attempt to recover his inheritance and arrangements made with the English quickly fell apart. De Mortimer was killed in Leinster and this impelled Richard to a second and disastrous expedition to Ireland in 1399. The defeated king soon returned to England to lose his throne to the Lancastrians and ultimately to lose his head. Great sweeps of eastern Ulster now fell to both the native Irish and the Scots of the Isles as the power of the English Crown was eroded by the deadly and wasting dynastic contest between the houses of Lancaster and York.

The most extensive area under complete and growing Gaelic control was centred on Ulster and known to the English – when they were not calling it the 'Land of War' – as the 'Great Irishry'. The north-west of Ireland was largely remote and unknown to the English and yet it was here that the place on the island most renowned across medieval Europe was to be found – Lough Derg. On 19 May 1396 King John of Aragon died suddenly, frightened to death, it was said, by the sight of an enormous she-wolf when he was out hunting alone. Ramon, Viscount of Perellós, had been the king's faithful courtier and now he feared that his royal master's soul would be in torment in hell, for the king had died without confession. Perellós made up his mind to go to Lough Derg: here a soul could be spared the pains of hell if the pilgrim could survive the dangers of Saint Patrick's Purgatory.

Pope Benedict III gave his blessing but, Perellós tells us, 'strongly advised me against it and he frightened me greatly, warning me that I should not do it for any reason whatsoever'. Leaving Avignon on 8 September 1397, Perellós travelled through Paris, sailed to England, where he was entertained by Richard II, and then chartered a ship for Ireland. In Dublin, de Mortimer urged him to halt his pilgrimage, for he would have to 'go through the lands of savage, ungoverned people', but Perellós got an escort to the frontiers of Ulster, where the soldiers would go no further. He rode on alone 'into the land of the savage Irish where King O'Neill reigned supreme'. Welcoming Perellós with a gift of ox meat; 'King O'Neill' – Niall Mór O'Neill of Tír Eóghain – and his retinue impressed the pilgrim:

The O'Neills appoint their chief; from a sixteenth-century drawing
BARBARA FAGAN

> He is the greatest king and he has forty horsemen. They ride without a saddle on a cushion and each one wears a cloak according to his rank. They are armed with coats of mail and round iron helmets like the Moors and Saracens . . . They are very courageous. They are still at war with the English and have been for a long time. The king of England is unable to put an end to it, for they have had many great battles. Their way of fighting is like that of the Saracens who shout in the same manner.

Perellós was taken across wild country to Lough Derg, where the monks warned him that he might not emerge alive from Saint Patrick's Purgatory. Taken to Saint's Island, he entered the pit there, where 'I almost lapsed into sleep because I had been feeling so ill'. Then follows his description of his journey to purgatory and the torments of those tortured by devils: 'There I spoke at great length to my lord the king who, by God's grace, was on the road to salvation.' Perellós returned from Lough Derg and spent the feast of Christmas with O'Neill:

A knight's helmet from Lough Henney, County Down
BARBARA FAGAN

> He held a great court in their fashion which to us seems very strange for

someone of his status ... his table was of rushes spread out on the ground while nearby they placed delicate grass for him to wipe his mouth.

After spending New Year's Day with the Countess of March in one of her castles, Perellós made his return in time to be present at the celebrations in Rheims given in honour of the Holy Roman Emperor Wenceslas in March 1398.

Over a dozen other pilgrims from as far away as Hungary left accounts of their visits to Lough Derg. Only Perellós, however, made any attempt to describe the Irish they encountered; his account opens a unique window on the life of the people of Ulster at a time when annals were concerned almost exclusively with military campaigns and births and deaths. It is not until the sixteenth century that this window is opened again.

Perellós did not mention that a famine was affecting Ireland at the time of his pilgrimage, which may explain his bleak impression of the people's diet. As 'a great gift', Niall Mór O'Neill sent him 'two cakes as thin as wafers and as pliable as raw dough. They were made of oats and of earth and they were black as coal, but very tasty.' He added:

> They do not eat bread, nor do they drink wine, for in that country there is none. However, the great lords drink milk as a sign of their nobility and some drink meat-broth. The common people eat meat and drink water ... But they have plenty of butter.

Butter was preserved in raskins, hollowed-out containers of wood, which were placed in bogs, acquiring a flavour the English disliked. On one occasion the O'Donnells fell upon Shane O'Neill's warriors while they were holding out their helmets to be served raw oatmeal with butter poured over it. Fresh milk was too precious to be drunk in quantity, but buttermilk was widely consumed. This diet was supplemented by game from the woods, mushrooms, watercress and wood sorrel. By the sixteenth century wine was imported by the Gaelic lords; otherwise ale was brewed from malted oats or distilled to make *uisce beathadh*, whiskey. Sir Josias Bodley in 1603 found priests in Lecale pouring 'usquebaugh down their throats by day and by night'.

The Ulster people, Perellós observed, 'are amongst the most beautiful men and women that I have ever seen anywhere in the world'. He gives this description of the dress of those he met in O'Neill's court:

> The great lords wear tunics without a lining, reaching to the knee, cut very low at the neck, almost in the style of women, and they wear great hoods which hang down to the waist, the point of which is narrow as a finger. They wear neither hose nor shoes, nor do they wear breeches, and they wear their spurs on their bare heels. The king was dressed like that on Christmas Day.

The common people wore what they could, but 'all the principal ones wear frieze cloaks and both the women and the men show their shameful parts

Harry Avery's Castle, County Tyrone, built by the fourteenth-century lord Henrí Aimhréidh O'Neill – one of the earliest stone castles built by the Gaelic Irish
HMSO (DEPARTMENT OF THE ENVIRONMENT, NORTHERN IRELAND)

without any shame'. Captain Francisco de Cuellar, an Armada castaway who took refuge on the shores of Lough Melvin, observed: 'The most of the women are very beautiful, but badly got up.'

Like later English writers, Perellós assumed that the people of Gaelic Ulster were nomads:

> Their dwellings are communal and most of them are set up near the oxen, for that is where they make their homes in the space of a single day and they move on through the pastures, like the swarms of Barbary in the land of the Sultan.

What he was seeing was the annual movement of cattle to and from summer pastures, either on the mountains or on the bogland: here the cows were milked and the butter churned. Below in the valleys the infield was fenced off to grow corn until in autumn the cattle returned to graze the long stubble left by the reaping hook and to manure the tilled ground with droppings. Flax was grown extensively for the making of linen tunics, and frieze was woven from wool to make the *falaing*, or mantle, which found a ready export market.

De Cuellar observed that the Irish 'lived in huts of straw', though these may have been temporary shelters on summer grazing grounds. There is little doubt that the majority of people in Ulster lived in post-and-wattle dwellings, usually oval or circular in shape, thatched and without chimneys. The Gaelic lords erected castles with such enthusiasm that Ireland became the most heavily castellated part of the British Isles. Some of the most impressive included Harry Avery's Castle, put up by Henrí Aimhréidh O'Neill; Fyn, Lifford and Donegal by the O'Donnells; Enniskillen by the Maguires; Doe by the MacSweenys; and Omagh by the O'Neills. Ireland was too disturbed to encourage the erection of undefended manor houses, as in England; tower houses, at least capable of fending off marauders, were preferred.

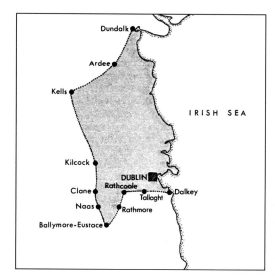

The Pale in 1515

James IV of Scotland: his
destruction of the
Lordship of the Isles led
to a heavy settlement of
MacDonnells and other
Gaelic-speaking Hebridean
Scots in the Glens of
Antrim
SIR FRANCIS OGILVY AND
NATIONAL LIBRARY OF
SCOTLAND

BEYOND THE PALE

In 1435 the Irish Council reported in desperation to Henry VI that 'his land of Ireland is well nigh destroyed, and inhabited with his enemies and rebels', with the consequence that the royal writ only ran in an area around Dublin 'scarcely thirty miles in length and twenty miles in breadth'. All that could be done was to construct the Pale: the Government put up fortifications, dug trenches, gave grants towards the building of tower houses, appointed guards to hold the bridges and assigned watchmen – paid by a tax called smokesilver – to light warning beacons when danger threatened.

By this time the Dublin government had resigned itself to the fact that, apart from Carrickfergus, Ulster was beyond the Pale. Emerging from their woody fastness of Glenconkeyne, the descendants of Áed Buidhe O'Neill – a former King of Tír Eóghain – crossed the lower Bann and carved out a new lordship for themselves from the shattered remnants of the earldom of Ulster. The Savages, driven out of the Six Mile Water valley, hung on precariously to the southern tip of the Ards. The Magennises and MacCartans engulfed central and southern Down, while Clann Aodha Buidhe emerged as the principal Gaelic lords of eastern Ulster, dominating a sweep of territory extending from Larne inland to Lough Neagh and taking in the castle of Belfast and north Down. This lordship the English called Clandeboye, after the ruling family which had conquered it. Carrickfergus was left isolated, described in 1468 as 'a garrison of war . . . surrounded by Irish and Scots, without succour of the English for sixty miles'.

In contrast with Gaelic Ulster, the lordship of the Isles was meanwhile succumbing to the power of Edinburgh. In 1476 James IV of Scotland forced the surrender of the MacDonnells, the ruling family, and absorbed the Isles into his kingdom. One branch of the MacDonnells, the Lords of Islay and Kintyre, found refuge in the Glens of Antrim. In 1399 John Mór MacDonnell had married Margery Bisset, the last heiress of a Norman family long settled there, and thus acquired a new territory for his people. With every reverse in Scotland a new wave of islanders brought their galleys south to Ulster. The MacDonnells brought with them MacNeills, MacAllisters, Mackays and Macrandalbanes from Kintyre and Gigha, and from the Rinns of Islay the Magees, after whom Islandmagee, County Antrim, is named. Others ranged backwards and forwards from the Isles to serve as mercenaries for the Gaelic lords of Ulster; these men were the Redshanks, so called, as a Highland priest explained to Henry VIII, because 'wee of all people can tolerat, suffir, and away best with colde, for boithe somer and wynter (except when the froeste is most vehemante), goinge alwaies bair-leggide and bair-footide'.

As the MacDonnells of the Isles strengthened their hold on the Antrim Glens, the English Crown viewed with alarm this linking of the military resources of Gaelic Scotland to those of Gaelic Ulster. Some of the king's advisers concluded that a concerted attempt would have to be made to conquer all Ireland, an undertaking which could be contemplated only after Henry Tudor had triumphed over the Yorkists at Bosworth Field in 1485.

Kilclief Castle, County Down, a typical fifteenth-century Ulster tower house HMSO (DEPARTMENT OF THE ENVIRONMENT, NORTHERN IRELAND)

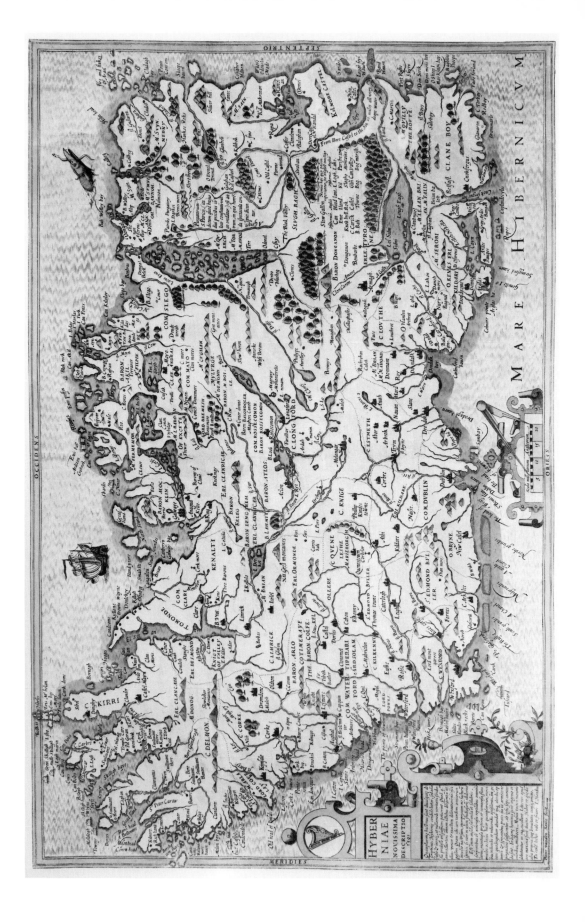

3

TUDOR CONQUEST
1486–1603

In the autumn of 1498 Henry VII's chief governor, Garret Mór Fitzgerald, 8th Earl of Kildare, led an army out of the Pale, joined forces with the O'Donnells and Maguires, and advanced into the heart of Tír Eóghain. The Annals of Ulster record:

> The castle of Dungannon was taken this year by the Deputy of the king of the Saxons in Ireland, namely, the Earl of Kildare . . . And Donal O'Neill, with his sons and all his friends, went with a host hard to count to meet the governor to the same castle and it was taken with guns on the morrow.

Thirteen years earlier Henry Tudor had defeated and killed Richard III at Bosworth. The wasting Wars of the Roses had been brought to an end and England became one of the most centralised states in Europe, growing rapidly in power and prosperity. This new era dawned with the O'Donnells and O'Neills once more coming to blows, fatally exposing them to the reinvigorated power of the English Crown.

Henry VII had no interest in extending his Irish lordship beyond the Pale and was content to let Kildare make decisions about what should be done to protect his interests. Henry VIII retained the services of Garret Mór, and after his death in 1513 those of his son Garret Óg. Eventually, however, the Fitzgeralds overreached themselves; Garret Óg's son, Silken Thomas, rose in rebellion in 1534, only to be crushed in a protracted campaign. From then on Henry ruled by lord deputy, a chief governor resident in Ireland throughout his term of office. What should the king do with Ireland? In 1515, a writer signing himself 'Pandor' had advised full-scale conquest:

> Yf the king were as wise as Salamon the Sage, he shalle never subdue the wylde Iryshe to his obeysaunce, without dreadde of the swerde, and of the myght and streynghthe of his power, and of his Englyshe subgettes.

If Ireland were subjected by force, he believed, 'hyt wolde be none other but a very Paradyce, delycious of all plesaunce, to respect and regard of any other land in this worlde'. The debate on policy had begun and the Tudor monarchy

Opposite:
1591 map of Ireland by Jodocus Hondius
LINEN HALL LIBRARY

vacillated until almost the end of the sixteenth century between conciliation and conquest.

SURRENDER AND REGRANT

Lord Deputy Leonard Grey believed in force and made war in Ulster several times. In 1539, for example, the Island Scots, swarming around Lecale, brought him north; there he took Dundrum, 'owt of whyche the sayd Scottys fled, and left mych corne, butters, and other pylfre, behinde them'. Grey, however, had made too many enemies, and had even driven O'Neill and O'Donnell to mutual assistance. Later in the same year he routed the O'Neills and the O'Donnells at Bellahoe near Carrickmacross in Monaghan. The deputy was recalled to face charges of corruption, and on conviction, had his head chopped off by order of the king.

Sir Anthony St Leger, Grey's replacement, believed that the Gaelic lords and their people, if treated with respect, would become loyal to the Crown and abide by English law. He persuaded Henry VIII to change his title from Lord of Ireland to King of Ireland; the Irish parliament gave its approval in June 1541 and the act was translated into Irish. A show of strength was needed before O'Neill and O'Donnell – all of Ulster in fact – would submit, for St Leger wrote that these two men 'had, in effecte, all the capitaynes of the north hanginge on their slevis'. An expedition to Lough Erne and a ruthless winter

Albrecht Dürer's
drawing of Irish
foot soldiers
NATIONAL GALLERY OF
IRELAND

campaign destroying corn and butter in Tír Eóghain were required before Manus O'Donnell and Conn Bacach O'Neill capitulated, Conn putting his x mark to a formal submission, confessing that 'for lack of knoweledge of my most bounded dieutye of allegeaunce, I have most grevouslye offended Your Majestie'.

Henry VIII was the first English king to lay serious claim to the whole island – the partition of Ireland between the 'Englysshe pale' and the 'Great Irishry' was to be erased, and all Gaelic lords were to hold their lands by English feudal law from the king. St Leger's scheme, known as Surrender and Regrant, was to persuade the lords to drop their traditional Gaelic titles and give up their lands, receiving them back from the king with English titles. This programme enjoyed initial success, with O'Neill leading the way in Ulster.

On Sunday 1 October 1542 Conn Bacach was in London to receive his new title of Earl of Tyrone. He put on his robes in the queen's closet at Greenwich; then he was led by two earls and a viscount before Henry VIII, 'and the King girt the said sword about the said Earl baudrickwise, the foresaid Earl kneeling ...' The new earl 'gave his thanks in his language, and a priest made answer of his saying in English'; then to the sound of trumpets he left carrying his letters patent before him like a prize. The succession of the title was now established in the English style, with Conn Bacach's illegitimate son Matthew, created Baron of Dungannon, named successor.

St Leger's policy seemed to be working well and had it been continued the Gaelic lords of Ulster might have adapted to become as much loyal agents of the Crown as the nobility of Wales. But others at court sought subjugation not co-operation and their advice gained favour. Manus O'Donnell was offered the title Earl of Tyrconnell but it was not until the reign of James I that an O'Donnell felt able to accept it. A potent factor adding to the unease of O'Donnell, O'Neill and their dependent chiefs was Henry VIII's determination to impose his Church revolution on Ireland.

In Gaelic Ulster the rule of celibacy was everywhere ignored, Church lands had fallen into the control of hereditary families and clergy often took sides in dynastic disputes. The Church continued to attract universal support but if Saint Malachy had been able to return to early-sixteenth-century Ireland, it is certain he would have found much to reform. Pandor was convinced that Irish souls fell to hell in showers,

> for ther is no archebysshop, ne bysshop, abbot, ne pryor, parson, ne vycar, ne any other person of the Churche, highe or lowe, greate or small, Englyshe or Iryshe, that useyth to preache the worde of Godde, saveing the poore fryers beggers.

The friars, dedicated to pastoral work amongst the people, enjoyed widespread support in Gaelic Ulster; friaries were built at Massereene, Lambeg,

Larne, Bonamargy, Donegal and elsewhere. Because of the reverence and affection the Gaelic people had for them, the friars were thus in a strong position to take a lead in resisting the Reformation.

'I entirely renounce obedience to the Roman Pontiff and his usurped authority,' Conn Bacach O'Neill agreed in 1542, recognising Henry VIII as supreme head of the Church in Ireland. Henry's break with Rome did not cause a great stir in Gaelic Ireland, for the Pope's authority was feeble there; the dissolution of monasteries within the Pale in 1539 was little regretted, for these communities had long ceased to provide education, hospitality and medical services. The destruction of relics did cause dismay, but there were no martyrs and no burnings. As yet there was little indication that religion would become a cause of strife in succeeding centuries. Protestant doctrine did not arrive until after the accession of Edward VI in 1547, and while it made some progress amongst colonists in Dublin, there was not a great deal for Mary to undo when she became queen in 1553, ordering the restoration of religious practice to that 'of old times used'. Elizabeth I, coming to the throne in 1558, imposed a Protestant settlement by law but she had neither the money nor the evangelists to make the new religious regime effective. As her reign wore on, trained priests returned to Ireland, not from Oxford as in former times, but from the seminaries of Louvain, Salamanca and Rome, bearing with them the combative zeal of the Counter-Reformation.

After vacillating for most of her reign, Elizabeth I determined on the complete conquest of Ireland in the 1590s.
LINEN HALL LIBRARY

Elizabeth could do little to dispel the view that the Reformation was simply an instrument used by the English monarchy to bring about Irish subjugation, for her government became more and more preoccupied with the objective of conquering the island from end to end. More than any other province, Ulster lay beyond the reach of the English Crown. The MacDonnells of the Isles strengthened their hold on the Antrim Glens and, despite repeated punitive expeditions from Dublin, Ulster chieftains could still launch damaging assaults on the Pale. In addition, there were alarming reports of Ulster's conspiracy with England's continental foes; until Ireland had been subdued entirely, the queen was advised by her courtiers, there would never be security for her realm.

In 1558 Elizabeth had no plan to conquer Ulster, but its position as an independent Gaelic province was in peril, as England grew more prosperous and powerful. Ulster, with a sparse population and an underdeveloped economy, attracted the English – particularly ambitious younger sons inheriting nothing at home – just as Spaniards were drawn to Mexico and Peru. For many years, however, the wildness of the borderlands gave Ulster effective protection, particularly when defended by such ruthless and resourceful warriors as Shane O'Neill.

SHANE THE PROUD

Brutal, vindictive and drunken, Shane O'Neill was an unlikely champion of an endangered culture. In 1559 he drove his aged father, Conn Bacach O'Neill, out of Ulster and into the Pale, where he died soon after. Shane had already murdered his half-brother Matthew, heir to the earldom of Tyrone. By English law Matthew's eldest son, Brian, was earl. Nevertheless, Shane remained unchallenged as The O'Neill.

To his own people O'Neill was Seáan an Diomuis, Shane the Proud, who was without rival in Tyrone and who aspired to dominate the O'Donnells of Tír Conaill, the Clandeboye O'Neills and the Antrim Scots. In May 1561 Shane overwhelmed Calvagh O'Donnell, Lord of Tír Conaill, at Glenveagh and bound him in chains: he had made war not only on a neighbour but on an ally of the English Crown. The Earl of Sussex, the queen's lord lieutenant, had Shane proclaimed a traitor in Dublin and invaded Tír Eóghain at the end of June. After weeks of futile campaigning, supplies ran out and the English were forced to make a humiliating retreat to Newry. In desperation Sussex concocted a plan to poison Shane, with a contingency scheme – as he frankly explained to Elizabeth – to murder the poisoner should he fail. Nothing came of this plan; instead a more ambitious incursion was prepared for the autumn. Sent an additional £2,000 and reinforcements from Berwick, Sussex advanced from Dundalk north-west to Omagh and Derry, but Shane repeatedly disengaged. The fleet of ships pressed from along the Lancashire coast to revictual his army failed to show up, so Sussex had to content himself with slaughtering Shane's brood mares and retire ignominiously the way he had come. Elizabeth felt she had no recourse but conciliation.

A nineteenth-century impression of Shane O'Neill
LINEN HALL LIBRARY

On 2 January 1562 Shane O'Neill entered London, accompanied by the Earls of Kildare and Ormond, and with an escort of fifty gallowglasses. The warriors – bare-headed, with hair flowing onto their shoulders, short tunics, heavy cloaks, and linen vests dyed saffron with urine – drew crowds of onlookers as large as those that had turned out to gape at native Americans and Chinese in the city a short time before. Only the enticement of £2,000 for expenses and guarantees from five Irish earls had persuaded Shane to cross the Irish Sea. Next day at Greenwich, in the presence of the ambassadors of

Sweden, Savoy, Spain and Venice and all the court, O'Neill threw himself to
the floor before Elizabeth; then rising to his knees, he made a passionate
speech in Irish, punctuated by howls which caused great astonishment. 'For
lack of education and civility I have offended,' the Earl of Kildare began,
translating Shane's words.

Would Shane be given recognition as The O'Neill and the title of Earl of
Tyrone? Weeks of indecision followed until the queen summoned Brian
O'Neill to London to help her make up her mind. On his way, at Carlingford,
Brian was slain. Had he been murdered on Shane's order? No proof could be
established and so Elizabeth hastened to make an agreement. Shane was
recognised as 'captain' of Tyrone; an English garrison was to occupy Armagh;
and O'Neill promised to be at peace with his Irish neighbours for six months.
Brian's brother Hugh was brought to the Pale for safekeeping, and Calvagh
O'Donnell, in chains in Tyrone, was still to have his future decided. For both
Elizabeth and Shane this was an unsatisfactory compromise. It demanded trust
on both sides – trust that was almost entirely lacking.

'I cannot scape neither by land nor by water, except God and your Lordship
do help me at this need' – so wrote Hugh Maguire, Lord of Fermanagh, in a
final frantic appeal to Sussex. Almost immediately after he had returned from
England, Shane had rapidly and violently reasserted his power across Ulster,
seizing thirty thousand O'Donnell cattle, plundering the O'Reillys and

*Dunluce Castle, County
Antrim: begun by the
MacQuillans and
extended by the
MacDonnells; nineteenth-
century view*
LINEN HALL LIBRARY

O'Hanlons, and forcing Maguire to capitulate after making a last stand on the islands of Lough Erne. Sussex launched a new offensive in Ulster early in 1563, only to have all his pack horses stolen at Armagh during a tempestuous downpour at night.

Ignoring Sussex's protests, Elizabeth authorised an interim agreement with Shane in the autumn of 1563. She abandoned Armagh but obtained Calvagh O'Donnell's release. For over two years Calvagh had been in bonds, his neck in a collar chained to fetters on his ankles, so that he could neither sit nor stand. Calvagh wept when he reached the Pale, recalling that Shane's irons had been 'so sore that the very blood did run down on every side of mine irons, insomuch that I did wish after death a thousand times'. Few in London or Dublin believed that Shane's ruthless ambition would allow the agreement to last.

It was Robert Dudley, Earl of Leicester, who advised Shane to win the queen's favour by driving the Scots from the Antrim Glens. Obtaining tacit approval from Dublin Castle, Shane advanced from the Fews, in south Armagh, during Easter 1565, and as he approached, the MacDonnells set their warning fires ablaze on Fair Head and the high ground behind Torr Point. The men of Kintyre seized their weapons and manned their galleys, but they were too late: as James MacDonnell steered into Red Bay he saw flames leap from his castle there. Sorley Boy MacDonnell, who had been leading the defence of the Glens, fell back to join his brother James and together they were overwhelmed on the slopes of Knocklayd. Dunseverick fell, Ballycastle was taken, and – after Shane threatened to starve Sorley Boy to death – Dunluce

Sir Henry Sidney: he shired Ulster and advocated all-out conquest; from Derricke's *Image of Irelande*

capitulated. Refusing appeals from both Elizabeth and Mary Queen of Scots to accept a ransom, Shane let James MacDonnell die of his wounds and ill-treatment. O'Neill had all Ulster in thrall, as he exultantly declared in a letter written in Latin to Sir Henry Sidney:

> My ancestors were Kings of Ulster, Ulster was theirs, and shall be mine. And for O'Donnell, he shall never come into his country if I can keep him out of it, nor Bagenal into the Newry, nor the Earl of Kildare into Dundrum or Lecale. They are mine; with this sword I won them, with this sword I will keep them. This is my answer.

Elizabeth in turn wrote to ask Sidney how 'such a cankred dangerous rebel' might be 'utterly extirped'.

In the summer of 1566, while Sidney advanced north from the Pale with a large army accompanied by Calvagh O'Donnell, a formidable English naval squadron sailed into Lough Foyle under the command of Edward Randolph, the queen's lieutenant of the ordnance. At first all went well for the Crown forces: Benburb was left a ruin; corn was burned; cattle were rounded up and slaughtered; Fermanagh was recovered; Randolph and Sidney rendezvoused at Lifford; and a new fort was built at Derry. Then in November, when Shane made an unsuccessful assault on the Derry garrison, Randolph was killed and Calvagh died after being thrown from his horse. The English began to run out of food and fall prey to disease. Finally, on 21 April 1567, a spark from the garrison's forge blew up the magazine and the English survivors sailed away soon after.

The queen's honour was saved by the men of Tír Conaill. Led now by Sir Hugh O'Donnell, Shane's nephew, the O'Donnells and MacSweenys made a furious attack on the O'Neills as they crossed the River Swilly at Farsetmore. The Annals of the Four Masters record:

> They proceeded to strike, mangle, slaughter, and cut down one another for a long time, so that men were soon laid low, heroes wounded, youths slain, and robust heroes mangled in the slaughter.

Shane's warriors retreated into the advancing tide, there to be drowned or cut down. In desperation he fled to the Scots in the Antrim Glens. It was an extraordinary decision but perhaps Shane hoped that by bringing Sorley Boy and Lady Agnes, widow of James MacDonnell, he could buy protection. The MacDonnells prepared a feast at Glenshesk in an apparent mood of reconciliation. They 'fell to quaffing', a quarrel broke out, and Shane was hacked to death. Captain Piers of Carrickfergus dug up the body, cut off the head and sent it 'pickled in a pipkin' to Sidney, who placed it on a spike over Dublin Castle's gate arch – the historian Edmund Campion found it still there four years later. It was an ignominious end for Shane the Proud.

ESSEX IN ULSTER

The fall of Shane O'Neill did little to increase English power in Ulster. Sidney had no intention of rewarding the MacDonnells and instead schemed to drive the Scots from the Glens and settle Englishmen on the coastlands of Antrim and Down. 'None will come from home,' Sidney reported in 1570, observing that prospective settlers for his 'Ulster Project' found the risks too great. Besides, the Tyrone O'Neills had a new chief, Turlough Luineach, who assumed the traditional title of The O'Neill, hired great numbers of Redshank mercenaries and established good terms with the O'Donnells. In any case, the outbreak of widespread rebellion in Munster in 1568 had left few English troops available for service to protect colonists in Ulster.

Sir Thomas Smith, provost of Eton and a privy councillor, was not to be

discouraged and he obtained letters patent entitling him and his son Thomas
to the lands of Clandeboye. The enterprise was doomed from the outset. Only
around one hundred colonists disembarked at Strangford village in August
1572, led not by Sir Thomas but by his even more inexperienced son. As the
expedition moved north towards Newtownards, Sir Brian MacPhelim
O'Neill, Lord of Lower Clandeboye, burned down buildings which might give
shelter to the English. Smith had to seek refuge in Ringhaddy Castle and it
was in vain that he appealed to Dublin for help. When Smith was slain by his
Irish servants in Comber the following year, a more grandiose enterprise was
already under way.

Walter Devereux, Earl of Essex, mortgaged most of his extensive English and
Welsh estates to finance his ambitious scheme to colonise Antrim, nearly all of
which had been granted to him by the queen. On seeing Essex arrive at
Carrickfergus with a thousand soldiers in the autumn of 1573, Sir Brian
MacPhelim made his submission. After a month the project was running into
difficulties, Essex complaining to Elizabeth that his gentlemen colonists were
'feigning excuses to repair home where I fear they give forth speeches in
dislike of the enterprise'. He fared no better the following year when he was
given the title of governor of Ulster; the earl did little more with his new
position than display deceit and cold-blooded cruelty. He hanged some Devon
men for attempted desertion and then set out to wreak havoc on the followers,
crops and cattle of Turlough Luineach, building a fort on the Blackwater. A
dispute with Sir Brian was patched up but this was to occasion a unique act

The submission of
Turlough Luineach
O'Neill to Elizabeth; from
Derricke's *Image of Irelande*

of treachery. Essex and his principal followers were invited to a feast in Belfast Castle in October 1574 and spent 'three nights and days together pleasantly and cheerfully'. The Annals of the Four Masters continue:

> At the expiration of this time, as they were agreeably drinking and making merry, Brian, his brother, and his wife, were seized upon by the Earl, and all his people put unsparingly to the sword . . . Brian was afterwards sent to Dublin, together with his wife and brother, where they were cut in quarters.

An act of equal barbarity was carried out the following summer. Essex was determined to break the power of Sorley Boy, one of the most astute politicians in the Gaelic world who could have become Elizabeth's ally had she been prepared to recognise the Mac-Donnells' rights to the Glens. On the morning of 22 July 1575 Essex's assault fleet, commanded by Francis Drake, reached Arkill Bay on the east side of Rathlin Island. Led by Captain John Norris, the English, Essex reported to the queen, 'did with valiant minds leap to land, and charged them so hotly, as they drave them to retire with speed, chasing them to a castle which they had of very great strength'. For four days the castle, containing many women and children, was pounded by ship's cannon. Then at dawn on 26 July the garrison surrendered on condition their lives were spared but, as Sidney reported:

Turlough Luineach O'Neill by Barnaby Googe, 1575. The lord deputy hoped in vain that he would drink himself swiftly to death.
BRITISH MUSEUM

> The soldiers, being moved and much stirred with the loss of their fellows that were slain, and desirous of revenge, made request, or rather pressed, to have the killing of them, which they did all . . . There were slain that came out of the castle of all sorts 200 . . . They be occupied still in killing, and have slain that they have found hidden in caves and in the cliffs of the sea to the number of 300 or 400 more.

Essex relayed to the queen information received from his spy, that Sorley had 'stood upon the mainland of the Glynnes and saw the taking of the island, and was like to run mad for sorrow . . . turning and tormenting himself, and saying that he had then lost all that he ever had'.

'For my part I will not leave the enterprise as long as I have any foot of land in England unsold,' Essex declared to the queen but, in spite of his ruthless bloodletting, there was no disguising his failure. Elizabeth withdrew her support and Essex retired to Dublin as Earl Marshal of Ireland, only to die there of dysentery in September 1576. That a favoured nobleman could ruin himself in such a way showed how the English still underestimated the difficulty of subjugating Ulster. Sidney was led to conclude that the settling there of loyal subjects was 'no subject's enterprise, a prince's purse and power must do it'. More than thirty years were to pass before such a scheme could be realised.

THE ARMADA AND ULSTER

Sidney believed that Turlough Luineach O'Neill would die soon because of his 'ill diet, and continual surfeit'. This prediction proved false and, by avoiding unnecessary conflict with his neighbours and the English, the wily chieftain kept Ulster generally at peace (helped also by the fact that after the Essex fiasco Elizabeth disbanded one third of her army in Ireland).
Nevertheless, Elizabethan administrators had the recurring nightmare that a coalition of Catholic warriors of the Isles, Mary Queen of Scots, the French and the Irish would put England in peril. For this reason, Sir John Perrott, appointed lord deputy in 1584, determined to drive the Scots from the province altogether. He besieged and captured Dunluce in September of that year but the Island Scots returned in their galleys, scaled the cliffs and ramparts, and recovered the castle on Hallowe'en night 1585. Appalled by the expense of her lord deputy's campaigning, Elizabeth sent a stinging reproof in her own hand:

> Let us have no more such rash, unadvised journeys without good ground as your last journey in the North … take heed ere you use us so again.

Perrott made peace with the MacDonnells and Sorley Boy came to Dublin in 1586 and prostrated himself before a portrait of Elizabeth, a small price to pay for recognition of his family's right to the Glens and the Route. Now over eighty years old, he planned to repair Dunluce – an undertaking completed with the help of Armada treasure salvaged from the *Girona*.

During the morning of 9 May 1588, the invincible Armada, 130 vessels in all, weighed anchor in the Tagus and steered into the open Atlantic. After years of vacillation Philip II of Spain had decided to cut off Elizabeth's aid to the Protestant Dutch and achieve victory for the Counter-Reformation by invading England. From the time the Armada entered the Narrow Seas, however, Philip's grandiose enterprise began to fail: harried by English culverins and scattered by fireships, the Spanish fleet was unable to transport the Duke of Parma's army in the Spanish Netherlands across the Channel. The Spanish ships sailed up the North Sea, around the Shetlands and westwards into the Atlantic. In the mountainous seas stirred up by autumn gales some vessels foundered and others were driven towards the rocky headlands of Ireland.

On 14 September *La Trinidad Valencera* sought shelter in the lee of the Inishowen peninsula. Despite being one of the greatest ships of the Spanish

The royal arms of Philip II on a massive siege gun recovered from *La Trinidad Valencera*, which foundered in Kinnegoe Bay, Inishowen, 1588
ULSTER MUSEUM

Armada, the vessel was dangerously overloaded (having rescued the entire crew of *Barca de Amburg* in mid-ocean) and had been shipping water in the wild south-westerly storm. The O'Dohertys did what they could for the stricken Spanish, taking out supplies in their currachs until suddenly the ship sank; forty men still below were drowned. Don Alonso de Luzon, the Maestro de Campo, saw that Inishowen could not for long support his company of 350 men, so he set off southwards with banners flying and drums beating.

Sir William Fitzwilliam, the lord deputy, had only two thousand men in the Irish army. Even a modest Spanish landing could occasion a major uprising and so his orders were clear: kill without delay any Spaniard cast ashore. Don Alonso's men got as far as Gallagh, just north of Derry, when they were overwhelmed by a force of Irish soldiers in English pay. At first light the Spaniards were taken into a field and butchered. About one hundred escaped, most of whom died of exposure, though some were given refuge by Catholic clergy and a few reached Scotland with the aid of the O'Cahans and MacDonnells. Some officers were kept alive for ransom, including Don Alonso, who was released in London in 1591.

Don Alonso Martinez de Leiva de Rioja, Knight of Santiago, Commander of Alcuescar, was general-in-chief of the land forces of the Armada entrusted with the conquest of England in joint action with the Duke of Parma. By September 1588 his only concern was to survive. His ship *Sancta Maria Rata Encoronada* foundered in Mayo. The survivors transferred to *Duquesa Santa Ana*, which was driven at night into the treacherous shallows of Loughros More Bay, 'where falling to anchor,' an Irishman on board recalled, 'there fell a great storm which brake in sunder all their cables and struck them upon ground'. Though his leg had been broken against the capstan, de Leiva rallied the survivors on an island in Kiltooris Lough. Hearing that other Spaniards were sheltering at Killybegs, the general and his men crossed the mountains to join them. There they agreed to make for Scotland in the one vessel still afloat, the *Girona*, a three-masted galleass with 36 oars pulled by 244 rowers.

With about 1,300 Spaniards crowded aboard, the *Girona* negotiated the wild waters off Bloody Foreland, only to have her rudder smashed by a northerly gale which blew the vessel onto the north Antrim coast. Just east of Dunluce the ship struck a long basalt reef and split apart. That terrible night the disaster at sea was so great that the death toll was only two hundred short of the number lost in the *Titanic* in 1912; only nine men survived. Three hundred and eighty years later the Belgian archaeologist Robert Sténuit brought the *Girona*'s treasures to the surface – the most complete piece of Armada archaeological evidence and a permanent reminder of the flower of the Spanish nobility who died with Don Alonso de Leiva, and the nameless sailors, conscripts and galley slaves who perished in these cold northern waters of Ulster.

'HE NEVER SAW READIER OR PERFECTER SHOT'

Captain Francisco de Cuellar, who survived shipwreck at Streedagh in County Sligo, fought with the MacClancys against Fitzwilliam's men on Lough Melvin. De Cuellar got back to Spanish Flanders via Coleraine and Scotland and wrote an account of his adventures, which includes this observation:

> The savages are well affected to us Spaniards, because they realise that we are attacking the heretics and are their great enemies. If it was not for those natives who kept us as if belonging to themselves, not one of our people would have escaped.

At one point there were perhaps three thousand Spaniards in Ulster. By 1589 nearly all had departed or been slain, though a handful remained to instruct the Irish in modern military techniques.

If 1588 had been a moment for action against the intrusion of English power in Ulster, that moment soon passed. Sir Brian O'Rourke of Bréifne (described by de Cuellar as 'an important savage') was executed at Tyburn; Sorley Boy did not wish to undo his recent agreement with the English Crown; Sir Hugh O'Donnell did not dare to help the Spaniards in Tír Conaill, as his son, Red Hugh, was held hostage in Dublin Castle; and Hugh O'Neill, recognised as Earl of Tyrone in 1585, helped to transfer some Spanish prisoners to the Pale.

The fate of the Spaniards and those who harboured them showed the extent to which English power had advanced in Ulster since Elizabeth had come to the throne. So far, Ulster chieftains had displayed little inclination to pull together in opposition to the Crown. A succession dispute amongst the MacMahons gave Fitzwilliam the opportunity in 1590 to partition all of Monaghan amongst five leading MacMahons, the chief of the MacKennas, other native freeholders and the Earl of Essex. It was a skilful application of the principle of divide and rule to extend English control. This approach had apparently worked well in Connacht a few years before and there seemed every reason to believe that the authority of the Crown could be extended piecemeal all over Ulster in a similar way. If, however, English officials felt confident about the progress of the queen's peace in Ulster, they reckoned without Elizabeth's own protégé, Hugh O'Neill.

Hugh O'Neill seemed to owe all he had to the English. It had been an English king who had given an earldom to his grandfather, Conn Bacach and, after the murder first of his father Matthew and then of his brother Brian, it had been Elizabeth who had affirmed Hugh as Baron of Dungannon in 1568. Carefully nurtured by the Crown and given a good English education in the

A seventeenth-century Italian portrait of Hugh O'Neill, Earl of Tyrone
LINEN HALL LIBRARY

Pale, Hugh had been proclaimed Earl of Tyrone in 1585. O'Neill seemed a valuable ally for Elizabeth, yet he was to become the most dangerous and astute of Elizabeth's opponents in all Ireland. Just when and for what reasons Tyrone turned against the queen is still veiled in mystery but it is certain he wanted power in Ulster and for a long time English help was essential in assisting him towards that objective. It took patience and skill to settle in at Dungannon while Turlough Luineach remained alive and while Shane O'Neill's sons were at large. It took vision to assuage the age-old enmity between the O'Neills and O'Donnells and make a firm alliance to his own advantage.

Lured on board an English vessel at Rathmullan in 1587, Red Hugh O'Donnell, the favoured heir to Tír Conaill, was held captive in Dublin Castle. During Christmas 1591 Hugh O'Neill organised his escape. At Ballyshannon physicians had to amputate Red Hugh's frost-bitten toes but in May 1592 he was proclaimed The O'Donnell, his aged father agreeing to step down. When Turlough Luineach died in 1595, Hugh O'Neill was duly inaugurated as The O'Neill at Tullahogue. The way was now clear for a coalition of the two most powerful rulers in Ulster. Tyrone's ambition was undoubtedly fed by the growing anxiety of the Gaelic Irish in Ulster: though not averse to sporadic mayhem themselves, they seem genuinely to have been appalled by Essex's massacres and the treacherous seizure of hostages. The division of Connacht and Monaghan and the encroachment of the queen's officials seemed to be pushing the Gaelic lords of Ulster to the end of the line. Armed resistance was their time-honoured reaction – not a national revolt in the modern sense but

English troops on the march during Lord Deputy Sidney's period of office; from Derricke's *Image of Irelande*

a struggle by an aristocratic caste to preserve an ancient way of life.

'I can but accurse myself and fortune that my blood, which in my father and myself hath often been spilled in repressing this rebellious race, should now be mingled with so traitorous a stock and kindred.' So wrote Sir Henry Bagenal, marshal of the queen's army, to the queen's secretary, Sir Robert Cecil, telling how his twenty-year-old sister Mabel had eloped with O'Neill, now fifty years old. That ill-feeling should not be discounted as a cause of the approaching war.

Bagenal and Tyrone campaigned together for the last time in 1593. Hugh Maguire, fearing an imposed redivision of lands in Fermanagh, had risen in rebellion against Elizabeth. Facing the combined forces of O'Neill and the marshal, Maguire was overwhelmed and his castle on the island of Enniskillen fell in February 1594. Maguire fought on, however, now with the support of Red Hugh O'Donnell. Tyrone made his first act of defiance and refused to give any further help – Maguire and Red Hugh, indeed, were his sons-in-law. Dangerously exposed, the English led by Sir Henry Duke were overwhelmed at the ford of Drumane over the Arney river. As the Annals of the Four Masters explain, 'the name of the ford at which this great victory was gained was changed to the Ford of the Biscuits, from the number of biscuits and small cakes left there to the victors on that day'. Maguire recovered Enniskillen the following year, by which time O'Neill was at war with the queen.

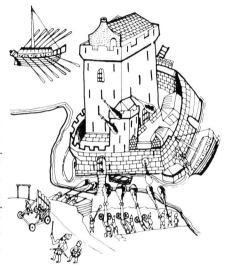

Siege of Enniskillen Castle, 1594, drawn by an Elizabethan soldier, John Thomas, subsequently killed in the campaign HMSO (DEPARTMENT OF THE ENVIRONMENT, NORTHERN IRELAND)

The skirmishing for Enniskillen showed how vulnerable were English garrisons planted in hostile territory. Retaining and provisioning forward positions proved far more difficult than setting them up in the first place; and yet Elizabeth's government could see no other way of taming the Ulster lords than by maintaining fortified posts in their territories. In February 1595 O'Neill carried out his first direct act of war against the queen when he destroyed the Blackwater Fort. This put the more southerly Monaghan garrison in peril. Bagenal relieved Monaghan in June but his force was ambushed by O'Neill as it returned near Clontibret church. Sir Edward York, in command of Bagenal's cavalry, observed 'that in no place whatsoever he had served in all his life he never saw readier or perfecter shot' and when the survivors got back to Newry it was admitted that there were 'more hurt men in the late service than was convenient to declare'.

Clontibret showed that Tyrone commanded a force more formidable and professional than Elizabeth's commanders had encountered in Ireland before. The vigilance of English pinnaces in the North Channel cut down the supply of Scots Redshank mercenaries and instead O'Neill raised a great Gaelic host in his own lands. Levies, known as *buannadha*, became as formidable as gallowglass professionals, and taught by deserters from the English and a few remaining Spanish survivors, they mastered the caliver or arquebus, and the heavier musket. All down to the poorest servants could be called up, including the *ceatharnaigh* or kerne, light foot soldiers who could muster from any part of Ulster within three days. O'Neill, his allied chiefs and their kinsmen, who formed the traditional aristocratic warrior caste, made up the cavalry of this Ulster army. With a force of some six thousand horse and foot, O'Neill was an adversary the like of whom the English had never yet encountered in Ireland.

O'Neill and O'Donnell knew that outside help was essential to ensure total victory. Philip II – hard-pressed in France and his government veering towards bankruptcy – was eager, nevertheless, to do what he could. In May 1596 his emissary, Alonso Cobos, sailed into Killybegs with munitions and returned with a letter from the Ulster lords asking Philip's son, the Prince of the Asturias, to 'aid in his clemency this most excellent and just cause, that of asserting Catholic liberty and of freeing the country from the rod of tyrannical evil'. It was late in October before Philip was ready; 81 vessels left Lisbon and were joined by 19 more from Seville; but the fleet was overwhelmed by a terrible storm – more than 2,000 men perished and at least 32 ships were lost. A year later another Armada sailed with 136 vessels and over 12,600 men but

English troops recovering Blackwater Fort in 1597: an attempt to relieve it in 1598 led to O'Neill's greatest victory at the Yellow Ford.
TRINITY COLLEGE DUBLIN

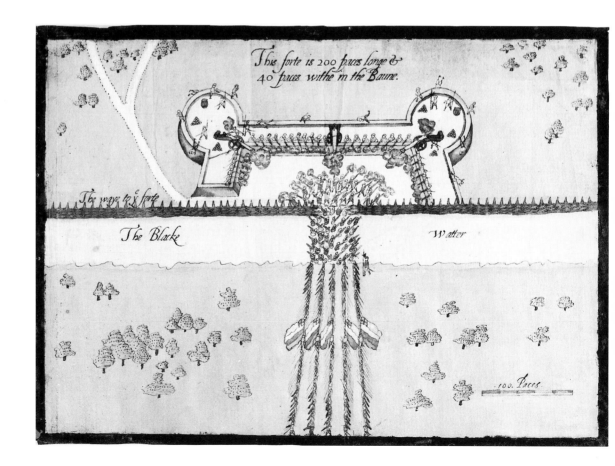

it too was dispersed by storms. Philip could not summon enough strength for a third attempt. O'Neill and O'Donnell would have to fight on, depending on their own resources.

THE YELLOW FORD AND AFTER

Appointed lord deputy in 1597, Lord Thomas Burgh was sure that if O'Neill 'be well pressed, all is got'. He led a force into Ulster, blundering as far as the Blackwater, where he built a new fort to replace the one Tyrone destroyed in 1595; it was, he wrote, 'my first child . . . an eyesore in the heart of O'Neill's country'. In fact, he had left a hostage to fortune and abandoned Armagh to sustain it. Meanwhile, the new governor of Connacht, Sir Conyers Clifford, was driven back over the Erne at Ballyshannon, many of his men swept to their deaths over the salmon leap. Burgh was forced to pull back to Newry where he died of famine fever on 13 October.

All the Gaelic lords of the north were joining O'Neill and O'Donnell. Shane MacBrian O'Neill, Lord of Clandeboye, took Belfast Castle and hanged and disembowelled all the English garrison. Sir John Chichester, governor of Carrickfergus, recovered the castle in July, 'without any loss to us, and put those we found in it to the sword'. The fall of Edenduffcarrick on the shores of Lough Neagh followed soon after, but Chichester failed to ensure good relations with the Antrim Scots. Sir James MacDonnell, who had succeeded his father Sorley Boy, had his castles besieged when he refused to give the governor a cannon retrieved from the wreck of the *Girona*. Sir James and his brother Randal counter-attacked and in a skirmish outside Carrickfergus Chichester was shot through the head and 180 of his men were killed. Now the MacDonnells, too, had become formidable opponents of the queen and the isolation of the Blackwater Fort was complete.

'I protest to God the state of the scurvy fort of Blackwater,' the Earl of Ormond remarked in his dispatch to Cecil, 'which cannot be long held . . . The fort was always falling, and never victualled but once (by myself) without an army.' He preferred the fort to be 'razed, or yielded upon composition, than the soldiers to be left to the uttermost danger'. The position of this garrison in the heart of Ulster was becoming desperate: fierce sallies had to be made to bring in wood and water, and the soldiers were reduced to eating grass growing on the ramparts. The Irish Council in Dublin, however, did not agree with Ormond, acting as the queen's lord general in absence of a deputy, and on the arrival of fresh troops in July 1598, Sir Henry Bagenal's offer to relieve the fort was accepted.

With three hundred horse and four thousand foot, the marshal arrived in Armagh without incident, leading one of the largest forces to have entered Ulster for many years. But from the moment he left Armagh early next morning Bagenal faced disaster. O'Neill had long prepared for this opportunity: he himself was in command on the left, O'Donnell on the right, Randal MacDonnell close by and Sir Hugh Maguire leading the horse. As Bagenal thrust across country his army was assailed by musket and caliver shot fired from the woods. Pack horses and four cannon dragged by bullocks impeded regiments marching behind, while the van advanced to near annihilation. O'Neill had a deep trench running almost a mile between two bogs. Behind, a heavy saker stuck in the bed of a stream oozing from a marsh – the yellow ford which gave the battle its name. Bagenal rode back to help extricate the gun but when he raised his visor he was shot in the face and fell

dying. The Irish closed in and the débâcle was complete when a soldier, refilling his powder horn, exploded two barrels with his match.

Hoping, perhaps, to ease negotiations for a truce, Tyrone stayed his hand and even allowed the men of the Blackwater Fort to march south to the Pale. As it was, 800 men and 25 officers in the invading force had been killed, together with 400 wounded and some 300 deserting to O'Neill's side. Many regard the Yellow Ford as the most disastrous defeat the English ever suffered at the hands of the Irish.

Elizabeth had no longer any wish to talk: the Yellow Ford convinced her that she must unstintingly use her treasure to defeat Tyrone. English rule, not only in the extremities but over the whole of Ireland, was in peril. Connacht was overrun by O'Donnell; the O'Mores furiously attacked the English settlement in the Midlands; the plantation in Munster disintegrated; and as many as twenty thousand Irish may have been in arms against the queen. Over the winter of 1598–9 troops were levied on an unprecedented scale

Robert Devereux, the 2nd Earl of Essex: despite commanding the largest English army yet seen in Ireland he failed to confront the Ulster lords in 1599; after a painting by Nicholas Hilliard.

across England and in April 1599 Robert Devereux, 2nd Earl of Essex, arrived in Dublin with the greatest English army yet seen in Ireland.

Essex spent the summer in an attempt to detach Leinster and Munster allies from O'Neill. As reports of aimless expeditions and inconsequential sieges were brought to Elizabeth, Sir John Harington observed, 'She walks much in her privy chamber, and stamps with her feet at ill news, and thrusts her rusty sword at times into the arras in great rage.' The news got worse. Clifford and his army were overwhelmed by the O'Rourkes in the Curlieu Mountains and his head was sent to Red Hugh. Then, when Essex at last set out for Ulster at the end of August 1599, he negotiated with Tyrone instead of fighting him. A six-week truce was agreed and the Ulster Irish retired having made no concessions whatever.

Elizabeth scathingly described the truce as a 'quick end made of a slow proceeding'. Essex then suddenly deserted his post, returned to London, and burst into the queen's bedchamber to beg forgiveness; he was committed to the custody of Lord Keeper Egerton. Elizabeth was determined to renew the fight and appointed Charles Blount, Lord Mountjoy, as her lord deputy in January 1600. Believing himself to be in constant bad health, Mountjoy wore three pairs of silk stockings with woollen stockings over them under his high linen boot hose and swaddled himself with three waistcoats under his coat. The new lord deputy, nevertheless, appeared fearless in battle and inspired his men with greater success than any of his predecessors. What is more, he had an army of 1,200 horse, many of them experienced soldiers, and the supply of munitions, provisions and fodder was better organised than before.

With this force, Mountjoy planned to break O'Neill's rebellion by an unceasing war of attrition; he preferred to fight in winter when it was more difficult for the Irish to hide in the leafless woods, their stores of grain could be burned and their cattle more easily seized. The lord deputy began by putting into effect the scheme Essex had failed to carry out – an amphibious operation to place a garrison at the head of Lough Foyle to drive a wedge between the territories of O'Donnell and O'Neill.

DERRY, MOYRY AND KINSALE

On 16 May 1600 a force of some four thousand foot soldiers and two hundred cavalry disembarked at Culmore on the south-western shore of Lough Foyle and threw up a fort there on the site of a ruined castle. In command was Sir Henry Docwra, who led his men up the lough to Derry. Docwra relates in his *Narration* that Derry was then an island:

Lord Mountjoy, the first English commander to conquer the entire island of Ireland; sixteenth century, after a painting by Juan Pantoja

> the River called loughfoyle encompassing it all on one side, & a bogg most commonly wett . . . This peece of Ground we possess our selves of without Resistaunce & iudging it a fitt place to make our main plantation in . . . I presentlie resolved to raise a fforte to keep our stoore of Munition & victuells in.

He avoided the temptation to march directly towards O'Neill's strongholds and instead concentrated on making Derry secure enough to 'sitt it out all winter'.

In September O'Neill joined Red Hugh and made a midnight attack from the bog next to the island. Irish muskets that were fired too soon gave the defenders time enough to drive off the attack, who 'takeing a fright, confusedly retyred as fast as they could'. The presence of such a large army produced the first hair cracks in the coalition of Ulster lords Tyrone had held together for so

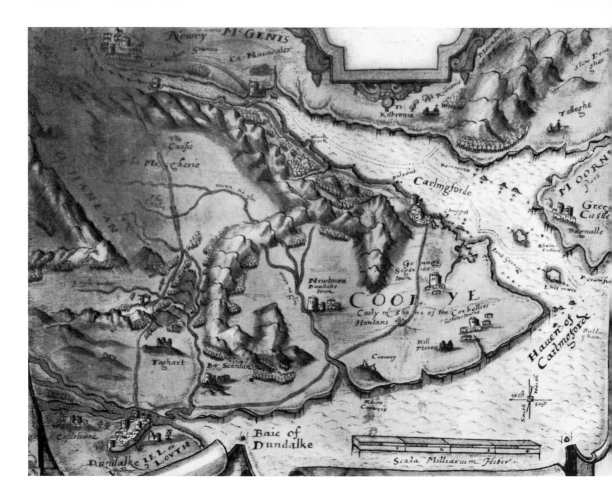

long. Art O'Neill, a son of Turlough Luineach, joined Docwra and on 3
October Niall Garbh O'Donnell, placed in command of Tír Conaill in Red
Hugh's absence, rode into Derry to offer his services to the English. The tide
of war was now turning for Elizabeth and O'Neill battled with the fierce
desperation of a commander forced to fight on several fronts.

Tyrone had long prepared to make a stand in the Moyry Pass and on viewing
the elaborate Irish defences, Mountjoy observed: 'These barbarous people had
far exceeded their custom and our expectation.' A spy told him that he found
O'Neill urging his people 'with great earnestness to work lustily and patiently', for if the lord deputy broke through, then it was 'farewell Ulster and
all the north'. In foul weather the English again and again attempted to break
through but without success, and one captain remarked on the Irish defences
that he never saw 'a more villainous piece of work, and an impossible thing for
an army to pass without an intolerable loss'.

Then, unaccountably, on 13 October O'Neill withdrew from the pass and
four days later Mountjoy marched through without opposition. Why did
Tyrone abandon such a strong defensive position? Was the decision made in
response to Red Hugh's frantic calls for assistance against Docwra? Whatever

the reason, O'Neill's retreat was probably the gravest strategic error made in nine years of war against the English. Thereafter, Mountjoy's tenacious winter campaigning, together with Docwra's steady success, wore down the forces of O'Neill and O'Donnell. Captain Josias Bodley (brother of Sir Thomas, founder of the Bodleian Library) took one of Tyrone's greatest strongholds, the *crannóg* fortress of Lough Lurcan. Sir Arthur Chichester, who had replaced his brother John as governor of Carrickfergus, ravaged Clandeboye, kept the MacDonnells at bay, and crossed Lough Neagh to create havoc on the western shores. In May 1601 he reported to Mountjoy:

> We have killed, burnt and spoiled all along the lough within four miles of Dungannon . . . in which journeys we have killed above one hundred people of all sorts, besides such as were burnt, how many I know not. We spare none of what quality or sex soever, and it hath bred much terror in the people.

Only timely and significant Spanish aid could change the course of the war.

On 21 September 1601 a fleet of Spanish vessels entered the Bandon estuary without opposition and seized the port of Kinsale. Don Juan del Águila, commander of the expeditionary force, would have preferred to disembark in Tír Conaill, but he had been overruled. With only 3,500 men in a province recovered by the English, and with all their ships sent home, the Spaniards could do little else but appeal to O'Neill and O'Donnell to march south.

A week later the Ulster lords were faced with an agonising decision – should they risk all to reach the Spaniards? If they stayed, the two Hughs could recover their position while Mountjoy marched south, but in the end O'Donnell persuaded the others to march to Munster. Mountjoy reached Kinsale before them with over 11,000 foot and 850 horse and camped before the walled town, allowing 'the garrison there neither quiet, rest, sleep, nor repose for a long time,' the Four Masters record. O'Donnell set out from Ballymote in Sligo on 2 November and gave the English the slip by crossing a frozen defile over the Slieve Felim Mountains. O'Neill made Lough Ramor in Cavan his rallying point and moved out cautiously on 9 November. The Ulster Irish covered over three hundred miles, wading river after river, often up to the chest, and drew up to Kinsale in good order, camping to the north and east of the English, severing Mountjoy's supply lines with Cork. As the English slightly outnumbered the combined forces of the Irish and the Spanish, O'Neill believed the best hope was to sit tight and starve the English into surrender. For weeks harsh weather and lack of provisions inflicted horrifying losses on both sides. Then Águila made a desperate appeal for help and Red Hugh implored O'Neill to attack.

The first hours of Christmas Eve were violently stormy, with lightning seen to strike some spears. The Irish army advanced in preparation for attack. The lord deputy had not gone to bed that night and, according to his secretary

Fynes Moryson, had been forewarned by a MacMahon in return 'for a bottle of Usquebagh'. In any case, the English could see the Irish lighting their

matches in the dark. Some of the Ulster men lost their way and, as the Gaelic host hesitated to regroup, Mountjoy launched a furious cavalry charge on the Irish infantry, knocking them off balance and then scattering them. In a couple of hours after dawn it was all over, and Águila's sally from the walls of Kinsale came too late.

Kinsale was Gaelic Ireland's Culloden: all of O'Neill's triumphs were now wiped out at a stroke and the complete conquest of the whole of Ireland was only a matter of time. Kinsale also tipped the balance of the European conflict in favour of England and the Netherlands, forcing Philip III to make terms by 1604. Before that could happen the final subjugation of Ulster had to be executed.

The remnant of the Ulster army retreated north with O'Neill, and Red Hugh sailed for Spain; the Tír Conaill chief was twice given an audience with Philip III but further help was not forthcoming. O'Donnell died in August 1602, poisoned it is thought by an English spy, and was buried at Valladolid. O'Neill sued for terms but Elizabeth refused, instructing Mountjoy: 'We do require you, even whilst the Iron is hot, so to strike.'

Mountjoy Fort, built in 1602, on the southern shore of Lough Neagh (which the English unsuccessfully attempted to rename Lough Sydney) .NATIONAL LIBRARY OF IRELAND

By the early summer of 1602 Mountjoy was in the heart of Tyrone, Docwra had reached Ballyshannon and, once Chichester had been summoned to join them, they entered the smoking ruins of Dungannon without resistance and destroyed the ancient coronation site of the O'Neills at Tullahogue. O'Neill, with only a few hundred men still by him, held out first in the fastness of Glenconkeyne and then in the woodlands of Fermanagh. Docwra was right to observe: 'The axe was nowe at the roote of the tree, & I may say, the Necke of the Rebellion as good as utterlie broken.'

Mountjoy laid waste the countryside, seizing cattle and destroying corn as harvest approached, reporting to London that 'for all Events we have spoiled and mean to spoil their Corn'. The inevitable consequence was a famine of great severity, as Moryson records:

> Now because I have often made mention formerly of our destroying the Rebels Corn, and using all Means to famish them, let me by two or three Examples shew the miserable Estate to which the Rebels were thereby brought. Sir Arthur Chichester, Sir Richard Moryson, and the other Commanders ... saw a most horrible Spectacle of three Children (whereof the eldest was not above ten Years old,) all eating and gnawing with their Teeth the Entrails of their Mother, upon whose Flesh they had fed 20 Days past, and having eaten all from the Feet upward to the bare Bones, roasting it continually by a slow Fire, were now come to the eating of her said Entrails in like sort roasted, yet not divided from the Body, being as yet raw.

Moryson describes 'Carcasses scattered in many Places, all dead of Famine'; common people surviving on 'Hawks, Kites and unsavory Birds of Prey'; and he concludes:

> No spectacle was more frequent in the Ditches of Towns, and especially in wasted Countries, than to see Multitudes of these poor People dead with their Mouths all coloured green by eating Nettles, Docks, and all things they could rend up above Ground.

The lord deputy looked forward to an end of O'Neill, 'the most ungrateful Viper to us that raised him', but as the English closed in, the queen cancelled her previous instructions to Mountjoy and commanded him to offer a pardon. Tyrone eagerly accepted the offer of a safe-conduct taken to him by Sir Garret Moore, who took him to his estate of Mellifont Abbey in March 1603.

The terms were more lenient than Tyrone could have dared to hope for: provided he renounced the title The O'Neill, he retained his lordship over most of his traditional territory. Mountjoy was eager for agreement, for he knew, and O'Neill did not, that Elizabeth had died six days earlier – the lord deputy could not be certain that James I would support him as the queen had done. The peace agreed at Mellifont had a poor chance of surviving intact. Too many had died and too many nursed bitter memories of suffering, betrayal and loss. The conquest had cost the Crown £2 million and war veterans, adventurers, merchant contractors and government officials were dismayed to find that the lands of Ulster were not available for dismembering. Great changes were certain to follow the Nine Years War, but it took the collapse of Mountjoy's treaty with O'Neill to effect a transformation of Ulster in the reign of the Stuarts.

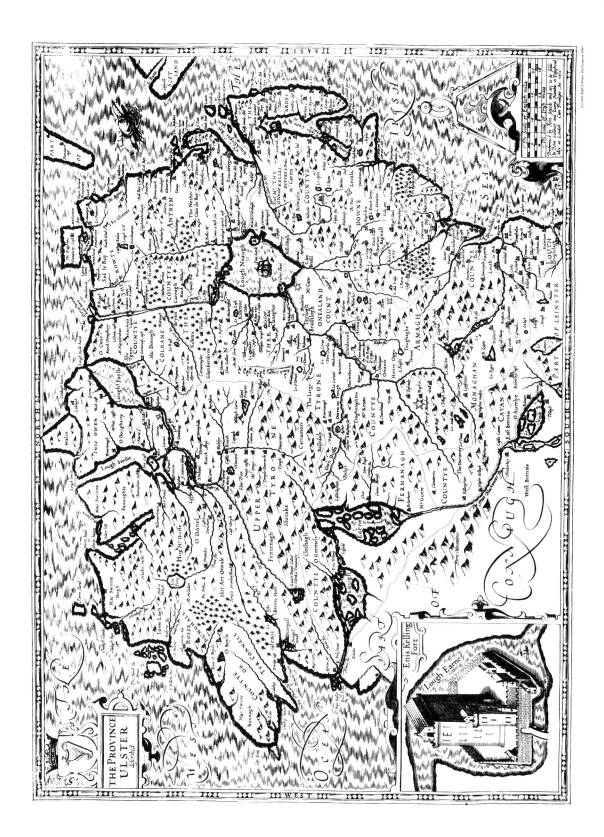

4

PLANTATION AND WAR

1604–1704

Sir John Davies, who survived being disbarred for breaking a cudgel over a fellow lawyer's head to become Irish attorney-general in 1606, yearned to impose English law on 'the Irishry in the Province of Ulster . . . the most rude and unreformed part of Ireland, and the seat and nest of the last great rebellion'. Hugh O'Neill and Rory O'Donnell, the brother of Red Hugh, created Earl of Tyrconnell, had been given a generous royal pardon which infuriated the servitors, those who had fought for the Crown in Ireland. Sir Arthur Chichester, appointed lord deputy in 1605, Davies and the servitors set out to undo the Treaty of Mellifont and undermine the overweening power of the northern Gaelic lords. Their scheme was more successful than they dared to hope.

Towards the end of August 1607, a Breton vessel steered into Lough Swilly and cast anchor off Rathmullan. At nightfall a messenger came ashore with gold and silver from the King of Spain. Cuchonnacht Maguire, Lord of Fermanagh, had planned this flight for more than a year, for he was certain the Gaelic lords would be beggared by the Crown. The lordship of Fermanagh had been partitioned between two hundred freeholders; the Earl of Tyrconnell was left only with mountainous and infertile lands and preferred the prospect of a military career in the service of Philip III; and traditional ways of levying tribute were being challenged by English law. Did O'Neill think of flight? He had apparently strengthened his direct control over sub-chieftains and tenants within his vast earldom but he chafed at the whittling away of his authority: in the lord deputy's words, 'now the law of England, and the Ministers thereof, were shackles and handlocks unto him, and the garrisons planted in his country were as pricks in his side'. If Tyrconnell and Maguire fled to Spain, would Tyrone be accused of staying behind to rouse the country against the king? He feared the Crown would make a new attempt to break his power, a view shared by the Spanish ambassador in London, who wrote to Philip, 'I know they wish to kill him by poison or by any possible means.'

With a heavy heart O'Neill decided he had no choice but to leave his native province. He returned from court sessions in Meath to gather as many

DISCOVERIE
OF THE
TRUE CAUSES
WHY
I R E L A N D
Was neuer entirely Subdued,
nor brought vnder Obedience
OF THE
Crowne of ENGLAND,
Vntill the Beginning of
His Maiesties happie Raigne.

Printed exactly from the Edition in 1612.

LONDON:
Printed for A. MILLAR, opposite Katharine
Street in the Strand. MDCCXLVII.

An influential book by Sir John Davies, Irish attorney-general: his view that massive confiscation should follow the conquest of Ulster prevailed over that of Sir Arthur Chichester, the lord deputy, who wanted to retain native proprietors in the hope that they would become Protestant and loyal to the Crown.
LINEN HALL LIBRARY

Opposite:
John Speede's map of Ulster, 1610: for the first time English cartographers were able to produce a reasonable representation of central and western Ulster.
LINEN HALL LIBRARY

The Flight of the Earls
in 1607 from
Rathmullan, Lough
Swilly
THOMAS RYAN

members of his family as he could in Dungannon. In haste they travelled all night over the Sperrins and shortly afterwards the cream of Ulster's aristocracy crowded aboard the vessel and sailed down Ireland's west coast. Contrary winds drove them to France, where they got permission to go to Spanish Flanders. The Earl of Tyrone wanted to lead a Counter-Reformation expedition to drive the English out of Ireland but instead there followed years of barren exile, a stream of letters to Philip, and the gradual realisation that Spain would not help. When Hugh O'Neill died in Rome in 1616, the Gaelic order in Ulster, which had flourished for a thousand years, was being swept away. 'Woe to the heart that meditated,' the Annals of the Four Masters lamented, 'woe to the mind that conceived, woe to the council that decided on, the project of their setting on this voyage.'

Chichester quickly grasped the opportunity presented by the Flight of the Earls. In September 1607 the lord deputy wrote to James I:

> If His Majesty will, during their absence, assume the countries into his possession, divide the lands amongst the inhabitants . . . and will bestow the rest upon servitors and men of worth here, and withal bring in colonies of civil people of England and Scotland . . . the country will ever after be happily settled.

Inheriting an immense debt from Elizabeth's Irish wars, James found much to attract him in Chichester's proposal. Davies had the earls 'attainted by outlawry' and in December 1607 lands of the departed lords were confiscated and preparations for a plantation began. Events the following spring were greatly to extend the scope of the project.

Sir Cahir O'Doherty of Inishowen had been foreman of the grand jury that had found a true bill for treason against the earls. Docwra had been replaced as governor of Derry by Sir George Paulet, who had none of his predecessor's diplomatic finesse and in a quarrel with O'Doherty hit him in the face. O'Doherty at once rose in rebellion, took Culmore Fort by a ruse on 18 April 1608, burned most of Derry to the ground the following night, destroyed Strabane soon afterwards and threatened to spread the revolt across Ulster as factions of the O'Cahans and O'Hanlons joined in. Chichester soon had the situation under control, however, pursuing the last of the rebels into the woods of Glenconkeyne. O'Doherty was killed at the Rock of Doon, near Kilmacrennan, on 5 July; Doe Castle fell but only after it had 'endured 100 blows of the demi-cannon before it yielded'; and the last resistance was overcome in an amphibious operation extending from Aranmore to Tory Island. Shortly afterwards, Chichester was granted Inishowen, a part of Ulster which he observed had been only recently as inaccessible as 'the Kingdom of China'.

Burt Castle, an O'Doherty fortress overlooking Lough Swilly; based on an original in State Papers Ireland, 1601
ULSTER JOURNAL OF ARCHAEOLOGY

While the campaign still raged in the Donegal highlands, Davies wrote to the king from Coleraine, informing him that he had six counties 'now in demesne and actual possession in this province; which is a greater extent of land than any prince in Europe has to dispose of'. He urged James to colonise the whole area thoroughly. The king was more than ready to agree to a full-scale plantation, for his enthusiasm had already been fired by the success of pioneering settlements in Antrim and Down.

Hugh Montgomery, 6th Laird of Braidstane, sent an agent from Ayr to Carrickfergus to rescue Conn MacNeill O'Neill, the Lord of Upper Clandeboye imprisoned for levying war against Elizabeth. The agent won the heart of the gaoler's daughter and 'ply'd his oar so well that in a few nights he had certain proofs of the bride's cordial love'. She opened the cell and Conn lowered himself down a rope to a waiting boat to be taken to Largs. In Scotland O'Neill readily agreed to share his estate if the king would pardon him.

The king gave the pardon and divided Upper Clandeboye between O'Neill, Montgomery and his secret agent, James Hamilton. Conn was fortunate to retain an estate of sixty townlands, because he was only one of several claimants. In the dramatically changed political climate other Gaelic lords in Antrim and Down made room for servitors and colonisers in return for a

Over-throw of an Irish rebell, in a late battaile:
Or
The death of Sir Carey Adonghertie, who murdred Sir George Paulet in Ireland; and for his rebellion hath his head now standing ouer Newgate in Dublin.

imprinted at London for I. Wright, and are to be sold at his shop neere Christ Church gate, 1608.

A contemporary pamphlet describing the suppression of O'Doherty's rebellion in 1608

The Hamiltons' castle at Killyleagh, County Down, built in the Dufferin, land formerly held by the MacCartans; from the *Dublin Penny Journal*
LINEN HALL LIBRARY

secure title in English law to their lands. Phelim MacCartan, for example, kept Kinelearty in south Down on condition that he passed 'the thirde part of all that his countrie' to the servitor Sir Edmund Cromwell. Sir Randal Mac-Donnell, though he had fought with Tyrone at Kinsale, won the king's favour by inviting Lowland Scots to settle in the Route and was created 1st Earl of Antrim in 1620.

After raising 'recruits of money' in Scotland, Montgomery built a harbour at Donaghadee: here arrived 'a constant flux of passengers coming daily over', ignoring 'evil report of wolves and woodkerns' to build new homes, repair old castles and till the land. In 1611 the plantation commissioners reported that at Newtownards he had 'made a good towne of a hundred houses or thereaboutes all peopled with Scottes'. Hamilton had built a mansion and '80 neowe houses all inhabited with Scotishmen and Englishmen' in Bangor and had fired 200,000 bricks to put up houses in Holywood.

Eager to set a good example on his own grant of lands in Lower Clandeboye, Chichester got the help of army officers who had fought with him to bring in colonists. The commissioners found Belfast with 'many famelyes of English, Scotish and some Manksmen already inhabitinge of which some are artificers who have buylte good tymber houses with chimneyes after the fashion of the English palle'. Moses Hill, a former lieutenant of Chichester's horse troop, built a fort at Stranmillis and brought in English colonists to settle the Lagan valley extensively upstream. Other busy planters included Ensign John Dalway, Captain Hugh Clotworthy at Massereene, Captain Robert Langford at Muckamore, Sir Thomas Phillips at Toome, and Sir Fulke Conway in Killultagh. Several of these men hoped to get more land west of the River Bann as the plantation of Ulster got under way.

THE PLANTATION OF ULSTER BEGINS

The summer assizes of 1608 judged that almost all of Tyrconnell, Coleraine, Tyrone, Armagh, Fermanagh and Cavan were in the king's hands. The so-called 'native plantation' of Monaghan was allowed to stand. This was a unique opportunity for James I to reward at little cost the many who had claims on his patronage and it would also be, the king observed to Chichester, a civilising enterprise which would 'establish the true religion of Christ among men . . . almost lost in superstition'. Besides, a plantation would quieten Ulster and reduce the risk of native rebellion and foreign invasion. This was the era of colonial expansion and it could be said that Virginia in America and Virginia in County Cavan were founded in the same spirit.

Sir Arthur Chichester, architect of the plantation of Ulster and the founder of Belfast
ULSTER JOURNAL OF ARCHAEOLOGY

Chichester headed a survey of the confiscated lands but this was little more than an inquiry and much confusion arose from different Irish divisions, ballybetaghs subdivided into townland units known as tates, polls and ballyboes. The 'Printed Book' of conditions for successful applicants for Ulster land was published in London in April 1610. Separation was the essence of the scheme, in which the largest group of colonists, known as undertakers, had to

Monea Castle, County Fermanagh: a planter castle, later seized by the Maguires during the 1641 rebellion – the garrison was massacred
JOHN STRANEY

clear their estates completely of native Irish inhabitants. The confiscated land was divided into 'precincts', each subdivided into large, middle and small 'proportions'. Undertakers had to be English or Scots Protestants, who were to pay rent of £5 6s. 8d. to the king for every thousand acres. Servitors and favoured native Irish were to have their estates in the same precincts, the theory being that ex-officers would be able to keep a watchful eye on rebellious Irish. Undertakers had to undertake to plant on every thousand acres twenty-four Protestant British from at least ten families, while those Irish granted proportions were to adopt English farming methods and pay £10 13s. 4d. per thousand acres. All classes of planters had obligations to build stone houses and defensive works; deadlines were set for arriving, colonising, building and rent payment; and conditions were laid down for founding towns, bringing in craftsmen, setting up schools and erecting parish churches.

The lord deputy was filled with a deep sense of foreboding; his advice to win the confidence of selected chieftains by creating a large class of anglicised and contented Irish landowners had not prevailed. The 'deserving' Irish were left only in possession of between one quarter and one fifth of the confiscated lands and some of these estates only during their lifetimes. The servitors, Chichester believed, had not been given enough – around one fifth of the land, not sufficient to carry out the defensive role expected of them. The undertakers had more than one quarter of the confiscated territory; Chichester doubted if they had the resources to carry out their obligations. Twenty years would pass before the lord deputy's anxieties were shown to be justified.

The great migration to Ulster began: servitors who had long sought a share in the province they conquered; younger sons of gentlemen eager for lands to call their own; Scottish nobles induced to plant 'for a countenance and strength to the rest'; relatives, neighbours, artisans and dependants of undertakers; rack-rented and evicted Lowland Scots farmers; and horse thieves and other fugitives from justice. The English had more capital but the Scots were the most determined planters, as Sir William Alexander observed:

> Scotland by reason of her populousnesse being constrained to disburden her selfe (like the painfull Bees) did every yeere send forth swarmes.

Most came from south-west Scotland, where lairds oppressed and evicted their tenants unable to make the down payments required under the 'feuing' land-letting system. Some came from the Borders, where the Earl of Dunbar's joint commission of English and Scots harried the cattle reavers. Later in the century the Reverend Andrew Stewart of Donaghadee claimed that

> from Scotland came many, and from England not a few, yet all of them generally the scum of both nations, who, for debt or breaking and fleeing from justice, or seeking shelter, came thither.

James I fretted that his plantation was making a slow start. The native Irish

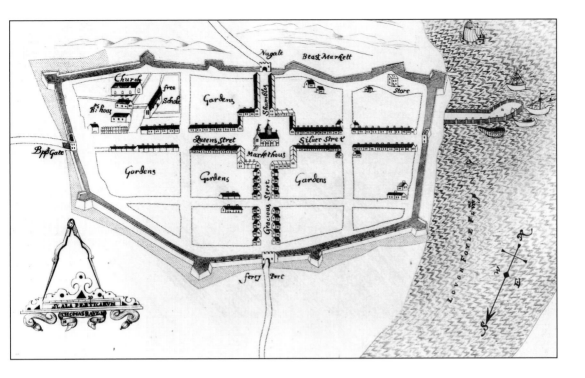

Labels on map: Church, free Schole, B: hou[se], Gardens, Shambles, Nugate, Beast Markett, Store, Queens Stret, Silver Stret, Markethous, Bpp Gate, Gardens, Gardens, Gracious Stret, Gardens, Ferry Port, Lovgh Foyle Fluvius, SCALA PERTICARUM, THOMAS RAVEN

Londonderry, the last walled city to be built in western Europe; from Raven's plan of 1625

were waiting to be moved or dispossessed and woodkerne lurked in the forests, threatening the settlements. And all this time rumours of O'Neill's return with Spanish help caused anxiety both in Ulster and in London. The king feared that not enough men of wealth had applied for land; to strengthen the plantation, therefore, he turned to the City of London.

Few undertakers had been attracted to the county of Coleraine, inhabited by resentful O'Cahans in the lowlands and woodkerne in the forests. Sir Thomas Phillips, who had been energetically developing his grants at Coleraine and Toome, persuaded the City aldermen to send a deputation to tour the county in the autumn of 1609. Impressed by the valuable woodland there, the Londoners agreed to plant. The Livery Companies could afford to dictate terms to the king: the City had underwritten much of the cost of conquering Ulster. James granted the London Companies not only all of County Coleraine but also the barony of Loughinsholin, detached from Tyrone, and some adjoining lands from Tyrconnell – now renamed County Donegal – and Antrim. By an agreement made in January the supervision of this huge area, named County Londonderry, was placed in the hands of City representatives in The Honourable The Irish Society.

On 17 December 1613, at a court of Common Council, a draw was held for the twelve proportions of the Londonderry plantation. The fifty-five London Companies arranged themselves into twelve associations and by the luck of the draw, taken by the City swordbearer, the Grocers, the Fishmongers and the Goldsmiths got the most fertile proportions. Work had begun on building Londonderry, the last walled city in western Europe, but progress was slow and in a damning report, Sir Josias Bodley in 1614 observed that the native Irish were still in the proportions.

James I was furious: the clearing of natives was 'the fundamental reason' for the plantation. It was in vain that the king raged against the undertakers; the failure to measure the confiscated lands resulted in proportions vastly greater in acreage than that stated in the grants. Planters could not find enough cash to colonise such extensive estates and kept on the Gaelic Irish, who themselves were prepared to pay high rents to avoid eviction. The king imposed fines and doubled the undertakers' rents; the colonists willingly paid up and so the grand plan to separate natives and newcomers had come to nothing.

With no security of tenure, their burdensome rents set by informal arrangements from year to year, and their status severely reduced, the Gaelic Irish in the north yearned for a return to the old order. They were confronted by alien planters adhering to a variety of Protestantism far distant from their own Catholicism and by Crown officials who took sporadic and ineffective but irritating measures against the Catholic Church. Meanwhile Franciscans increased their numbers and, together with priests returning from seminaries on the European mainland, instilled a new zeal amongst Old English and native Irish Catholics alike. In Ulster, therefore, the uncompromising spirit of the Counter-Reformation faced the inflexible determination of the Puritan settlers. Hostility, suspicion and uncertainty created a dangerously unstable atmosphere in the province.

THE REBELLION OF 1641

Thomas Wentworth, Earl of Strafford: he alienated planters and natives alike and ended on the scaffold; after a painting by Van Dyck

Charles I did not share his father's enthusiasm for the Ulster plantation. Instead he sought money which did not have to be sanctioned by parliament in order to increase his personal power. Thomas Wentworth was sent to Ireland in 1633 to raise funds for the royal coffers and to enforce High Church conformity. Imperious and indefatigable, Wentworth soon alienated every interest group in the country. A Commission for Defective Titles sent ripples of alarm through the landed classes; the London Companies were fined heavily for failing to evict the Irish from their lands; and the Presbyterians of the north were harassed unrelentingly.

Protestant clergy who refused to recant their Presbyterianism were deprived of their offices and many, with their followers, took refuge in Scotland. There they played their part in rallying support for the Covenant, a bond of union among the king's Scottish opponents. Many Scots in Ulster needed no encouragement to sign the Covenant and Wentworth lost no time in taking action against them, drafting a command that they take an 'oath of abjuration of their abominable covenant' – the Black Oath – and sending troops to Ulster to enforce it.

The king's military reverses in Scotland and the growing power of the Commons at Westminster led to Wentworth's execution in 1641 – the treatment of the London Companies and the Presbyterians contributed powerfully to his downfall. Charles I's waning power and the emergence of a hostile parliamentary opposition gave discontented Gaelic lords an opportunity to recover their position which they had not had since Elizabeth's time. They found it hard to adapt to British methods of estate management and most were in dire financial straits by 1641. These descendants of 'deserving natives' loathed Wentworth's regime; at a time when they had been impoverished by the harvest failures of 1629–32, the lord deputy levied 'recusancy' fines to the letter of the law for non-attendance at Established Church services and drastically lowered the value of their estates by questioning land titles. The O'Reillys of Cavan told the Dublin administration that they were oppressed with

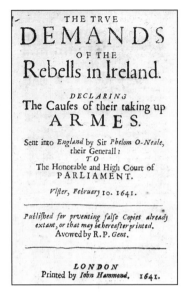

THE TRVE
DEMANDS
OF THE
Rebells in Ireland.

DECLARING
The Caufes of their taking up
A R M E S.

Sent into *England* by Sir *Phelom O-Neale,*
their Generall :
T O
The Honorable and High Court of
PARLIAMENT.

Vlfter, February 10. 1641.

Publifhed for preventing falfe Copies already
extant, or that may be hereafter printed.
Avowed by R. P. *Gent.*

LONDON
Printed by *Iohn Hammond.* 1641.

Sir Phelim O'Neill presents his demands before going into rebellion in 1641
LINEN HALL LIBRARY

> grievous vexations, either to the captivating of oure consciences, our looseinge of our lawfull liberties, or utter expulsion from our native seates, without any just grounds given.

Rory O'More, with lands in Armagh, led the conspiracy of the Ulster lords which matured fitfully from February 1641. Returned émigré officers instilled Counter-Reformation zeal into the plot, and final arrangements were made on 5 October at Lough Ross in County Monaghan: Dublin Castle would be seized on 23 October, while Sir Phelim O'Neill, Lord of Kinard in south Tyrone, would lead a simultaneous revolt in Ulster.

On the night of Friday 22 October 1641 Owen O'Connolly sat drinking with his foster brother Hugh MacMahon in Winetavern Street in Dublin. There O'Connolly learned of the Ulster lords' plot and having been instructed in Protestant doctrine by Sir John Clotworthy, he had no hesitation in informing the Government. Dublin Castle rallied its defences and MacMahon, Lord Maguire and other conspirators were imprisoned in the fortress they had planned to capture. The plot had been foiled but that same night the rebellion in Ulster had begun.

Just before eight o'clock on that Friday evening Sir Phelim O'Neill called

S.ʳ *Phillom O*
Cheife Traytor
Neale
of all Ireland

Sir Phelim O'Neill, leader of the 1641 rebellion and executed in Dublin in 1652
LINEN HALL LIBRARY

Atrocities committed against
the colonists in Ulster in
1641; propaganda woodcuts
from Sir John Temple's
The Irish Rebellion
LINEN HALL LIBRARY

on his neighbour Lord Caulfield at Charlemont and invited himself to dinner. Once inside Sir Phelim and his men seized the fort and imprisoned the garrison; then they galloped to Dungannon, which had fallen by a similar ruse, reaching it by midnight. Before nightfall on Saturday Sir Conn Magennis had led a successful assault on Newry and Lurgan was in flames. On Sunday Sir Phelim issued a proclamation from Dungannon, declaring that the rising

> is noe wayes intended against our Soveraine Lord the King, nor the hurt of any of his subiets, eyther of the Inglish or Schotish nation, but onely for the defence and liberty of our selves and the Irish natives of this kingdom.

So far the rebellion had limited objectives and no appeal had been made to foreign powers. Under the direction of native Irish gentry the insurgents had shed comparatively little blood. Within days the insurgents were striking south to Dundalk, north to Moneymore which had been seized by the O'Hagans, and west towards Fermanagh, where the Maguires had risen.

Robert Lawson, a merchant returning from Killyleagh, beat a drum through the streets of Belfast, raised about 160 men, and reached Lisburn on 25 October. Magennis, having burned Dromore, approached Lisburn that night but 'making show of six or seven lighted matches for every piece, to astonish the enemy', Lawson's men forced him back. It was to no avail that the Irish drove four hundred head of cattle at the gates next day. Belfast, Lisburn, Carrickfergus, Antrim and Larne were thus saved but elsewhere in the province the insurgents seemed to sweep all before them. Portadown fell, all Cavan was overwhelmed, Armagh capitulated and in Fermanagh all the planter castles were besieged by the Maguires. Only Enniskillen, commanded by Sir William Cole, held out in the west.

Everywhere the Catholic gentry depended on an uprising of the Gaelic peasantry and after the first fortnight they lost control. Hungered by harvest failures, and listening to wild prophecies and rumours of a Puritan plot to massacre them, they threw themselves with merciless ferocity on the settlers. The Irish victories were so rapid in the first few days that they did not know what to do with those who surrendered. Many settlers were 'turned naked, without respect of age or sex, upon the wild barren mountains, in the cold air' and perhaps a majority of those who died perished from exposure and hunger. Others, like Viscount Caulfield, were simply shot dead. The massacre at Portadown is well authenticated; there Manus O'Cahan drove about eighty men, women and children from Loughgall to the Bann

> and there forced them to goe upon the Bridge which was cut down in the midst and then striped the said people naked and with theire pikes and swords and other weapons thruste them down headlong in to the said river and immediately they perished and those of them that asayed to swim to the shore the rebels stood to shoot at.

William Clark, a 'British Protestant', gave this sworn evidence in Dublin, where in Trinity College there are over thirty manuscript volumes filled with depositions by survivors. Robert Maxwell, writing in August 1642, claimed that 154,000 were killed in Ulster – a wild exaggeration as this figure exceeds the entire Protestant population of the province at the time. Hilary Simms in a meticulous study concludes that the maximum number of people massacred and murdered in County Armagh 'including all hearsay evidence and rumour is 1,259'. There is no doubt that large numbers of settlers were slaughtered, often in appalling circumstances. At Shewie, a mile from Legacorry, Protestants were herded into a thatched house and burned alive; in Fermanagh the Maguires killed the garrison of Tully Castle after promising mercy; and dozens of people taken away from Armagh, just before it was set on fire, were massacred at Charlemont in 1642.

Neither side gave quarter in this war. Sir William Cole killed some two hundred captured in a sally from Enniskillen and nearly four hundred Scots who surrendered were put to the sword near Augher. In north Antrim some Catholic Scots joined the rebellion, slaughtering settlers at Portna; over five hundred Ulster colonists took refuge on the Isle of Bute alone and in the presbyteries of Ayr and Irvine some four thousand others were in danger of starving. Meanwhile, the Scots were cautiously considering an urgent plea to send a relief army to Ulster.

Major-General Robert Monro, a hardened veteran of the Thirty Years War, landed at Carrickfergus on 3 April 1642 and set out southwards with his Scots army in pursuit of the Irish. He simply slaughtered his captives, first at Kilwarlin, then at Loughbrickland, and finally at Newry, where he hanged or shot sixty men and his soldiers threw women in the river and used them as targets. Marching north again, Monro slaughtered any Irish men, women and children that he found – 'nits make lice' was a popular cry of those who justified the killing of native children. Mountjoy and Dungannon were recovered, and in desperation the Ulster Irish prepared to capitulate. Just then, at the end of July 1642, Owen Roe O'Neill disembarked at Doe Castle in north Donegal. Nephew of Hugh, the Great O'Neill, Owen Roe now used

Carrickfergus Castle, held by the Scots until 1649 when it was captured by Cromwellian troops led by Colonel Robert Venables
LINEN HALL LIBRARY

his prestige and military experience in Spanish Flanders to stiffen the ranks of the Irish. The task was not easy, for Ulster, the province he had left forty years before, 'not only looks like a desert, but like Hell'.

In August 1642 the English Civil War began and Irish politics became labyrinthine in its complexity in the years following. Ulster Catholics and Protestants were each, at various times and for different reasons, opponents and allies of the king, but almost always opposed to each other. The formal approval given to the rebellion by the Catholic Church in March 1642 led the Old English, native Irish and clergy to pool their resources and form 'the Confederate Catholics of Ireland' at Kilkenny in October. The Catholic Old English, however, were eager for a deal with Charles I and a 'cessation' was agreed in 1643. The native Irish in Ulster wanted to fight on but without resources they could do little more than skirmish with Monro. Then in 1645 Giovanni Battista Rinuccini arrived as papal nuncio with impressive supplies of arms, thus giving Owen Roe a chance to put the Ulster army he had trained into action.

At the beginning of June 1646 Monro moved southwards with some six thousand men and six field pieces drawn by oxen. Near Armagh he learned that Owen Roe threatened his rear just north of the Blackwater at Benburb. Force-marching his men almost twenty miles, Monro crossed the river at

Caledon on 5 June and began with a brisk cannonade. Owen Roe harangued his men: 'Let your manhood be seen by your push of pike. Your word is Sancta Maria , and so in the name of the Father, Son, and Holy Ghost advance!' With no guns but with an equal number of men, the Irish army steadily pressed the exhausted Scots back to the river, slaughtering them. Monro escaped only after he had cast away his coat, hat and wig; and between one third and one half of all the Scots were killed, the Irish sustaining only trifling losses. When the news reached Rome Pope Innocent X himself attended a Te Deum in Santa Maria Maggiore: it was the greatest and most annihilating victory in arms the Irish ever won over the British. 'For ought I can understand,' Monro ruefully observed, 'the Lord of Hosts had a controversie with us to rub shame in our faces.'

Giovanni Battista Rinuccini: the papal nuncio who brought arms to Ulster but divided the insurgent command by his inflexibility
BRITISH LIBRARY

CONFISCATION AND RESTORATION

The victory at Benburb was thrown away. Though all Ulster was now at his mercy, Owen Roe instead turned south to help Rinuccini seize control of the Catholic Confederacy in Kilkenny. The three-year truce was broken and war was resumed against the Protestants, Royalist and Parliamentarian alike. Indecisive campaigning was brought to an abrupt end by the execution of Charles I in January 1649 and Cromwell's arrival in August. After taking Drogheda on 11 September, Cromwell put the garrison of some 2,600 to the sword, and captured priests, by his own account, 'were knocked on the head promiscuously'. He explained that this was retribution for the Ulster massacres of 1641, 'the righteous judgement of God upon those barbarous wretches who have imbrued their hands with so much innocent blood'. A second massacre was carried out in Wexford a month later when around two thousand were killed.

Colonel Robert Venables was sent by Cromwell to recover the north, where the Lords Hamilton and Montgomery declared for Charles II, as had nearly all Scots. He had only the support of Sir Charles Coote, commander of the Derry garrison; but his men were seasoned veterans of Naseby, and Newry and Belfast were taken without difficulty. Early in December 1649 Venables and Coote cut the settlers' army to pieces near Lisburn, killing one thousand men, many hacked down in a relentless cavalry pursuit. General Tam Dalyell then surrendered Carrickfergus. Owen Roe O'Neill died in November and Bishop Heber MacMahon of Clogher was elected to lead Catholic resistance. The Irish had no answer to the Ironsides, however:

Owen Roe O'Neill: he failed to follow up his victory at Benburb in 1646
LINEN HALL LIBRARY

MacMahon was routed near Letterkenny in June 1650 and hanged at Enniskillen; Charlemont Fort surrendered in August; and guerrilla warfare was ended in April 1653 when the O'Reillys capitulated after an assault on Lough Oughter.

The Pourtrature of his Excellency
The Right Honorable
OLIVER CROMWELL
Lord Gôvernour of Ireland &c.

Oliver Cromwell: in 1649 he and his Ironsides took merciless revenge for the Ulster massacres of 1641.
LINEN HALL LIBRARY

The Commonwealth exacted a harsh retribution. Hundreds were executed; around 12,000 were transported to the West Indies; 3,400 soldiers were exiled; and millions of acres were confiscated. Only those landowners who could prove 'constant good affection' to the parliamentary cause were not punished. In practice, Protestants were absolved if they paid fines, but almost all Catholic landowners disappeared in Ulster, many obtaining smaller estates in Leitrim as compensation. In Ulster the biggest confiscations were in the east and south of the province: 41 per cent of the land of Antrim; 26 per cent of Down; 34 per cent of Armagh; and 38 per cent of Monaghan. Only 4 per cent of Tyrone was confiscated and Cromwell's charter restored Derry property to the City of London, showing that the Ulster plantation was largely undisturbed. A fresh set of landlords and jobbers arrived, but this time there was no real attempt to remove the native cultivators. The Gaelic aristocracy, already shattered by the Ulster plantation, was all but wiped out and the foundations of the Protestant Ascendancy had been firmly laid.

General George Monck, who for a time had held Belfast with Parliamentarian troops against Scots royalists, proclaimed the restoration of Charles II in 1660. Although he had no wish to go on his travels again, the king felt that something would have to be done for Irish Catholics who had remained loyal to the Crown through all its troubles. The 1662 Act of Settlement declared that land had to be found for 'innocent Papists'. But who was innocent? The Earl of Antrim, languishing in the Tower mainly to protect him from his creditors, was restored to his estates at the behest of the dowager Queen Henrietta Maria. Protestants in Britain and Ireland were so outraged that Charles shrank from any serious attempt to overturn Cromwell's land settlement. By 1688 less than 4 per cent of counties in Ulster, other than Antrim, was owned by Catholics.

Once more, men who had lost everything withdrew to the woods and the hills. The name given to a landless outlaw in this period was 'tory', an anglicised version of an Irish word meaning 'pursuer' – a word of abuse subsequently applied by the Whigs to their political opponents in the Westminster parliament. Draconian legislation by the Commonwealth failed to extirpate the tories, who continued to terrorise much of Ulster during the reign of Charles II. The most notorious of all was Redmond O'Hanlon of Poyntzpass, who, after being imprisoned for horse stealing, bribed his way out of Armagh gaol and – according to the author of a popular biography – 'despairing of mercy or pardon, he resolved to abandon himself to all Lewdness and to become a perfect bird of Prey'. Landowners paid a force of thirty men ninepence a day for three months to track down this tory to no avail and reports of O'Hanlon's daring appeared in London as he and his 'pack of insolent bloudy outlaws' plundered Down, Leitrim and Roscommon in October 1679. It took the viceroy himself to bring about O'Hanlon's fall: in return for a pardon and £200, Art O'Hanlon shot dead his foster brother Redmond at Eight Mile Bridge near Hilltown, County Down, on 25 April 1681. In the years following, nearly all the remaining tories were tracked down and killed. On 17 March 1683 Sir William Stewart, of Newtownstewart in County Tyrone, wrote to the Duke of Ormond:

> There was never such a winter for country sports as the last and I have enjoyed them in much perfection. I had very good hawks and hounds but we have not had more success in any sport than Tory hunting. The gentlemen of the country have been so hearty in that chase that of the thirteen in the county where I live in November, the last was killed two days before I left home.

In the same year that Redmond O'Hanlon was killed the Catholic primate of all Ireland was executed. This judicial murder in 1681 of Archbishop Oliver Plunkett, hanged, drawn and quartered at Tyburn, was the climax of the 'Popish Plot', in which Catholics were supposed to be planning to assassinate the king. Under Cromwell's regime, Catholics endured much persecution: around one thousand priests were banished and outlawed worship was confined to a 'Mass rock' in a remote place. However, the accession of Charles II ushered in a new era of toleration. The Government ceased to interfere with the Presbyterians who accepted the *regium donum*, a grant from the king for the upkeep of their ministers, and Catholic worship became public again and religious orders began to return. A Protestant jury in Dundalk had no difficulty in throwing out trumped-up charges against Plunkett; it was English rather than Irish Protestant frenzy that sealed the primate's fate. The Popish Plot did not have an Irish counterpart and, taken as a whole, these were years when religious tensions eased perceptibly, peace prevailed and striking economic progress was achieved.

Oliver Plunkett, Catholic archbishop of Armagh, who was executed in London during the Popish Plot in 1681
NATIONAL GALLERY OF IRELAND

In 1682 Dr William Molyneux in Dublin was commissioned to collect

statistical accounts of Irish districts for inclusion in Moses Pitt's 'Grand Atlas'.
The publication fell through before it got to Ireland but a few manuscript
descriptions survive and they paint a picture of a province which was settled
and growing in prosperity. In his account of Oneilland barony in north
Armagh, William Brooke observed:

> The vast quantity of wheat that is yearly carried hence into the County of
> Antrim, besides the maintenance of above two thousand Familys with bread
> . . . do plainly demonstrate it to be the granary of Ulster, and one of Ceres's
> chiefest barns for Corn . . . so it challenges the preference for fruit trees, good
> sider being sold here for 30 shillings the hogshead.

In and about Lurgan 'is managed the greatest Linnen manufacture in Ireland',
and Brooke concludes, 'the fertility of the Soile, the curious inclosures, the
shady Groves and delicate seats, that are everywhere dispersed over this Barony
doe all concur to make it a Paradise of pleasure'. William Montgomery
described the Ards peninsula, where 'the Inhabitants doe Manure & Dung the
land with sea oar by them called Tangle which being spread on it and plowed
down makes winter grain & summer Barly grow in aboundance'. And in his
eccentric description of County Antrim Richard Dobbs estimated Islandmagee to be 5,500 acres, 'whereof 5000 I am sure is fit for fork and scythe, nor
did I ever see better ground for so much together, whether for grain or cattle'.

These accounts paint an excessively rosy picture. In fact Ulster had been in
a wretched economic condition on the accession of Charles II and recovery
was not helped by export restrictions imposed on Ireland by Westminster. Yet
rapid recovery did take place – the rising prosperity of England and her
colonies, together with growing trade opportunities on the European mainland, kept up the momentum. By 1683 Belfast was exporting more butter than
any other port in Ireland and was soon to bypass Limerick to become the
fourth largest town in Ireland. The City of London suffered huge losses during
the Plague of 1665 and the Great Fire of 1666, and Derry had its own serious
fire in 1668; The Irish Society had little money to spare, therefore, to
reinvigorate its plantation. Coleraine and Derry had depended heavily on
exports of timber, but now the woods had almost all gone. However, the
salmon fisheries there were self-sustaining and remained profitable; salted
salmon were exported as far as Venice and Bilbao, and in 1684 Spain imported
1,885 barrels of salmon from Derry alone. In short, the plantation in Ulster
flourished for most of Charles II's reign and, despite the growing attractions of
English colonies in America, the province drew in a steady flow of English and
Scots. Then in 1685 the accession of a Catholic king, James II, sent tremors of
alarm not only through the length and breadth of England but also through
the Protestant settlement in Ireland.

One of the few Catholics to survive Cromwell's massacre at Drogheda was

Richard Talbot, who had risen from being the sixteenth child of an impoverished Kildare gentleman to become James II's principal agent in promoting
the revival of Catholic fortunes in Ireland. Created the Earl of Tyrconnell in
1685, Talbot arrived in Dublin as lord deputy in February 1687 and immediately began promoting Catholics to all positions of importance and purging
Protestant officers from the army. Some dismissed officers left Ireland to serve
William of Orange, but for the present, Ulster Protestants were content to sit
tight and await developments.

William of Orange had good reason to believe that
Louis XIV of France aimed at nothing short of European domination and intended the invasion of Holland.
As he drew together a defensive alliance, including
Catholic princes such as Leopold I of Austria and the
Elector Maximilian of Bavaria, the nobility of England
– seeing that James II was attempting to reduce parliament to a cipher – turned to the ruler of Holland for
aid. William seized this opportunity to win the backing
of a powerful neighbour and disembarked at Brixham
on 5 November 1688 with an imposing Dutch army.
After fatal vacillation James fled to France just before
Christmas and the following February William and his
wife Mary, James's eldest daughter, were declared joint
sovereigns of England, Scotland and Ireland. This
bloodless revolution gave the Westminster parliament
new constitutional powers but members were not
stirred to action until news came in March that James
had arrived in Ireland with a formidable French army.
'If Ireland be lost, England will follow,' one MP
observed, and another declared: ''Tis more than an Irish

William of Orange; portrait
by an unknown artist
LINEN HALL LIBRARY

war, I think 'tis a French war.' For a brief moment in history the fate of much
of Europe turned on events in Ireland.

Early in 1689 a Council of Protestant Gentlemen – representing Monaghan,
Armagh, Down and Antrim – met at Loughbrickland under the leadership of
Lord Mount-Alexander to organise resistance to Tyrconnell. Their efforts were
too dilatory: an assault on the Catholic garrison in Carrickfergus failed
completely; led by Richard Hamilton, the Jacobites – those who remained
loyal to King James – swept northwards and overwhelmed the Protestants at
the 'break of Dromore' in March; and it looked as if all of Ireland would fall
under James's control, whose progress to Dublin was a triumph. In the west
only Enniskillen held out: there Gustavus Hamilton organised the defence and
his men's long-range fowling pieces kept Lord Galmoy and his Jacobites at a
respectful distance. In the north-west Lord Antrim approached Derry with

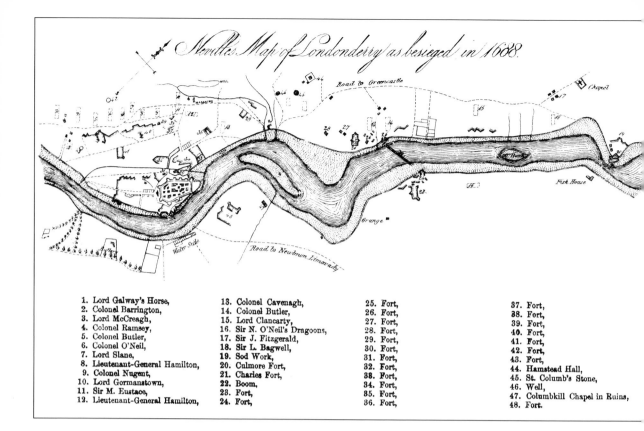

Nevilles Map of Londonderry as besieged in 1688.

Map of the siege
of Derry, 1689
LINEN HALL LIBRARY

1,200 Catholic Redshanks; when they entered the Waterside and began to cross the Foyle, thirteen apprentice boys ignored the advice of Ezekial Hopkins, bishop of Derry, to admit the troops, raised the drawbridge at Ferryquay Gate and closed the gates. The resolution of the apprentice boys, Captain Thomas Ash recalled,

> acted like magic and roused an unanimous spirit of defence; and now with one voice we determined to maintain the city at all hazards, and each age and sex conjoined in the important cause.

For William III everything now depended on whether or not the Protestants in Enniskillen and Derry could hold out long enough until he could send aid.

'NO SURRENDER'

Inside the walls of Derry confidence in Lieutenant-Colonel Robert Lundy, military governor of the city, was ebbing rapidly. Whether or not he was hedging his bets between James and William, or secretly supported James, or was simply incompetent, Lundy was no man to command the defence of a beleaguered city. After the Jacobites had overwhelmed Protestants entrenched at Lifford, Long Causey and Cladyford, and Lundy refused the support of two regiments sent out from Liverpool, the suspicion that the governor was a traitor became a certainty. Adam Murray, a farmer from the Faughan valley, led a citizens' revolt and overthrew Lundy. Joint governors were appointed in his place: Major Henry Baker, a professional soldier from County Louth, and the Reverend George Walker, Church of Ireland rector of Donoughmore. Both were to provide inspired leadership.

King James, exhilarated by news of the victory at the fords upstream of the city, joined his besieging army. On 18 April he advanced towards the walls and offered terms; he was greeted with cries of 'No surrender!' and a fierce and sustained barrage of shot and ball. Just out of range, James sat motionless on his horse for several hours in the pouring rain. Then at the entreaty of his French advisers the king returned to Dublin, where Louis XIV's ambassador, Comte d'Avaux, observed that James 'appears to me to be very mortified over his latest proceeding'.

The Jacobites were ill-equipped for a long siege. One regiment inspected by James had only one matchlock in a hundred fit for service; a single mortar was the only artillery piece the besiegers possessed; and one French supply officer reported that 'most of the soldiers in front of Derry have still only pointed sticks, without iron tips'. It was not until the end of May that a siege train of heavy guns sent by James arrived to intensify the bombardment of the city. The rain of shells, bombs and cannon balls never threatened to breach the walls, but it did exact a heavy toll of life from the densely packed defenders. Captain George Holmes recalled that 'one bomb slew seventeen persons. I was in the next room one night at my supper (which was but mean) and seven men were thrown out of the third room next to that we were in, all killed and some of them in pieces.'

After months of siege the defenders were starving. Walker provides a price list for July: 'Horse-flesh 1/8d a lb; quarter of a dog 5/6 (fattened by eating the bodies of the slain Irish); a dog's head 2/6; a cat 4/6; a rat 1/0; a mouse 6d; a small flook [flounder] taken in the river; not to be bought for money . . .' George Holmes observed:

> I believe there died 15,000 men, women and children, many of which died for want of meat. But we had a great fever amongst us and all the children died, almost whole families not one left alive.

Because of the fever, another survivor wrote, 'people died so fast at length as could scarce be found room to interr them'.

Major-General Percy Kirke sailed into Lough Foyle on 11 June with thirty vessels, but for the next six weeks he refused to risk the Jacobite guns of Culmore to bring relief to Derry. Another deterrent was a floating boom across the Foyle at Brookhall, completed just a week before his arrival; made of fir

Reverend George Walker, hero of the siege of Derry, subsequently killed at the Battle of the Boyne, 1690

A nineteenth-century impression of the *Mountjoy* breaking the boom across the Foyle to relieve Derry in 1689

LINEN HALL LIBRARY

beams fastened with chains, it seemed an insuperable barrier below the city. After a vain attempt to draw Jacobites away from the siege by landing troops at Inch, Kirke received a stiff note from London ordering him to attempt relief forthwith.

At 7 p.m. on Sunday 28 July 1689, while the *Dartmouth* engaged Culmore, a longboat and three small vessels – the *Mountjoy*, the *Phoenix* and the *Jerusalem* – sailed up the Foyle. The wind dropped completely but the flowing tide pushed the *Mountjoy* against the boom, snapping its chains. The shore gunners were drunk with brandy and fired wildly, the Jacobite author of *A Light to the Blind* observed bitterly; he continued:

> What shouts of joy the town gave hereat you may easily imagine, and what pangs of heart it gave to the loyal army you may as easily conceive ... In the interim those gunners lost Ireland through their neglect of duty.

The siege of 105 days was the last great siege in British history, and the most renowned. 'The Lord, who has preserved this City from the Enemy,' Captain Thomas Ash recorded in his diary, 'I hope will always keep it to the Protestants.' For the Protestants of Ulster this epic defence gave inspiration for more than three centuries to come. For King William the steadfast refusal of Derry to surrender provided a vital breathing space in his war with Louis XIV and gave him a base in Ireland to drive out King James in a campaign that had just begun.

General Richard Hamilton, in command of the Jacobites at Derry, realised that the defenders could be regularly provisioned now that the boom had been broken and on Wednesday 31 July he decided to raise the siege. That same day the Williamites based in Enniskillen won a notable victory. Reinforced by two troops of horse and six companies of foot from Sligo, the garrison felt strong enough to strike out at the Jacobites before they could lay siege to the island town. Military parties plundered Trillick, Augher and Clones in April; routed the Jacobites at 'break of Belleek' and relieved Ballyshannon in May; and kept Enniskillen well supplied with food.

On the evening of 28 July – when the *Mountjoy* was breaking the boom at Derry – a desperate appeal arrived from Colonel Crichton that Lieutenant-General Justin MacCarthy and his formidable Jacobite army were bombarding Crom Castle. The Enniskillen garrison hurried south along the heavily indented eastern shores of Upper Lough Erne and, after routing some Jacobites near Lisnaskea, advanced on MacCarthy at Newtownbutler, adopting as their battle cry 'No Popery!' With over three thousand men facing an army of two thousand, MacCarthy should have won, but a confused order to his cavalry caused them to turn tail. Of five hundred Jacobites who tried to swim the lough, only one survived and the rest of the foot were hunted down and slain; quarter was given only to around four hundred officers and almost two thousand rank-and-file were put to the sword. The Comte d'Avaux wrote to Louis XIV in disgust that MacCarthy had been taken prisoner and his 'cavalry and dragoons fled without firing a pistol, and after some of them had burst their horses with the force of flight, they took to their feet and threw away their weapons, their swords, and jackets, that they might run more swiftly'.

West of the Bann, Ulster was soon cleared of Jacobites and in Antrim and Down the forces of King James were thrown on the defensive. The Duke of Schomberg's Williamite army met no opposition as it came ashore at Ballyholme Bay on 13 August 1689 to be greeted by Protestants 'falling on their knees with tears in their eyes thanking God and the English for their deliverance'.

After a brisk bombardment, the Jacobite garrison in Carrickfergus capitulated and, his army augmented by fresh arrivals to nearly twenty thousand, Schomberg then marched south to face the Jacobites entrenched at Dundalk. Almost certainly Schomberg lost the opportunity for a quick victory; but the duke – a seventy-four-year-old veteran – was loath to take risks. The price he paid for his caution was that his army, camped by a marsh, was ravaged by fever: the Williamite chaplain George Story estimated that 'we lost nigh one

The Duke of Schomberg: he took Belfast and Carrickfergus but failed to dislodge James II at Dundalk. He was killed at the Battle of the Boyne.
TENTH DUKE OF LEEDS'S WILL TRUST

The Battle of the Boyne,
1 July 1690; from an
engraving by Theodore Maas
ULSTER MUSEUM

half of the Men that we took over with us'. With a heavy heart, King William realised that he had no choice but to go to Ireland himself.

THE BATTLE OF THE BOYNE AND AFTER: 1690–1

Sir Cloudesley Shovell's squadron of warships escorted William's fleet of about three hundred vessels across the Irish Sea into Belfast Lough on 14 June 1690. The king stepped ashore at Carrickfergus and drove with Schomberg in a coach along the lough shore to Belfast. Close to the North Gate, William met Walker, hero of the siege of Derry, and accepted a verse address from the Belfast Corporation, urging him to 'Pull the stiff kneck of every Papist down'. This pale asthmatic monarch, his face lined with the constant pain of fighting ill health, told the 'great concourse of People' there that he had not come to let the grass grow under his feet.

Meanwhile, an army of continental size was disembarking. There were over forty pieces of artillery and more than a thousand horses to draw them, and £200,000 in cash for William to pay his men. On the evening of 19 June King William set out for Lisburn and, after a brief skirmish in the Moyry Pass, deployed his troops on the north side of the Boyne, just west of Drogheda on Monday 30 June. Numbering some 36,000, the Williamites were at least 10,000 stronger than the Jacobites and represented the Grand Alliance against France: here were regiments of English, Dutch, Danes, French Huguenots, Germans, and Ulster Protestant skirmishers, 'half naked with sabre and pistols hanging from their belts,' Story remarked, '. . . like a Horde of Tartars'. Although recently re-equipped by a French fleet, James's army, commanded by the Comte de Lauzun, was also greatly inferior in firepower.

William was superstitiously opposed to doing anything important on a Monday and waited until the morning of Tuesday 1 July before beginning the battle with an artillery barrage. He decided on a frontal assault across the river at Oldbridge, while he sent his right wing upstream in a feint which most successfully drew the French away. The Dutch Blue Guards had to wade up to their armpits at Oldbridge, opposed fiercely by Tyrconnell's cavalry, but in the end the Williamites triumphed by superior firepower. Schomberg was killed by mistake by a French Huguenot and the Reverend George Walker also died in the fighting. To the alarm of Sir Robert Southwell, William 'weares his Star and Garter and will not disguise who he is . . . ' He continued:

> His Maj^{ty} was here in the crowd of all, drawing his swoard & animating those that fled to follow him, His danger was great among the enemyes guns which killed 30 of the Inniskillingers on the spott.

The Battle of the Boyne was not a rout, for the Irish and French retired in good order to fight doggedly behind the Shannon for another year. Yet the battle was decisive: it was a severe blow to Louis XIV's pretensions to European hegemony; James, who made a precipitate flight, could no longer think of Ireland as a springboard for recovering his throne; for the English, the Glorious Revolution and parliamentary rule were made secure; for the Old English, the defeat dashed hopes of recovering their estates; and for Ulster Protestants, the battle ensured the survival of their plantation and a victory for their liberty to be celebrated from year to year.

The Right Honble Godart Baron de Ginkel etc. Comander-in-Chief of all their Maties Forces in Ireland & Earle of Athlone.

Baron de Ginkel, who routed the Jacobites at Aughrim on 12 July 1691

Tyrconnell wanted to make terms with William III but the Jacobite army preferred the advice to fight on given by Patrick Sarsfield, a dashing cavalry commander and grandson of the 1641 leader Rory O'More. As the Jacobites prepared to hold a line along the Shannon, William followed and laid siege to Limerick early in August 1690. Deprived of his heavy guns, destroyed in a daring raid on his siege train at Ballyneety, the king failed in his assault on the city and returned to direct affairs from London. Godard van Reede, Baron de Ginkel, now commanded the Williamite army and in May 1691 the Jacobites acquired a new general, Charles Chalmont, the Marquis de Saint-Ruth. Saint-Ruth's considerable reputation was severely shaken when in June he failed to stop Ginkel's men fording the Shannon near Athlone. Sixteen miles to the south-west, near the village of Aughrim, Saint-Ruth attempted on 12 July to lure the Williamites into a treacherous bog in front of his line. At first this tactic seemed to work, especially after Ulster Jacobites, led by Gordon O'Neill,

spiked a battery of enemy guns. 'They are beaten, *mes enfants*,' Saint-Ruth cried out, but a cannon ball fired at extreme range took off his head and Ginkel made a devastating flanking assault over a narrow stretch of dry ground. Over seven thousand Jacobites were killed in this the bloodiest battle ever fought on Irish soil.

When news of the victory spread north, the Protestants of Ulster set bonfires ablazing, as they would do every year thereafter: over time the Williamite triumphs of 1 July 1690 and 12 July 1691 fused into one celebration. As Ginkel renewed the siege of Limerick even Sarsfield knew that he would have to sue for peace and on 3 October 1691 the Treaty of Limerick was signed: fifteen thousand soldiers – the Wild Geese – were allowed to sail away to serve Louis XIV; those who stayed and gave their allegiance to William and Mary were to keep their lands; Catholics were to have such freedom of worship 'as they did enjoy in the reign of King Charles II'; and only Protestants were to live inside the walls of Limerick and Galway.

The Protestant gentry vented their fury at the Treaty of Limerick when William III summoned his first Irish parliament in 1692. If the Glorious Revolution meant anything, it meant that the monarch had to bow to the wishes of elected representatives. Ginkel's treaty was not ratified and more land confiscations were agreed both in Dublin and at Westminster. In Ulster the Catholics did not have much more to lose, except, that is, for the Earl of Antrim who was fortunate in being restored once again to his estates.

Peace returned with remarkable speed – indeed, it could be said that the broken Treaty of Limerick inaugurated the longest peace Ulster has ever known. It was the completeness of the Williamite victory, however, which ensured the century of calm that followed it. Catholics in Ireland had retained 22 per cent of the country in 1688 but the confiscations of the 1690s reduced the proportion to 14 per cent. By 1776 Arthur Young, the agricultural improver, was estimating that Catholics had only 5 per cent of the land of Ireland, even though they formed three quarters of the population. This further decline was due almost entirely to the Penal Laws.

The Irish parliament, almost exclusively representing the landed gentry of the Established Church, was convinced that the victories of the Williamite War could only be maintained by keeping Catholics in subjection. It began the Penal Code in 1695 by preventing Catholics from bearing arms, educating their children and owning any horse above £5 in value. William – anxious not to alienate Leopold I, his Catholic ally against Louis XIV – was able to stave off the banishment of monks and friars, but his death in 1702 removed the final constraints. Queen Anne's government found parts of the bill to Prevent the Further Growth of Popery unnecessarily vindictive, but it had no wish to quarrel with the Irish parliament and the proposals became law in 1704. Westminster did stifle more extreme propositions such as that made in 1719 to castrate unregistered priests. The Irish privy council explained:

> The Commons proposed the marking of every priest who shall be convicted of being an unregistered priest . . . remaining in this Kingdom after 1st May 1720 with a large 'P' to be made with a red hot iron on the cheek. The council generally disliked that punishment, and have altered it into that of castration which they are persuaded will be the most effectual remedy.

The final penal law, depriving Catholics of the vote, did not enter the statute book until 1728.

The Penal Laws were directed principally at Catholic men of property and the most effective legislation deprived them of political and economic power. Catholics could not buy land, and estates had to be divided equally amongst sons; Catholics could not have leases running for more than thirty-one years; the lucrative legal profession, the army and all public offices were closed to Catholics; and Catholics could not vote, be members of parliament or of municipal corporations, or sit on grand juries. The enforcement of these measures helped to create a highly privileged élite, aptly described in the 1790s as the Protestant Ascendancy.

The most unworkable clauses of the Penal Laws were those concerned with worship. Jesuits, monks and friars were exiled and there was no Catholic archbishop of Armagh between 1692 and 1714; yet even after

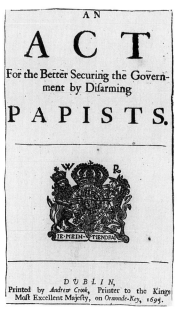

The Penal Code: examples of laws imposing many restrictions on Catholics
LINEN HALL LIBRARY

the most determined period of persecution there were fourteen bishops in Ireland at the close of Queen Anne's reign. Pilgrimages – including that to Lough Derg specifically outlawed in the 1704 act – continued without interference. Priests were not prevented from saying Mass provided they registered with the authorities. Only thirty-three priests out of around one thousand took an oath, imposed in 1710, abjuring the authority of the pope, and for some time most priests were therefore unregistered and forced to resort once again to Mass rocks. Only a few Protestants showed any enthusiasm for attempting to convert Catholics and religious restrictions fell into abeyance as the century advanced.

Catholic labouring men, unable to buy land or obtain any but the shortest of leases, were hardly touched by the Penal Laws; but even if this code was widely ineffective it kept vivid the memory of defeat and confiscation. The majority of the country's inhabitants – and more than half the people of Ulster – were at the very least second-class citizens and, unlike similar laws imposed on Huguenots in France and Protestants in Silesia, the Penal Code was applied by a minority to a majority. As the eighteenth century advanced the Enlightenment began to touch Ulster with its liberal hand, helped by growing prosperity; but fear and resentment had been etched into the folk memory in the previous century with baleful consequences for the future.

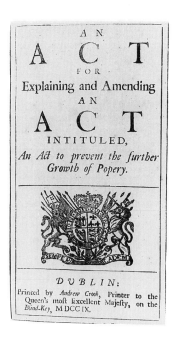

5

PROSPERITY, REVOLUTION AND REACTION

1705–1800

The triumph of William of Orange was so complete that it was followed by the longest peace Ulster had ever known. From being the poorest of the four provinces, Ulster became the most prosperous: the population rose; the province acquired an extensive road network and its first canal; market towns flourished; and, above all, the striking success of the linen industry spread a new prosperity over a wide region. In the early decades of the eighteenth century the benefits were slow enough in coming and, in any case, expectations were rising: great numbers of Ulster Presbyterians were to choose to make a new life for themselves in North America.

Presbyterian Scots were pouring into Ulster even before the Williamite War was at an end. It was observed that 'vast numbers of them followed the Army as Victuallers . . . and purchased most of the vast preys which were taken by the Army in the Campaign and drove incredible numbers of cattel into Ulster'. A string of harvest failures in the 1690s brought about such a terrible famine in Scotland that perhaps one quarter of the population died. Many survivors sought to make a new start for themselves on the far side of the North Channel and the Presbyterians in Ireland recorded a doubling of their congregations between 1660 and 1715. Any satisfaction the Government derived from this strengthening of the plantation was short-lived: these Presbyterians acquired a taste for migration and as the eighteenth century got under way – just at the time that the coming of Scots into Ulster had almost completely ceased – great numbers of them set out across the Atlantic.

'No papists stir,' wrote Archbishop William King in 1718, '. . . The papists being already five or six to one, and being a breeding people, you may imagine in what condition we are like to be in.' His view that emigration would drain Ireland of its Protestant settlers was shared by Primate Hugh Boulter who informed the Duke of Newcastle in 1728:

> The humour has spread like a contagious distemper, and the people will hardly hear any body that tries to cure them of their madness. The worst is that it

Primate Hugh Boulter, the British government's trusted representative in Ireland who was alarmed by the Ulster Presbyterian migration to America
NATIONAL PORTRAIT GALLERY

affects only protestants, and reigns chiefly in the north, which is the seat of our
linen manufacture.

The reality was that most Catholics had neither the resources nor the
inclination to go to the colonies, which were, in any case, still overwhelmingly
Protestant. The momentum of Presbyterian emigration gathered pace in the
1720s to reach a peak in 1728–9. Thomas Whitney, a seaman waiting to sail
from Larne Lough, wrote in July 1728:

> Here are a vast number of people shipping off for Pennsylvania and Boston,
> here are three ships at Larne, 5 at Derry two at Coleraine 3 at Belfast and 4 at
> Sligo, I'm assured within these eight years there are gone above forty thousand
> people out of Ulster and the low part of Connacht.

This was a wild overestimate but certainly the outflow was enough to alarm
the Government. An *Address of Protestant Dissenting Ministers to the King* of 1729
argued that the sacramental test was found by Ulster Presbyterians to be 'so
very grievous that they have in great numbers transported themselves to the
American Plantations for the sake of that liberty and ease which they are
denied in their native country'. This test had been added in 1704 by the
English privy council to the bill to Prevent the Further Growth of Popery: it
stated that any person holding public office must produce a certificate proving
that he had received the sacrament of the Lord's Supper 'according to the usage
of the Church of Ireland'. Henceforth Presbyterians could no longer be
members of municipal corporations or hold commissions in the army or the
militia. This was an irritant rather than a major grievance, however. The Justices
of Assize for the North-West Circuit of Ulster, reporting in 1729, were closer
to the truth in listing as reasons for Protestant emigration rent increases, clergy
using 'vigorous methods in payment of their tithes', and the success of agents
sent around the province by ships' masters who assured the people 'that in
America they may get good land to them and their posterity for little or no
rent, without either paying tithes or taxes'. It was also certain that many
Presbyterians, in addition to Catholics, were finding it difficult to make ends
meet in the harsh economic climate of the early eighteenth century.

'SCARCE A HOUSE IN THE WHOLE ISLAND ESCAPED FROM TEARS'

Arriving in Derry in the summer of 1718, Bishop William Nicolson found
'dismal marks of hunger and want' on the faces of people in his diocese, and a
few years later, when one of his coach horses was accidentally killed, some fifty
people fell on the carcass, hacking off pieces with choppers and axes to take
home for their families. 'We seem to be brought to the brink of a famine,' he
wrote. 'God defend us from the pestilence.' A scarcity of 1726–7 was followed
by a severe famine in 1728–9. Then at the end of 1739 a sharp frost set in and

Feb. 1. Buried Matthew Son of John Lavery of Drumnaferry.
1. Buried Susanna Wife of James Macoun of Edenballycoggill.
4. Buried Murthagh Heany from Hilwardlin
6. Married David Bell and Margaret Parker of Ballym^t^nean.
10. Buried Mary Dau: of Edward & Susanna Nagle of Magheralin.
13. Buried A Child of John Jenkins of Maralin Shoemaker.
14. Buried A Child of Bryan Lavery's from Moyrah Parish.
17. Buried Elizabeth Dau: of Widow Conky of Maralin.
18. Buried A [____] Dau: of Bryan M^c^Ilboy of Drumnaferry.
19. Buried Elinor Dau: of Widow M^c^Clatchy of Maralin.
19. Buried Richard Demply of Maralin.
19. Buried Hugh Dales of Edenmore.
19. Buried Dimund Lavery from Ballenderry.
20. Buried Jean Dau: of Thomas & Cathrine Walker of Dromo & D[__]
22. Buried Margaret Wife of Rocher Lavery of Denmore
23. Buried Jean Dau: of Hugh Walker of Tullyard.
23. Buried Margaret Read a poor Woman from the Glebe.
24. Buried Andrew Son of Dan & Mary Campbell of Dromo & D[____]
25. Buried Patrick Son of Patrick M^c^Keonan of Lissmean.

lasted for seven weeks: potatoes in store and in clamps in the fields were destroyed; cattle died; water-powered cornmills could not operate; and an ox was roasted on the ice on the frozen River Foyle. Shortage of seed and further bad weather led to a terrible famine in 1741; in the words of the author of *The Groans of Ireland*, a pamphlet written in that year:

> Want and misery in every face . . . the roads spread with dead and dying bodies; mankind the colour of the docks and nettles which they fed on; two or three, sometimes more, in a car going to the grave for want of bearers to carry them.

In the wake of this famine, at its most severe in Ulster, fever exacted a fearful toll during the hot summer of 1741:

> The universal scarcity was ensued by fluxes and malignant fevers which swept off multitudes of all sorts; whole villages were laid waste by want and sickness and death in various shapes; and scarce a house in the whole island escaped from tears and mourning.

The Irish called this *bliadhain an áir*, year of the slaughter; perhaps around three

The Year of the Slaughter: parish register of Magheralin, County Down, graphically showing the impact of the 1741 famine on one locality
PUBLIC RECORD OFFICE OF NORTHERN IRELAND

Flax growing at
Hillsborough, County
Down: in the foreground a
man is lifting a beet of flax
from the lint hole; behind
him a woman, standing,
holds two beets in her
arms, and another woman,
sitting, is rippling a sheaf to
remove the seeds; in the
right background a woman
pulls the flax from the
ground while another loads
the beets onto a wheel car;
engraving by Hincks.
LINEN HALL LIBRARY

hundred thousand died, a death toll in proportion as terrible as the Great
Famine of the 1840s. The meagre documentary record of this calamity is an
indication that such acts of God were still considered a normal feature of the
human condition in north-western Europe in the early eighteenth century.

Ulster was then an unpromising province for farming compared with other
extensive regions in Ireland. Not only is it the coldest province but half its area
is above three hundred feet; an underlay of carboniferous limestone extends
only a little way into southern Ulster; and even there its sweetening effect is
offset by poor drainage, leaving the soil cold and sticky even when it is not
covered by tracts of bog and lakeland. Yet from the 1740s onwards the
population of Ulster began to rise rapidly and living standards improved. Even
the most advanced agricultural improvements of the day could not have
brought about such striking progress. It was the success of the linen industry
that made Ulster the most prosperous part of Ireland for the remainder of the
century and beyond.

THE DOMESTIC LINEN INDUSTRY

From very early times the Irish had grown their own flax and made their own 'bandle linen'; it gets scant attention in Gaelic records, however, for it was woven up by people who were low born. Bandle linen was still made for local sale in the eighteenth century, but its width was too narrow for the export market. Some of the leading planters encouraged their tenants to grow and spin flax, and many of the colonists – particularly Quakers from the north of England – were skilled weavers who knew what sold best in Britain. The Government, too, was keen to foster an industry which did not conflict with English commercial interests and removed import duties on unbleached linen in 1696. The Irish parliament set up the Irish Linen Board in 1710 to give grants to inventors, subsidies to bleachers, bounties on the export of sailcloth, spinning wheels to the poor and tuition fees to spinning schools. Partly as a result, exports rose dramatically from two and a half million yards in the 1720s to eight million yards in the 1740s and seventeen million yards by the 1800s.

A County Down water-powered bleach mill: boiling and bucking is going on in the wing from which smoke is issuing; the section with louvred windows houses the beetling engine, rub boards and wash mill; men are working on cloth in a long wooden trough; and lengths of linen are laid out and pegged out on the grass; engraving by Hincks.
LINEN HALL LIBRARY

The making of linen in Ulster was essentially a domestic industry carried on
for the most part by people who divided their time between farming and the
making of yarn and cloth. After being pulled in August, the sheaves, or beets,
were dried and then put in a pond to rot for about a fortnight. Only after the
flax had been dried again, and 'broken', 'scutched' and 'hackled' – each process
in itself intensely laborious – could the fibres be made into yarn: long fibres
produced fine linen yarn, while short fibres were suitable for coarse cloth. After
being wound on a clock reel, the yarn was ready for the weaver – usually a
man, for weaving was heavy work. Preparing the loom was time-consuming
and only when it was tackled and the warp threads dressed with tallow and
flour, was the weft ready to be placed in the hand shuttle. Linen cloth was
usually woven into a web, a roll of cloth a yard wide and twenty-five yards in
length. Washing, bleaching and smoothing the webs was almost as labour
intensive as the making of the cloth itself and took around six months. These
finishing processes were the first to become mechanised, drapers raising capital
in Dublin to harness the streams to drive engines by water power.

The drapers made sure that Ulster had an important and early role to play
in Europe's first industrial revolution. The heart of the industry was the 'linen
triangle', extending from Dungannon, east to Lisburn, and south to Armagh;
then, as output increased, Newry was drawn in. Within this area and later
beyond it, drapers sought out suitable sites for their vertical water wheels and
bleach yards along rivers such as the Upper Bann, the Lagan, the Callan, the
Agivey, the Main and the Sixmilewater. On the Callan there were no bleach
works until 1743, and yet by 1771 there were thirty-six bleach yards along its
banks and tributaries, finishing 108,500 pieces totalling 2,712,500 yards. Rub
boards – corrugated wooden boards which were pushed backwards and
forwards by water power while wet soaped cloth was drawn between them –
came into use as early as 1705 and were a local invention. The wash mill, an
adaptation from the English fulling mill, was introduced in the 1720s. The first
beetling engine – for closing the weave and giving the cloth a sheen – seems
to have been set up at Drum Bridge on the Lagan in 1725, with a Dutchman
as manager. A striking improvement on hand beating, this technology was soon
adopted by all the drapers. Water power was also harnessed in scutch mills to
break flax between pairs of revolving grooved rollers and to beat off unwanted
pith and skin by fast-turning wooden blades.

In the 1750s dilute sulphuric acid replaced buttermilk sour, urine and other
home-made concoctions to whiten the cloth; and then in 1785 the bleaching
power of chlorine was discovered, which greatly speeded up finishing. In
between repeated washing, rubbing and soaking operations the linen pieces
were laid out on spread fields to bleach further in the sun, wind and rain,
carefully guarded from watch houses. That a vigilant eye had to be kept on the
bleaching webs is clear from this *Belfast News-Letter* report of 11 April 1783:

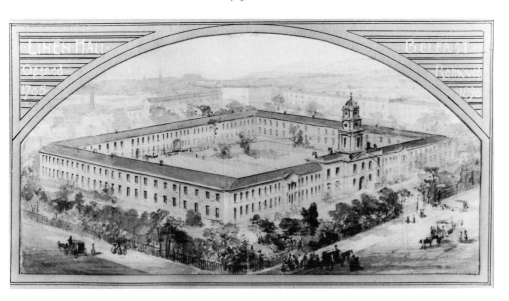

At the assizes for the county of Down, which ended on Wednesday last, the following persons were capitally convicted . . . George Brown (to be executed at Downpatrick 1st June next) for stealing linen out of the bleachgreen of Samuel McAlester of Lisnamore . . . and John Holmes (to be executed at Downpatrick on the 1st June next) for receiving said linen knowing it to be stolen.

The White Linen Hall in Belfast, completed in 1784 and home to the Linen Hall Library from 1802 to 1892, when it was demolished to make way for the City Hall
LINEN HALL LIBRARY

Drapers bought cloth unbleached, thus giving weavers a quicker return for their work, and finding the Linen Board too bureaucratic, they stopped taking their cloth to Dublin and decided to market it in Ulster. White linen halls were built in Newry and Belfast in 1783, but they were not a success, for by this time drapers had both the contacts and the funds to deal directly with English merchants. Rivalry between drapers could be softened by commercial interdependence, family connection and friendship. In 1795 lines of verse were enclosed with a pack of linen sent from Thomas Stott and Company, Dromore, to James Gilmour, Garvagh:

> The lawns we fear ye'll no think cheap
> Though we by them smal' profit reap.
> The cambrics, tho' they luk but lean
> Will make a shift to haud their ain.
> On baith to this bit paper joined
> The bill o' parcels ye will find . . .

This flourishing industry not only brought prosperity to those directly engaged in it but also stimulated the whole economy of the north by providing a ready market for the produce of farms across the province.

POTATOES, PEATS, RABBITS, GEESE, WHALES AND FISH

For weavers, who were also farmers, the first priority was to rent land as close as possible to the main linen markets and for this they were prepared to pay exceptionally high rents. They generally kept a few cows but, for fear of roughening their hands and snapping threads on the loom, they left tillage to labourers, or cottiers, to whom they sublet for a year at a time to grow flax and potatoes. The steady rise in the population of the linen triangle provided an immense market for food – the incentive to increase the yield of the soil and to bring waterlogged lands, scrub and mountain sides into full cultivation was therefore strong.

The great forests of Glenconkeyne, Killultagh and the Dufferin had been swept away and the settlers had so recklessly squandered the woodlands that, losing their habitat, the native red deer became extinct in the north and the last wolf was killed in the Sperrins in the 1760s. In 1780 a mighty tree forty-two feet in girth, known as the Royal Oak, was felled on the Conway estate near Antrim. Part of it was sawn up to build a fifty-ton vessel for Lough Neagh but – as a striking illustration of the soaring price of wood products – the bark alone of this single oak was sold for £40.

Forest clearance did, nevertheless, increase land available for farming. Together with the maintenance of peace, two vital ingredients made possible the intensive exploitation of wetlands, scrub and mountain: potatoes and turf. The potato, which tolerates a wide range of soils, was considered the best crop for clearing land and provided an abundant staple diet – it was reckoned that one Irish acre could feed eight people for a year. The most characteristic implement for preparing and cultivating new land was the loy, from the Irish

Cultivating potatoes in
lazy beds in Glenshesk,
County Antrim,
c. 1900
ULSTER MUSEUM

laighe, a spade with a long shaft, one foot rest and a narrow iron blade. Potatoes were grown on raised ridges known, inappropriately, as lazy beds: sods were carefully turned over, ashes from burned sods spread over these, potatoes planted on top and then covered with mould from the adjacent furrow. The root crop became part of the rotation with barley and oats and, if the soil could be made fertile enough, flax.

Turf from the bog (known as 'peats from the moss' in areas of dense Lowland Scots settlement) not only provided hard-won but abundant firing and building material (in the form of sods and bog oak) but also found a ready market in the valleys to heat the bleachers' boilers. Cash earned in this way could buy limestone or marl to be taken back up to the hills, there to be burned in kilns to sweeten acid soils. Coastal farms could draw on the bounty of the sea and even today shell sand is still highly prized for spreading on peaty, acid soils. Seaweed was rightly seen as an excellent manure and was gathered along every shore; native Irish speakers in Donegal carefully distinguished between the various species, while English speakers referred to seaweed as wrack, sea bar and kelp. Kelp blown in from the deeps during storms was burned to ash for bleaching and fertiliser. Arthur Young noted that some gentlemen rented stretches of shoreline and that kelp ashes sold for forty or fifty shillings a ton.

An Irish cabin, sketched by the agricultural improver, Arthur Young, in 1776: as late as the 1840s about a quarter of the Irish people lived in hovels such as this one; engraving by Hincks.
LINEN HALL LIBRARY

Outside the main linen producing area, the north-west depended heavily on farming. Much of the land was poor and unyielding. In Magilligan, a flat sandy headland in north County Londonderry, salt spray damaged grass and crops, and to prosper, the people had to supplement their income in other ways. Here the sand dunes and marram grass were home to the most extensive rabbit warren in Ulster; the local people sold the carcasses in the region for about 4d. each and found the buyers eager to take the skins for Dublin's large hatting trade. By the beginning of the nineteenth century the annual take was around 2,500 dozen animals, selling at thirteen shillings a dozen. In winter barnacle geese flying from the north could be trapped at night, as Dean Henry observed in 1739:

Ploughing in Clanbrassil, County Down: only better-off farmers could afford to plough with four horses. A man is broadcasting seed and, in the background, two oxen draw a harrow; engraving by Hincks.
LINEN HALL LIBRARY

In the months of October, November and December there come into it vast flights of Barnacles, which as they fly low along the Southern Shore, are taken on Nets Erected on long poles.

Magilligan farms often paid part of their rent in honey and this coastline was already attracting summer visitors seeking good health.

Nearly all the barley in the north-west was grown for making whiskey and by the 1780s there were no fewer than forty legal distillers in County Londonderry, with Coleraine second only to Dublin in importance. The making of illegal poteen flourished, particularly on the Inishowen peninsula and at Magilligan, where stills could be hidden behind the dunes from gaugers' eyes.

In times of harvest failure the prolific coastal and inland waters helped to save people from starvation. In 1744 historian Walter Harris observed of the County Down coast that 'such Quantities of Sand Eels have sometimes been taken on it, particularly in the late Season of scarcity, that the Poor carried them away in Sack fulls'. Young noticed that 'the whole barony of Ards are fishermen, sailors and farmers, by turns' and that Portaferry alone had 110 fishing boats. The herring fishery in County Donegal was on a much larger scale. Between mid–October and Christmas the shoals were immense; Young learned that the herring 'swarmed so, that a boat which went out at 7 in the evening, returned at 11 full, and went out on a second trip. The fellows said it was difficult to row through them.' County Donegal was also the centre of Ireland's whaling industry. Thomas Nesbit of Kilmacrennan claimed to have invented the harpoon gun, taking whales with it when Dutch, Danish and British vessels failed to get any, along with forty-two basking sharks in a week, extracting a ton of oil from each fish. Lough Neagh had its own species of white fish, known as pollan, and trout called dollaghan, which still run the feeder streams to spawn, up to thirty pounds in weight. At Coleraine, Young just missed seeing 1,452 salmon taken in one drag of one net, but 'I had the pleasure of seeing 370 drawn in at once', and at the leap he noted straw ropes hung in the water to give elvers coming from the sea a route past the falls on their way to Lough Neagh; on their return, the eels were trapped at Toome to the value of £1,000 a year.

THE SPOILED CHILDREN OF FORTUNE

Sarah Siddons, the celebrated actress, visited her friend Lady O'Neill at Shane's Castle in 1783:

> It is scarce possible to conceive the splendour of this almost Royal estab-
> lishment, except by recollecting the circumstances of an Arabian Night's
> entertainment . . . The table was served with a profusion and elegance to which
> I have never seen anything comparable . . . A fine band of musicians played
> during the repast. They were stationed on the Corridor, which led from the
> dining room into a fine Conservatory, where we plucked our dessert from
> numerous trees of the most exquisite fruits.

After the turbulence of the seventeenth century, the great landowners were now reaping the material rewards of victorious peace. The rise in prosperity and in the population – between 1753 and 1791 the number of houses paying hearth tax in Ulster almost doubled – gave northern landlords a unique opportunity to lease their estates to give them a much higher income, especially in the linen triangle. Most of the great landed proprietors in Ulster – even those badly in debt – lived as lavishly as French aristocrats, building sumptuous mansions and laying out extensive gardens.

The classical style became the vogue when Sir Gustavus Hume, high sheriff of County Fermanagh, invited the Huguenot architect Richard Cassels to build his country seat by Lower Lough Erne in 1728. It cost Armar Lowry-Corry, 1st Earl of Belmore, some £90,000 to build Castle Coole. He charted a brig to bring Portland stone from the Isle of Wight to a specially constructed quay at Ballyshannon; from there the blocks were carted ten miles to Lough Erne to be taken by barge to Enniskillen, and more bullock carts were used

Shane's Castle, on the
northern shore of
Lough Neagh, the seat of
Lord O'Neill
LINEN HALL LIBRARY

for the last two miles to complete the delivery. Lord Belmore's extravagance was exceeded by that of the 'Earl-Bishop', Frederick Augustus Hervey, who, after being appointed bishop of Derry, succeeded his brother as Earl of Bristol. Favouring wild romantic settings, he built at Downhill, on the rugged Londonderry coast, a huge, rather forbidding, palace costing £80,000 and a Grecian-style temple close by, dedicated to his pretty cousin Frideswide Mussenden, perched on a 180-foot cliff. Then he threw himself into a new project to build another great house by Lough Beg at Ballyscullion. Ballyscullion was never completed and in 1791 Hervey left Ireland for ever to collect art treasures for his houses. Well might Chevalier de Latocnaye conclude:

> Oh, what a lovely thing it is to be an Anglican bishop or minister! These are the spoiled children of fortune, rich as bankers, enjoying good wine, good cheer, and pretty women, and all that for their benediction. God bless them!

Frederick Hervey,
the 'Earl-Bishop',
a champagne radical
painted by the Italian artist
Batoni in the 1770s
M.A. NICHOLSON

Other lavish mansions of the period include Lissanoure at Ballymoney, Tollymore, Glenarm Castle, Caledon House, Florence Court, Shane's Castle and Castle Caldwell. Great sums were spent on gardens and demesnes; Sir Arthur Rawdon, for example, built the first hothouse in Ireland at Moira and sent a ship to Jamaica to get plants to fill it.

Still possessing more capital and credit than merchants, the gentry and nobility were the principal developers of towns. William Stewart, the Tyrone MP, laid out Cookstown in 1736, giving it a splendid tree-lined main street a mile and one quarter long; the Southwell family restored Downpatrick; and

Lord Hillsborough rebuilt Banbridge on a cruciform plan and hired an English brickmaker to make the town of Hillsborough one of the most elegant in the

north. Rebuilt after being destroyed by fire in 1707, Lisburn was described by William Molyneux as 'one of the beautifullest towns perhaps in the three kingdoms'. Richard Robinson, who became Baron Rokeby in 1777, was the first primate of the Established Church to make Armagh his permanent residence. When appointed in 1765 he found the city with only three buildings with slate roofs and he threw himself into an ambitious programme to make Armagh a centre of elegance and learning: he restored the cathedral, built a splendid archbishop's palace, founded an infirmary, cut freshwater channels, sank wells, made sewers and paved and lit the streets.

Archbishop Richard Robinson, Baron Rokeby, who made Armagh the most handsome city in Ulster; portrait by Joshua Reynolds
CHRIST CHURCH COLLEGE, OXFORD

Ulster's largest towns were still its ports. Cut off from its natural hinterland by the Foyle, Derry was slow to grow until a wooden bridge erected by Cox and Thompson of Boston brought immediate economic benefits. The Needham family made Newry for a time the principal town of the north, widening the Clanrye river and building quays. The town was grand enough to invite Handel to conduct his *Alexander's Feast* in 1742 and to build a theatre in High Street, opening with George Farquhar's *The Inconstant* in 1769. Yet in the final decades of the eighteenth century Newry had to relinquish its premier position in Ulster to Belfast.

'I live in the neighbourhood of Belfast,' Lord Massereene wrote in 1752, 'and know it to be in a ruinous condition.' Ever since Belfast Castle had been gutted by fire in 1708, the Chichester family remained absentee and it was left to the 5th Earl of Donegall to launch a major rebuilding of the town to strictly specified standards. He put up a new parish church, covered over the Farset river to make High Street a wide thoroughfare, built an Exchange and the Assembly Rooms, and donated ground for the White Linen Hall, opened in 1784. In 1777 Robert Joy formed a partnership to build the town's first cotton mill in Francis Street, an initial step towards making Belfast the centre of Ireland's cotton industry. The Joy family also owned the *Belfast News-Letter*, the province's most forthright and influential newspaper. By 1791 Belfast had a population of eighteen thousand, just bypassing Newry to become the most successful port in Ulster. Both these towns owed their prosperity not only to overseas trade but also to their ability to draw in business from the heart of the province by inland waterways.

CANALS, ROADS AND POPULAR DISTURBANCES

In east Tyrone small amounts of coal had been dug out of the ground from the middle of the seventeenth century, but the sinking of deep shafts at Brackaville, soon to be known as Coalisland, in the 1720s revealed deposits on a scale not yet found anywhere else in Ireland. Meanwhile, the population of Dublin had increased sevenfold since 1660, a mushroom growth not possible without massive importation of British coal. With the optimistic hope that the Tyrone coalfield could supply the capital's needs, the Irish parliament set up the Commissioners of Inland Navigation to subsidise the Newry Navigation. Begun in 1731, the canal was completed in 1742 and on 28 March in the same year the *Cope* and the *Boulter* of Lough Neagh sailed into the port of Dublin with cargoes of Tyrone coal.

A canal of fifteen locks, including the first stone lock chamber in Ireland, the Newry Navigation crossed eighteen miles of rough country to connect Lough Neagh with the sea – the earliest true summit-level canal, pre-dating the Sankey Cut at St Helens and the Bridgwater Canal to Manchester. Never before in peacetime had so many men been put to work on a single project in Ireland. The Tyrone coalfield never achieved what was expected of it, however, largely because severe faulting made mining difficult. Yet the Newry canal prospered and stimulated the domestic industry in central Ulster by providing an inexpensive route for imported bleachers' potash and exported cloth. The Lagan Navigation, begun in 1756, became equally important, the first lighter reaching Lisburn in September 1763; by December 1793 the canal had reached Lough Neagh, joining it at Ellis's Gut.

Roads were a local responsibility and a source of mounting friction. A major grievance shared by merchants, weavers and farmers was that all decisions on the levying of local taxes were made by the gentry and aristocracy of the Established Church. From 1710 county grand juries could levy a cess, or local rate, to make new roads, and turnpike trusts could be set up from 1733. There was much jobbery, corruption and inefficiency, but the legacy of the eighteenth century is that Ulster still has one of the best secondary road networks available anywhere. However, a burdensome cess brought social tensions to the surface. In 1761 bands of weavers and farmers calling themselves the Hearts of Oak tore down toll gates on the turnpikes and when the cess was increased in 1763 the disorder spread and intensified, requiring the army to quell the turbulence in the north Armagh barony of Oneilland in 1772. Eighteenth-century progress was accompanied by violent fluctuations – the trade downturn of the 1770s was especially acute, triggering popular revolt.

On the morning of Sunday 23 December 1770 angry farmers gathered at Templepatrick Meeting House and, armed with firelocks, pistols and

The Newry Navigation; from a map by Walter Harris

pitchforks, set out for Belfast. Calling themselves the Hearts of Steel and numbering some 1,200, they besieged the barrack, set fire to houses in Hercules Lane and forced the release of a comrade held on the charge of maiming cattle. The immediate cause of this assault was the eviction of tenants by the Upton family; poor tenants had been ejected and replaced by speculators who had been able to outbid them when leases had expired. At the same time Lord Donegall was causing unrest by passing heavy fines for the renewal of leases.

The 'houghing' of cattle – deliberately laming the animals by cutting their leg tendons – became so prevalent that the *Belfast News-Letter* reported it to be carried on 'even at noonday undisguised'. The revolt spread and merged with the Hearts of Oak resistance to the cess in Armagh. Eventually troops were brought in, men were tried and hanged, and some insurgents drowned while attempting to escape to Scotland in open boats. Lord Townsend, the viceroy, ordered a general pardon in November 1772 and privately condemned the landlords, whose rents were 'stretched to the utmost'. In their Proclamation of March 1772 the Hearts of Steel blamed the 'heavy rents which are become so great a burden to us that we are not scarcely able to bear', and continued:

> Betwixt landlord and rectors, the very marrow is screwed out of our bones . . . they have reduced us to such a deplorable state by such grievous oppressions that the poor is turned black in the face, and the skin parched on their back.

Behind these disturbances were severe harvest failures and a catastrophic slump in the linen trade. 'The good Bargins of yar lands in that country doe greatly encourage me to pluck up my spirits and make redie for the journey, for we are now oppressed with our lands at 8s. an acre,' David Lindsay explained to his Pennsylvanian cousins in 1758. Increasing rents helped to keep up a steady annual outflow of Ulster people prepared to face the hazards of an Atlantic crossing. When the economic crisis struck in 1770, emigration to America reached a new peak of about ten thousand a year. The governor of North Carolina, Arthur Dobbs of Carrickfergus, was only one of many colonial land developers anxious to attract Ulster families to the American back country. Ulster Presbyterians – known as the 'Scotch–Irish' – were already accustomed to clearing and defending their land and were prepared for frontier skirmishing. 'Get some guns for us,' James Magraw urged his brother in Paxtang. 'There's a good wheen of ingens about here.' Magraw was writing from the Cumberland Valley, where the fertile soil attracted many Scotch-Irish pioneers; from there they pushed to the Appalachians and on to Kentucky and Tennessee. Perhaps one quarter of a million Ulster people had settled in the American colonies when the peak of emigration was reached in the first half of 1773. Then, as Thomas Wright informed his fellow Quaker Thomas Greer in a letter from Bucks County on 14 June 1774:

> The Colonies at present is in a very dissatisfied position by reason of the impositions of Great Britain; Boston is entirely blocked up . . . some here is apprehensive the event will be attended with much bloodshed.

Emigration abruptly ceased as the American revolution began.

'ENGLAND HAS SOWN HER LAWS LIKE DRAGON'S TEETH'

On 13 April 1778 Paul Jones, the American privateer, sailed his ship *Ranger* into Belfast Lough and engaged *Drake*, a Royal Navy sloop stationed there. After an obstinate fight off the Copeland Islands, the British vessel struck its colours and was seized. The American Revolutionary War, now more than two years old, had been brought to the very shores of Ulster. Informed by Dublin Castle that only half a company of invalids and a troop of dismounted horse were available to defend Belfast, the citizens of the town flocked to join a Volunteer company formed on Saint Patrick's Day.

When the American revolution broke, the sympathy of the northern Protestants was with the colonists. Early in 1778, however, France had joined the war against Britain and Ulster Protestants had no difficulty in recognising the traditional enemy, and, determined to defend the country from invasion, Volunteer companies formed rapidly across the province and in the rest of the island. The Government's position was fast becoming desperate. The lord lieutenant, the Earl of Buckinghamshire, was forced by threat of bankruptcy to suspend all salaries, pensions and parliamentary grants. Tax receipts were sharply down, for the country was in crisis. The depression begun in the early 1770s was now aggravated by the dislocation of war and government trade embargoes. The Government would find no money to finance a militia when Ireland was all but stripped of regular troops to fight in America. The defence of Ireland now depended on the Volunteers and, after much heart-searching, Buckinghamshire agreed to give out to them the sixteen thousand militia

James Caulfield, Earl of Charlemont: leader of the Patriots in the Irish House of Lords and commander-in-chief of the Volunteers; from an engraving by Samuel Ferguson
LINEN HALL LIBRARY

muskets he had in store – in doing so, he advertised his government's acute financial embarrassment and greatly strengthened the Volunteers over whom he had no control. In a few weeks the number of Volunteers leaped from twelve thousand to forty thousand, half of them in Ulster. Such a large independent army was certain in a crisis to wield formidable political influence.

Ireland's constitutional position closely resembled that of some of the American colonies now in revolt. Westminster alone controlled imperial and foreign affairs, and the viceroy and other members of the Irish executive were appointed, not by the parliament in Dublin, but by the government of the day in London. The Irish parliament – utterly unrepresentative except of the leading landed interests – met only every other year and had its powers emasculated; Poyning's Law allowed for the alteration or suppression of Irish bills by the English privy council; and the 1720 Declaratory Act gave Westminster authority to legislate for Ireland, a right most frequently used to regulate trade. Loose interest groups opposed to the Government and calling themselves Patriots had no thought of severing the British connection, but they did want to obtain more genuine power for their parliament. Ulster grandees were well represented in the Patriot opposition, led in the Irish Lords by Lord Charlemont, who not only obtained Ulster seats for the Patriot spokesmen Henry Flood and Henry Grattan but also was commander-in-chief of the Volunteers.

'Talk not to me of peace; Ireland is not in a state of peace; it is smothered war,' the Patriot Hussey Burgh proclaimed in the Irish Commons; 'England has sown her laws like dragon's teeth, and they have sprung up in armed men.' By November 1779 the Government was helpless before menacing demonstrations of Volunteers and a united Patriot majority. The beleaguered Tory ministry at Westminster, reeling from news of disastrous defeat in America, had no choice but to lift major trade restrictions on Ireland. The Volunteers now threw themselves into a campaign to change Poyning's Law and to get rid of the Declaratory Act.

Henry Grattan, leader of the Patriots, and later an unwavering champion of Catholic emancipation
LINEN HALL LIBRARY

On the morning of 15 February 1782, 242 delegates, representing 143 Volunteer companies in Ulster, marched two by two down the streets of Dungannon, lined by the local infantry company to the parish church. There, between noon and eight that evening, propositions were debated and voted on. The motions passed at the convention were a clarion call for legislative independence:

> Resolved unanimously, That a claim of any body of men, other than the King, Lords and Commons of Ireland, to make laws to bind this kingdom, is unconstitutional, illegal, and a Grievance.

> Resolved (with one dissenting voice only), That the powers exercised by the Privy Councils of both kingdoms, under, or under colour or pretence of, the Law of Poyning's, are unconstitutional and a Grievance.

These were but two of twenty resolutions approved, including agreement to send an address of support to the Patriots:

> In a free country, the voice of the People must prevail. We know our duty to our Sovereign, and are loyal. We know our duty to ourselves, and are resolved

The Lisburn and Lambeg
Volunteers firing a *feu de
joie* in the Market Square,
Lisburn, in honour of the
1782 Dungannon
Convention
LINEN HALL LIBRARY

to be Free. We seek for our Rights, and no more than our Rights; and, in so
just a pursuit, we should doubt the Being of a Providence, if we doubted of
success.

The Volunteers and Patriots did have success: a few weeks later the Tory
government fell and the new Whig ministry granted all that was demanded.
From now on the Irish parliament could make its own laws, but for some
Ulster radicals, legislative independence was only the first victory. The
parliament in Dublin did not represent the people of Ireland: in county
elections Protestant freeholders were completely dependent on their landlords;
and in the north all the towns with representation, with the exception of
Carrickfergus and Derry, were 'close' boroughs controlled by patrons, with
electorates as small as thirteen in Belfast and thirty-six in Coleraine. Catholics
had no part to play whatsoever.

Flushed with their recent victories, northern Volunteers pressed strongly for
parliamentary reform in 1783. Divisions between radicals and moderates at a
Volunteer convention in Dublin weakened the campaign, and the moment for
action passed as the American war ended. Volunteer pressure had been vital,
however, in removing most of the Penal Laws in 1778 and 1782 and at the
Dungannon Convention the resolution had been passed, 'that, as men and as
Irishmen, as Christians and as Protestants, we rejoice in the relaxation of the
penal laws against our Roman Catholic fellow subjects'. Catholics were still
excluded from the legal profession, parliament and from voting. It was in

Belfast and surrounding districts that they found their most ardent champions.

Over most of Ireland, Protestants were in a small minority, concerned to defend their privileges; over much of Ulster, Protestants and Catholics were roughly equal in number, and the old rivalries were still strong; only east of the Bann did Protestants have such an overwhelming majority that they had no fears of a Catholic resurgence. Here Presbyterians of Antrim and Down had a long tradition of defending their rights against clergy and landlords of the Established Church. In Belfast an energetic and confident middle class passionately debated new political ideas coming in with their cargoes from Scotland, America and France. Their delegates had been bitterly disappointed that they had failed to convince their fellow Volunteers in 1783 that Catholics should be given the vote and, the following year, the Belfast 1st Volunteer Company attended Mass at St Mary's chapel, which they had largely paid for, and defiantly invited Catholics to enlist in their ranks. These Presbyterian liberals were challenging the exclusiveness of the Ascendancy and the outbreak of the French Revolution gave them a fresh opportunity to puncture the complacency of the Ascendancy's monopoly of power.

The opening of St Mary's, the first Catholic church in Belfast, on 30 May 1784: Belfast Volunteer companies parade to demonstrate their support; an early-twentieth-century postcard issued by the Dungannon Clubs

LINEN HALL LIBRARY

UNITED IRISHMEN, DEFENDERS AND PEEP O' DAY BOYS

On the afternoon of 14 July 1791 the Belfast Volunteers set out from the Exchange, 'together with such a multitude of our unarmed inhabitants as no former event ever was the means of assembling', to celebrate the second anniversary of the Fall of the Bastille. On their arrival at the White Linen Hall three volleys were fired into the air, answered between each by salvoes from their four brass six-pounders; then Volunteers and citizens formed a circle and solemnly agreed to send their declaration to the National Assembly of France.

> If we be asked, what is the French revolution to us? we answer; – MUCH. Much as MEN – It is good for human nature that the grass grows where the Bastile stood . . . As IRISHMEN. We too have a country, and we hold it very dear . . . so dear to us its *Freedom*, that we wish for nothing so much as a real representative of the national will.

This exuberant commemoration had been organised by the reviving

Dr William Drennan, the
originator of the United
Irishmen; portrait by Robert
Home in 1786
PUBLIC RECORD OFFICE OF
NORTHERN IRELAND

AN

ARGUMENT

ON BEHALF OF THE

CATHOLICS OF IRELAND;

——————

RE-PRINTED BY ORDER OF
The Society of United Irishmen of
BELFAST.

——————

1791.

This pamphlet drew the
attention of Belfast radicals
to Wolfe Tone
LINEN HALL LIBRARY

Volunteers and the Northern Whig Club, formed in the town the previous year at the request of Lord Charlemont. Though it was more outspoken than its Dublin parent, the club did not go far enough for some Belfast radicals.

On Friday 14 October 1791 the Society of United Irishmen of Belfast was founded in Crown Entry, the brainchild of Dr William Drennan, son of the minister of the 1st Presbyterian Church in Rosemary Street. Much of the initial planning was done by Drennan's brother-in-law, Samuel McTier, and its first secretary was Robert Simms, owner of the Ballyclare paper mill. A special guest, and the man who named the society, was Theobald Wolfe Tone, a Dublin lawyer who had deeply impressed northern reformers by his recently published *Argument on Behalf of the Catholics of Ireland*. They were joined by Henry Joy McCracken, a Belfast cotton merchant. The United Irishmen sought 'a cordial union among all the people of Ireland', and a complete reform of the Irish parliament, which must 'include Irishmen of every religious persuasion'. They were not yet revolutionaries but believed that the 'extrinsic power' of England could be 'resisted with effect solely by *unanimity, decision and spirit in the people*'. In January 1792 they launched the *Northern Star* to promote the radical cause, with Samuel Neilson, owner of Belfast's largest woollen drapery business, as editor.

When, in February 1793, Britain was drawn into the French revolutionary war, northern radicals seemed little better than traitors to Dublin Castle. The lord lieutenant suppressed the Volunteers, troops were let run amok in Belfast, and a militia was raised to defend the country from a possible French invasion. However, the United Irishmen had achieved much in its first two years. William Pitt's government was eager to make concessions in Ireland in case the ties between northern Presbyterian radicals and Catholics should become dangerously strong. In 1792 Catholics won the right to enter the legal profession and in the following year the Irish legislature was cajoled into giving Catholics the vote. Reformers now believed that full Catholic emancipation would follow. It did not. Lord Fitzwilliam, taking office as lord lieutenant in 1795, was recalled from his post for openly supporting Grattan's bill to allow Catholics to sit in parliament. Dublin was at a standstill as Fitzwilliam sailed down the Liffey and the *Belfast News-Letter* reported that the people 'saw his Lordship, ashamed to betray the most amiable weakness, and with his handkerchief, endeavouring to conceal pure tears springing from an undefiled heart'. In Belfast, the *Northern Star* observed, 'There was not a Shop or Counting-house open during the whole day – all was one scene of sullen indignation.'

Middle-class Presbyterians and Catholics, confident of emancipation, were shattered by this turn of events; they were 'upon the recall of Lord Fitzwilliam,' the chief secretary remarked, 'led to despair of anything effectual without the assistance of the French'. Tone was caught negotiating with a French spy and exiled; in May 1795, just before he left Belfast for America, he climbed the Cave Hill overlooking the town, as he recorded in his diary:

> Russell, Neilson, Simms, McCracken, and one or two more of us, on the summit of McArt's fort took a solemn obligation – which I think I may say I have on my part endeavoured to fulfil – never to desist in our efforts until we had subverted the authority of England over our country and asserted her independence.

Such idealists represented only a small proportion of Ulster Protestants. Over much of the province the defeat of Catholic emancipation was warmly welcomed and in County Armagh sectarian rivalries were so intense that they led to open conflict.

Drunken affrays in the vicinity of Markethill between gangs known as 'fleets' had become openly sectarian by 1786. The combatants regrouped, Protestants becoming Peep o' Day Boys and Catholics the Defenders, and, for the next decade and more, sectarian warfare raged in County Armagh. Better armed, the Peep o' Day Boys at first swept all before them – a 'low set of fellows,' Lord Gosford, governor of Armagh, observed, '. . . who with Guns and Bayonets, and Other Weapons Break Open the Houses of the Roman Catholicks, and as I am informed treat many of them with Cruelty'. The violence fanned out from the 'Low Country' to the uplands of south Armagh; here the Catholics had the advantage of numbers and turned on the Protestants with a ferocity not seen for more than a century. A horrific climax was reached when Defenders attacked a schoolmaster and his family in Forkhill on 28 January 1791, described by the Reverend Edward Hudson, Presbyterian minister of Jonesborough:

> In rushed a Body of Hellhounds – not content with cutting & stabbing him in several places, they drew a cord round his neck until his Tongue was forced out – It they cut off and three fingers of his right hand – Then they cut out his wife's tongue . . . She I fear cannot recover . . .

Ancient hatreds gushed to the surface as the violence spilled over into neighbouring counties – in the words of Hudson, 'the same hereditary Enmities handed down from generation to generation'. Defenderism, the form of a co-ordinated network of oath-bound clubs, spread southwards and in 1794 there was a furious uprising in County Cavan. In north Armagh, however, General William Dalrymple found many Catholics 'preparing for flight the moment their little harvests are brought in, some are gone to America, others to Connaught – Their houses are placarded, and their fears excessive.'

Lord Fitzwilliam: the viceroy recalled because of his open support for Catholic emancipation in 1795

NATIONAL LIBRARY OF IRELAND

Peep o' Day Boys searching for Defender arms in a Catholic household; an early-twentieth-century impression
LINEN HALL LIBRARY

In September 1795 Defenders assembled near Loughgall in north Armagh at the crossroads known as The Diamond to face the Peep o' Day Boys in battle. When the Protestants were reinforced, however, the Catholics took their priest's advice and agreed to a truce. Both sides withdrew but on 21 September a fresh body of Defenders arrived from County Tyrone determined to fight. The Peep o' Day Boys, on home ground, quickly reassembled and took position on the brow of a hill overlooking The Diamond; then, according to William Blacker, a local landowner, they opened fire

> with cool and steady aim at the swarms of Defenders, who were in a manner cooped up in the valley and presented an excellent mark for their shots. The affair was of brief duration . . . I am inclined to think that not less than thirty lost their lives.

The victorious Peep o' Day Boys then marched into Loughgall and there, in the house of James Sloan, the Orange Order was founded. This was a defensive association of lodges pledged to defend 'the King and his heirs so long as he or they support the Protestant Ascendancy'. At first the order was a parallel organisation to the Defenders – it was oath bound, used passwords and signs, was confined to one sect, and its membership comprised mainly farmer-weavers. William Blacker was one of the very few of the landed gentry who joined the order at the outset. He did not approve, however, of the immediate outcome of the Battle of The Diamond:

James Sloan's house in Loughgall, County Armagh, where the Orange Order was founded in September 1795
GRAND ORANGE LODGE OF IRELAND

> Unhappily . . . A determination was expressed of driving from this quarter of

the county the entire of its Roman Catholic population . . . A written notice was thrown into or posted upon the door of a house warning the inmates, in the words of Oliver Cromwell, to betake themselves 'to Hell or Connaught'.

The 'wreckers' smashed looms, destroyed homes and drove some seven thousand Catholics out of Armagh in just two months. Many did flee to Connacht. On 28 December 1795 Lord Gosford spoke to local magistrates, saying that 'It is no secret, that a persecution . . . is now raging in this county.'

'To the ARMAGH PERSECUTION is the Union of Irishmen most exceedingly indebted,' leading state prisoners were to claim in 1798. Following the recall of Fitzwilliam, the United Irishmen had become a secret oath-bound revolutionary body, pledged to fight for an Irish republic with the assistance of the French. Now tens of thousands of Defenders clamoured to be part of the coming revolution for, far from shattering the movement, the Orangemen seem to have hastened recruitment by scattering highly political Catholics to the west and the south. The United Irish leaders could not spurn such a vast field army, for, until now, their organisation was confined to bourgeois radicals in Belfast, Lisburn and Dublin, and Presbyterian farmers in Antrim and Down. Hopes for success were high – news was reaching Ireland that the French were ready to bring aid.

INSURRECTION IN ANTRIM AND DOWN

On 16 December 1796 a formidable French fleet – with 14,450 soldiers and 41,644 muskets – sailed out of Brest and steered north-west to Ireland:

> The French are in the Bay! they'll be here without delay,
> And the Orange will decay, says the Shan Van Vocht.

The French entered Bantry Bay on 22 December, but their commander was missing and as a result of mismanagement and storms no landing was made. 'Well, England has not had such an escape since the Spanish Armada,' Wolfe Tone truthfully wrote in his journal on board the *Indomptable*. News of the appearance of the French, nevertheless, electrified the United Irishmen and their Defender allies. In Ulster, United Irish membership doubled in the first four months of 1797: this may well have been the best moment for insurrection but, believing another French expedition was imminent, the revolutionary leaders held back their men. It was left to the Government to seize the initiative: only the most rigorous methods, swiftly applied, Dublin Castle decided, could stifle the coming rebellion in the north.

'Nothing but terror will keep them in order,' Lieutenant-General Gerard Lake wrote on taking up his post in Belfast. 'It is plain every act of sedition originates in this town.' On 13 March 1797 he proclaimed martial law and, following military searches reaching out to Loughbrickland and Armagh, 5,462 firearms were seized, together with an immense number of pikes in the first ten days alone. Seven tumbrils left Belfast in April laden with prisoners; in May the Monaghan Militia silenced the *Northern Star* by demolishing its premises in Belfast; and in the countryside the newly formed yeomanry were let loose, striking terror by burning houses and flogging suspects. The Reverend Robert Magill watched men flogged at Broughshane:

> I saw Samuel Bones of Lower Broughshane receive 500 lashes – 250 on the back and 250 on the buttocks. I saw Samuel Crawford of Ballymena receive 500 lashes. The only words he spoke during the time were 'Gentlemen, be pleased to shoot me'; I heard him utter them. I saw Hood Haslett of Ballymena receive 500 lashes. I believe he was only about nineteen years of age. Before he had received the 500 lashes I heard him exclaiming, 'I am cutting through . . .'

Almost fifty prisoners were executed, including William Orr, a farmer of Farranshane convicted of administering unlawful oaths: his 'Dying Declaration' was printed and distributed in thousands:

> If to have loved my Country, to have known its Wrongs, to have felt the Injuries of the persecuted Catholics and to have united with them and all other Religious Persuasions in the most orderly and least sanguinery Means of procuring Redress; – If these be Felonies I am a Felon, but not otherwise.

By the end of 1797 Lake's ruthless campaign had almost obliterated the United Irishmen in Ulster, where previously they had been strongest. Far from snuffing out rebellion in the south, however, Lake helped to provoke it there in 1798. When the storm broke in the province of Leinster towards the end of May, the revolutionaries in Ulster were in a state of confused impotence.

JOSEPH CUTHBERT,

TAYLOR AND LADIES' HABIT-MAKER,

(Now confined in Kilmainham Jail, on a charge of High Treason,)

SOLICITS the continuance of his numerous Friends and Cuſtomers to his Houſe, as the Buſineſs is now conducted by a ſkilful Foreman. He hopes the unmerited perſecution he has ſuffered, on his being ACQUITTED by a Jury of his Country, to be immediately detained upon a new Warrant, that the uſual liberality of Belfaſt will be now exerted in his favour. He requeſts thoſe Indebted to him to Pay Mrs. CUTHBERT. Dublin, May 10, 1797.

JACOB NIXON,

FORMERLY SURGEON AND APOTHECARY,

In Bridge-ſtreet, Belfaſt,

Now a Priſoner in Kilmainham goal, on a charge of High Treaſon,

CONTINUES to carry on the *Apothecary Buſineſs* in his former Shop, by his Apprentice, Mr. SAMUEL STEWART, who has laid in an extenſive Aſſortment of freſh Drugs; and as he can depend upon Mr. Stewart's attention and diligence, he hopes his former Friends will continue to favour him with their commands.

Kilmainham Gaol, May 11, 1797.

MR. O'NEIL,

(Now a Priſoner in Kilmainham,)

BEGS Leave to Inform his Friends of Belfaſt, and the Public in General, that his Academy will be conducted as formerly, by approved Teachers; and the better Accommodation of the Pupils, a French Claſs will be Opened on the 15th inſt.

O'NEIL has too long known the integrity of Belfaſt, to be ſuſpicious of their deſerting him now.

Dublin—Kilmainham, May 5th, 1797.

Belfast tradesmen, imprisoned for their United Irish activities, appeal to their customers not to desert them; *Northern Star*, May 1797
LINEN HALL LIBRARY

The northern revolutionaries were utterly disorganised when the insurrection began in the south on the night of 23 May. Even when the peasantry of Kildare, Carlow and Wexford swept to victory, the Ulster leaders could not agree to act; and it was only when Henry Joy McCracken arrived from Dublin that the most determined decided to rise on 7 June. McCracken had no intention of attempting an assault on his home town of Belfast, now the second largest garrison in the country. Instead he ordered his men to seize their local towns and then join him in an attack on Antrim.

The first shots of the rebellion in Ulster were fired by the United Irishmen

March	Mr Donnel Thomas	0.0		
Decem	Mc Cornuch Edw	5.5		
July	McClenaghan Wm	1.7.1	Dead	
Sept	McCracken Henry Joy	1.6.1	Miss McCracken admitted	in his place 1st Nov 1790
	Mc Crum John	5.5		
	McCracken William	1.10.4	forfeited	
March	McDonnel Doctor	3.3		
Sept	McCracken Francis	4.4	Abroad	

in Larne as darkness fell on 6 June. After driving the Tay Fencibles back to their barrack, they drew off to join their comrades on Donegore Hill. The insurgents forced the surrender of Ballymena by placing burning tar barrels against the Market House after a brisk battle. Meanwhile, Randalstown fell by a similar device and the bridge at Toome was laboriously broken down to prevent the military further west from crossing the Bann. McCracken set out from Craigarogan Fort near Roughfort with a small band of followers and, as they advanced north through Dunadry and Muckamore singing 'La Marseillaise', they were joined by United men from all over south Antrim. But barely half of those pledged to rise turned up and they had only one cannon, a brass six-pounder long hidden under the floor of Templepatrick Meeting House and now mounted on the wheels of an old chaise.

The garrison at Antrim fired two cannon so inaccurately that the grapeshot merely cast up gravel in the faces of the rebels entering the town; the Templepatrick gun fired two deadly rounds and then fell off its mounting; making a cavalry charge, the dragoons merely transfixed themselves on the insurgent pikes; and men from Ballyclare were fighting their way forward down Bow Lane. It was in this last action that Lord O'Neill – once the darling of the Presbyterian freeholders now in combat against him – was killed near the Market House. A column force-marched from Blaris, under Colonel James Durham of the Fife Fencibles, now bombarded the town from Sentry Hill and then poured into the streets, scattering insurgents.

As the soldiery finished off any wounded rebels they found and summarily executed thirty others captured in arms, McCracken attempted to rally the fleeing rebels, but to no avail. Randalstown and Ballymena were abandoned. After hiding out on Slemish and the Cave Hill, McCracken, from the slopes of Collin Mountain, watched Saintfield burn and heard the distant guns at Ballynahinch. The County Down uprising had begun.

From the earliest list of members of the Linen Hall Library, Belfast: it includes Henry Joy McCracken, replaced after his death by his sister Mary Ann.
LINEN HALL LIBRARY

Henry Joy McCracken, the Belfast cotton salesman who led the United Irishmen at Antrim and was executed at the Market House, on the corner of High Street and Cornmarket, in July 1798
LINEN HALL LIBRARY

The Battle of Ballynahinch,
11 June 1798; a painting by
Thomas Robinson
DEPARTMENT OF ARTS,
CULTURE AND THE
GAELTACHT, IRELAND

On Saturday 9 June Colonel Chetwynd Stapylton, commanding the
Newtownards Yeoman cavalry, volunteers led by three Church of Ireland
clergy, and 270 York Fencibles, was ambushed by insurgents near Saintfield.
Before he was driven off, Stapylton lost 3 officers, 5 sergeants, 1 clergyman, 2
drummers and 45 other ranks; a York Fencible veteran of the French wars later
recalled that 'for danger and desperation this skirmish exceeded anything he
had before witnessed'. News of this victory spread rapidly and, despite earlier
reverses at Portaferry and Newtownards, United Irishmen hurried to join the
rebel camp at the Creevy Rocks near Saintfield. Here Henry Monro, a Scottish
merchant from Lisburn, agreed to head the Down insurrection. Monro
ordered his rebel army south to Ballynahinch, where a new camp was made at
Montalto, with an entrenched forward position on Windmill Hill.

The weather was perfect on 11 June, as it had been for days. James Thomson,
then a boy of twelve and later the father of the scientist Lord Kelvin,
accompanied women carrying food to the rebel encampment, where he found

> a considerable number sheltering themselves from the scorching rays of a
> burning sun under the shade of the trees . . . They wore no uniforms; yet they
> presented a tolerably decent appearance being dressed, no doubt, in their
> 'Sunday clothes' . . . The only thing in which they all concurred was the
> wearing of green . . . on a sudden an alarm was given . . . In a moment all was
> bustle through the field.

The piking of Protestants on Wexford Bridge, 1798: reports of such atrocities turned Ulster radicals away from revolution.
GEORGE CRUIKSHANK

Major-General George Nugent, commander of the government forces, had burned his way south from Belfast; now he began pounding the rebel positions with his eight guns. The insurgents on Windmill Hill were overwhelmed and when darkness fell Ballynahinch was occupied by the Monaghan Militia, who were soon drunk and out of control. Monro launched a dawn attack with some success but at around 7 a.m. rebel ammunition ran out and Nugent's army then overwhelmed the United Irish on Ednavady Hill. No quarter was given as the cavalry in relentless pursuit hacked down those in flight through lanes and byways. Monro, captured and condemned to death, was taken to the market place in Lisburn. An officer present recalled: 'I stood very near him when at the foot of the gallows, and he settled his accounts as coolly as if he had been in his own office, a free man . . . This done, he said a short prayer . . .'

The reprisals following the Battle of Ballynahinch were fearful, yet Nugent behaved with more humanity than Lake in Wexford. Indeed, news of atrocities against Protestants at Scullabogue and on Wexford Bridge did much to dampen swiftly the embers of revolt in the north. One of the last to be executed was Henry Joy McCracken, taken at Carrickfergus and hanged in Belfast's Cornmarket on 17 July 1798.

There was no northern response to the French invasion at Killala, County Mayo, towards the end of August, even after Lake had been routed at Castlebar. A final French expedition of ten warships was caught by Sir John Warren's squadron off Lough Swilly in a storm. The first to step ashore from the captured *Hoche* at Buncrana was Wolfe Tone. Sent to Dublin, condemned and denied military execution, Tone slit his throat in prison and died seven days later. Meanwhile, Lord Cornwallis had been sent from Westminster as lord lieutenant with instructions to force through legislation bringing the life of the Dublin parliament to an end.

Wolfe Tone, in his French army uniform: portrait drawn shortly after the Battle of Lough Swilly, when Tone stepped ashore from the *Hoche* at Buncrana, County Donegal, and was arrested on 3 November 1798.
LINEN HALL LIBRARY

'JOBBING WITH THE MOST CORRUPT PEOPLE UNDER HEAVEN': THE UNION

The self-confidence of the Ascendancy was reeling in the wake of the Ninety-eight insurrection and the government of Ireland had become utterly dependent on British military and financial support. The first vote on the Union bill, in January 1799, was discouraging; it was rejected by a margin of two votes and for such a crucial measure a large majority was essential. Cornwallis wrote letter after letter cajoling and urging borough owners to change their minds. 'My occupation is now of the most unpleasant nature, negotiating and jobbing with the most corrupt people under heaven,' he wrote; 'I despise and hate myself every hour for engaging in such dirty work.'

Cornwallis delegated the main task of building up a majority to Robert Stewart, Lord Castlereagh. Originally elected a radical by the freeholders of County Down, Castlereagh had deserted the opposition and been appointed chief secretary in 1798. Now he worked on the abstainers, in particular, with consummate skill. Both Cornwallis and Castlereagh hoped that full Catholic emancipation could be included in the Union Bill, but hardliners in the Irish government persuaded Pitt to drop this proposal. Pitt did, however, promise to carry emancipation after the Union and for this reason Catholic men of

A majority for the Union in the Irish parliament was partly obtained by bribery and the creation of peerages, as this contemporary cartoon indicates.
LINEN HALL LIBRARY

property supported the bill. For the same reason most members of the Orange Order campaigned to preserve the 'Protestant constitution'. On the whole, however, the Union was a burning issue only with the narrow élite of the Ascendancy.

Early in 1800 the Union Bill passed through the Irish Commons and Lords by comfortable majorities. Westminster gave its approval and on 1 January 1801 the new Union flag, incorporating Saint Patrick's cross, was run up poles in all the principal towns. For the great majority of the people of Ulster it was an event of no consequence – far more important were the hardships brought about by wartime inflation and harvest failures. Some forty years were to pass before the Union moved centre stage in the theatre of Ulster politics.

Robert Stewart, Lord Castlereagh: as Irish chief secretary he built up a majority for the Union in the Irish Commons.
LINEN HALL LIBRARY

Lord Cornwallis: he survived crushing defeat at Yorktown in 1781 to oversee the final suppression of rebellion in 1798 and the passing of the Union Bill in 1800 as lord lieutenant of Ireland.
LINEN HALL LIBRARY

The Reverend Dr Henry
Cooke's challenge to
Daniel O'Connell when
the 'Liberator' accepted
an invitation to come
to Belfast in 1841 to
address a repeal meeting
in the town.
LINEN HALL LIBRARY

6

POVERTY AND PROGRESS

1801–1870

'The most Jacobinical thing I ever heard of!' George III shouted out during his levee at Windsor on 28 January 1801. The secretary of war had just reminded him of the Government's pledge to emancipate the Catholics, and the king continued: 'I shall reckon any man my personal enemy who proposes any such measure.' As a result, Pitt was unable to keep his promise and resigned on 3 February. Later, when George III was in his straitjacket impotently gnashing his gums, the Prince Regent made clear his view that if Catholics were allowed to sit in parliament, the British constitution would be in peril.

Irish Catholics of education and property felt cheated; as in 1795, their hopes had been raised and then dashed. The Union, which had been in effect a no-confidence vote in the ability of the Protestant Ascendancy to govern Ireland, now seemed to shore up that élite. As late as 1828, for example, jobs and offices paid or subsidised by the Crown numbered 3,033 but Catholics had only 134 of them. 'I care no more for a Catholic than I care for a Chinese,' one MP remarked. If Westminster remained indifferent, then the Catholic bourgeoisie would force Ireland to the top of the agenda. Daniel O'Connell, the Kerry landowner and lawyer, brought together priests, the middle class and peasantry into one formidable agitation and his Catholic Association, founded in 1823, created a sophisticated local administrative network never before achieved by an Irish political organisation. Such a movement, so obviously Catholic, soon aroused intense passions in Ulster.

Ribbonmen swearing an oath
LINEN HALL LIBRARY

The sectarian turbulence of the 1790s continued into the new century, though on a reduced scale. Ribbonmen – so called because they tied long white handkerchiefs round their waists – were simply Defenders with a new name and were strongest in Ulster. Ignoring vehement denunciations by the Catholic clergy, the Ribbonmen looked forward to the time when 'locusts from the bottomless pit' – the Protestants – would meet their end. They pledged themselves to aid a prophesied Protestant downfall, as their oath in Ulster shows:

> I, A.B., Do Swear in the presence of My Brethren and by the † of St Peter and of Our Blessed Lady that I will Aid and Support Our holy Religion by Destroying the Heriticks and as far as my power & property will Go not one Shall be excepted . . .

Meanwhile, the Orange movement gained in strength. At the height of the Napoleonic Wars 25,000 regular troops and 31,000 yeomen were on active service in Ireland; 20,000 of the yeomanry were stationed in Ulster and nearly all were Orangemen. The order gained respectability as more and more of the Protestant gentry were persuaded to enrol and the Government was grateful for services rendered during and after the Ninety-eight rebellion. Continued reports of intimidation and the blatant partiality of Orange magistrates caused mounting alarm in Westminster, however, and the Unlawful Societies Act of 1825 which put down the Catholic Association also suppressed the Orange Order. This ban was accepted with calm resignation by the order's leaders in Britain and Dublin, but the organisation remained intact in Ulster, where it was reconstituted as the Brunswick Clubs. In Antrim and Down Presbyterian radicalism was wilting before the growing self-confidence of Irish Catholicism. The 1835 Ordnance Survey Memoir for the district of Connor observed that the people there almost to a man had been 'engaged in the rebellion of 1798 . . . However, since that time their politics have changed, and now they seem indifferent and careless on the subject.' Militant Protestantism mobilised as the drive for emancipation reached its climax.

In the autumn of 1828, Jack Lawless, the Belfast journalist who was one of O'Connell's most energetic lieutenants, announced the 'invasion of Ulster' – he and his supporters would advance from town to town in the province, holding public meetings and rallying support for emancipation. He arrived in Carrickmacross, the frontier town of County Monaghan, on 17 September and declared that he would enter Ballybay six days later with fifty thousand followers. Some eight thousand armed Orangemen rallied in Ballybay, which was then almost exclusively Presbyterian. 'The state of the country at the present crisis is truly awful,' the *Northern Whig* observed, after Lawless had announced that his next venue was to be Armagh. Armed Protestants poured into the city only to hear that local Catholics had successfully pleaded with their leader to stay away. Huge Brunswick Club demonstrations followed, the largest at Tandragee with forty thousand attending; after the one at the Moy, a group went to a nearby townland, where all but two families were Catholic and there the loyalists' approach

> was announced by drums, fifes, bugles, and by playing party tunes, such as 'Holy Water', 'Croppies lie down', and 'Kick the Pope before Us' . . . till two in the morning, when they marched back, playing the same tunes, huzzaing, and firing shots.

O'Connell had mobilised such a formidable display of Catholic power in the rest of Ireland, however, that Wellington's government felt it had no choice but to give way. In 1829 Catholics won their emancipation. Contrary to the general view, Irish Protestants in the north did not accept emancipation as inevitable and henceforth most saw themselves as a beleaguered people. Ulster was turbulent that summer: violent sectarian incidents were reported from across the province, including twenty murders in Portglenone, County Antrim, alone. The *Northern Whig* had observed about Lawless: 'As to his reconciling the Catholics and Orangemen – the idea is Quixotic.' The truth of that view was to be demonstrated with the passing of every year.

Daniel O'Connell
LINEN HALL LIBRARY

THE REPEALER REPULSED

In July 1830 blood flowed in the streets of Paris once more as the hated Bourbons were driven out and, as the fire of revolution spread to Brussels and into central and southern Europe, the Whigs took office at Westminster for the first time in over twenty years, only to face an alarming English agricultural labourers' revolt. Ulster was turbulent, too, as regular troops were withdrawn from the province to quell a bloody campaign against the tithe in Leinster. The local yeomanry proved violent and partisan; on 18 June 1831, for example, after being taunted by a large crowd in Newtownbarry, County Cavan, the yeomen opened fire, killing seventeen people and wounding twenty.

Daniel O'Connell called for repeal of the Union – the return of a Dublin parliament. The Whigs adamantly rejected this solution but they were grateful for his support for the 1832 Reform Act and entered into a parliamentary alliance with him, formalised in 1835. The Government steadily chipped away at the privileges of the Ascendancy, extending the constabulary set up in 1814, appointing Catholic magistrates, reducing the tithe, creating corporations elected by ratepayers and establishing National Schools. The Reverend Dr Henry Cooke, who united most Presbyterians into the orthodox General Assembly, raged against 'this close-compacted phalanx of infidelity and Popery'; at a great Conservative demonstration at Hillsborough on

30 October 1834 he 'published' the banns of marriage between Presbyterianism and the Establishment and declared that repeal was 'just a discreet
word for Romish ascendancy and Protestant extermination'.
While many liberal Presbyterians denounced Cooke's proposed
union, more and more believed the time had come to make
common cause against the rising tide of Irish nationalism. The
new alliance of Conservative Protestants, already dismayed by
the Whig reforms, was galvanised into action in 1840 when
O'Connell broke his parliamentary alliance and launched a
new mass movement for repeal of the Act of Union.

The Reverend Dr Henry
Cooke who united Ulster
Presbyterians and Anglicans
in common opposition to
the drive to give Ireland a
parliament of her own
LINEN HALL LIBRARY

'When you *invade* Ulster, and unfurl the flag of *Repeal*, you
will find yourself in a new climate,' Cooke declared, '. . . I
believe you are a great bad man, engaged in a great bad cause.'
O'Connell had accepted an invitation in January 1841 to speak
in Belfast: he never ceased to hope that northern Presbyterians
would join him in his campaign for a Dublin parliament.
Though the plan for a procession into Ulster was dropped, the
Government took no chances and rushed artillery, mounted
and foot police, and more than two thousand regular troops,
northwards.

O'Connell did, indeed, find himself in a new climate in
Belfast. On Tuesday 19 January he attempted to address the public from the
balcony of Kern's Hotel in Donegall Place. 'The fraternal force of liberty,
presaging prosperity,' he bellowed, 'will rise from Connemara to the Hill of
Howth – will pass from Cape Clear to the Giant's Causeway; and the men of
Belfast will gladden, in pleasing gratitude, as the joyous sound passes them.' But
he could not be heard:

> Yells, hisses, groans, cheers and exclamations of all descriptions were blended
> together in the most strange confusion imaginable . . . 'Ha, Dan, there's Dr
> Cooke coming' – 'No Pope' – 'No Surrender' – 'Come down out of that ye big
> beggarman, till we shake hands with ye' . . . Dan O'Connell for ever' – 'Hurrah
> for Repeal', etc.

That evening, as O'Connell attended a soiree in the May Street Music Hall, a
stone-throwing battle raged outside, while a 'still larger body of people
traversed the town, shouting and yelling', smashing windows of the homes of
known repealers. Next morning O'Connell needed the protection of four cars
full of police and a body of police cavalry as he set out to catch the cross-
channel steamer at Donaghadee.

O'Connell's discomfiture was celebrated at two 'Grand Conservative
Demonstrations' in Belfast on 21 and 22 January. At the first Cooke concluded
his long peroration with these words:

THE CHALLENGE.

Look at the town of Belfast. When I was myself a youth I remember it almost a village. But what a glorious sight does it now present – the masted grove within our harbour – (cheers) – our mighty warehouses teeming with the wealth of every climate – (cheers) – our giant manufactories lifting themselves on every side – (cheers) – our streets marching on … And all this we owe to the Union. (Loud cheers.) … Yes Mr. O'Connell, we will guard the Union as we will guard our liberties … Look at Belfast, and be a Repealer – if you can. (The Rev. Doctor then retired amid the most enthusiastic cheering, and loud shouts of approbation, which continued for several minutes.)

Despite impressive displays of strength at 'monster meetings' in the south, O'Connell's drive for repeal came to grief in 1843. By then the state of the economy was of far more immediate concern than the political future of the country.

COTTON, LINEN AND RAILWAYS

Cooke was right: nowhere was hectic growth more evident than in Belfast. The town's population increased by almost 47 per cent between 1801, when it was 19,000, and 1811, when it was nearly 28,000; viable banks and reliable insurance helped firms ride out the violent fluctuations in Ulster's economy; and in 1810 Belfast's exports included over 15 million yards of linen, 63,561

A Conservative view of the power of Cooke's arguments against repeal: one of O'Connell's supporters wields the axe of the 1832 Great Reform Act which had inceased the representation of Repealers in the Commons to around forty.
LINEN HALL LIBRARY

hundredweight of bacon, 51,547 firkins of butter and 1,884 kegs of ox tongues. Yet it was the manufacture of an exotic import – cotton – for sale to the home market that was the most arresting feature of Belfast's expansion in these years. Clustering round Belfast Lough for the most part, to be close to sea-borne supplies of fuel and raw material, mills spun cotton by steam and water power; this yarn was then 'put out' to handloom weavers to be made into cloth. By the end of the Napoleonic Wars in 1815 Belfast was taking half of Ireland's cotton wool and yarn. Thereafter, the industry found it increasingly difficult to compete with Lancashire, and by 1836 parliamentary com-

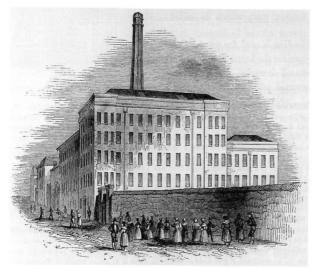

missioners declared that the cotton industry in Ireland was almost extinct. Once a luxury material, cotton had become the cheapest of all textiles and this threatened the very survival of the Ulster linen industry.

In 1805 the linen board had offered a subsidy to anyone who could erect machinery 'for spinning hemp or flax for sail-cloth ... to be worked by steam or water, ten shillings per spindle'. It was not until 1825 that John Kay of Preston developed a wet-spinning process to spin flax by power machinery. James and William Murland of Annsborough, near Castlewellan, made the first commercially successful application of this technique in Ulster in 1828 and, in the same year, Mulholland's York Street mill in Belfast,

York Street flax-spinning mill, Belfast, in 1842
LINEN HALL LIBRARY

after a disastrous fire, was rebuilt not for cotton-spinning but for the power-spinning of flax. The cotton manufacturer Hugh McCall observed:

> The profits of the York Street concern exceeded the dreamiest imaginings of the proprietors ... Several of the far seeing merchants of the Northern Athens began to surmise the truth respecting the new El Dorado that had been discovered in York Street, and no long time elapsed until other tall chimneys began to rise in different parts of the town.

The threatened collapse of Ulster's linen industry was thus averted by the enterprise of firms capable of competing with Manchester on its own terms by mass-producing linen of ever-improving quality at a steadily falling cost. The capital, business skills and technical expertise earlier acquired by drapers and cotton manufacturers were now redeployed to make eastern Ulster the one part of Ireland where the industrial revolution made spectacular progress in the nineteenth century. By 1850 there were sixty-two wet-spinning mills in the province, with a total horsepower of 19,000. Outside Belfast, several proprietors laid out purpose-built mill villages: they included Barbours at

Plantation, near Lisburn; Herdmans at Sion Mills; Dunbar McMaster at Gilford; and Richardsons at Bessbrook. For such concerns, cheap and rapid access to overseas markets was essential and they pressed strongly for an improvement in the province's internal communications.

Towards the end of July 1837 *Express and Fury*, two 2-2-2 locomotives built by Sharp, Roberts and Company of Manchester, were drawn up from the Belfast quays by ten horses to Glengall Place, the *Belfast News-Letter* reported, 'attended by immense crowds of spectators, who incessantly cheered their progress through the streets'. For the past two years a line had been laid between Belfast and Lisburn. On 12 August the line was formally opened, and the *Belfast News-Letter* gave this account:

> The crowds assembled in the neighbourhood of the Railway were immense, and universal enthusiasm prevailed at the success with which this truly national undertaking has been hitherto prosecuted. The number of passengers during the day amounted upwards of three thousand, while hundreds were disappointed in obtaining places.

There were some who alleged that smoke from the engines would frighten cows into refusing milk and the Belfast Presbytery condemned the running of trains on the Sabbath; one minister told his congregation he 'would rather join a company for theft and murder than the Ulster Railway Company, since its business is sending souls to the devil at the rate of 6d a piece', and that every blast of the railway whistle was 'answered by a shout in Hell'.

The Ulster Railway Company was not to be halted by such objections and by 1842 the line had reached Portadown via Lurgan and Seagoe. On 1 March 1848 the first train arrived at Armagh 'amid the acclamations of many of the townspeople', after crossing the Upper Bann by a great wooden viaduct of five

The impressive Portadown Railway Station, built in 1861–2, was demolished in the 1970s.
NATIONAL LIBRARY OF IRELAND

The Antrim Coast Road, which ended the isolation of the Glens, was completed in 1842.
ULSTER MUSEUM

thirty-nine-foot spans. Other companies laid down track to reach Ballymena by April 1848, Holywood by August 1848 and Newtownards by May 1850, and work was already under way on joining the Dublin to Drogheda line with the Ulster Railway, connecting at Portadown. Opening up the interior was more important to Ulster businessmen than establishing links with the south, and the result was to draw more and more of the province's commerce towards Belfast.

For a time the advent of the railways stimulated mail and coach services. For example, the Enniskillen Day, the Omagh Day and the Portadown Fair Trader brought in passengers from the countryside to the main stations, while the Belfast Night Mail picked up travellers from Drogheda on the arrival of the Dublin train at 7 p.m. and drove to catch the Belfast train at Lisburn at five o'clock next morning. Grand juries continued to extend the network of roads, being subsidised by the Board of Works, set up in 1831, for major projects. The most spectacular undertaking in these years was the opening up of the Glens by the Antrim Coast Road. This was just being completed when William Makepeace Thackeray travelled it in 1842:

> The 'Antrim coast road' . . . besides being one of the most noble and gallant works of art that is to be seen in any country, is likewise a route highly picturesque and romantic . . . The road, which almost always skirts the hill-side, has been torn sheer through the rock here and there; and immense work of levelling, shovelling, picking, blasting, filling, is going on along the whole line.

On the other side of Ulster, the wilder coast of Donegal was less well served but improvements were being made, the Board of Works being motivated more and more by the need to provide seasonal employment in a countryside becoming ever more impoverished.

'STRUGGLING THROUGH LIFE IN POVERTY AND WRETCHEDNESS'

For the great majority in the Ulster countryside mechanisation spelled disaster, for the power-spinning of flax destroyed a vital supplement to the family incomes of labourers, cottiers and small farmers. Lieutenant P. Taylor, in his memoir for the parish of Currin in south-west Monaghan in 1835, noted that the 'most industrious and active spinner cannot earn more than 2d. a day', and a weaver giving evidence to the Ordnance Survey concluded: 'The machinery has thrown our families idle.' As Thomas Beggs, a weaver who died in the Famine wrote:

> But the guid auld times are gane out o' sight,
>   An' it mak's the saut tear aften start to mine e'e;
> For lords o' the Mill and Machine ha'e decreed
>   That bodies like me maun beg their bread.

In short, when the whole domestic linen industry was in a state of near collapse in the 1830s, tens of thousands of people in Ulster continued to be dependent on it for survival. The mass production of cheap cotton cloth in Britain had depressed the price that could be asked for linen, the competing textile. As hand-spinners lost their work, the status and income of linen weavers were steadily pushed down. The desperation of the poor prepared to work for barest subsistence, combined with competition from cotton woven by power, reduced earnings to between three and eight shillings a week by the 1840s. Weavers found themselves on a par with the poorest cottiers and labourers, forced to work almost every waking hour to survive. Even such miserable earnings, however, gave significant protection from the disasters which were to strike those now utterly dependent on what the land could yield.

'Till men of property set some plans on foot to alleviate the condition of the poor, there can be no chance of improving their situations,' James McEvoy wrote in 1802, drawing attention to the plight of cottiers and labourers in County Tyrone. During the Napoleonic Wars the rising

A handloom linen weaver
LINEN HALL LIBRARY

demand for Irish corn in Britain encouraged owners of estates to raise rents and shorten leases as soon as they expired. The rapid increase in the numbers of cottiers and labourers in turn intensified competition for land sublet from farmers – without the protection of leases these wretched people bid against each other from year to year. 'Armagh is indisputably, in proportion to its size, the most populous county in Ireland,' Sir Charles Coote wrote in his survey of 1804; so dense was the population here that the turf bogs 'are very much exhausted . . . we cannot conceive there is a sufficiency of bog for the demand'. At least shortage of turf was not a problem in the wilder and more mountainous parts of Ulster. Here only the potato made possible the cultivation of such marginal land; in County Tyrone, McEvoy observed, 'we meet with innumerable small patches throughout the country, in many parts up to the summits of the highest mountains'. Potatoes in this period failed no more often than oats or barley and a family could eke out an existence on little more than half an acre of this crop; if potatoes could be supplemented with buttermilk, they very nearly provided a balanced though monotonous diet. In the absence of terrible epidemics or ruinous war, the population rose to the limit the land could bear.

It was an Ulsterman, Lord Castlereagh, who was largely responsible for negotiating the 1815 Treaty of Vienna which ushered in the longest era of peace Europe had hitherto enjoyed. The close of almost one quarter of a century of continuous warfare, however, was followed by a severe slump and steadily falling agricultural prices thereafter. In 1821 Ulster's population of two million was almost equal to the whole of Scotland, yet the province remained more rural than either Leinster or Munster – the 1841 census showed that 'fewer than 10 per cent of its people lived in towns of two thousand inhabitants or more'. In spite of Belfast's dramatic growth, there was not yet enough urban employment to draw in all the destitute from the countryside. Because of the ever-rising demand for land, rents failed to fall at the same pace as agricultural prices and the relentless subdivision of land continued, a disastrous trend when earnings from the domestic linen industry crashed in the years following Waterloo.

In the autumn of 1824 the Ordnance Survey staff arrived at Phoenix Park in Dublin to begin mapping the whole of Ireland on a scale of six inches to one statute mile. In addition to this great undertaking, a detailed memoir was ordered for every parish but alarm at the costs involved caused the abandonment of this part of the project. These unpublished memoirs survive for much of Ulster and provide striking evidence of the increasing misery of those living at the bottom of the social pyramid. In 1835 Lieutenant Taylor described the level to which the people of Currin had been reduced:

> The wretched hovels, scantily covered with straw, surrounded and almost entombed with mire, which everywhere present themselves throughout the

'The Battle of Magheracloon' (1843); police fire on tenants in County Monaghan demonstrating against rent increases.
LINEN HALL LIBRARY

parish, sufficiently testify that the total absence of all activity in industry is one source of the wretchedness and misery which almost overwhelms the land.

Not only the collapse of rural linen production but also the 'practice of sub-dividing farms into small tenures, and subletting the same to insolvent tenantry' caused this poverty, Taylor believed. Lieutenant J. Greatorex, in his memoir for Aghalurcher in County Fermanagh, also observed the prevalence of subdivision and early improvident marriages in the cottier and labouring classes:

> It is customary as soon as the children of a family grow up for them to marry, usually at an early age, and begin the work on their own account, building mud huts wherever a few acres of land are to be obtained, and struggling through life in poverty and wretchedness, but apparently contented and cheerful.

The author of the memoir for the parish of Drummaul in County Antrim commented that in the labouring classes marriages 'of women under 17 and of men under 21 are not unusual'. He also castigated the manner in which Lord O'Neill treated his tenantry: 'The number of ejectments annually served on his estate are almost incredible, and in the depth of winter many a family is annually turned adrift.'

Despite the striking advance of industrialisation, all over Europe landlords continued to monopolise economic and political power; and at least the rural poor of Ulster were not subjected to mass clearances, as in Scotland, and they were not serfs as were most of the peasantry in the Austrian and Russian empires. Even the serfs of Russia, however, had community rights, whereas in Ireland the cottiers and labourers were given no long-term interest in the holdings and potato gardens they tilled. With no guarantee that they could remain on their scraps of land for another year, with no property of any consequence, and with no marketable commodity other than the strength of their bodies, they had no incentive to build more comfortable and permanent dwellings and no inducement to delay marriage.

One result of the congestion was pressure on the land so intense that little room was left for wildlife. 'Foxes, badgers and hedgehogs are very rare,' it was remarked of the parish of Ballybay, and in neighbouring Aghabog it was reported that 'the extermination of partridges and hares is almost complete . . . the otter and the badger have become entirely extinct'. Outside the walled demesnes the land had become almost bereft of trees. Cabins could only be made of sods, mud or stone, for timber was beyond the means of the cottier. Wage labourers, seeking wages of 8d. or 9d. a day, rented even smaller pieces of the land than the cottiers and for higher rents – as high as £9 per acre in County Cavan, for which the farmer paid only twenty-five to thirty shillings. As it could be difficult to get enough work locally, labourers often became migrant workers after planting their potatoes, while their families took to the roads to beg.

Perhaps the poorest region in Ulster was west Donegal. In 1837 a National School teacher, Patrick McKye, wrote a memorial to the lord lieutenant on behalf of the inhabitants of West Tullaghobegley; there the population of some 9,000 possessed between all of them only 1 cart, 1 plough, 16 harrows, 8 saddles, 20 shovels, 7 table-forks, 27 geese, 8 turkeys, 3 watches and 2 feather beds. In the whole parish there was not a single wheel car, not a pig, not a clock, and not a pair of boots. He continued:

> If any unprejudiced gentleman should be sent here to investigate . . . I can show him about one hundred and forty children bare naked, and was so during winter, and some hundreds only covered with filthy rags, most disgustful to look at.

Long storms had ruined their crops and now they faced starvation; many could afford only one meal every three days and McKye found 'their children crying and fainting with hunger, and their parents weeping, being full of grief, hunger, debility and dejection'. In reality the population here had become so dense by the 1840s that the people could not afford to pay rent at all. The survival of such a large number of inhabitants on such poor land was made possible only by the successful cultivation of the potato. When that crop failed mass starvation could be the only outcome.

THE FAMINE

In the middle of September 1845 the maturing potato crop began to rot over much of Ireland. The damage was only partial and losses in the counties of Fermanagh, Tyrone and Londonderry were the lowest in the country.

Nevertheless, the medical officer for Coleraine workhouse reported, 'Nothing else is heard of, nothing else is spoken of . . . Famine must be looked forward to . . .' The potato crop had often failed before but this was a new disease, *Phytophthora infestans*, a microscopic fungus for which there was then no remedy and which struck again with virulent force in the summer of 1846. The Reverend Samuel Montgomery, rector of Ballinascreen in County Londonderry, made this entry in the parish register:

> The tops were first observed to wither and then, on looking to the roots, the tubers were found hastening to Decomposition. The entire crop that in the Month of July appeared so luxuriant, about the 15th of August manifested only blackened and withered stems. The whole atmosphere in the Month of September was tainted with the odour of the decaying potatoes.

Underneath his signature he wrote, 'Increase the fruits of the earth by Thy heavenly benediction.'

'Rotten potatoes have done it all,' the Duke of Wellington remarked to the diarist Charles Greville; 'they put Peel in his d—d fright.' Sir Robert Peel, the prime minister, had repealed the Corn Laws in June of that year in an attempt to free the market and encourage the importation of cheap grain into Ireland. It was an act of political suicide: the Tory grandees rounded on this jumped-up cotton magnate and in July Lord John Russell headed a new Whig government. Peel had acted promptly by the standards of the day, advancing loans to grand juries to give the destitute employment and buying American maize for Ireland at cost price. Now the Whigs turned for advice to Charles Trevelyan, permanent head of the treasury, who recommended a drastic reduction of subsidised food and a major extension of public works. 'The supply of the home market may safely be left to the foresight of private merchants,' he observed in a memorandum to the cabinet. Closely following Trevelyan's advice, the Government agreed to maintain corn depots, managed by the army commissariat, only along the Atlantic seaboard north to Donegal.

'A famine, with all its baneful consequences, presses, if the people be not immediately relieved,' the Glenties Board of Guardians informed the commissariat on 29 August 1846. In the middle of September the coastguard officer at Loughros Point, Mr Moore, could endure no longer the heart-rending sight of the famished vainly seeking food at nearby Ardara; he sailed to the depot at Sligo and reported after he returned:

> I never saw anything like it, and I hope I never will. People came 18 miles for a little meal, which I could not give. 14 tons, all but one bag, went in a day.

The new system of public works, which were not to compete with capitalist

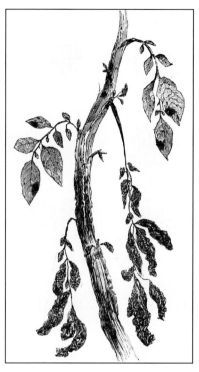

The potato blight: neither the cause of the disease nor the ways to control it were understood during the Famine; from the *Illustrated London News.*
LINEN HALL LIBRARY

enterprise, were confined to building walls, roads, bridges, causeways and fences. Unlike Peel's subsidised scheme, the relief works were to be financed entirely out of the county cess – Irish property was to pay for Irish poverty. There were agonising delays before the cumbersome operation got under way and there were alarming signs of disorder. At Ballyconnell, County Cavan, a mob locked up the grand jury to force the magistrates to vote a high level of cess for relief work; around Newry people held meetings to discuss the withholding of rent; in County Armagh 'there has recently sprung up a considerable trade in fire-arms'; sacks of biscuit were pillaged in Killybegs; and poultry houses, turnip fields and flour carts were robbed on the Inishowen peninsula. By early December, when the snow lay six to eight inches deep, the officials' reports became more urgent: in County Armagh 'the misery and destitution of the people is extreme'; in County Fermanagh the 'distress is, I am sorry to say, on the increase'; and in County Monaghan 'the destitution is awful, and, I fear, increasing . . . The clergy of all denominations are pressing for employment for their followers . . . in short, I am beset, morning, noon and night.' Indeed, there was every sign, as the atrocious weather continued, that the whole system of relief by public works was collapsing.

The winter 1846–7 was as cold and as long as any in living memory. From the north-east blew 'perfect hurricanes of snow, hail and sleet', which, when they did not bring the relief works to a standstill, caused ill-clad and famished labourers to drop from exposure. Men returned from hill-cutting at Ballinaleck, Captain Handcock reported from Fermanagh, 'are so weak and infirm that they could not do a day's work so must be put to break stones . . . and the general cry when they are put to stone breaking is, that the cold of sitting on stones kills them'. Yet more people were applying to the public works than could be taken on. From all over Ulster came reports of a deteriorating situation. On 17 January George Dawson, brother-in-law of Sir Robert Peel, wrote from Castledawson to Sir Thomas Fremantle, a former Irish chief secretary:

My dear Fremantle,

I really have not had heart to write to you before, for I had nothing to communicate except the heart rending scenes of misery which I daily witness. I wish I had never come here . . .

    I do not exaggerate when I tell you that from the moment I open my hall door in the morning until dark, I have a crowd of women and children crying out for something to save them from starving . . . So great is their distress that they actually faint on getting food into their stomachs . . . We are also visited by hordes of wandering poor, who come from the mountains or other districts less favoured by a resident gentry; and worst of all, death is dealing severely and consigning many to an untimely tomb . . . I see enough to make the heart sick . . . hundreds will die of starvation.

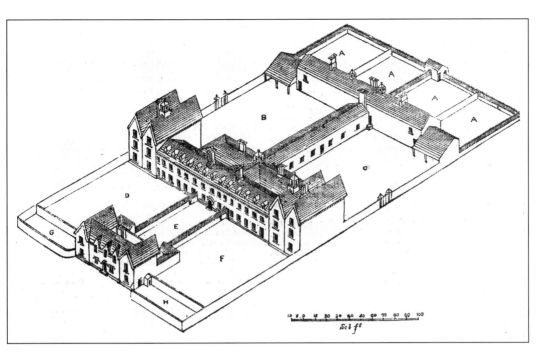

From early February 1847 there were fresh and heavy falls of snow, and in the vicinity of Omagh 'the weaker and worst clad, and perhaps badly fed workmen, were not able to endure it', and when the snow on the roads became three feet deep, the relief works had to be stopped.

The English Poor Law system had been applied to Ireland in 1838 and nearly all the workhouses were operational by the time the Famine began. Outdoor relief was refused to the able-bodied and only a tiny proportion of the destitute were accepted indoors, where work was hard and families were split up. Previously avoided, these refuges of last resort were now overflowing. The death rate in Lurgan workhouse, County Armagh, was so appalling at the end of January 1847 that the Poor Law commissioners demanded an explanation. Dr Bell, the medical officer, wrote that the workhouse was grossly overcrowded, with the result that

> it has been impossible to provide dry beds in many instances in cases of those wetted by weak ill children and by persons in a sickly state. This sleeping upon damp beds has increased fever and bowel complaints which have in many instances proved fatal.

The Reverend W.P. Oulton, the chaplain, blamed the 'dreadful mortality which has swept our workhouse' on sour bread and putrid broth made of rotten beef, 'like the flesh of an animal that had died of disease'.

In February 1847 the Government made, in effect, an open admission that its policies had failed: henceforth relief would be provided by the free distribution of soup, the main cost to be borne by the ratepayer. No more corn would be bought by the Government and the export of food would not be prohibited. 'We think it far better,' Russell explained to parliament, 'to leave the

Bird's-eye view of a Union workhouse, 1841, for the accommodation of eight hundred men, women and children; from the *Irish Penny Journal* LINEN HALL LIBRARY supplying of the people to private enterprise and to the ordinary trade.' As a formidable new bureaucracy was being created to administer the soup kitchens, people, weakened by starvation, were falling victim to fever and dying in their thousands.

Hordes of the poor brought disease into eastern Ulster and a great many impoverished weavers fell victim. Dr Andrew Malcolm, who worked day and night to treat those stricken by fever, recalled the influx of the starving into Belfast:

> Famine was depicted in the look, in the hue, in the voice, and the gait. The food of a nation had been cut off; the physical strength of a whole people was reduced; and this condition, highly favourable to the impression of the plague-breath, resulted in the most terrible epidemic that this Island ever experienced.

Leading citizens set up a Board of Health in May 1847, sheds were put up beside the Frederick Street Hospital when it overflowed, the workhouse infirmary was enlarged, and a temporary hospital was erected in the grounds of the Belfast Academical Institution. 'Yet hundreds,' the *Belfast News-Letter* reported, '– for whom there remains no provision – are daily exposed in the delirium of this frightful malady, on the streets, or left to die in their filthy and ill-ventilated hovels.'

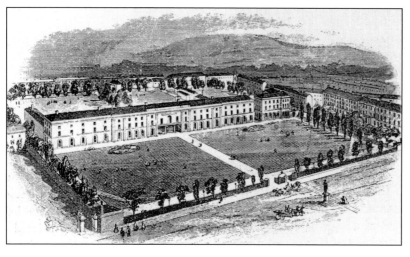

The fine summer of 1847 ensured that the grain harvest was excellent and kept the blight at bay, but the acreage planted with what few tubers had survived two years of famine was so small that the poor

The Belfast Academical Institution: a temporary hospital of tents was erected in its grounds during the Famine.
ROYAL BELFAST ACADEMICAL INSTITUTION

still faced mass starvation. None the less, the Government stopped the distribution of soup in almost all districts in September. From now on the burden of relief was to fall entirely on the workhouses – unquestionably the harshest decision made by Westminster during the Famine. Rates were often impossible to collect and many workhouses became bankrupt. The early months of 1848 saw not only heavy falls of snow but also a resurgence of fever, which spread with fearful speed through the densely packed poorhouses. The Enniskillen workhouse, accessible only by boat in the winter, was particularly hard hit. The medical officer's report for January 1848 included:

> Tuesday [January] 11th – Have to report that the roof of the temporary fever

hospital further gave way on the 7th instant; in consequence was obliged to
have most of the patients brought across the lake, in the rain, at 11 o'clock at
night, to their great injury.

The roof still had not been fixed when Temporary Inspector d'Arcy reported
on 2 March. He came upon twenty-nine patients sharing beds in one room,
eighteen feet long by sixteen feet wide, and he reported:

> Immediately previous to my visit there had been *five children in one bed, three of
> whom were in fever and two in small-pox* . . . No statement of mine can convey an
> idea of the wretched condition the inmates of this house were in; I have
> frequently heard the horrors of Skibbereen quoted, but they can hardly have
> exceeded these.

Hunger was the main driving force behind the revolutions which convulsed
much of Europe in 1848. 'Ireland's opportunity, thank God and France, has
come at last!' Charles Gavan Duffy announced on 4 March: 'We must die
rather than let this providential hour pass over us unliberated.' Duffy, son of a
Catholic bleacher in Monaghan, had helped to found Young Ireland in 1842
to promote the romantic nationalism now sweeping much of mainland
Europe. As editor of the *Nation*, Duffy employed the Banbridge solicitor John
Mitchel as a leading contributor. Born in County Londonderry, the son of a
Presbyterian minister, Mitchel published the *United Irishman* in 1848, appealing
to the spirit of Ninety-eight and calling for an immediate mass uprising. A
starving people, however, had no interest in insurrection and Ireland's sole
contribution to the 'Year of Revolutions' was the 'Battle of Widow
McCormack's Cabbage Patch', in which a small force of police dispersed some
fifty insurgents in a County Tipperary farm house at the end of July. Mitchel
was arrested without difficulty and sentenced to fourteen years' transportation.

The harvests were good in central Europe, and as the peasants left the
barricades to reap their corn, the forces of reaction began to recover. But in
Ireland constant rain produced the worst grain harvest for many years and
hastened the spread of blight, once more destroying the potato crop. The
Government had decided the Famine was over but the workhouses were still
overflowing and the destitute were still dying a year later. Yet even now – while
famine still stalked the land and cholera reaped a fearsome harvest – men of
property in Belfast celebrated the completion of a major engineering
enterprise which would make their town a great imperial port.

At 1.30 p.m. on Tuesday 10 July 1849 the Belfast Harbour Commissioners,
members of the Town Council, the Council of the Chamber of Commerce,
the principal gentry and merchants of Belfast, Major-General Bainbrigge and
officers and men of the 13th Regiment stepped on board the royal mail
steamer *Prince of Wales*. They had come to open the new channel running from
the Garmoyle Pool in Belfast Lough to the quays, which would enable large

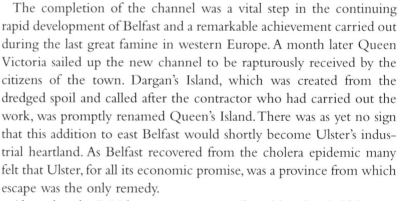

The opening of the Victoria Channel, Belfast, on 10 July 1849
LINEN HALL LIBRARY

William Dargan who constructed the Victoria Channel, a vital development for the future of Belfast as a port
LINEN HALL LIBRARY

vessels to come up the Lagan at any state of the tide. 'Along the whole line of the opposite quay,' the *Belfast News-Letter* reported as the ship steamed along, 'loud huzzas from a dense multitude of spectators rent the air.' William Pirrie, chairman of the commissioners, made a short speech, poured a libation of champagne into the river 'as the rite of inauguration', and named the new cut the Victoria Channel.

The completion of the channel was a vital step in the continuing rapid development of Belfast and a remarkable achievement carried out during the last great famine in western Europe. A month later Queen Victoria sailed up the new channel to be rapturously received by the citizens of the town. Dargan's Island, which was created from the dredged spoil and called after the contractor who had carried out the work, was promptly renamed Queen's Island. There was as yet no sign that this addition to east Belfast would shortly become Ulster's industrial heartland. As Belfast recovered from the cholera epidemic many felt that Ulster, for all its economic promise, was a province from which escape was the only remedy.

Altogether the British government contributed less than half the cost of famine relief, the rest being raised from Ireland itself. Overall the balance of Westminster's contribution was some £7 million: from one point of view, no European state had ever taken such vigorous action to cope with a natural disaster; but another view is that this sum was paltry when it is considered that landlords were able to collect around 75 per cent of their rents, that the ports were not closed, that the United Kingdom's annual tax revenue in the late 1840s was around £53 million, and that £69.3 million were expended on fighting the Crimean War. It was not until the publication

An emigrant ship leaving
Belfast in 1852, bound for
North America
ULSTER MUSEUM

of the census returns of 1851 that the full impact of the Famine on the population was revealed: one million had died and one million had emigrated. The number of Ulster's inhabitants fell by 374,000 between 1841 and 1851, a drop of 15.7 per cent compared with 19.9 per cent for the whole of Ireland. The north had fared better than the south and west but not as well as Leinster. Ulster suffered around 224,000 'excess deaths'; that is, the number over and above those who would have died from the usual causes. Economic historian L.A. Clarkson calculates that in addition to excess deaths in the province about a further two hundred thousand 'loss of births' must be accounted for, resulting from the death of marriage partners and amenorrhoea among women brought on by hunger and disease. He also estimates that famine deaths in the province were almost exactly equalled by the number of emigrants.

Many saw emigration as the only hope of staying alive during the Famine. One such was Michael Rush of Ardglass, County Down, who wrote to his parents in America:

> Now my dear father and mother, if you knew what hunger we and our fellow-countrymen are suffering, you would take us out of this poverty Isle . . . if you don't endeavour to take us out of it, it will be the first news you will hear by some friend of me and my little family to be lost by hunger, and there are thousands dread they will share the same fate.

Had there not been unique opportunities for flight overseas, the effects of the potato harvest failures would have been even more horrific – opportunities rarely available today to victims of destitution, disease and natural disaster across the world. Around 1.2 million left the country between 1846 and 1851. Though the proportion of emigrants from Connacht doubled during the

Famine, Ulster was still in the lead, providing 40.6 per cent of those leaving in 1847–8.

America was the preferred ultimate destination amongst emigrants from every country. Lax standards on British ships kept fares to Canada as low as £3 per person, one third of the cost of going to New York: these were the infamous 'coffin ships', grossly overcrowded and inadequately provided with food and clean water, where louse-borne famine fever flourished. Stephen de Vere noted in his diary what he saw when vessels anchored at the quarantine station at Grosse Isle in the St Lawrence:

> . . . water covered with beds, cooking vessels etc. of the dead. Ghastly appearance of boats full of sick going ashore never to return. Several died between ship and shore. Wives separated from husbands, children from parents, etc.

Many better-off Protestants stayed in British North America, but the great majority of Catholics pressed on southwards to the United States. The price of a fare to America could be had for less than could be raised from the sale of a heifer or from a summer's earnings in the fields. Yet for many this was more than could be saved. Great numbers poured into ports and industrial towns on the British mainland. In Glasgow and Liverpool, where for a time the immigrant Irish formed one fifth of the population, Orange and Green divisions were firmly implanted, leading at times to violent clashes. Emigration to Australia was quite beyond the means of the ordinary tenant or labourer; and financial assistance from landlords, eager to clear their estates of scrapholders, was essential. Some Ulstermen were to travel to the southern hemisphere as convicts in chains:

> He brought me back to Omagh Jail, in the County of Tyrone,
> From that I was transported from Erin's lovely home . . .
> There are seven links upon my chain, and every link a year,
> Before I can return again to the arms of my dear.

The immense outflow steadily reduced population pressure on the land, thus ensuring a rise in living standards. Those who had survived the horrors of the Famine, however, were determined that never again would landlords have such total control over their destiny.

LANDLORDS AND TENANTS

'Sir, I send herewith a list of Tenants from which Notices to Quit can be filled,' an agent wrote from Markethill, County Armagh, in March 1847 to his employer William Cotter Kyle, requesting that evictions be carried out 'as easily as convenient'. Between 1849 and 1854, 49,000 families – amounting to almost one quarter of a million persons throughout Ireland – were permanently dispossessed in the post-Famine clearances. Eviction seems to have been particularly relentless in the counties of Armagh, Antrim and Monaghan. Those tenants who had fallen behind in rent payments were naturally most vulnerable but prompt payment was no protection if a landlord (often close to bankruptcy himself) was determined to consolidate the farms on his estate. Patrick Murphy, a tenant on the Wingfield estate near Monaghan town, wrote in protest to his agent:

> I have lived on this land for forty years and have worked hard. I was never behind with my rent. I do not know why I was ejected.

Concerted action against landlord power began not with the wretched evicted smallholders but amongst more substantial tenants, many of whom had come through the potato harvest failures largely unscathed. Their aim was to defend the Ulster tenant right – a custom long accepted in the north that there would be no eviction if the rent was paid and that a tenant giving up his holding could demand a lump-sum payment (often as high as £10 an acre) from the incoming tenant. This custom was a valuable form of insurance, providing the outgoing tenant, for example, with enough cash to take his family to America.

In 1847 the Ulster Tenant Right Association was launched by William Sharman Crawford of Crawfordsburn, County Down, the Radical MP for Rochdale who had helped to draft the People's Charter in 1838 and who had striven indefatigably but unsuccessfully to persuade Westminster to give legal force to the Ulster Custom. Similar organisations were formed in the south and in August 1850 Charles Gavan Duffy created a national movement, the Irish Tenant League. It seemed a unique moment

William Sharman Crawford of Crawfordsburn, County Down: the Chartist who founded the Ulster Tenant Right Association in 1847
LINEN HALL LIBRARY

in Irish history when north and south, and Protestant and Catholic, were working together for one cause. Monster meetings were planned and the league's president, Dr James McKnight, editor of the *Londonderry Standard*, crystallised its aims into the '3 Fs': fair rent (in effect, a reduction of rent set by tribunals); free sale (the extension of the Ulster Custom to the whole island); and fixity of tenure (no eviction if rent had been paid). This was the programme which was to guide the Irish land reform movement for the next thirty years.

For a time independent MPs, known as the Irish Brigade, supported the aims of the league but there was no hope of success at Westminster until the political grip of Conservative landlords had been loosened by secret voting and extensions of the franchise. The agitation died down partly because farmers were now enjoying a prosperity they had never known before. From 1853 agricultural prices began to rise and received a further fillip the following year with the outbreak of the Crimean War. Britain was now at her zenith as the world's greatest naval, trading and industrial power, and the burgeoning urban population of the manufacturing regions provided a ready market for farm produce carried regularly and speedily across the Irish Sea. Horse-drawn hay sweeps, churning machines, all-metal swing ploughs and mechanical reaper-binders helped to raise living standards but price increases were probably more important. As farmers increased their incomes, the relative position of landlords slipped. Landlord power, however, was still formidable. As late as 1876 almost 80 per cent of Ulster was held by 804 owners, though there were 190,973 occupiers of land, of whom only 18 per cent had leases. Landlords like the Marquess of Downshire, the Duke of Abercorn, the Marquess of Hertford, the Marquess of Conyingham and Lord O'Neill were as rich as German princes and together they formed a mighty vested interest. There was nothing the law could do to restrain a proprietor from imposing swingeing rent increases or clearing his estate of

Glenveagh Castle, County Donegal: built in 1870 by John George Adair, the perpetrator of the Derryveagh evictions of 1861
LINEN HALL LIBRARY

unwanted tenants. No event in this period gave farmers a sharper reminder of the legal power of the landlord than the Derryveagh evictions of 1861.

John George Adair, a Queen's County landowner, bought the north Donegal estates of Gartan, Glenveagh and Derryveagh in stages from 1857 onwards. Scottish sheep and shepherds were brought in clearly with the intention of supplanting the native peasantry and Adair was high-handed from the outset: he impounded straying animals, raising £368 in fines for their release over two years; he quarrelled with almost everyone, including another landlord and the police; and he had tenants evicted without paying them the full value of their tenant right. When his steward was murdered in November 1860, Adair was convinced that local people were responsible and determined to evict all his Derryveagh tenants. On Monday 8 April 1861 Sub-Sheriff Samuel Crookshank, accompanied by two hundred police and a party of Adair's men shouldering crowbars, moved up into the high country at Lough Barra by the foot of Slieve Snaght. Then, as the *Londonderry Standard* reported, 'the terrible reality of the law suddenly burst with surprise on the spectators', as the eviction party started on a farm held by a widow and her six daughters:

> Six men, who had been brought from a distance, immediately fell to level the house to the ground. The scene then became indescribable. The bereaved widow and her daughters were frantic with despair. Throwing themselves on

the ground they became almost insensible, and bursting out in the old Irish wail
– then heard by many for the first time – their terrifying cries resounded along
the mountain side for many miles . . . with bleak poverty before them, and only
the blue sky to shelter them, they naturally lost all hope, and those who
witnessed their agony will never forget the sight.

Moving from house to house across country down to the shores of Lough
Gartan, the sub-sheriff and Adair's men took three days to evict 244 people
from 46 households and to unroof or level 28 homes over an area of 11,602
acres. There was no resistance of any kind, and it was observed, 'the police
officers themselves could not refrain from weeping'. It was later demonstrated
that Adair's steward had been murdered by one of the Scottish shepherds and
not by the tenants.

Meanwhile, on the other side of the province there was also misery and
acute deprivation in Belfast, where the impoverished, pouring in from the
countryside, crowded into alleys, courts and entries. Possessing nothing, they
sought work: that was to be provided by the town's burgeoning industries.

LINEN AND SHIPS

'You will see by the papers that we have rather exciting times here now,' the
Larne emigrant Andrew Greenlees wrote from the state of Illinois in March
1856. He continued:

> Slavery and freedom seem ready for a fight . . . A civil war would not be
> anything unnatural to look for, and if it be the means by which slavery is to be
> done away with, the sooner it comes the better.

Five years later his predictions were proved correct and Greenlees kept his
Ulster relations informed. The Union fleet imposed an effective blockade on
cotton exports from the Confederate States across the Atlantic and then in
1864 – as the Prussians invaded Denmark and sectarian riots raged in Belfast
– Union troops advanced south, devastating the cotton plantations. Starved of
their raw material the Lancashire cotton mills fell silent. Linen was the nearest
substitute for cotton and thus Ulster faced the challenge of making up the
shortfall in the British market.

Specialist firms in Preston, Blackburn and Bury had mastered the problems
caused by linen yarn's lack of elasticity and had developed power looms just in
time for Ulster to meet the challenge. A boom followed in the province's linen
industry quite without equal in the nineteenth century. In June 1865 the
Northern Whig reported:

> New mills and factories are springing up on all sides, while as fast as they can
> be got started, orders flow in and such a thing as manufacturing for stock is
> almost unknown.

William Ewart and Son
Limited, one of the largest
linen firms in the world
LINEN HALL LIBRARY

Contrasting with the tall spinning mills, the new single-storey weaving factories covered extensive ground. The vibration caused by a heavy shuttle thundering across each power loom 160 times a minute made it unsafe to place such machinery on upper storeys. The boom continued beyond the Union victory in 1865, the United Kingdom exporting 255 million yards the following year, most of it from Ulster. The recovery of the cotton plantations inevitably led to what the *Linen Trade Circular* described as 'a cataclysmic reversal of fortune', but Ulster was now firmly established as the greatest centre of linen production in the world.

The making of linen by power machinery was labour intensive (a linen mill required up to four times as many operatives as a cotton mill with the same number of spindles) and it was therefore the united opinion of employers that wages must be kept down, especially as mills in Russia, Austria-Hungary, Belgium and France were becoming more competitive. Wages in the industry were consistently lower than in other textile factories in the United Kingdom. 'It will ruin our trade, and perhaps leave Belfast a forest of smokeless chimneys': this was the *Belfast News-Letter*'s comment on the 1874 Factory Act which raised the minimum starting age at the mill from eight to ten years and reduced the working week for adults to fifty-six hours. In 1855 Ulster linen manufacturers joined the National Association of Factory Occupiers (Charles Dickens called it the 'Association for the Mangling of Operatives') which opposed legislation to fence off dangerous machines. It was not until well into the 1870s that damning reports by Dr C.D. Purdon, certifying surgeon of the Belfast factory district, drew attention to the damaging effect of flax dust, heat and moisture on the health of mill workers.

Characterised as they were by low rates of pay, the linen mills and factories could not alone have given Belfast the prosperity it enjoyed in the late nineteenth century. For this the higher wages of the engineering industry were vital, in particular those earned in the spectacularly successful shipyard on Queen's Island.

On 1 October 1855 Edward Harland completed his first iron vessel, the *Khersonese*, and a few months later launched the 1,387-ton *Circassian*, the largest ship ever to have been built in Ireland. At the age of twenty-three, this engineer from the Tyne had come to manage Robert Hickson's ailing ironworks on Queen's Island. The Ulster Bank foreclosed and in September 1858 Hickson offered Harland the yard for £5,000. Harland was able to accept Hickson's offer only because he had the full financial backing of Gustav C. Schwabe, a partner in John Bibby and Sons of Liverpool who had been deeply impressed by the young man's engineering prowess. Schwabe's nephew, Gustav Wolff, had already joined Harland as personal assistant.

A high proportion of ocean-going vessels built by Harland and Wolff, as the company was named from 1861, were to orders from the Bibby line. Disparagingly called 'Bibby coffins', these craft caused a sensation in the shipping world because of their revolutionary design 'of increased length, without any increase in the beam'. As Harland explained: 'The hull of the ship was converted into a box girder of immensely increased strength.' The characteristic square bilge and flat underside of the hull soon became known in the trade as the 'Belfast bottom'. Business was brisk during the American Civil War when the Confederate States were eager to buy fast steamers capable of running the Union blockade. The Harbour Commissioners greatly improved facilities on Queen's Island during this time by building the Hamilton graving dock and the Abercorn basin, nearing completion as the *Istrian, Iberian* and *Illyrian* – the finest of this Bibby series – were being launched in 1867.

Sir Edward Harland
BELFAST HARBOUR
COMMISSIONERS

The shipyard on Queen's Island was now of worldwide importance and its success was the outcome of international expertise and enterprise. Belfast appeared to have few of the assets needed to become a great shipbuilding centre, and credit must first be given to the Harbour Commissioners for making the most of what advantages it did have. Just across the sea, Scotland and the north-west of England supplied inexpensive coal and iron; the Clyde provided indispensable specialist engine-making and metal-working; and Liverpool beckoned as the gateway of the fast-growing empire. In addition, the population time bomb continued to send its shock waves eastwards, now reaching the Russian Empire and the Balkans. Tens of thousands sought a better life in America – not to speak of the added impulse given by the suppression of Poland in 1863, Bismarck's wars, Bulgarian horrors and tsarist pogroms – thus creating a market of unprecedented size in the transport of emigrants across the ocean.

The very vessels launched from Queen's Island drew the north of Ireland into closer contact with ideas and movements overseas. Not all of these were concerned with material progress: the great campaign for Christian spiritual renewal launched in America in 1858 surged across the Atlantic and reached the shores of Ulster early in the following year. Here it struck a chord deep in the hearts of many Protestants who had remained faithful to the beliefs of their forefathers when so many of their co-religionists across the Irish Sea had long since abandoned theirs.

PROTESTANT REVIVAL AND CATHOLIC RENEWAL

'A revival is now passing over the churches of America such as has not been known since Apostolic times,' the *Irish Presbyterian* reported on 1 June 1858, and soon after, the General Assembly held a special session which agreed to send out a circular letter commending the new movement. With tireless zeal, the Reverend S.J. Jones got the revival under way in mid-Antrim, holding as many as a hundred prayer meetings a week in Connor and Ballymena. From there the movement spread rapidly to neighbouring counties and as far south as Cavan and Monaghan. The Reverend David Adams of Ahoghill, County Antrim, remembered the spring of 1859:

> In the end of April and the beginning of May the wind of the Spirit calmed, but about the middle of May it blew a heavenly hurricane, and the mighty wave of mercy swelled gloriously mountain high, sweeping across the dead sea of our rural population, and washing the rocky hearts of formal worshippers.

Huge prayer and praise meetings followed in Ballymena, Fair Hill at Coleraine, Portrush, Randalstown, Lurgan, Portadown and Armagh. The largest of several open-air meetings in Belfast took place on Sunday 29 June 1859 when some forty thousand crowded into the Botanic Gardens. The Reverend John Johnston of Tullylish, moderator of the Presbyterian General Assembly, presided. Since not all could hear him, about twenty other meetings sprang up before people left the gardens at 3.30 p.m. to catch their special trains.

The 1859 revival was merely the high point of a sustained evangelical movement begun by John Wesley, who had visited Ireland twenty-one times in the previous century. Often referred to as the Second Reformation, it was accompanied by a new drive to convert Catholics to Protestantism. This galvanised Catholic bishops, led by Paul Cullen, archbishop of Armagh, to launch a campaign of renewal. Nowhere did the Catholic Church seem in more urgent need of regeneration than in Ulster, even though Catholics still formed a majority of the population – 50.5 per cent in the 1861 census. Regular church attendance was lower than in the rest of Ireland; illegitimacy rates were higher; and folk religion was prevalent. In part this was due to the fact that Catholics in the province were overwhelmingly confined to the lower rungs of the social ladder, literally unable to afford to participate in institutional devotion.

Soon after his consecration in 1865 as bishop of Down and Connor, Patrick Dorrian launched a general mission in Belfast. Twelve additional priests were brought in to help the eight parish clergy of the town hear confessions for ten hours a day over a month beginning on 21 October. Further missions were held about every three years; parochial societies, confraternities, and lending libraries of religious books sprang up; by 1877 the St Vincent de Paul Society alone recorded over two thousand boys attending its Sunday schools; and adults who had missed confirmation as children were now confirmed in great numbers. All over Ulster Dorrian's example was followed and, perhaps for the first time, regular attendance at Mass became universal. Many chapels were replaced by larger, more flamboyant, buildings.

Dr Patrick Dorrian: the Loughinisland parish priest who become bishop of Down and Connor and spearheaded the Catholic renewal in the north-east
LINEN HALL LIBRARY

The Catholic and Protestant revivals were remarkably similar in character. Both displayed intense religious fervour and a triumphalist assertiveness. Both laid a new emphasis on faith, regular prayer, private devotions, participation in church services and Sunday instruction for children. Both accepted infallibility, one of the Pope and the other of the literal truth of the Bible as God's word, and both – with the help of rising living standards – adopted 'Victorian morality' with a greater enthusiasm than the English themselves. And yet most Catholics and Protestants were acutely aware of what divided them. The party fight at Dolly's Brae near Castlewellan, County Down, on 12 July 1849 when the Famine still raged, in which Orangemen burned Catholic homes and killed about fifty Ribbonmen, demonstrated the surviving intensity of sectarian feeling in the countryside. This animosity was transferred by industrial development to Belfast, where the frontiers of religious enclaves were kept unstable by the massive influx of newcomers from the countryside. The working classes, packed into such warrens as the Pound and Sandy Row, had chosen where they had settled with care: the invisible dividing lines running through these districts were primarily a reflection of sectarianism imported from rural Ulster. Here, where the low-paid majority eked out a wretched existence, religious hatreds had ample opportunity to fester in brutalising conditions.

On Monday night, 12 July 1857, while mobs hurled stones and insults at each other across wasteland by Albert Street, Catholics at Millfield wrecked a spirit grocer's store and beat two Methodist ministers with sticks. On Tuesday night Sandy Row Protestants made a determined attack on the Pound, smashing windows and setting houses on fire. Meanwhile, Catholics destroyed a Methodist church on the Falls Road, and the hussars arrived only to be pelted by 'kidney pavers' dug up from the streets. The violence was particularly severe on Saturday 18 July, when the mills stopped work at two o'clock: the police were swept aside as the mobs clashed in ferocious combat in front of the Pound and gunfire continued into Sunday night – Head-Constable Henderson from Quadrant Street saw a ditch 'closely lined with men, having guns levelled, firing without intermission'. Rioting resumed in August when sectarian passions were inflamed by street preaching from the Custom House steps. Here, journalist Frankfort Moore remembered, there was a 'warm interchange of opinion on a basis of basalt'.

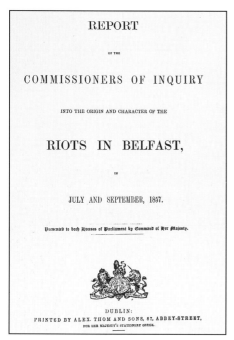

REPORT

OF THE

COMMISSIONERS OF INQUIRY

INTO THE ORIGIN AND CHARACTER OF THE

RIOTS IN BELFAST,

IN

JULY AND SEPTEMBER, 1857.

Presented to both Houses of Parliament by Command of Her Majesty.

DUBLIN:
PRINTED BY ALEX. THOM AND SONS, 87, ABBEY-STREET,
FOR HER MAJESTY'S STATIONERY OFFICE.

The first of many reports on sectarian riots in Belfast
LINEN HALL LIBRARY

After a few years of calm, intercommunal warfare flared up again. Throughout the month of August 1864 the fighting was so severe and continuous in Belfast that many mills and factories were forced to close. The destruction by the mobs was so widespread on Friday 12 August that the *Belfast News-Letter* commented: 'The whole thing seemed like a burlesque on an invasion by a Gothic horde on a Roman province.' Dublin Castle sent up a special train of twenty-seven wagons carrying two field guns and substantial reinforcements of constabulary, cavalry and infantry. Yet gun battles continued to rage. The funeral of John McConnell, a Sandy Row father of five killed by a constabulary volley, was turned into a massive parade of loyalist strength. 'I think every man had a pistol,' James Kennedy JP recalled, and as the hearse passed down Donegall Place, Belfast's most fashionable street, the *Northern Whig* reported: 'The guns fired continuously, the bullets pierced the air, whirr after whirr, in a continuous volley.' Astonishingly, no one was killed in this incident. The arrival of the great government force, together with what Frankfort Moore called 'the usual autumn monsoon', at last brought the riots to an end. The overall official figure of twelve dead was almost certainly too low.

There were riots also in Derry, Portadown and Lurgan, but these were minor in comparison with those in Belfast. The proportion of Catholics in Belfast fell back from around a third in the 1830s to a quarter as the century drew to a close, but Protestant feelings of insecurity were heightened by the growing confidence and strength of Irish nationalism.

7

HOME RULE AND WORLD WAR
1870–1918

'**M**y mission is to pacify Ireland,' William Ewart Gladstone remarked in 1868 as he set off for Windsor to be accepted by Queen Victoria as her prime minister. Ireland had elected sixty-six Liberals, though only four of them had been returned from Ulster, and Gladstone felt a strong moral obligation to take immediate action. He had been deeply affected by the conspiracies of the Irish Republican Brotherhood, a revolutionary organisation better known as the Fenians, dedicated to the establishment of an Irish republic by force of arms. In 1867 an attempt by Irish exiles in America to send help was thwarted; skirmishes at Tallaght, outside Dublin, and in the south and west were swiftly ended by constabulary volleys; following the killing of a police sergeant during a rescue attempt in Manchester in September, three men were publicly executed; and twelve people had died in December when Fenians blew in the wall of Clerkenwell prison in London. Only a vigorous legislative programme to give justice to Ireland, Gladstone believed, would sap the Fenians of popular support and ensure the stability of the United Kingdom.

William Ewart Gladstone in the early 1870s: he strove harder than any other British prime minister to solve the Irish Question.
RECTOR DREW SCHOOL, HAWARDEN

'So long as that Establishment lives,' Gladstone warned, 'painful and bitter memories of Ascendancy can never be effaced.' In the spring of 1869 he pushed through his bill to disestablish the Irish Church; though generous compensation was paid to the Church of Ireland and the Presbyterians, many Ulster Protestants were appalled that an important branch of the Union had been lopped off. The following year Gladstone pressed on with a Land Act which attempted to give legal force to the Ulster Custom throughout Ireland. Yet it was legislation for the whole of the United Kingdom that had the most profound impact on Ireland: secret voting was introduced in 1872. At a stroke, the grip of the landlords on the electorate had been released.

On 19 May 1870 the Home Government Association was formed in Dublin to demand, in the words of Isaac Butt, 'full control over our domestic affairs'. Butt, the son of a Donegal clergyman who had become a Dublin University professor and then a Conservative MP, seemed an unlikely leader of a new movement seeking the restoration of a Dublin parliament. However, his brilliant legal defence of Young Irelander and Fenian prisoners had won the respect of a wide range of Irish nationalists. For nearly a quarter of a century the issue of repeal of the Union had been all but dead; now it was revived by an uneasy alliance of Conservatives disgusted at the disestablishment of their Church, Irish Liberals bitterly disappointed by the Land Act, which fell far short of the promised reforms, former repealers, and Fenians searching for an alternative to futile revolution. Butt was returned as a Home Rule MP for Limerick in 1871, and then the general election of 1874 – the first to be carried out by secret ballot – delivered a deadly and irreversible blow to Liberal representation in Ireland with the election of fifty-nine Home Rulers.

Joseph Biggar, Fenian and Nationalist MP, successfully obstructed business in the Commons with long, boring speeches.
PUBLIC RECORD OFFICE OF NORTHERN IRELAND

Only in Ulster was something of the previous pattern retained. 'This country, in my opinion,' Joseph Biggar declared, 'can never rise from her present state of stagnation until she has once again a native parliament.' Biggar, a Presbyterian pork merchant from Belfast, was one of two Home Rulers elected in County Cavan, but he knew the movement to restore a Dublin parliament was so far weak in the north, and there, the bogey of Home Rule proved invaluable to the Conservatives. In February 1874 the *Belfast News-Letter* declared:

> Home rule is simple Rome rule, and, if home rule were accomplished tomorrow, before that day week Rome rule would be evident.

The 1874 election brought no advantage to Home Rulers. Disraeli's Conservative government, largely absorbed by foreign crises and imperial adventures, almost completely ignored Irish affairs. Biggar began obstructing the business of the Commons to force the House to pay attention to Ireland. With a harsh, grating voice and in a Belfast accent few could follow, Biggar read interminable extracts from Statutes of the Realm in a tedious monotone. On 22 April 1875 he spoke for four hours, with extended boring readings, concluding with the remark that he was 'unwilling to detain the House any longer'. As he sat down a member newly returned in a County Meath by-election entered the chamber: his name was Charles Stewart Parnell. Soon

Parnell was joining Biggar in parliamentary obstruction. Butt strongly disapproved of this tactic, but by now an infrequent attender, and criticised for his dissolute life style, he was gently pushed aside.

There was every reason why Westminster should give Ireland more of its attention: from 1877 the country was assailed by an agricultural crisis of such dimensions that it evoked vivid reminders of the Great Famine.

One-roomed dwelling in Gweedore, County Donegal, *c*. 1870
ULSTER FOLK AND
TRANSPORT MUSEUM

CRISIS ON THE LAND

Unremitting rain throughout August 1877 destroyed the oats and rotted the potatoes in the ground, especially in the west and north-west. Many smallholders could not pay their rents, and evictions, negligible in the good years, leaped to 406 in 1877 and to 843 in 1878. Then the indifferent harvest of 1878 was followed by a disastrous season, the worst since the Famine. The year 1879 was the wettest and coldest since records began. The potato crop was ravaged by blight and smallholders in the west faced starvation. To make matters worse, prices for all agricultural output slid down relentlessly as cheap grain and frozen beef arrived in ever-increasing quantities from America. Evictions for failure to pay rent jumped to 1,098.

On behalf of the Society of Friends, James Hack Tuke returned to Ireland in February 1880, retracing his steps in County Donegal and battling through blizzards of snow and sleet as he had done in 1847. On this occasion the people were not dying of starvation but there was great want and misery. Tuke spoke to Patrick Burns near Kilcar who owed three years' rent and his county cess; he had 'neither cow, nor calf, nor ewe, nor lamb, nor baste that treads the earth . . . only ten fowls which left a few eggs'. Another family with a similar story added, 'we must not grumble', even though all they had left was the cat – 'Yes, we must keep that.'

Tuke reckoned eight thousand families in the Glenties Union needed help until the next harvest. He was scathing about the failure of the Poor Law to provide real help: 'The guardians do not incline to tax themselves, it seems.' He found the landlords of Donegal a singularly unprepossessing lot who regularly refused to vote money for public works or relief. 'It is touching to see how patiently they bear their want,' Tuke said of the distressed people, and added that he found 'simple well-bred courtesy' everywhere. However, the smallholders of the west determined not to submit tamely as they had done in the Famine of the 1840s: there was widespread intimidation of bailiffs; and some resorted to murder.

William Clements, 3rd Earl of Leitrim, had property amounting to 94,535 acres, including an estate of 54,352 acres in north Donegal. No man in Ireland so perfectly matched the nationalist caricature of the predatory landlord: he ejected Protestants and Catholics with equal enthusiasm; he removed all the tenants of Rawros to build his castle at Manorvaughan; he forced a farmer keeping goats against his rules to kill them on the spot before his eyes; and he

forced himself on his tenants' daughters, causing one girl, it was said, to drown herself in sorrow in a nearby lough. Like his neighbour, John George Adair, he quarrelled with almost everyone, including the Presbyterian minister of Milford and the lord lieutenant, the Earl of Carlisle, who stripped him of his post as justice of the peace. This last incident made Leitrim a pariah even within his own class.

The men of Fanad launched no fewer than three attempts on Leitrim's life, one failing because the assailant due to fire the blunderbuss fainted at the crucial moment. Then on the morning of 2 April 1878 the earl was ambushed at Woodquarter on his way to Milford. The first shot killed Leitrim's driver, two more shots mortally wounded his clerk and further rounds gravely wounded the earl. With no time to reload, the men overpowered the seventy-two-year-old Lord Leitrim and clubbed

A predatory County Donegal landlord murdered by the men of Fanad: William Clements, 3rd Earl of Leitrim; from the *Illustrated London News.*
BELFAST CENTRAL LIBRARY

him to death with a musket butt. Large sums were offered as reward to find the murderers. Yet the money was never collected. The police knew who the assailants were, but could find no one prepared to give sufficient evidence for a conviction.

Neither bloody murder nor armed revolution brought down landlordism in Ireland. During the years of prosperity, an alliance of Presbyterian and Catholic farmers in Ulster kept alive the peaceful agitation for tenant right. Now, as the agricultural crisis struck hard, the lead was taken over by a remarkable mass

movement of smallholders in the west. Home Rule MPs had no choice but to
ally themselves with the farmers and assist in the formation of the Irish
National Land League in 1879. American Fenians, organised in Clan na Gael
led by John Devoy, gave their enthusiastic backing to the new movement.

The general election of 1880 swept Gladstone back to power but he failed
to take decisive action to calm the land agitation. In Connacht the movement
reached a new peak of intensity in the autumn of 1880, as the people took
Parnell's advice to shun the offending landlord 'as if he were a leper of old'.
Captain Charles Boycott, agent for Lord Erne's Mayo estate, became a
celebrated victim when he described his plight in a letter to *The Times*. Ulster
Conservatives determined to lead an armed expedition of Orangemen to lift
Boycott's potato crop and thrash his corn. The alarmed Chief Secretary
William E. Forster rushed seven thousand troops to Mayo and limited the
Orange labourers to fifty.

Before the eyes of the world's press, the Protestant labourers from Monaghan
and Cavan trudged through the driving rain from Claremorris railway station
to Ballinrobe and on to Lough Mask House. Here they slept in army tents, and
sang loyalist songs round campfires as they cooked potatoes, for which Captain
Boycott, the *Belfast News-Letter* admitted, meanly charged them 9d. a stone.
Then in the torrential November rain the work began.

The relief of Captain Boycott was a pyrrhic victory, for it had cost £10,000
to save his crops. To rescue every beleaguered landlord in this way would be
quite impossible. 'The bright Irish have invented a new word,' *Le Figaro*
reported, 'they are currently saying to boycott somebody, meaning to ostracise

Captain Boycott, wearing a
deerstalker hat, thanks the
Orange labourers from
Cavan and Monaghan on
the steps of Lough Mask
House; from the *Illustrated
London News*.
BELFAST CENTRAL LIBRARY

him.' Boycotting proved an extremely effective tactic and the Land League went from strength to strength, now rallying support in Ulster.

During most of 1880 and 1881 Protestants as well as Catholics thronged to attend Land League meetings. Michael Davitt, a Fenian prisoner released in 1878, addressed thousands across the province at venues ranging from Saintfield in County Down to Letterkenny in County Donegal. 'The land question can be definitely settled only by making the cultivators of the soil proprietors,' Davitt told his audience at Saintfield on 23 October 1880. No longer would the '3 Fs' be enough. The landlords themselves must go. On 3 December 1880 the Presbyterian journal *Witness* observed:

> The flag of the Land League is now unfurled in the very heart of the Protestant north, and the standard bearers are now busy beating up recruits amongst the loyal men of Down and Antrim . . . The Land League is with us, yet Ulster is at peace.

'Most of the Presbyterians, the younger Methodists, and I may say all the Romanists go in the "whole length of the unclean animal" with the Land League,' the Reverend D.C. Abbott observed with disgust.

Michael Davitt, founder of the Land League: for a time he had the support of both Protestant and Catholic tenant farmers in Ulster.
NAPOLEON SARONY

In a desperate attempt to curb mounting rural disorder in the west, the Government steered coercive legislation through parliament early in 1881 while Gladstone prepared a far-reaching Land Bill, which he said had to be 'what the brewers would call treble x'. The '3 Fs' were granted in full: fair rent would be set by land courts; free sale enforced compensation for improvements; and fixity of tenure gave protection against eviction provided the rent was paid. In Ulster, tenants associations and Liberals greeted the act with acclaim. There, farmers rushed to have their rents judicially fixed by the new Land Commission. Some landlords agreed on reductions without judicial haggling and when the agent of the Carrickatee property in County Monaghan announced reductions of up to 40 per cent, his car was pulled from Ballybay station to his hotel and his bailiff was carried shoulder high.

In the rest of Ireland the response to the act was mixed, for the legislation fell far short of the league's aim to abolish landlordism. Extreme speeches by Parnell against coercion landed him in gaol in October 1881, where he joined other leading 'suspects'. The violence which raged over much of the south during Parnell's imprisonment did much to dismay Presbyterian members of tenants associations. Even when Gladstone released Parnell and calm returned to the countryside, Protestant and Catholic farmers in the north continued

to drift apart, especially when Parnell launched a new movement to concentrate on winning Home Rule for Ireland.

Butt had died in 1879 and Parnell had been elected leader of the Home Rulers the following year. Now this Protestant landlord was creating a modern, highly disciplined party, known as the Irish Parliamentary Party, with its MPs generally referred to as Nationalists, with a capital N. Home rule, not land reform, was made the first objective.

Tim Healy, Parnell's lieutenant, put himself forward as a Nationalist candidate in a by-election in County Monaghan in 1883 and won the seat. The Liberal vote all but collapsed and it was quite clear that all the Catholics had voted for Healy and nearly all the Protestants for the Conservative candidate. In Belfast and the other principal towns of Ulster, politics had been polarised on sectarian lines for years. Now the polarisation of the northern countryside was well under way, especially when the Nationalists announced a new drive to extend their party all over Ulster in the autumn of 1883. Nationalists assumed that because so many Ulster Protestant farmers had joined them in the Land League they would now back their campaign for a parliament in Dublin. When all thirty-nine Irish Parliamentary Party MPs trooped through the lobby to vote with the Conservatives against the Government, and a general election became inevitable in 1885, that assumption was put to the test.

No one could predict the outcome. Gladstone's parliamentary reforms had tripled the Irish electorate by giving labourers the vote, and parliamentary divisions had been redistributed. Passions, fears and hopes ran high. Party scrutineers were fiercely vigilant during the extraordinarily high turnout, reaching over 93 per cent in some constituencies. Liberal representation in Ireland was completely wiped out. In Ulster the Conservatives held sixteen of their seats and the Nationalists won seventeen, failing to take West Belfast and Londonderry City by only a few dozen votes. All the Conservative MPs were Protestant and all the Nationalist MPs in the north were Catholic. Henceforth, all elections would be fought on the issue of the Union, for or against. It was the most significant election in Ulster's history.

The Irish Parliamentary Party won eighty-six seats: Parnell's party now held the balance of power in the governing assembly of the world's greatest trading power, the world's most extensive empire. The Liberals in Britain won

TENANT-FARMERS
OF ARMAGH
Who are Your Friends?

Since the Election of 1874, there have been

15 Divisions in the House of Commons

Upon the several LAND BILLS brought in by Mr. BUTT, Mr. CRAWFORD, Professor SMYTH, and others; and out of 15 DIVISIONS upon these Bills, the ARMAGH REPRESENTATIVES voted as follows :--- .

E. WINGFIELD VERNER, M.P. - 10 Times, all AGAINST the Tenants
MAXWELL C. CLOSE, M.P., - - 10 Times, all AGAINST the Tenants
G. D. BERESFORD, M.P., - - 9 Times, all AGAINST the Tenants

VOTE FOR

RICHARDSON & TENANT-RIGHT

James Richardson headed the poll in County Armagh in the 1880 general election.
LINEN HALL LIBRARY

eighty-six seats more than the Conservatives, a margin exactly equalled by the size of the Irish Parliamentary Party. The Conservatives would not offer Home Rule – what would the Liberals do? Parnell seemed to have an unassailable mandate from Ireland for a parliament in Dublin. Even a majority of MPs in Ulster, the most Protestant province, had pledged themselves to Home Rule.

'IS THEM 'UNS BATE?': THE FIRST HOME RULE BILL, 1886

Lord Randolph Churchill: he played the Orange card; from the *Illustrated London News.*
BELFAST CENTRAL LIBRARY

Possessed by a genuine feeling of high moral purpose, Gladstone concluded that Britain now had a duty to right past wrongs: Home Rule, he felt sure, was the only real way to pacify Ireland. It was therefore with some distaste that Queen Victoria accepted Gladstone as her prime minister for the third time on 30 January 1886, disinclined as she was to 'take this half-crazy and in many ways ridiculous old man for the sake of the country'. Only two days later, at Dungannon, the Conservatives in Ulster launched their campaign against Home Rule. Binding themselves more closely to the Orange Order, they brought their demonstrations across Ulster to a climax with a 'Monster Meeting of Conservatives and Orangemen' in the Ulster Hall in Belfast on 22 February.

The principal speaker at the Ulster Hall was to be the wayward Lord Randolph Churchill: not long before, he had told Lord Salisbury, the Conservative leader, that 'these foul Ulster Tories have always ruined our party', but by 16 February he had decided that if Gladstone 'went for Home rule, the Orange card would be the one to play. Please God it may turn out the ace of trumps and not the two.' 'Ulster will fight, and Ulster will be right,' he proclaimed to cheering supporters at Larne, and greater numbers turned out to greet him in Belfast as he made his way to the Ulster Hall. For one and a half hours he held the rapt attention of his audience, urging them to organise, so that Home Rule might not come upon them 'as a thief in the night'.

Not since the second reading of the Great Reform Bill in 1832 was the Commons so packed and so tense as when Gladstone introduced the Home Rule Bill on 8 April 1886. The prime minister spoke for two and a half hours: 'he seemed so passionately sincere and earnest,' the journalist Frank Harris recalled, 'that time and again you might have thought he was expounding God's law conveyed to him on Sinai'. His proposals were complex: the Dublin parliament was to consist of two 'orders' which would normally sit together as one chamber; the lower order would be elected on the franchise of the day; and the upper order, intended to give special representation to Protestants, was to be made up of twenty-eight Irish peers and seventy-five members elected by voters with a high property qualification. By later standards Gladstone was offering Ireland a very limited form of devolution – little more than control over the police, civil service and judiciary – but, whatever their private reservations, Nationalists gave him their unreserved backing.

Major Edward J. Saunderson, once a Liberal MP for County Cavan, now led the Irish Conservatives and, without difficulty, got his colleagues across the Irish Sea to support him. At St James's Hall on 15 May a Conservative demonstration gave three cheers for Ulster, and Lord Salisbury remarked: 'You would not confide free representative institutions to the Hottentots, for example,' explaining to his audience that the Celtic Irish were unsuited to self-government and that 'democracy works admirably when it is confined to people who are of Teutonic race'. He concluded by observing that Irish loyalists would be justified in using violence in defence of their political faith.

'Think, I beseech you,' Gladstone implored during the final debate, 'think well, think wisely, think not for the moment but for the years that are to come before you reject this bill.' During the first hours of 8 June 1886 the decision was taken: ninety-three Liberal MPs voted with the Conservatives against the bill, which was defeated by a margin of thirty votes. The hostility of the Whig right wing was expected, but it was the mass desertion of fifty-five left-wing Liberal MPs led by Joseph Chamberlain that sealed the fate of Home Rule. Frankfort Moore was one of the journalists who got the news in Belfast by electric telegraph. As he walked home at 4 a.m. he was met by scores of workmen in Sandy Row who

Major Edward Saunderson: he led the Ulster Unionists until his death in 1906.
LINEN HALL LIBRARY

> put to me in their own idiom and staccato pronunciation the burning question:
> 'Is them 'uns bate?'
> And when I assured them that the unspeakable Nationalists had been beaten
> by a good majority, once more cheers were raised.

That fine morning was just a calm interlude in a conflict started four days before and which, as it intensified, was to be the worst violence experienced anywhere in Ireland in the nineteenth century.

Rioting began at the Belfast docks on 4 June 1886 when a thousand shipwrights descended on Catholic navvies who had driven out a Protestant the previous day. As the violence spread to the brickfields Sir Edward Harland, the mayor, telegraphed Dublin Castle on 7 June, requesting reinforcements to assist the 525 men of the Royal Irish Constabulary based in Belfast. As news spread the following day of the defeat of the Home Rule Bill, Protestants left their work early and, while Orange bands played loyalist airs, they lit bonfires and tar barrels in jubilation. To lament the bill's failure, Catholics set fire to their chimneys. The combined result, the *Belfast News-Letter* noted, was a pall over the town 'as thick as a London fog'. That evening Protestants in the

Shankill began attacking public houses owned by Catholics.

Next day, Wednesday 9 June, some of the bloodiest fighting took place. While most of the police were attempting to restore order in Donegall Street, other constables were engaged in a losing battle on the Shankill. After they had been driven back by a mob of some two thousand, three civil magistrates, seventy-two constables, several police officers and a reporter took refuge in the small, two-storey Bower's Hill barracks. The besieged came under ferocious and prolonged attack. According to the *Belfast News-Letter*, kidney pavers had been

> strewn over the road by a number of vicious young women who carried them
> in their aprons . . . and when the stone-throwing waned for a moment girls and
> women came to the front and uttered the most desperate threats to the men
> who desisted.

A salvo of paving stones destroyed the telegraph apparatus, and in desperation the defenders opened fire on the mob, killing seven people, only two of whom were rioting.

Many Protestants became convinced that Gladstone's government was intent on punishing them for opposing Home Rule. The fact that most of the police were southern Catholics, officered though they were by Protestants, only reinforced that conviction. Battles between loyalists and the constabulary, and sectarian engagements in the brickfields, raged all summer. When at last the riots subsided in mid-September the official death toll was thirty-one, though the actual number killed, according to George Foy who made surgical reports on the riots, was probably around fifty. By then the Conservatives, supported by Liberal Unionists, had returned to office. Lord Salisbury, the prime minister, stated firmly that what Ireland needed was twenty years of resolute government. His nephew Arthur Balfour, appointed Irish chief secretary in March 1887, soon proved that he could administer Ireland with a firm hand. At the same time he concluded that some reform might have the effect of 'killing Home Rule with kindness'.

'A GREAT, WIDE, VIGOROUS, PROSPEROUS, GROWING CITY'

Two minutes before noon on Saturday 13 October 1888 the discharge of fog signals on the Great Northern Railway line warned of the imminent arrival of a special train from Dublin. As the locomotive steamed into Belfast's Great Victoria Street terminus one hundred men of the Gordon Highlanders presented arms and the band of the Black Watch played 'God Save the Queen'. Then Charles Vane-Tempest-Stewart, 6th Marquess of Londonderry and lord lieutenant of Ireland, stepped out of the viceregal saloon carriage onto red carpet to be greeted by the mayor of Belfast, Sir James Haslett. The lord lieutenant was certain of a warm welcome here in the heart of the loyalist north, particularly as he was one of the many Ulstermen in these years who occupied high office in the British Empire. Belfast had become a thriving imperial city and it was to give formal recognition to this status that the marquess was making his state visit.

The *Pictorial World* the following year observed that Belfast had become 'a great, wide, vigorous, prosperous, growing city, already covering no less than 6,805 acres, and at present throwing out its arms eagerly asking for more broad stretches of both Antrim and Down'. In 1891, the year in which the census confirmed that Belfast had bypassed Dublin to become the largest city in Ireland, *The Industries of Ireland* found that the

> business-like aspect of the city is particularly impressive . . . Here in these crowded rushing thoroughfares, we find the pulsing heart of a mighty commercial organisation, whose vitality is ever augmenting, and whose influence is already world-wide.

In 1894, when there were nine hundred thousand spindles in use in Ulster's linen industry, the president of the Belfast Chamber of Commerce, H.O. Lanyon, made this estimation:

> I find the length of yarn produced in the year amounts to about 644,000,000 miles, making a thread which would encircle the world 25,000 times. If it could be used for a telephone wire it would give us six lines to the sun, and about 380 besides to the moon. The exports of linen in 1894 measured about

An advertisement in the 1892 *Linen Trade Directory*: Belfast became the greatest centre of linen production in the world.
LINEN HALL LIBRARY

156,000,000 yards, which would make a girdle for the earth at the Equator
three yards wide . . .

The lion's share of this remarkable productive capacity was based in Belfast.
The emergence of a successful engineering industry in the city was fostered
by the growing needs of the linen and shipbuilding firms. By 1892 Mackie's
was making one hundred spinning frames a year; John Rowan and Sons
invented piston rings still in use; and by the end of the century Davidson's
Sirocco Works had become the world leader in the manufacture of ventilation,
fan and tea-drying machinery. Belfast was rapidly becoming a world centre for
the production of aerated waters – an extraordinary achievement considering
the water was obtained by boring artesian wells through the
foul sleech of Cromac. The city had four large distilleries and
by 1900 Belfast exported 60 per cent of Ireland's whiskey.
Thomas Gallaher had transferred his tobacco firm from Derry
to Belfast in 1867 and by 1889 he was importing raw tobacco
to the value of £480,000 and employing six hundred people.
Marcus Ward had one of the largest printing and paper-making
firms in the British Isles and claimed to have pioneered the
mass production of Christmas cards.

ROSS'S ROYAL
(AROMATIC)
GINGER ALE
AND OTHER WORLD-RENOWNED
AERATED TABLE WATERS.
The only Gold Medal for Ginger Ale awarded at Liverpool
International Exhibition, 1886.

Ross's vied with Cantrell
and Cochrane in Belfast to
be the biggest maker of
aerated waters in the
world: the company refused
to supply the licensed trade
LINEN HALL LIBRARY

By far the most striking evidence of Belfast's economic
power, setting the city apart from any other in Ireland, were the
huge shipbuilding yards on Queen's Island. The decade of the
1890s was one of spectacular growth, pushing Harland and
Wolff forward to become the greatest shipyard in the world,
launching the world's largest ships. The *Oceanic* – the second
ship of that name built for the White Star line – was launched in January 1899:
thirteen feet longer and eight feet deeper than Brunel's *Great Eastern*, she was
the largest ship afloat. The *Freeman's Journal*, often scathing about Belfast's
pretensions, described the launch as

the greatest event of its kind the world has ever witnessed, and in a certain
sense, perhaps the most epoch-making incident of the century.

Belfast's emergence as a leading industrial port owed much to the dramatic
growth of the European economy during the second half of the nineteenth
century. While much of Ulster west of the Bann benefited but little, this
quickening reached out to the north-west of the province to bring about a
remarkable revitalisation of Derry. The invention of steam-driven machines for
both cutting and sewing brought shirt-making into factories, the most
impressive being a five-storey block in Foyle Road, erected in 1857 by two
Scots, William Tillie and John Henderson. By 1902 there were 38 factories in
Derry, with 113 rural branches, paying out more than £300,000 a year in
wages to some 18,000 employees, more than half of whom were outworkers

Launched in 1899, the *Oceanic* was the largest ship built in the world in the nineteenth century.
ULSTER FOLK AND TRANSPORT MUSEUM

in rural County Londonderry and County Donegal, Inishowen in particular. Attempts were made to make Derry a shipbuilding centre: W.F. Biggar built twenty-six sailing vessels and six steamers between 1882 and 1892 at Penny-burn, and the yard, taken over by Swan and Hunter in 1912, prospered in a small way. The city's economy was diversified by busy corn and saw mills, foundries, tanneries, tobacco manufacture, salmon netting, oyster fishing and whiskey distillation – A.A. Watt's Abbey Street distillery was for a time the largest in Ireland.

Celebrated across the world by the ever-popular 'Londonderry Air' (also the brand name of a perfume made by Glendenning's Medical Hall in Strand Road), Derry had nevertheless acquired urban sectarian problems similar to those of Belfast. Catholics clustered and spread out from the Bogside west of the walls and by 1891 they formed a majority of 4,500 over Protestants living in the city. Knife-edge parliamentary contests and fierce disputation in the registration courts, together with traditional festivals, helped to heighten sectarian passions. Factory owners staggered closing times in an attempt to stem almost daily taunting by both sides and severe rioting was a frequent occurence, notably in 1868–70 and 1899.

During the second half of the nineteenth century and for much of the twentieth century, Ireland was unique in being the only country in Europe to experience a fall in population. Between 1841 and 1911 there was a decrease of 46 per cent: apart from the Famine, emigration was the principal cause; Ulster's population fell 34 per cent, from 2.4 million to 1.6 million. Because this decline was less severe than in the other three provinces, Ulster's share of the inhabitants rose from 29 per cent to 36 per cent in this period. West of the Bann, population decline was similar to the rest of the island: Cookstown, Omagh, Derry, Strabane and Bundoran were the only five growing towns in the western half of Ulster.

In some towns local industries wilted before the onslaught of more competitive goods made in Belfast and brought in by rail. This happened in Armagh, which was overtaken in size by Lurgan in 1871 and by Portadown in the 1890s. Portadown, little more than a village at the beginning of the nineteenth century, flourished by being the junction for four busy railway lines, becoming an important market town for all of southern Ulster. As well as Cookstown and Omagh, the railway also stimulated growth in Ballymoney and Ballymena. By the end of the century the Braidwater Spinning Mill, employing one thousand people, was only one of several flourishing linen firms in Ballymena. Coleraine had a diversified economy and enjoyed modest expansion, but Newry failed to fulfil the promise of the eighteenth century and by the 1890s it had ceased to grow. Like Holywood, Lisburn was close enough to Belfast to become a dormitory town but its population of twelve thousand by the end of the century was largely sustained by its own commercial and industrial success. Economic progress created a prosperous middle class, which became accustomed to taking summer holidays by the sea. Bangor with a population of 7,800 by 1911 was the largest resort; Portrush grew rapidly from the 1880s to over 2,000; and Bundoran in south Donegal made spectacular growth in the first years of the twentieth century. The sea-fishing industry never fulfilled the hopeful predictions of economists, partly because Cornish and Scots boat owners were usually better equipped. However, the seasonal appearance of mackerel and herring shoals did provide a modest prosperity to Kilkeel, Ardglass and Annalong, in County Down, and Killybegs, in County Donegal.

With its mix of modern industry, family farms, traditional crafts and efficient communications, Ulster in many respects looked like several provincial regions of the British mainland. In the peculiar nature of its divided society, however, it seemed to have more in common with provinces of the Austro-Hungarian, Russian and Turkish empires.

TWO NATIONS?

More clearly now than at any time since the seventeenth century the inhabitants of Ulster seemed divided sharply into two ethnic groups with profoundly divergent aspirations. Some, indeed, were convinced that Protestants and Catholics there formed two separate nations. Protestants had no difficulty in accepting the theory that they were Anglo-Saxon in race, possessing the inherited virtues of thrift, capacity for hard work and respect for law and order. Nationalists, though they might add adjectives such as 'dour', largely accepted Protestants' assumption of racial separateness, for they at the same time were emphasising their Gaelic origins and laying claim to inherent characteristics such as hospitality, passion and love of poetry. Such views are still widely accepted today – were these theories of racial separation justified?

There is growing scholarly evidence that seventeenth-century planters and their descendants did not separate themselves from the native population as much as was formerly believed. British settlers in western Ulster sometimes married local women and within a generation their descendants could well be speaking Irish. On the other side of the province the incoming flood of colonists encouraged many native Irish to embrace Protestantism, speak English and drop the prefix 'O' or 'Mac' from their surnames. A cursory glance at registers in segregated schools past and present will show many 'British' surnames, such as Adams and Hume, in Catholic roll books, and 'Irish' surnames, such as Maginnis and McCusker, in Protestant ones.

Genealogists have uncovered a far greater degree of religious conversion and

The Derry team, Ulster hurling champions, 1902–3: formed in 1884, the Gaelic Athletic Association excluded from membership soldiers and police and those who played 'foreign games'.
DERRY COUNTY GAA

An Orange band from
Derry at the beginning of
the twentieth century
LINEN HALL LIBRARY

native–planter, Catholic–Protestant intermarriage than might be expected. The
nineteenth century saw a dramatic fall in the number of people who could
speak Irish and, as surnames were anglicised, translated or given pseudo-
translations, the memory of ancestral connection was often lost. Many
Donnellys (originally Ó Donnghaile) in the Coleraine district became
Donaldsons; Laverys (Ó Labhradha) on the eastern shore of Lough Neagh
became Armstrongs; and the Johnston and Johnson surnames, of Scots and
English origin, were borrowed by MacKeowns, MacShanes and Bissetts. Even
the dropping of a prefix could invalidate conclusions on regional origin, in the
absence of other evidence: the common Ulster surname Neill is borne by
people who could descend from the Scots Neilsons or MacNeillies; from the
MacNeills of the Isles; or from any branch of the Ulster O'Neills; or from Mac
an Fhilidh, 'son of the poet', which had also been anglicised as MacNeilly,
Neely, MacAnelly, MacAnilly and MacNeely.

In short, by the late nineteenth century, descendants of natives and planters
had become so intermingled that it would be quite wrong to conclude – as
so many do – that the great majority of Catholics are of Gaelic origin and that
most Protestants are of British colonial stock. Detailed investigation would
surely reveal a similar lack of clarity in the ethnic distinctions then so

passionately espoused in the Austro-Hungarian, Turkish and Russian empires. What mattered was that Serbs, Croats, Slovenes, Czechs, Bulgars, Poles and others *felt* themselves to be separate nations. Similarly, the vast majority of Ulster Catholics thought of themselves as part of an Irish nation, worthy of self-government; and Ulster Protestants, with a few notable exceptions drawn largely from the intelligentsia, saw themselves as Britons, who should not be cut loose from the United Kingdom. These clashing aspirations continued to generate eddies of turbulence, sometimes becoming dangerous cyclones, for many years to come. Politicians, however, often displayed a striking inability to recognise the portents of storm.

'WE SHALL DEFEAT THIS CONSPIRACY': THE SECOND HOME RULE BILL, 1893

Gladstone in opposition was still at the helm of the Liberal Party, with Home Rule remaining at the top of his agenda. Unionists were watchful but, with Lord Salisbury in power, their determination was not yet put to the test. Besides, the Irish Parliamentary Party was riven by a bitter quarrel when the details of Parnell's liaison with Katharine O'Shea were revealed to the world in 1890. Parnell, ousted from the leadership, toured the country in all weathers in an attempt to recover his position but, exhausted, he died in Katharine's arms on 6 October 1891. The split in the party he had so skilfully put together survived his death for almost a decade.

If Nationalist quarrels brought comfort to Unionists, it was short-lived. The electorate in Britain was impatient for change and Gladstone was confident of victory in the general election called for the summer of 1892. The prospect of another Home Rule Bill galvanised Ulster Unionists: plans were laid for an orderly and dignified convention in Belfast to demonstrate to the world the strength of loyalist feeling in the north. Unionist leaders were determined to erase the memory of the vicious rioting that had so besmirched the opposition to Home Rule in 1886. This time twelve thousand delegates had been elected by Unionist associations across the province and they were to meet indoors on the plains of Stranmillis in a specially constructed convention hall, described by the *Northern Whig* as 'the largest which has ever been erected in Great Britain or Ireland for political purposes'. The proceedings on 17 June were begun by the archbishop of Armagh asking God to send down 'Thy Holy Spirit to guide our deliberations for the advancement of Thy Glory, the safety of the Throne, and the integrity of the Empire'. Then, led by a male-voice choir, all sang the versified Psalm 46:

> God is our refuge and our strength,
> In straits a present aid;
> Therefore, although the earth remove,
> We will not be afraid . . .

The Ulster Unionist Convention of 1892 in the Botanic Gardens, Belfast: Ulster Unionists then unhesitatingly regarded themselves as Irish.
ULSTER MUSEUM

With the backing of both Nationalist factions – the Parnellites and the anti-Parnellites – Gladstone was able to form a government in August 1892 with a majority of forty MPs. Almost at once he set about preparing his second Home Rule Bill. No bill in the nineteenth century occupied so much parliamentary time: fighting the provisions clause by clause, Unionists spoke 938 times for a total of almost 153 hours over 82 days. All this effort notwithstanding, the House of Commons passed the bill. The Lords gave their verdict on 9 September 1893 and it was said that only two Unionist peers were absent without valid excuse – one shooting lions in Somaliland, the other killing rats at Reigate. They threw out the bill by 419 votes to 41, rejecting the will of the elected representatives of the people. A constitutional crisis should have followed, but as John Morley, the Irish chief secretary, observed: 'The temperature of feeling for the Irish task was not by any means uniform or equable.'

Exhausted and dispirited after his second failure to set Home Rule for Ireland, Gladstone retired in March 1894 and his successor, Lord Rosebery, let Home Rule drop out of his government's programme. Meanwhile, the Nationalists were too demoralised by their bitter internal squabbles to conduct an effective campaign outside Westminster. The Conservatives returned to power in 1895 and were to stay in office for the ensuing decade without a break. Lord Salisbury had no doubt that his government should leave 'Home Rule sleeping the sleep of the unjust'.

The Conservative policy of killing Home Rule with kindness was renewed, but since there did not seem to be much to kill, the kindness could be rationed to no more than what the British electorate considered just. The Congested

Districts Board subsidised local crafts, built harbours and promoted agricultural improvements in the west, including County Donegal and small stretches of Fermanagh and Tyrone, but, in spite of considerable sums expended, no impressive results flowed from these efforts – even the rapid adoption of an effective potato spray and of disease-resistant tubers was due mainly to the farmers' own initiative. The Local Government Act of 1898 was the outcome of crisis management and not of forward planning. Stung by a report of a royal commission that Ireland was overtaxed, Irish Unionists and Nationalists briefly united to sweep away grand juries and give democracy to rural Ireland. Unfortunately the new local government jobs thus created were not thrown open to public competitive examinations and the result was the rapid entrenchment of petty local patronage, with baleful consequences for Ulster in the decades to come.

The most far-reaching reform was promoted by George Wyndham, appointed Irish chief secretary in November 1900. Great-grandson of Lord Edward FitzGerald, he seemed to have inherited some of his forbear's revolutionary zeal as, to the treasury's alarm, he outlined his plans to wipe out poverty, rehouse a third of the population and get rid of landlordism. In 1902 he backed the recommendation of a conference of landlords and tenant representatives that a massive scheme of land purchase be undertaken at once by the Government. The following year Westminster passed Wyndham's Land Bill, which encouraged landlords to sell entire estates, the money being advanced to tenants by the treasury to be repaid over 68.5 years at the rate of 3.25 per cent. The act was an immediate success, though it took further legislation in 1909 to compel all landlords to sell. The land issue virtually dropped out of the Irish Question. Landlords, generally eager to sell, either retained only their demesnes or cleared off altogether: such a revolution was to be accomplished in many other European states only by violence and bloodshed.

George Wyndham: the Irish chief secretary who took the land question out of politics
LINEN HALL LIBRARY

Wyndham was eager to demonstrate to all the benefits of the imperial connection to Ireland – an island, he felt certain, best governed in the manner of a Crown Colony. He was, however, incautious, imperious and overconfident, and was loathed by the northern Unionists. Wyndham for his part disliked 'Orange uncouthness' and found 'the parochialism of the Ulster right-wing . . . beyond belief'. By 1904 he was remarking: 'My contact with the Ulster members is like catching an "itch" from park pests.' That autumn it was revealed that Dublin Castle was drafting proposals for devolution in Ireland. As T.P. O'Connor, the Nationalist MP for Liverpool, gleefully pointed out, devolution was simply the Latin word for

Home Rule. Ulster Unionists angrily called for Wyndham's removal, and Nationalist MPs, frustrated by the lack of concessions to them, joined in the hue and cry. Wyndham denied having seen the devolution proposals but he was not convincing and recent research has shown that he was lying. He resigned in the spring of 1905, to dissolve rapidly in alcohol thereafter. Constructive unionism was in ruins.

IRISH IRELANDERS AND MILITANT REPUBLICANS

'I am very sorry to say,' John Dillon remarked about his fellow Nationalist MPs in 1898, 'that an increasing number of them are prepared to throw themselves into oceans of whiskey and into nothing else.' In 1900, however, the Irish Parliamentary Party reunited under the leadership of the Parnellite MP for Waterford, John Redmond. Redmond appeared to have little option but to await the return of the Liberals and an opportunity to hold the balance of power in the Commons once more.

Not all Irish nationalists were prepared to be patient. Some sought to emphasise the cultural separateness of the island: the Gaelic League, founded in 1893 to promote the revival of the Irish language, had acquired around one hundred thousand members by the beginning of the new century; and the Gaelic Athletic Association, formed in 1884 and taking root in rural areas, tended to be divisive, as it excluded from membership soldiers, police and anyone associated with 'Britishness', including those who played cricket, rugby and other 'foreign games'. The Gaelic revivalists roundly condemned what they saw as the corrupting influence of urban, materialistic, secularist and liberal culture emanating from Britain. The movement therefore blended easily with the continuing Catholic revival, which now combined a proselytising puritanism with romantic zeal. Ulster Protestants – notably Samuel Ferguson, William Reeves and George Sigerson – had done much to get the Gaelic revival under way; now most were repelled by these new interpretations of cultural identity which made them feel alien in their own land. A few, such as Francis Joseph Bigger, Roger Casement and Sir Shane Leslie, espoused the 'Irish Ireland' movement but they were swimming against a strong local tide.

It was in the very heart of the Protestant north-east that militant re-publicanism retained most vigour. In the early years of the twentieth century, Belfast had the most active cells of the Irish Republican Brotherhood in Ireland. At a time when the brotherhood was moribund in Dublin, the piano-tuner Denis McCullough revitalised the separatist movement in the heart of Unionist territory. He weeded out the faint-hearted - including his own father – and worked with unremitting zeal to enrol in the brotherhood young men determined to fight for a republic. He was joined by the Protestant journalist from Holywood, Bulmer Hobson, and together they launched the Dungannon

Club in 1905 to revive republican feeling. Named to evoke memories of the Dungannon Convention of 1782, the club merged in 1907 with Arthur Griffith's separatist but non-violent Sinn Féin (meaning 'ourselves', a name suggested by Edward Carson's Gaelic Leaguer cousin, Maire Butler). The dedication of these northern republicans attracted the attention of John Devoy, head of the IRB's American counterpart, Clan na Gael. Rejecting constitutional nationalism after the fall of Parnell, Devoy had despaired of revitalising physical-force republicanism in Ireland until these young Ulstermen came to his notice.

Devoy sent money and instructions to prepare for armed rebellion. On the eve of the First World War his northern zealots – by then including Sean MacDermott, Thomas Clarke, Dr Patrick McCartan and Sir Roger Casement – had seized complete control of the IRB, toppling the Dublin leadership opposed to insurrection – a task made easier by the massive campaign of resistance conducted by Ulster Unionists against the third Home Rule Bill.

The momentous general election of January 1906 dashed the Irish Parliamentary Party's rising expectation that Home Rule would soon be clearly on the horizon. The Conservative and Unionist vote crashed so dramatically that Sir Henry Campbell-Bannerman, the new Liberal prime minister, had no need of Nationalist support. Besides, the Liberals were nervously reluctant to put Home Rule near the top of their agenda.

Jim Larkin, leader of the 1907 Belfast dock strike
LINEN HALL LIBRARY

Nevertheless, tentative proposals for a limited form of devolution, the creation of an Irish Council, rejected though they were, sent a frisson of alarm through loyalist ranks in Ulster. Party machinery was streamlined by the Ulster Unionist Council, formed in 1904 'with a view to consistent and continuous political action'. This reinvigoration across the province tacitly excluded southern Unionists: from now on they would have to fend for themselves. The need to hold together urban supporters was particularly urgent as the labour movement was growing rapidly in strength. The Irish Trades Union Congress had been set up in 1894, and by 1899 half the affiliated trade unionists for the whole island were working in Belfast and its environs. The Belfast Labour Representation Committee's candidate, William Walker, came close to winning the North Belfast seat in 1905. Sent over to the city as organiser for the National Union of Dock Labourers, Jim Larkin achieved conspicuous success in recruiting unskilled men of both sects and in May 1907 engaged the employers in a titanic struggle which paralysed Belfast until August and was briefly supported by a police mutiny. Fortunately for the Unionists,

Motor vans delivering
goods and protected by
police: Belfast dock
strike, 1907
LINEN HALL LIBRARY

Nationalists shared their conservative horror of socialism, and from the moment that Larkin moved to Dublin in 1908, the solidarity of those who sought a Dublin parliament was constantly challenged by labour militancy.

The 1907 Belfast Dock Strike ended in victory for the employers, but for a time Catholics and Protestants had campaigned shoulder to shoulder. It would take more than trade-union loyalty to detach them from their traditional political allegiances, however. Besides, events at Westminster were shortly to arouse the people of Ulster to passionate defence of, or opposition to, Home Rule.

HOME RULE PROMISED AND LOYALIST RESISTANCE PREPARED

When Campbell-Bannerman died in 1908 and Herbert Asquith took his place as prime minister, Britain was entering the most dangerous constitutional crisis since the Glorious Revolution. After emasculating bills sent up from the Commons for three years, the Lords rejected the 1909 'People's Budget': Asquith had no choice but to take the issue to the people, and a general election followed in January 1910. The Liberals won but with such a reduced majority that they were now dependent on forty Labour and eighty-two Nationalist MPs to stay in power. The Lords gave way and accepted the budget only to face a Parliament Bill designed to deny peers the right to reject bills from the Commons for more than three successive sessions. Once again there was a constitutional impasse which could only be resolved by another election. In December 1910 the Conservative and Unionist Party won exactly the same number of seats as the Liberals but Asquith remained as prime minister with the support of forty-two Labour MPs and eighty-four Nationalists.

Now was the moment for Redmond to exact the price of his support: Asquith had announced that the Irish Question could be solved only 'by a policy which, while safeguarding the supremacy and indefeasible authority of the imperial Parliament, will set up in Ireland a system of full self-government in regard to purely Irish affairs'. Uncertain of Tory resolve at Westminster and disgusted by the apparent indifference of the British electorate, northern loyalist leaders firmly embarked on an unconstitutional course. 'With the help of God, you and I joined together . . . will yet defeat the most nefarious conspiracy that has ever been hatched against a free people.' From a platform overlooking Belfast Lough, Sir Edward Carson addressed these words to fifty thousand men from Unionist Clubs and Orange lodges from all parts of Ulster. 'We must be prepared,' he warned, '. . . the morning Home Rule passes, ourselves to become responsible for the government of the Protestant Province of Ulster.' One of the most brilliant lawyers of his day, Carson had become a household name in 1895 when he brought down Oscar Wilde. He had served as Balfour's solicitor-general and was a southern unionist who was certain that the welfare of the island as a whole depended on the maintenance of the Union. He now agreed to lead Ulster loyalists in the belief that if he could prevent Home Rule being applied to Ulster, then Home Rule could not be applied to the rest of Ireland, for Redmond would never accept a divided island. Captain James Craig was Carson's partner rather than his second-in-command; Craig had already demonstrated his courage and organisational flair as an officer in the Boer War. To a greater extent than Carson, Craig shared the prejudices and fears of the Ulster Protestants he represented. Carson wanted to maintain the Union for all of Ireland; Craig wanted to maintain the Union in order to save Protestant Ulster. Events were to prove that Craig's objective was the more realistic of the two.

Sir Edward Carson: the southern Unionist who led Ulster's resistance to Home Rule; from the *Illustrated London News*

> The dark eleventh hour
> Draws on and sees us sold . . .

So Kipling began an indignant poem, 'Ulster 1912', published in the *Morning Post*, showing that British Conservatives were rallying to the Ulster Unionist cause. Andrew Bonar Law, born in Coleraine, had become leader of the

ULSTER LIBERAL ASSOCIATION.

Unreserved 1/-

The Right Hon. LORD PIRRIE, K.P., H.M.L.

The Right Hon. WINSTON CHURCHILL, M.P.

Mr JOHN REDMOND, M.P.

CELTIC PARK FOOTBALL GROUNDS, FEBRUARY 8th, 1912.

Meeting at 1 o'clock.   Doors open at 12 o'clock.

Belfast Corporation refused to let Liberal Home Secretary Winston Churchill speak in the Ulster Hall where his father, Lord Randolph, had warned that Home Rule could arrive like 'a thief in the night'. After the 1916 rebellion Lord Pirrie opposed Home Rule.
LINEN HALL LIBRARY

opposition in 1911. Determined to save Protestant Ulster, he spoke to one hundred thousand loyalist demonstrators at the Balmoral showgrounds in Belfast on Easter Tuesday 1912, and assured them:

> Once again you hold the pass, the pass for the Empire . . . The Government have erected by their Parliament Act a boom against you to shut you off from the help of the British people. You will burst that boom. That help will come . . .

There was more here than a desire to be revenged on the Liberals for recent humiliations: a formidable body of British opinion saw Home Rule as a deadly threat to the empire. The Home Rule Bill about to be introduced might well be a modest measure of devolution, but as Nationalist leaders themselves suggested, it could be extended at a later date – this was just what was feared on both sides of the Irish Sea.

On 11 April 1912 the Home Rule Bill was introduced and members of the Irish Parliamentary Party seemed to have been brought to their promised land. Bonar Law spoke with exceptional bitterness at a great Unionist rally at Blenheim Palace, saying that if Ulster loyalists resorted to force, they would have his backing: 'I can imagine no length of resistance to which Ulster can go in which I should not be prepared to support them.' Passions were running high in Ulster and the danger of outright sectarian warfare loomed large. Only by a series of massive displays of loyalist solidarity, the Ulster Unionist Council believed, could British sympathy be won and violence be avoided. Carson

began by addressing forty thousand on Portora Hill in Enniskillen on 18 September 1912, launching the campaign to sweep eastwards across the loyalist heartlands to Belfast.

On the morning of Saturday 28 September all over Ulster the Protestant people emerged from churches and meeting halls, pledging themselves

> to stand by one another in defending for ourselves and our children our cherished position of equal citizenship in the United Kingdom and in using all means which may be found necessary to defeat the present conspiracy to set up a Home Rule parliament in Dublin.

In Belfast City Hall Carson was the first to sign Ulster's Solemn League and Covenant, and when he re-emerged the reverential hum of the vast crowd changed to tempestuous cheering. Then bowler-hatted stewards struggled to regulate the flow of men eager to sign. A double row of desks stretching right round the building made it possible for 550 to sign simultaneously. Women signed their own separate declaration. Altogether 471,414 men and women who could prove Ulster birth signed either the Covenant or the declaration, over 30,000 more women, in fact, than men. That night at Donegall Quay Sir Edward was saluted by a fusillade of shots as he was welcomed aboard *Patriotic*. As the vessel steamed into the Victoria Channel, bonfires in Great Patrick Street sprang to life, a huge fire on the Cave Hill threw a brilliant glare over the sky, fifty other bonfires blazed from hills and headlands round Belfast Lough, and salvoes of rockets shot up into the air. Redmond had said that

As the Unionists were against female suffrage, women signed their own separate declaration against Home Rule. More women signed the declaration than men signed the Covenant; from the *Illustrated London News*
x
BELFAST CENTRAL LIBRARY

Ulster Unionists were only engaged in 'a gigantic game of bluff and blackmail'. J.L. Garvin, reporting for the *Pall Mall Gazette*, now concluded: 'No-one for a moment could have mistaken the concentrated will and courage of those people.'

Early in 1913 the Home Rule Bill passed the Commons only to be rejected by the Lords by 326 votes to 69. Soon after, the Nationalists recovered Londonderry City, tipping the balance of MPs in Ulster in their favour, seventeen to sixteen. Undeterred, the Ulster Unionist Council had already decided to use 'all means which may be found necessary' to stop Home Rule: the scheme for setting up the provisional government of Ulster was ready and the Ulster Volunteer Force, to be recruited from men who had signed the Covenant, was formally instituted. Making Belfast's Old Town Hall its headquarters, the UVF grew to ninety thousand men by the end of the year. Could the UVF stop Home Rule unless it was fully armed? Could Ulster Unionist resistance force Asquith to modify his bill?

Captain T.C. Agar-Robartes MP first proposed partition at Westminster. He was killed in action in 1915; from the *Illustrated London News.* BELFAST CENTRAL LIBRARY

'I have never heard that orange bitters will mix with Irish whiskey,' T.C. Agar-Robartes, an English Liberal MP, had observed at an early stage in the Home Rule debate. Then his amendment to exclude the four most Protestant counties from the bill's operation had been decisively rejected. During the final months of 1913, however, Asquith seriously considered partition and put forward a complicated amendment early in 1914 allowing each Ulster county to opt out of Home Rule for six years. 'We do not want sentence of death with a stay of execution for six years,' Carson told the Commons on 9 March and left London ten days later to set up the Provisional Government of Ulster.

Winston Churchill, first lord of the Admiralty, ordered a large naval cordon into position and the war minister, Colonel John Seely, asked the commander-in-chief in Ireland to strengthen the approaches to Ulster at Enniskillen, Dundalk and Newry. Uncertain of its next step, the Liberal government then quickly lost the initiative. Seely yielded to senior army pressure and gave cavalry officers at the Curragh army camp a written assurance that the Government did not intend to crush political opposition in the north. The war minister was dismissed but it was too late. Fully alerted, the UVF moved its headquarters to a heavily sandbagged Craigavon at Craig's Strandtown estate.

The Unionists' fateful decision to resort to arms was taken earlier than is generally acknowledged: in November 1910 the Ulster Unionist Council had formed a secret committee to oversee the buying of weapons from arms dealers. Acting as the council's agent, Major Fred Crawford, secretary of the Ulster Reform Club, had written in the same year to five arms manufacturers, including Deutsche Waffen und Munitionsfabriken, seeking quotations for twenty thousand rifles and a million rounds of ammunition. Only by one daring stroke, Crawford persuaded the Unionist leaders, could enough modern weapons and ammunition be run into Ulster to equip the entire UVF. 'Crawford,' Carson said, 'I'll see you through this business, if I should have to go to prison for it.'

On the night of 19–20 April 1914, 216 tons of arms were transferred off the Tuskar Rock to the SS *Clydevalley*: Crawford had bought 24,600 German, Austrian and Italian rifles and 5 million rounds of ammunition in Hamburg and taken them via the Kiel Canal and the Baltic to the south-east of Ireland. That same night instructions had been issued for a full test mobilisation of the UVF. Only twelve men knew for certain the elaborate plan for landing and secretly distributing the arms. On 24–5 April, while the authorities investigated a decoy ship sent into Belfast Lough, the guns were brought in without interference at Larne, Bangor and Donaghadee, and loaded on to motorcars, which then sped through the night distributing them to prepared dumps all over the province. Probably for the first time in history motor vehicles had been used on a large scale for a military purpose, and with striking success.

Major Fred Crawford: the UVF's swashbuckling gun-runner
LINEN HALL LIBRARY

THE GREAT WAR

'Trust in the old party – and Home Rule next year,' Redmond had promised at a great rally in Dublin in March 1912. Now it looked as if the Unionist threat of violence was about to thwart the wishes of the great majority of the Irish people. Eoin MacNeill, the Irish history professor from the Glens of Antrim who had helped to found the Gaelic League, argued that nationalists should defend legislative independence as the eighteenth-century Volunteers had done. Persuaded by the republican leader Bulmer Hobson, MacNeill presided at a meeting in Dublin's Rotunda concert hall on 25 November 1913 which launched the Irish Volunteers. Unknown to MacNeill, key positions on the executive were held by men who were members of the IRB.

General von Bernhardt in Berlin was certain that the critical situation in Ireland would paralyse Britain 'if ever it comes to war with England'. By May 1914 the Irish Volunteers numbered 129,000, with 41,000 of them in Ulster. In an effort to prevent civil war, George V called an all-party conference at Buckingham Palace in July; according to Churchill the delegates 'toiled round the muddy byways of Fermanagh and Tyrone', but no agreement was reached. On Sunday 26 July a consignment of obsolete single-shot Mausers was bought in Hamburg and taken by yacht to Howth near Dublin. Soldiers, who had attempted to take some of the rifles from the Irish Volunteers, opened fire on a taunting crowd, killing four people and wounding a further thirty-seven.

German arms being driven from Larne, 24–5 April 1914; sketches by Carey and Thompson of Belfast for the *Illustrated London News*

UVF gun-runners on the road, 24–5 April 1914: there were only about 200 motorcars in County Antrim and nearly all of them carried arms that night; sketches by Carey and Thompson of Belfast for the *Illustrated London News*

Nationalists were intensely bitter when they compared their treatment with that of the UVF. Field Marshal Conrad von Hötzendorff was sure that the Ulster crisis would give him a free hand in Serbia, but his punitive expedition there began to escalate and by 4 August 1914 the United Kingdom was at war.

'All officers, non-commissioned officers and men who are in the Ulster Volunteer Force . . . are requested to answer immediately his Majesty's call, as our first duty as loyal subjects is to the King': with this telegram Carson pulled his followers back from the brink of civil war. 'The armed Catholics in the South will only be too glad to join arms with the armed Protestant Ulstermen,' Redmond declared in the Commons. With evident relief Sir Edward Grey, the foreign secretary, said that 'the one bright spot in the very dreadful situation is Ireland'. The martial fever that gripped so many parts of Europe was not slow in infecting Ireland as tens of thousands of nationalists and loyalists flocked to join up.

On 15 September Asquith told the Commons that the UVF's patriotic spirit made the coercion of Ulster 'unthinkable', but that in three days' time the Home Rule Bill would become law. Nevertheless, he continued, Home Rule would not be implemented until the end of the war and amending legislation later on would make special provision for Ulster. Carson stumped out in protest and the entire opposition followed him. Redmond, however, had as much reason for anxiety as the Unionists: as the war became a bloody and

The UVF at Craigavon,
Sir James Craig's home in
east Belfast; from the *Graphic*
BELFAST CENTRAL LIBRARY

inconclusive slogging match in the trenches, Home Rule receded into an uncertain future.

Protected by the Royal Navy and far out of range of Zeppelins, the farms, mills, workshops and shipyards of Ulster strove to meet the insatiable demands of the Allied war effort. Never had the people been so prosperous and rarely had the island known such domestic peace. News that a rebellion had broken out in Dublin on Easter Monday 1916, came, therefore, as a complete surprise. Even Dr Patrick McCartan, a member of the IRB supreme council, wrote from County Tyrone that 'the whole business was like a thunderbolt to me'.

This was the conspiracy of a tiny minority: the decision to go ahead with the rising was taken solely by two Ulstermen, Thomas Clarke and, the real organiser, Sean MacDermott. No more than two thousand took part, most of them Irish Volunteers who refused to support the war and around two hundred men and boys of the Citizen Army, a republican socialist force led by James Connolly. 'We have failed in Tyrone – miserably failed – but it is not the fault of Tyrone but of Dublin. They did not let me know till the last minute . . .' So wrote McCartan in a letter written on the back of fourteen blank cheques, in hiding, after the men of Carrickmore had been dispersed and their store of weapons seized. The insurrection in Dublin, nevertheless, cost 450 lives, 2,614 wounded, and £3 million worth of damage. The cost in other respects was incalculable. As military tribunals in Dublin condemned insurgent leaders to execution by firing squad, the power base of the Irish Parliamentary Party was being eroded away.

The severity of the British government's reaction to the rebellion reflected the Allied fear that victory was not in prospect. All hopes were pinned on a massive offensive being prepared for the early summer along the River

Somme. The heaviest bombardment the world had yet seen neither cut the
German wire nor knocked out the enemy machine-gun nests. Exposed to
relentless fire and mistakenly shelled from their own side, whole companies
were wiped out. During the first two days of the Battle of the Somme, 1–2
July 1916, 5,500 men of the Ulster Division had been killed or wounded.
Ulster's tight-knit Protestant community would never forget the terrible
sacrifice that had been made.

Soon after replacing Asquith as prime minister in December 1916, David
Lloyd George announced an amnesty for suspects interned after the Easter
Rising. Several of those released threw themselves into a drive to form a new
coalition of advanced nationalists, called Sinn Féin. Arthur Griffith's original
Sinn Féin had all but expired by 1916 but now, the spring of 1917, the name
was applied to this broad organisation serving as an umbrella for all those
seeking Irish independence, ranging from dissatisfied Home Rulers to militant
republicans, some of them survivors of the rising. When Redmond died in
March 1918 the party he had helped to reunite was in disarray and in one by-
election after another Sinn Féin candidates were victorious – assisted by a
British government attempt to impose conscription and by the imprisonment
of seventy-three of the leading Sinn Féin activists.

Enniskillen may have been the first town in the United Kingdom to hear of
the armistice. Having picked up a faint radio message at 6.30 a.m., troops in
the military barracks there spread the news by launching rockets and soon
church bells rang out to greet crowds gathering for the hiring fair. According
to the *Irish News*, Belfast witnessed 'a display of enthusiasm, amounting almost
to emotionalism, on the part of the public such as has never been witnessed in

The Ulster Division Memorial at Thiepval, France
LINEN HALL LIBRARY

this city'. The *Belfast Telegraph* reminded its readers 'the gladness of this hour is chastened by the thought of the vacant chair'. Around 170,000 Irishmen enlisted during the war and about half of them were from Ulster. Of the forty to fifty thousand who had given their lives in the fighting, at least half were Catholics.

Lloyd George called a general election for 14 December 1918. Eight years had passed since the previous poll and few could predict the outcome, all the more so since the latest parliamentary Reform Act had almost tripled the Irish electorate. In addition, there was a long overdue redistribution of seats. The Irish Parliamentary Party was annihilated, retaining only six seats out of the sixty-eight they held on the eve of the poll. Four of these were in Ulster, three of them partly as the result of an electoral pact with Sinn Féin, arranged by Cardinal Logue, in constituencies where Unionists were certain to win if there had been three-way contests. The Ulster Unionist representation leaped from eighteen to twenty-three, to which could be added two from Trinity College and one from County Dublin. In the whole of Ireland Sinn Féin had captured seventy-three seats and now claimed to be 'the great representative organisation of the Irish people in Ireland and throughout the world'.

The prediction made by John Dillon, now leader of the remnant of the Irish Parliamentary Party, that there would be only republican separatists and Ulster loyalists representing Ireland had all but come true. The island was about to be plunged into violence on a scale not seen since 1798 and, at its most intense in Ulster, bringing with it momentous political changes, resulting in the partition of both the country and the historic nine-county province.

8

PARTITIONED PROVINCE
THE EARLY YEARS
1919–1939

Early in 1919 Carson received a summons in Irish to attend Dáil Éireann, an assembly of the elected representatives of the Irish nation, in Dublin's Mansion House which met for the first time on 21 January. The amused Ulster Unionist leader kept it as a souvenir and there was laughter in the Dáil when the reading out of his name at roll call was greeted by silence. Thirty-four Sinn Féin deputies were not present either, as they still being detained at His Majesty's pleasure. Nevertheless, nationalist Ireland had voted overwhelmingly for Sinn Féin and the Dáil felt justified in making its Declaration of Irish Independence, stating that 'the Irish Republic was proclaimed in Dublin on Easter Monday 1916'. The Dáil put all its faith in its 'Message to the Free Nations of the World', an appeal to the Paris Peace Conference which had opened the previous day.

Sinn Féin had no plan for conciliating or compromising with the Protestant majority in the north-east. Dáil deputies seemed to have assumed that the whole island of Ireland would be the unit chosen for the application of the self-determination principle espoused by the American president, Woodrow Wilson. At the peace conference, George Gavan Duffy, grandson of the Young Ireland leader, and Sean T. O'Kelly were again and again rebuffed in their attempt to get international recognition for an all-Ireland republic. The conference was swamped by dozens of delegations – including one led by Ho Chi Minh seeking independence for the Vietnamese in French Indo-China – all lobbying for self-determination. Wilson, himself of Ulster Presbyterian extraction, was baffled by Europe's ethnic complexity and had no wish to embarrass Britain, the United States' closest wartime ally, by agreeing to the Dáil's demands.

Sean T. O'Kelly was rebuffed in Paris when he called at Georges Clemenceau's office in a vain attempt to have Dáil Éireann represented at the Peace Conference in 1919.
LINEN HALL LIBRARY

Agreed since 1916 that the partition of the six north-eastern counties was the most practical political solution, Ulster Unionists felt exceptionally confident in 1919. Although Lloyd George was still prime minister, he now led a coalition of 520 MPs, 400 of whom were Conservative and Unionist, possessing an absolute majority in the Commons. Such men were unlikely, it was thought, to betray their allies in Ulster. Besides, the Sinn Féin MPs refused to sit at Westminster; the Irish Parliamentary Party had all but disappeared; and Carson, Craig and Lord Londonderry all had places in the Government, and were therefore in a strong position to influence legislation for Ireland.

An early decision made in Paris was the confirmation of Luxemburg's independence. Since that state was smaller than County Antrim, the prospect looked bright for a partitioned Ulster in 1919–20 as Lloyd George's government readdressed the problem of sorting out Ireland's constitutional future. The exclusion of all nine counties of the province was no longer seriously contemplated. Should the excluded territory include all of the counties of Fermanagh and Tyrone, both with large tracts inhabited overwhelmingly by Catholics? The problem was essentially the same as it had been in 1912–14, as Churchill reminded the House of Commons in his most celebrated speech on Ireland:

> The whole map of Europe has been changed. The position of countries has been violently altered. The modes of thought of men, the whole outlook on affairs, the grouping of parties, all have encountered violent and tremendous changes in the deluge of the world. But as the deluge subsides and the waters fall short we see the dreary steeples of Fermanagh and Tyrone emerging once again. The integrity of their quarrel is one of the few institutions that has been unaltered in the cataclysm which has swept the world.

As Lloyd George laboured on the details of the Bill for the Better Government of Ireland through the year 1920, that quarrel became openly violent. On 21 January 1919, the day the Dáil had first met, two RIC constables had been shot dead by masked Volunteers in County Tipperary. Irish Volunteers, now calling themselves the Irish Republican Army, grew ever more restless and when Lloyd George declared the Dáil illegal in September 1919, the restraining hand of constitutional politicians was removed. By 1920 full-scale guerrilla warfare had developed over much of the south; as the year advanced it spread northwards, inflaming ancient hatreds, plunging Ulster into the most terrible period of violence the province had experienced since the eighteenth century.

The civil war, postponed by a general European war in 1914, had begun.

OUTRIGHT INTERCOMMUNAL WARFARE

The sustained slaughter of the First World War seemed to accustom men to the regular use of violence to advance a cause, redress grievances and enforce the will of government. After the armistice, blood continued to flow on the European mainland: British, French and Polish troops intervened against the Bolsheviks in Russia only to intensify the miseries of a civil war there which left millions dying of typhus and starvation; squads of Fascist ex-servicemen and revolutionary socialists fought each other for supremacy on the streets of northern Italian cities; Spartacists and disbanded soldiers of the Freikorps threatened to stifle the infant Weimar Republic in its cradle; Admiral Horthy crushed the Communists in Budapest with an army invading from Transylvania; and in the new states emerging from the wreck of the Austro-Hungarian, German and Russian empires, ethnic rivalries flared into violent struggles. Now men came back from the front to Ireland to renew their fighting; Robert Lynd reported for the *Daily News* that 'soldiers who fought for the Allies as they return home are becoming converted by the thousand into Sinn Féiners', some, like Tom Barry, to become leading men in the IRA; and others played a crucial role in reviving the UVF. 'I had thought my soldiering days were over,' wrote Captain Sir Basil Brooke, the Fermanagh landlord awarded the Military Cross during the war; '. . . I was to become a soldier of a very different sort . . . but I had the added stimulant of defending my own birthplace.' As IRA attacks spread northwards Brooke took a lead in organising Protestant resistance, while, at the same time, Lloyd George recruited ex-servicemen to revive the demoralised RIC, and thus unleashed the notorious Black and Tans and the Auxiliaries on the southern Irish countryside. As the Anglo-Irish War edged into Ulster it triggered off a sectarian conflict more vicious and lethal than all the northern riots of the previous century put together.

In the 1920 local government elections, the first in the United Kingdom to be conducted under a system of proportional representation, the Unionists lost control of Londonderry Corporation for the first time ever. Hugh O'Doherty, the city's first Catholic mayor, in his inaugural speech declared uncompromisingly: 'Ireland's right to determine her own destiny will come about whether the Protestants of Ulster like it or not.' Here, loyalist fears of abandonment were particularly acute. In the middle of April rioting began at the corner of Long Tower Street, described by the *Derry Journal* as 'a great storm centre in party fights in the city'. Shots were fired into the Bogside on 18 April and on 14 May trouble flared up again: in a four-hour gun battle the local head of the RIC special branch, and a Catholic returned from the trenches gassed and wounded, were killed. Worse violence followed in June when the UVF seized control of The Diamond and Guildhall Square, and began firing down from the old city walls. By the time 1,500 troops had arrived on 23 June, 8 Catholics and 4 Protestants had been killed. The army imposed a curfew and directed machine-gun fire into the Bogside, killing six more Catholics; and, as

shootings, assassinations and reprisals continued, the death toll for the city eventually reached forty. A striking feature of the army's intervention in Derry was its close co-operation with the local UVF.

In Belfast, shipyard workers met outside the gates of Workman Clark's south yard on 21 July 1920 and there the call to drive out 'disloyal' workers was enthusiastically supported. At the end of the meeting hundreds of apprentices and rivet boys marched into Harland and Wolff's yard and ordered out Catholics and socialists. Some were kicked and beaten, others were pelted with rivets, and some were forced to swim for their lives. At the same time, after being driven out of local mills and factories, virtually the entire Catholic populations of Banbridge and Dromore in County Down were forced by loyalists to flee. Catholics were attacked in Bangor also but it was in Belfast that the most ferocious fighting ensued. After three days and nights of outright intercommunal warfare, troops restored order by firing on both sides. Seven Catholics and six Protestants had died violently in east Belfast but the killing in the city had only begun. Then on Sunday 22 August District Inspector Oswald Swanzy was shot dead in Lisburn and in the next three days Protestants attacked and burned sixty Catholic-owned public houses and business premises and finally drove out of the town almost all the Catholic residents. Fred Crawford, now a lieutenant-colonel, visited the town but he had little sympathy for the victims:

> Lisburn is like a bombarded town in France . . . All this is done by Unionists as a protest against these cold-blooded murders . . . It has been stated that there are only four or five R.C. families left in Lisburn; others say this is wrong that there are far more. Be that as it may there certainly are practically no shops or places of business left to the R.C.s.

Intense violence erupted again in Belfast and all the usual sectarian flash points were engulfed in protracted rioting. In east Belfast troops ended the turmoil only by drastic means; the *Irish News* reported in heavy type that 'the Newtownards Road was absolutely swept by machine gun and rifle fire in both directions'.

The Conservative *Birmingham Post* warned Unionists in Ulster that the ill-treatment of Catholics would 'alienate the sympathies of the great masses of people who desire to help her'. The *Westminster Gazette* published a cartoon of Carson 'watching the Orange glow in Belfast', while the opposition press was more outspoken, the *Daily Herald* remarking: 'The bloody harvest of Carsonism is being reaped in Belfast.' Unionist leaders themselves were alarmed that their cause would be ruined by further unconstrained assaults on the Catholic population. They eagerly sought a political settlement while the balance at Westminster was still in their favour.

THE CREATION OF NORTHERN IRELAND

The intensification of the Anglo-Irish War caused consternation amongst loyalists in rural Ulster. In Armagh, John Webster, a local merchant, brought in arms from Scotland and from UVF headquarters 'to form a type of security or protective patrol to operate at night in the city'; a vigilante patrol formed by Lieutenant-Colonel George Liddle repelled an IRA attack on Lisbellaw in County Fermanagh on the night of 8–9 June 1920; and Sir Basil Brooke took out UVF rifles from their hiding place in Colebrooke House and formed another vigilante patrol. Brooke wrote to General Sir Nevil Macready, the commander-in-chief in Ireland, urging recognition of loyalist paramilitaries, otherwise the 'hotheads will take matters into their own hands'.

At a joint meeting between the cabinet and the Irish administration on 23 July 1920, Churchill proposed the formation of a special constabulary. Dublin Castle officials were aghast and even the diehard Lord Curzon described this as 'a most fatal suggestion'. Setting aside protests, Lloyd George decided in September to form the Ulster Special Constabulary – he had not been able to prove his own assertion that he had 'murder by the throat', and such a force,

B Specials in 1920: uniforms
had not yet been issued
IMPARTIAL REPORTER

he believed, would give some relief to the RIC, the Auxiliaries, the Black and
Tans, and the army, in their war against the IRA. The new constabulary was
divided into three categories: 2,000 A Specials, full-time and paid like the RIC;
19,500 B Specials, part-time and unpaid, serving only in their own areas; and
an unspecified number of C Specials, an unpaid reserve force only to be called
out in dire emergencies. All 'well-disposed citizens' were invited to apply but
no determined effort was made to get Catholics to join. 'The Chief Secretary
is going to arm pogromists to murder the Catholics,' Nationalist leader Joseph
Devlin said in his bitter denunciation made in the Commons. Though the
chief secretary denied this at Westminster, it was clear that the special
constabulary would operate only in the six north-eastern counties – an
indication that the Better Government of Ireland Act was about to partition
Ulster.

During the years 1919–21 the map of Europe was redrawn in a series of
peace treaties. In 1920 the United Kingdom also acquired a new frontier
running through the province of Ulster, though by the decision of parliament
rather than by international accord. The Treaty of Versailles allowed the exact
positioning of Germany's borders of Upper Silesia, Schleswig, Marienwerder
and Allenstein to be agreed after holding plebiscites. The British government
rejected any thought of a referendum in Ulster and Balfour argued that
plebiscites were only suited to vanquished enemies: 'Ireland is not like a

conquered state, which we can carve up as in Central Europe.' Thus, with the absence of any Sinn Féin MPs in the Commons and only a half-dozen demoralised Irish Parliamentary Party MPs, Ulster Unionists essentially got the constitutional arrangement they desired.

The Better Government of Ireland Bill proposed two Irish parliaments, one for the six north-eastern counties to be called Northern Ireland and another for the other twenty-six counties to be known as Southern Ireland. Since ultimate responsibility was to be reserved to Westminster, both parts of Ireland were to continue to send representatives there. As a gesture towards the self-determination principle, the bill proposed a Council of Ireland, made up of twenty representatives each from the Dublin and Belfast parliaments, 'with a view to the eventual establishment of a parliament for the whole of Ireland'.

The Ulster Unionist Council was somewhat unconvincing in asserting that loyalists would be making a 'supreme sacrifice' by accepting a parliament in Belfast. Captain Charles Craig, brother of James and MP for South Antrim, said in the Commons that 'without a parliament of our own constant attacks would be made upon us, and constant attempts would be made . . . to draw us into a Dublin parliament'. Getting the council to agree to a six-county Northern Ireland was much more difficult. An amendment to partition off the entire province, proposed by the 11th Baron Farnham on behalf of Unionists in Donegal, Monaghan and Cavan, was rejected by delegates in March 1920 so brusquely that Sir James Stronge, the County Armagh landowner, felt that 'the three counties have been thrown to the wolves with very little compunction'. Essentially, most delegates were not convinced that a nine-county parliament would have a sufficiently secure Unionist majority.

Lord Farnham: his proposal to include all nine counties of Ulster in Northern Ireland was decisively rejected by the Ulster Unionist Council in March 1920.
LINEN HALL LIBRARY

Did Northern Ireland have to engulf the six north-eastern counties intact? The question was hardly considered in 1920. James Craig suggested a boundary commission in 1919 but then thought better of it; yet the drawing of a frontier to enclose the most Protestant areas would have been no more difficult than the task facing boundary commissioners negotiating a line between Poles and Germans in Upper Silesia. The Ulster Unionists, facing negligible opposition at Westminster, set out to get as much territory as they could without endangering their majority in order to bring as many outlying Protestants as they could into their fold. Their behaviour was similar to that of other postwar winners, such as the Italians in Istria, the Greeks in Thrace, the Romanians in Transylvania and the Poles east of the Vistula, when negotiating their political orders.

Sinn Féin rejected the 'Partition Act' out of hand and carried on the struggle to make the Dáil the parliament of the thirty-two-county Irish republic.

Nevertheless, the Better Government of Ireland Act, receiving the royal assent on 23 December and due to come into force on 1 May 1921, was to become, in effect, the constitution of Northern Ireland for the next fifty years. Thus it was that the part of Ulster that had fought hardest against Home Rule was the only part of Ireland to get Home Rule.

> I could not have allowed myself to give to Ireland by deputy alone my earnest prayers and good wishes in the new era which opens with this ceremony, and I have therefore come in person . . .

Cardinal Logue: he refused an invitation to attend the state opening of the Northern Ireland parliament by George V in 1921.
LINEN HALL LIBRARY

With these words George V began his crucial speech in Belfast City Hall at the state opening of the Northern Ireland parliament on 22 June 1921. The Northern Ireland elections had been held the previous month and in an 89 per cent poll, 40 Unionists, 6 Sinn Féiners, and 6 Nationalists had been returned. Sir James Craig – he had been knighted in 1917 – had given up his junior ministerial post at Westminster to become Northern Ireland's first prime minister. Now the king addressed only Unionist MPs, for the Nationalists and Sinn Féiners held to their pledge 'not to enter this north-eastern parliament' and Cardinal Logue had also refused to attend.

The royal speech was intended to reach far beyond the walls of the city hall:

> This is a great and critical occasion in the history of the Six Counties, but not for the Six Counties alone, for everything which interests them touches Ireland . . . I speak from a full heart when I pray that my coming to Ireland to-day may prove to be the first step towards an end of strife amongst her people, whatever their race or creed.

Lloyd George had helped to compose the speech and he had seized this opportunity to offer an olive branch to Sinn Féin: British public opinion was impatient for a settlement and he had been told that it would cost £100 million to achieve victory in Ireland. The IRA flying columns were now hard-pressed and short of arms and on 11 July 1921 a truce between the IRA and the British government came into force. Eamon de Valera, president of the Dáil, went to London for talks, and a cautious peace settled on Northern Ireland.

Fearful that concessions would be required of him, Craig turned down Lloyd George's entreaties to join discussions between the Dáil and Westminster and 'explore to the utmost the possibility of a settlement'. He also refused to join the formal negotiations that began in London on 11 October between the British government and plenipotentiaries sent over by the Dáil, led by Arthur Griffith. There followed weeks of deadlock. At different times the prime minister fumed that he wanted 'a complete smash-up of the revolutionists'; Churchill was spotted 'breathing fire and slaughter'; and Bonar Law was heard muttering down the corridor that 'the Irish were an inferior race'. Nevertheless, at 2.10 a.m. on 6 December 1921, the Dáil plenipotentiaries signed the Anglo-Irish Treaty, Churchill recalling that 'Michael Collins rose looking as if he was going to shoot somebody, preferably himself'.

The treaty set aside the Government of Ireland Act for the twenty-six counties, now to be known as the Irish Free State and having the same constitutional relationship with Britain as that of the dominion of Canada. How had Lloyd George been able to get Sinn Féin to sign? The answer lay in Article XII, which provided for a boundary commission. Convinced that this could tear great lumps out of Northern Ireland, Craig went immediately to London to protest. In a letter to the assistant secretary to the cabinet, Sir Maurice Hankey, Thomas Jones wrote:

> Sir James Craig was closeted with the P.M. . . . He then went off to his Doctor to be inoculated – I suppose against a Sinn Fein germ. Anyhow, yesterday he charged the P.M. with a breach of faith . . . Carson . . . wrote a nasty letter.

For all its success in the South, the truce of July 1921 had not stopped the killing in the North. In Belfast one horrific incident followed another and by the end of the year the death toll in the city for the previous twelve months had reached 109. To make matters worse, the Dáil kept up its 'Belfast Boycott' of goods exported to the South, originally imposed in protest at the shipyard expulsions. The new year saw the unleashing of pent-up forces in Northern Ireland as the terms of the treaty were being hotly debated inside the Dáil and by the general public all over the island.

No. 8.

What the Peace Treaty Gives Ireland—

1. A PARLIAMENT elected by, and responsible to, **the Irish people alone.**

2. An EXECUTIVE GOVERNMENT responsible to that PARLIAMENT.

3. Hence, after Centuries of Struggle, DEMOCRATIC CONTROL of all Legislative Affairs is, in the ultimate, **in the hands of the Irish people themselves.**

4. Power to make laws for every Department of National Life.

5. An Irish legal system, controlled and administered by Irishmen.

6. An IRISH ARMY.

7. An IRISH POLICE FORCE.

8. Complete control of Education; with complete freedom to foster the Irish language, Irish literature, art and culture.

9. A National Flag.

10. Freedom of opinion.

11. Complete fiscal freedom—commercial, industrial and financial.

12. Complete control of land systems of the country.

13. Power and freedom to develop the resources and industries of the country.

14. Freedom to frame a Democratic Constitution.

15. An IRISH STATE organisation to express the will and the mind of the Nation.

16. A recognised place as a separate State among the Nations.

Dublin Castle has Fallen !
British Bureaucracy is in the dust !
Is this Victory or Defeat ?

Support the Treaty

A pro-Treaty election hand bill, June 1922
LINEN HALL LIBRARY

CIVIL WAR NORTH AND SOUTH

Rising in the Dáil to second the motion to approve the treaty, Deputy Sean MacEoin said: 'To me symbols, recognitions, shadows, have very little meaning. What I want, what the people of Ireland want, is not shadows but real

Michael Collins (right) at a
Sinn Féin demonstration in
Armagh in September 1921:
he had been elected MP for
Armagh in the northern
parliament and this was his
first public appearance since
the truce in July 1921.
PUBLIC RECORD OFFICE OF
NORTHERN IRELAND

substances . . .' Yet in fifteen days of debate symbols seemed to be the central issue. For both sides the position of the Irish Free State within the empire was of far greater concern than the fate of Ulster. Whether for or against the treaty, deputies were complacent about the vague terms of reference for the Boundary Commission. On 7 January 1922 the Dáil approved the treaty by the uncomfortably narrow margin of sixty-four votes to fifty-seven. De Valera flounced out of the chamber with his supporters, not to return until 1927. Thus it was that Griffith became chairman of the Provisional Government of the Irish Free State.

Article XII of the treaty may well have been a diplomatic masterstroke in London, but in Ulster it immediately magnified uncertainty and unrest. Loyalists living near the border were now gripped with apprehension that soon they would fall under the jurisdiction of the Free State. Suddenly nationalists believed that so much territory would be transferred that Northern Ireland could not possibly survive. In fact, the main outcome of the treaty in Northern Ireland was intense disorder and bloodshed. Augmented by releases from prison, the IRA units were united in their determination to destabilise Northern Ireland whatever their views on the treaty.

The IRA campaign, launched in January 1922 when eleven IRA men from

Premises in Belfast,
destroyed by the IRA
in May 1922
ULSTER MUSEUM

County Monaghan were arrested, intensified in February after forty prominent loyalists were seized in the counties of Fermanagh and Tyrone in retaliation and taken south; and when A Specials were attacked after their train halted at Clones, a sergeant, three constables and an IRA commandant were killed. The situation deteriorated further in March when both sides in Belfast perpetrated assassinations and reprisals of frightful barbarity. Altogether sixty-one people died in the city during that month. Isolated Catholic and Protestant families were particularly vulnerable, and intimidation, houseburning, rioting and assassinations drew the lines between the two communities in Belfast more tautly than ever. The very survival of Northern Ireland seemed to be at stake as the IRA went on the offensive in the countryside, killing constables, burning flax mills, raiding houses and seizing RIC barracks.

Constables of the RUC in 1922
PUBLIC RECORD OFFICE OF NORTHERN IRELAND

'I say to the Government, "Take whatever powers you require and we will give them to you",' Captain Mulholland declared in the northern parliament. On 5 April 1922 the Royal Ulster Constabulary was formed. It was closely modelled on 'the old RIC that every Irishman was proud of', as Lloyd Campbell described the force to the applause of fellow Unionists. To this gendarmerie would be added the augmented Special Constabulary – now controlled by the Northern Ireland government but still financed by Westminster – until by the early summer there were fifty thousand regular and part-time policemen; that is, one policeman for every six families in the region, or put another way, one policeman for every two Catholic families. On 7 April the Civil Authorities (Special Powers) Bill became law, giving the minister of home affairs authority to detain suspects and to set up courts of summary jurisdiction. The special courts could hold suspects without trial for unspecified periods, impose sentences of penal servitude or death, and 'in addition to any other punishment which may lawfully be imposed, order such a person, if a male, to be at once privately whipped'. The *Manchester Guardian* denounced

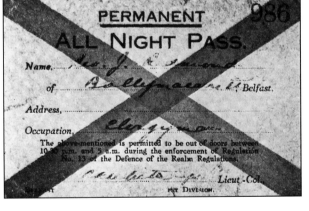

Curfew permit for the Reverend John Redmond, vicar of St Patrick's in Ballymacarrett: his attempts to halt sectarian conflict in east Belfast in 1920–2 were unsuccessful.
SAINT PATRICK'S CHURCH, BALLYMACARRETT

Shane's Castle, County Antrim, burned by the IRA in 1922; from the *Graphic*
BELFAST CENTRAL LIBRARY

the 'envenomed politicians' who

> are voting themselves power to use torture and capital punishment against citizens whom they forbid to defend themselves while they scarcely attempt to protect them from massacre . . .

Robert Lynn, Unionist MP for Belfast Central and editor of the *Northern Whig*, argued that the question at issue was simple: 'Is civilisation going to be allowed to exist, or is there going to be anarchy?'

In an attempt to relieve the pressure on Catholic enclaves in Belfast, the IRA launched an intensified campaign in the countryside in May 1922: 'big houses', including Shane's Castle, were burned down; flax mills and railway stations were destroyed; and three policemen were killed in Desertmartin – there seven Catholics were murdered in reprisal and, after their homes and businesses had been burned, all the Catholic residents of this County Londonderry town were driven out. The tempo of killing in Belfast increased. Among the victims was W.J. Twaddell, Unionist MP for Woodvale; his murder led to the immediate imposition of internment. All the two hundred men arrested in the first sweep were Catholics. Though a curfew was imposed, the killing and destruction continued: altogether forty-four Catholics and twenty-two Protestants met with violent deaths in Belfast during the month of May.

Soon after, a frontier incident put Anglo-Irish relations under severe strain. The IRA occupied a triangle of territory between Belleek and Pettigo and forced fifty A Specials to withdraw from Magherameenagh Castle up Lower Lough Erne by pleasure boat. Churchill in his capacity as colonial secretary ordered several hundred troops, with artillery and armoured cars, to converge on this corner of County Fermanagh. The two villages were surrounded and shelled by howitzers, three IRA men and one Special constable were killed, and a portion of Free State territory was occupied by British soldiers. The impression that the IRA was attempting to force border revision by violence was reinforced soon after by the murder of six Presbyterians near Newry on 17 June. Reprisal killings followed, leaving seven Catholics dead.

The Provisional Government of the Irish Free State shrank from a confrontation along the border, for by now open conflict over the treaty threatened: the IRA had been split down the middle and the 'Irregulars', those opposed to the treaty, had seized barracks and public buildings. Then the whole situation was transformed by the murder in London of Field Marshal Sir Henry Wilson, military adviser to the Northern Ireland government, on 22 June. Prompted by Churchill's threat of military intervention, the Provisional Government took action. On Collins's order, at 4.29 a.m. on 28 June a field gun fired across the Liffey at the Irregular garrison in the Four Courts and moments later a torrent of bullets poured from both sides. The Irish Civil War had begun.

After fierce fighting in the centre of Dublin, the Irregulars took their campaign into the countryside in a guerrilla war more bitter and deadly than the recent conflict against the British. In August 1922 Collins was killed in an ambush in his native County Cork. The great majority of the IRA in the North stayed loyal to the Provisional Government; as these men were under orders not to confront security forces in Northern Ireland, Ulster now became the most peaceful province in the country. Its most disturbed county was Donegal where

Guarding a new frontier: troops of the Lincolnshire Regiment on the borders of Fermanagh and Leitrim; from the *Graphic*
BELFAST CENTRAL LIBRARY

Argenta: moored first in Belfast Lough and then in Larne Harbour, this vessel held internees between June 1922 and November 1923.
SAINT PATRICK'S CHURCH, BALLYMACARRETT

Commandant-General Joe Sweeney led National Army troops to round up groups of Irregulars in the mountains. Sean Larkin, from County Londonderry, and Commandant-General Charles Daly were shot by firing squad in Drumboe Castle on 14 March 1923, eight months after their capture. Eight weeks later, on 24 May, de Valera issued this message to the Irregulars: 'Soldiers of the Republic . . . Military victory must be allowed to rest for the moment with those who have destroyed the Republic.'

The civil war was a remarkable stroke of good fortune for the Northern Ireland government. As IRA activists disengaged or withdrew to fight each other across the frontier, incidents of violence steadily declined in the North and by 1923 it could be said that the region was at peace. The price in blood had been heavy: between July 1920 and July 1922 the death toll in the six counties was 557 – 303 Catholics, 172 Protestants and 82 members of the

An armoured car accompanies the funeral procession of four members of the MacMahon family, Catholics murdered in north Belfast in March 1922; from the *Graphic*.
BELFAST CENTRAL LIBRARY

security forces. Catholics had suffered most and their relief organisations estimated that in Belfast up to 11,000 Catholics had been driven out of their jobs, that 23,000 Catholics had been forced out of their homes, and that about 500 Catholic-owned businesses had been destroyed. Protestants believed that Catholics were aiming for nothing less than the destruction of the state, but they formed one third of the population of Northern Ireland and the Government was now faced with the problem of what policy to adopt towards such a substantial alienated minority. The government of the Irish Free State, facing the awesome task of reconstruction, could not put the implementation of the Boundary Commission at the top of its agenda. This was another stroke of luck for Craig. Yet another had been the fall of Lloyd George in October 1922 and his replacement by the man he once described as 'meekly ambitious', Andrew Bonar Law, the Ulster Unionists' most unwavering friend at Westminster. As a result, Craig had now a period of remarkable calm in which to shape the future of Northern Ireland.

THE FAILURE TO CONCILIATE

Parallels can be drawn between Northern Ireland and states emerging from collapsed empires in central Europe. Of these only Austria had a fairly homogeneous ethnic composition and it has been estimated that more than 25 million found themselves as national minorities after 1919. Only two thirds of the inhabitants of Poland spoke Polish, for example, and there were 4.6 million Germans, Poles, Ruthenes and Magyars in Czechoslovakia out of a total population of 14.3 million. Here language was the badge of distinction, unlike Ulster. Yet closer similarities with Northern Ireland's divided society can be found. Relations were severely strained between the Czechs and Slovaks who spoke the same language, though in different dialects. Craig had emerged from Downing Street just after the signing of the treaty, saying, 'There's a verse in the Bible which says Czecho-Slovakia and Ulster are born to trouble as the sparks fly upwards.' Whether or not he understood the full implications of his remark is difficult to say.

An even closer parallel could be sought in Yugoslavia, where ethnic tensions threatened to destroy the new state. Here Serbs, Croats and Muslims shared the same tongue but were bitterly divided by cultural traditions and religion. Catholic Croats could be compared with Ulster Protestants, regarding themselves as more civilised and prosperous than the more numerous Orthodox Serbs, and fearful that they would be dominated in a united South Slav state. Ethnic groups in Yugoslavia claimed to be able to distinguish each other by smell just as people in Ulster had their own equally bogus means of identifying 'the other sort'.

Northern Ireland, however, did set out with assets several central European states did not possess. The evils of landlordism, which had largely been swept away in Ireland by land purchase, remained as virulently as before in Hungary, Poland and Romania. Like Czechoslovakia, but unlike most of the other successor states, Northern Ireland had a developed industrial base, experience of participation in representative institutions, and a substantial middle class from which competent public servants could be recruited; and, unlike Czechoslovakia, Northern Ireland had a powerful neighbour ready to provide support in times of crisis.

The restoration of peace in 1923 gave the Northern Ireland government a unique opportunity to attempt a healing of wounds and to woo at least some of the minority into an acceptance of the new regime. That opportunity was not taken. Ulster Unionists felt embattled and isolated, their magnanimity in victory eroded by the IRA campaign and mounting criticism from the British press. Members of the Government had limited horizons; in part this was because Ulster unionism was by its nature defensive, tending to throw up leaders who were dogged, reliable and conservative, rather than imaginative and innovative.

Though deeply conservative on social and financial matters, easily the most broad-minded and outward-looking members of the Government were Hugh Pollock (Finance), Lord Londonderry (Education) and James Milne Barbour (Commerce). Milne Barbour was in favour of engaging substantial numbers of Catholics in the civil service, 'though it may be a risky thing politically to say'.

Craig, however, frequently met deputations which complained that Catholics were getting preference in public appointments in spite of incontrovertible evidence that civil servants were drawn overwhelmingly from the Protestant section of the community. Wilfrid Spender, postwar commander of the UVF and now cabinet secretary, was exasperated in 1934 by the 'vile persecution' of a Catholic gardener employed on the Stormont estate, even though he had a distinguished war record and a personal reference from the Prince of Wales. Asked to investigate by Craig, who had listened to complaints about this man from the Orange Order, Spender responded bluntly:

> I think the only course would be for the Government to come out in the open and say that only Protestants are admitted to our Service. I should greatly regret such a course.

In reply to a question put to him in Fintona, County Tyrone, Edward Archdale, the agriculture minister, stated that he 'had 109 on his staff and so far as he knew there were four Roman Catholics. Three of these were Civil Servants turned over to him, whom he had to take when he began.' John Andrews, minister of labour, on returning from holiday in 1926 found two 'Free Staters' on his staff and straight away ordered that such men be disqualified immediately, even though they had impeccable British Army records.

G.C. Duggan, a senior civil servant, recalled that Richard Dawson Bates, minister of home affairs, 'made it clear to his Permanent Secretary that he did not want his most juvenile clerk or typist, if a Papist, assigned for duty to his ministry'. Hearing that a Catholic telephonist had been appointed, he refused to use the telephone for important business until he had succeeded in getting this employee transferred. There is little doubt that Craig's appointment of Bates to such a crucial ministry as Home Affairs made it exceedingly difficult to conciliate the Catholic minority. Bates openly regarded Catholics as enemies and he set a low standard in public life by his blatant disregard for impartial procedures in, for example, the granting of contracts.

The minority was antagonised by the abolition of proportional representation in local government elections in 1922, though Bates's main reason for doing so was to wipe out labour representation in Belfast, Lurgan, Lisburn and Bangor. Nationalists and Sinn Féin, except in Irvinestown, County Fermanagh, and Ballycastle, County Antrim, refused to meet the commission to rearrange local government boundaries the following year. The result was that Unionists were able to dictate the positioning of boundaries with meticulous care to their own complete satisfaction. The results speak for themselves. Since many Catholics abstained in 1924, the best comparison is between the local election results of 1920 and 1927. In 1920 opposition parties won control of 24 local authorities out of 27, but by 1927 Unionists had a majority in all but 12 councils. Westminster made no attempt to interfere in what had been a blatant exercise in gerrymandering.

The parochial, narrow and partisan character of life in Northern Ireland was demonstrated as much in disputes over education policy as it was in politics. Lord Londonderry, the minister of education, set out to create a system of elementary schools drawing pupils from all parts of the community. The managers of Catholic schools expressed their hostility by stating their opinion that 'the only satisfactory system of education for Catholics is one wherein Catholic children are taught in Catholic schools by Catholic teachers under Catholic auspices'.

Protestant opposition was slower in coming. In part this was due to the complexity of the Education Bill, which Londonderry steered through parliament with remarkable ease considering the outcome. 'Protestant teachers to teach Protestant children' was the watchword of clergy who resented their loss of control over appointments and campaigned for compulsory Bible instruction in the state schools. The United Education Committee of the Protestant Churches, founded in 1924, distributed a hand bill with the title PROTESTANTS AWAKE in large red letters, arguing that the Londonderry act threw open the door 'for a Bolshevist or an Atheist or a Roman Catholic to become a teacher in a Protestant school'. While Londonderry was in England in March 1925, Craig capitulated and rushed through an amending bill with indecent speed to give clergy a say in the appointment of teachers in state schools and to compel teachers there to give 'simple Bible instruction'. Not surprisingly, Londonderry resigned the following year.

Lord Londonderry: as minister of education he failed to realise his scheme to have Catholics and Protestants educated together and resigned in 1926; painting by William Conor
QUEEN'S UNIVERSITY BELFAST

Catholic 'voluntary' schools got teachers' salaries paid and a contribution towards heating, lighting and cleaning, but nothing towards capital costs. In the 1930 Education Act they won 50 per cent grants for building but the Protestant character of state schools was reinforced: education authorities were now compelled to provide Bible instruction in compulsory attendance hours. It was not until 1945 that J.C. MacDermott, the Northern Ireland attorney-general, declared that this legislation broke the terms of the 1920 Government of Ireland Act, in which Section 5 made it illegal 'to establish or endow any religion'. There is no doubt that Westminster had allowed the Unionist government with its unassailable majority to discriminate against Catholics in education provision.

'NOT AN INCH': THE BOUNDARY COMMISSION

In March 1924 the British government received 'a stiff letter' from Dublin insisting that the Boundary Commission be set up forthwith. Having temporised as long as he could, Craig flatly refused to appoint a commissioner when pressed on 10 May. It was not until October that J.R. Fisher, a Unionist and former editor of the *Northern Whig*, was appointed by Ramsay MacDonald to represent the Northern Ireland government. Justice Richard Feetham of the South African Supreme Court had already agreed to become Westminster's representative and chairman. The Free State government appointed Eoin MacNeill, now minister of education, as their commissioner. The first meeting was held on 6 November 1924: there all three commissioners decided on strict secrecy.

At the end of 1924 the commissioners spent a fortnight touring the border and on one occasion, after getting completely lost on a minor road, they were put back on course by an RUC patrol. Much of 1925 was spent in receiving deputations. The wording of Article XII of the 1921 treaty was extraordinarily vague: it set the commission the task of determining, 'in accordance with the wishes of the inhabitants, so far as may be compatible with economic and geographic conditions, the boundaries between Northern Ireland the rest of Ireland'. Feetham interpreted this article in a narrow, legalistic way and placed economic and geographic conditions well to the fore, accepting, for example, the Unionist argument that Newry was within Belfast's commercial orbit.

Members of the Boundary Commission, 1924–5
Left to right:
F.B. Bourdillon (secretary); J.R. Fisher (Northern Ireland government representative); Justice Richard Feetham(chairman); Eoin MacNeill (Free State government representative); and C. Beerstecher (private secretary to Justice Feetham)
F.X. MARTIN

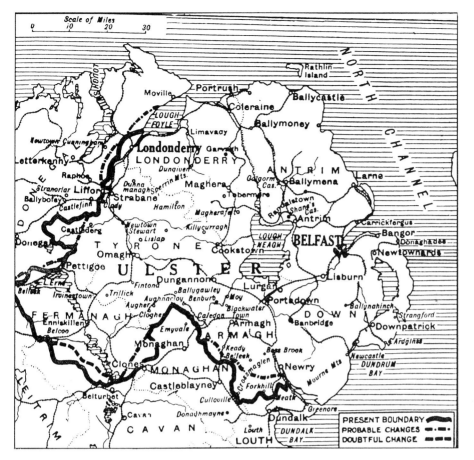

Map published in the
Morning Post on
7 November 1925: by
revealing that only minor
adjustments to the frontier
were intended, the map
precipitated the crisis
which led to the
suppression of the
Boundary Commission
report.

Meanwhile, Dawson Bates drafted a memorandum listing the forces at the Northern Ireland government's disposal should it be necessary to confront either the British Army or Free State troops; full test mobilisations of B and C Specials were held in the counties of Fermanagh, Tyrone and Armagh; and Craig's cabinet agreed to order 156 Vickers and Lewis machine guns and 14 million rounds of ammunition – enough for 'a small war', Assistant Under-secretary Sir Ernest Clark observed in alarm. Seeking 'a pronouncement by the people while the Commission is sitting in their midst', Craig called an election in April 1925. Devlin announced his intention to sit in the Northern Ireland parliament – a view supported by the Catholic electorate which returned ten Nationalists and only two abstaining Sinn Féiners. Craig did not get the overwhelming mandate from Protestants he had hoped for but at least the Unionist vote was up in the constituencies touching the border. There, loyalists had heeded Craig's election cry, 'Not an inch' – would the Boundary Commission do the same?

On 7 November the *Morning Post* published a 'forecast' of the Boundary Commission's report with a map which was a remarkably accurate indication of the forthcoming award. In short, Fisher had broken his pledge of secrecy. The press leak caused an immediate crisis in Dublin. Only minor territorial adjustments were to be made and both Newry and Derry were to remain in

Northern Ireland. MacNeill resigned and Irish premier William Thomas Cosgrave hastily arranged a meeting in London with Prime Minister Stanley Baldwin and Craig: there it was agreed to suppress the Boundary Commission report. When Craig returned to Belfast on 5 December shipyard workers gave him a gold mounted portion of a foot rule – the inch he had not surrendered. Cosgrave was glad to have escaped from 'this barren question of the Boundary' and he frankly admitted the 'half-truth' of the 'taunt of having sold the Roman Catholics in Northern Ireland'.

The suppression of the Boundary Commission forced the Catholic minority to accept, whether they liked it or not, that they were citizens of Northern Ireland. Devlin took his seat in 1926 and by 1928 there were ten Nationalists, three Labour MPs and a couple of Independents sitting on the opposition benches. Meanwhile, de Valera had led Fianna Fáil, the newly formed anti-treaty party, into the Dáil. North and south, the spirit of the Locarno and Kellogg pacts seemed to settle on Ireland as parliamentary debates took on an air of reality they had not possessed before, and on both sides of the border abstentionist Sinn Féin found itself cold-shouldered by electorates almost wholly won back to constitutional politics. Reconciliation, however, was as fragile in the North as it was on the European mainland.

Craig, raised to the peerage as Lord Craigavon in 1927, abolished proportional representation in parliamentary elections in 1929. 'It will make it the more difficult for minorities to secure representation,' declared Sam Kyle, leader of the Northern Ireland Labour Party, with much justification, but the most bitter denunciations came from the Nationalists. Devlin described it as 'a mean, contemptible and callous attempt' to rob the minority of safeguards in the 1920 act. Westminster, however, was not concerned to intervene. Devlin said in the northern Commons in March 1932:

'Wee Joe' Devlin, leader of the Nationalist Party until his death in 1934
LINEN HALL LIBRARY

You had opponents willing to co-operate. We did not seek office. We sought service. We were willing to help. But you rejected all friendly offers . . . You went on on the old political lines, fostering hatreds, keeping one third of the population as if they were pariahs in the community.

Two months later Devlin led all of the Nationalists out of the chamber and for the rest of the decade they pursued a policy of intermittent and erratic abstentionism. Nationalists ignored the celebrations in November 1932 when the Prince of Wales opened the Northern Ireland parliament's permanent home at Stormont – a fine neo-classical structure in a magnificent setting,

which was, in Pollock's words, 'the outward and visible proof of the permanence of our institutions; that for all time we are bound indissolubly to the British crown'.

The quality of debate at Stormont never even began to match the grand surroundings: MPs were often embarrassingly inarticulate, badly informed, and concerned only with petty local matters. Craig himself seemed largely concerned to preserve the status quo and the impression of uncoordinated drift became more evident in the 1930s. Moreover, the 1920 act gave the Northern Ireland parliament little room for manoeuvre, particularly in financial affairs. The United Kingdom's first experiment in devolution might have worked more successfully had not the financial provisions been drafted during the high point of an uninterrupted ten-year economic boom. Then it seemed that with a buoyant economy, the regional government would have no difficulty paying its way. When Northern Ireland came to birth, however, Ulster was assailed by an unremitting depression lasting two decades.

BOOM, SLUMP AND DEPRESSION

Belfast had been the fastest-growing shipbuilding region in the United Kingdom ever since 1878 and in 1914 Harland and Wolff was responsible for almost 8 per cent of world output. Unrestricted submarine action ensured that

The Parliament Buildings at Stormont, opened by the Prince of Wales in November 1932
NORTHERN IRELAND ASSEMBLY LIBRARY, STORMONT

orders flowed in during the war. The firm invested £1 million in 1917 primarily to build a new yard on the east side of the Musgrave Channel, and, during 1918 alone, Harland and Wolff launched 201,070 tons of merchant shipping, 120,000 tons more than the firm's nearest United Kingdom rival.

	NUMBER OF RIVETS	ACCUMULATING TOTALS
1ST HOUR	1167	1167
2ND ..	1101	2268
3RD ..	1071	3339
4TH ..	1187	4526
5TH ..	1267	5793
6TH ..	1328	7121
7TH ..	1409	8530
8TH ..	1276	9806
9TH ..	1403	11209
TOTAL		

A record never broken: the greatest number of rivets ever driven home by one man – J. Moir – in a single day at Workman Clark in June 1918

Workman Clark built boom defence vessels, patrol boats, sloops and cargo ships totalling 260,000 tons during the war. All the traditional export industries prospered, the Belfast Ropeworks, for example, producing 50 per cent of the Royal Navy's cordage requirements and the Derry shirt-making firms winning War Office contracts averaging nearly £830,000 each year of the war. At the same time the numerous small farmers of Ireland successfully defied government attempts to regulate prices in a seller's market and enjoyed a prosperity they had never experienced before. After that the province thrived in the postwar boom fuelled by the need to replace what had been destroyed, by pent-up consumer demand, and by desperate food shortages in central and eastern Europe. The *Belfast News-Letter* concluded that 'in the long history of the linen industry, 1919 may in future be called the annum mirabilis'. Never before and never again were there so many spindles and looms at work in Ulster.

In the winter of 1920 the boom shuddered to a halt; nearly 23 per cent were unemployed in 1922 and for the rest of the decade on average around one fifth of all insured workers had no jobs. The slump developed into a protracted depression as the region's traditional staple industries continued to contract. Here, in the most economically disadvantaged part of the United Kingdom, the Depression began early. The real problem was that the war had brought about traumatic changes in world trading conditions: in these years Northern Ireland was producing and attempting to sell goods of which there was a surplus abroad.

On 23 October 1929 security prices on the Wall Street stock market crumbled in a wave of frenzied selling and in less than a month the securities lost more than 40 per cent of their face value. The collapse of business confidence after the great speculative orgy of 1928–9 in America was followed by an unrelieved world depression lasting ten years. Heavily dependent on a limited range of exports, Northern Ireland was particularly vulnerable. As world trade contracted and foreign governments raised prohibitive tariffs to protect their ailing industries the numbers out of work rose alarmingly: by 1932 the official unemployment rate was 28 per cent, or seventy-two thousand registered out of work, to which could be added another thirty thousand unregistered unemployed. Not a single ship was launched at Queen's Island between 10 December 1931 and 1 May 1934, and the number of employees in Belfast was reduced from 10,428 in 1930 to 1,554 in 1932. The world crisis was too much for Workman Clark: after the delivery of the tanker *Acavus*, ship number 536, in January 1935, the 'wee yard' had no more orders and was forced to close down. Around one third of workers in the linen industry became unemployed and smaller firms went to the wall.

As many were out of work for extended periods, they lost their eligibility for unemployment benefit and were forced to turn to the Poor Law as the only official alternative to starvation. The Belfast Board of Guardians, in particular, applied the old workhouse test with rigour. In Britain in 1928 Neville Chamberlain had swept away Boards of Guardians and introduced cash payments as of right. The Northern Ireland government did not follow suit, but it did put through a bill in 1929 forcing the guardians to extend relief. Still the Belfast board resisted, being congratulated for its stand against this 'wastrel class' by a delegation of four Protestant clergymen who called on the guardians 'to cut off grants to parasites'. By October 1932, however, the *Belfast News-Letter* was giving this warning:

> We are told that those on Outdoor Relief are on the verge of starvation; unless something is done and done quickly, conditions will become tragically worse.

For a time the prevailing distress in Belfast brought together working-class people of both religions in common protest. The lead was taken by men resurfacing the streets in task work, without which the unemployed could not qualify for relief payments. Over the summer of 1932 the Unemployed Workers' Committee had organised an impressive series of public meetings and marches, causing Dawson Bates to advise the cabinet:

> There can be no doubt that unless some ameliorative measures are adopted there will be a large body of the population driven to desperation by poverty and hunger . . . the situation is rapidly approaching a crisis.

On Monday 3 October the outdoor relief workers began a strike to force their demand for an increase in assistance and that evening sixty thousand from all over Belfast marched from Frederick Street Labour Exchange to a torch-lit rally at the Custom House. Demonstrations followed every day, some of which led to repeated police baton charges.

The Government banned all marches when the Unemployed Workers' Committee planned a great protest demonstration for Tuesday 11 October. That day the police converged on the five assembly points, starting in east Belfast. Here, *The Times* correspondent watched 'dense crowds of strikers congregating . . . things were looking very ugly when police reinforcements in a caged car appeared on the scene'. When the men began advancing down Templemore Avenue, the *Belfast Telegraph* reported, 'an order was given: "Draw – Ready – Charge!" Men in the crowd went down like nine-pins, and the rest fled helter skelter.' There were further baton charges as Catholics from Seaforde Street attempted to rescue largely Protestant strikers being driven away in police 'cages'.

Baker Street, Belfast, during the 1932 Outdoor Relief riots: the cobblestones have been pulled up for ammunition.
PUBLIC RECORD OFFICE OF NORTHERN IRELAND

The worst violence was in the lower Falls, where the people put up barricades in an attempt to impede the police, who used their firearms freely. It was here that Samuel Baxter, a Protestant flower-seller, was shot dead; John Geegan, a Catholic from Smithfield, was mortally wounded; and fourteen others suffered gunshot wounds. News of the fighting reached the Shankill and soon people were fighting the police and shooting at them. Order was restored by the imposition of a curfew. The last major eruption was in the York Street area the following evening when police armed with rifles opened fire on crowds of looters. John Kennan of Leeson Street was shot dead. By now the thoroughly alarmed government was forcing the guardians to relent and on 14 October substantial increases in relief were announced.

The Depression was unrelenting – this was no temporary downswing in the economy. Between 1931 and 1939, 27 per cent of the insured workforce was unemployed, the lowest point being reached in July 1935 when 101,967 in the region were out of work.

Dr James Deeny, in an investigation of the health and financial circumstances of 205 women in Lurgan in 1938, reported what would seem obvious today: that there was a very close relationship between unemployment, sickness and

poverty. Those from families dependent on state benefits, in his view, simply did not have enough income to pay for the bare necessities of life, though they 'were not the poorest in Lurgan by any means; in fact, they could be regarded as industrial aristocrats'. A survey in Belfast carried out during the winter of 1937–8 by the Methodist Church showed that: 76 per cent of 705 households investigated were below the poverty line set by Seebohm Rowntree in 1936; 40 per cent of these households were totally reliant on state benefits; and of these, 89 per cent fell below the poverty line.

The poor were endlessly resourceful to make ends meet. Sam McAughtry remembered that in Belfast

> money for food was so scarce that kids like myself were sent down to John McCollum's bakery off York Street on a Monday morning to queue up for the bread and buns kept in the shop over the weekend. Stales, we used to call them, and in my case they were collected in a clean pillowcase, half filled for about a tanner.

Fresh sweet milk was a luxury and the working class had condensed milk or buttermilk as alternatives – 'a penny in the gas and the gas tube in the buttermilk really made a nice intoxicating drink,' Charlie Hull observed.

When compared with six British cities, Belfast had the lowest infant mortality rate in 1901 but in 1938 it had the highest rate, ninety-six per one thousand live births compared with, for example, fifty-nine in Sheffield.

Ultraviolet treatment for rickets, a common ailment amongst the poor between the wars
NEWTOWNABBEY
METHODIST MISSION

'Maternity is a more dangerous occupation in Northern Ireland than in the Free State or in England,' Professor R.J. Johnstone MP accurately observed, for maternal mortality actually rose by one fifth between 1922 and 1938. Whooping cough, influenza and measles killed around three times as many in Belfast in the late 1930s than in similar cities across the Irish Sea. Pneumonia was the deadliest disease but the main killer of young adults was tuberculosis: the mortality rate from this disease was 20 per cent higher in Northern Ireland than in the rest of the United Kingdom. Anne Boyle remembered:

> There were whole families wiped out with tuberculosis. I remember the sexton of Sacred Heart chapel, Paddy McKernan; all he had was four daughters, and those four daughters died within a couple of years. They were teenage girls.

Of the many causes of the high death rate for tuberculosis, cramped and poor-quality housing was very high on the list. The deeply conservative population of the region ensured the return of councillors intensely hostile to rate increases. Northern Ireland refused to follow the rest of the United Kingdom step-by-step in housing policy: local authorities generally did their best to evade what responsibilities they did have and Belfast Corporation proved it was barely fit to undertake them. Dawson Bates timidly refused to take action when a report of 1926 revealed gross corruption in Belfast's housing committee. The corporation put up a mere 16 houses by direct contract and only subsidised the building of 2,600 more in the whole interwar period. Not a single labourer's cottage was built by the public authorities in County Fermanagh during the same period. The Government steadily reduced subsidies, largely because its financial position was becoming desperate. Devolution enabled Westminster to save a great deal of money because it was not obliged to treat the region with the same generosity as other unemployment blackspots, such as Wales and Clydeside. Northern Ireland budgets were balanced only by what one treasury official described as 'fudges', 'wangles', and 'dodges and devices'. One result was that the Northern Ireland government was paralysed into virtual inaction.

'HE WHO SOWS THE WIND SHALL REAP THE WHIRLWIND'

The brief co-operation between Protestants and Catholics in Belfast in 1932 did not signal a healing of sectarian divisions. Indeed, deteriorating relations between Dublin and London seem to have aggravated religious tensions. Fianna Fáil came to power in 1932 and a tariff war ensued when de Valera removed the oath of fidelity to the Crown from the Irish constitution and withheld payment of the land annuities to Britain. Though a massive increase in smuggling renders the figures suspect, exports from north to south, according to official statistics, had dropped by 1936 to one third of the 1931 level. Fianna Fáil gave little thought to the effect their actions would have on

Catholics in Northern Ireland: a Nationalist wrote to his leader Cahir Healy, complaining of de Valera's 'mad policy' and concluded that 'what is a border today will be a frontier tomorrow'.

Special trains and buses returning with pilgrims from the International Eucharistic Congress in Dublin in June 1932 were attacked at Loughbrickland, Banbridge, Lurgan, Portadown, Kilkeel, Lisburn and Belfast. During the summer marching season resolutions were carried denouncing 'the unchanging bigotry of Rome' and at the Poyntzpass 12 July demonstration the prime minister declared defiantly: 'Ours is a Protestant government and I am an Orangeman.' A more notorious speech by a member of the Government, Sir Basil Brooke, was given exactly a year later at Newtownbutler, County Fermanagh. As reported in the *Fermanagh Times*, Brooke said:

> There were a great number of Protestants and Orangemen who employed Roman Catholics. He felt he could speak freely on this subject as he had not a Roman Catholic about his place . . . He would point out that the Roman Catholics were endeavouring to get in everywhere . . . He would appeal to Loyalists, therefore, wherever possible, to employ Protestant lads and lassies (cheers).

The speech was condemned in public by a prominent County Fermanagh landlord, Captain T. T. Verschoyle, who said:

A Eucharistic Congress arch in Fahan Street, Derry, in 1932
DAVID BIGGER AND TERENCE McDONALD

He who sows the wind shall reap the whirlwind . . . it remains to be seen whether the Colebrooke Hitler will receive a well-merited rebuke from a responsible member of the government.

There was no rebuke. 'I would not ask him to withdraw one word,' Craigavon said at Stormont and responded to criticism of the Orange Order by saying:

> I have always said I am an Orangeman first and a politician and Member of this Parliament afterwards . . . The Hon. Member must remember that in the South they boasted of a Catholic State. They still boast of Southern Ireland being a Catholic State. All I boast is that we are a Protestant Parliament and a Protestant State.

In November 1933 a Catholic publican, Dan O'Boyle, was shot dead in York Street in Belfast. This was the first sectarian murder since 1922. As the bitter quest for work continued, religious hatreds were easily brought to the surface. Violent incidents became more frequent in 1934 and in 1935 feelings ran high when Protestants triumphantly celebrated George V's jubilee. On the eve of the Twelfth of July, Dr John MacNeice, Church of Ireland bishop of Down, made this appeal:

> Forget the things that are behind. Forget the unhappy past. Forget the story of the old feuds, the old triumphs, the old humiliations.

At the Belmont 'Field' the Orange grand master, Sir Joseph Davison, referred directly to the bishop's words: 'Are we to forget that the flag of the Empire is described as a foreign flag and our beloved King insulted by Mr. De Valera? Are we to forget that the aim of these people is to establish an all-Ireland Roman Catholic State?'

'Forget the story of the old feuds, the old triumphs, the old humiliations': Dr John MacNeice, Church of Ireland bishop of Down and father of the poet Louis MacNeice, on the eve of the 1935 riots
DAN MacNEICE

Towards the end of the day, as the Orangemen paraded home down Royal Avenue into York Street, violence began. Ferocious rioting raged that night: 2 people were killed, 14 houses were set on fire and 47 other dwellings were wrecked. Troops were called in and a curfew was imposed, but night after night the violence continued. It was nearly the end of August before the rioting ceased, by which time eight Protestants and five Catholics had been killed. At an inquest on riot victims the city coroner observed:

> It is all so wanton and meaningless . . . The poor people who commit these riots are easily led and influenced . . . there would be less bigotry if there was less public speechmaking of a kind by so called leaders of public opinion . . . It is not good Protestantism to preach a gospel of hate and enmity towards those who differ from us in religion and politics.

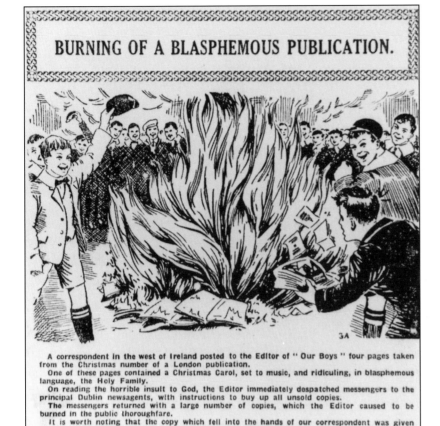

BURNING OF A BLASPHEMOUS PUBLICATION.

A correspondent in the west of Ireland posted to the Editor of " Our Boys " four pages taken from the Christmas number of a London publication.

One of these pages contained a Christmas Carol, set to music, and ridiculing, in blasphemous language, the Holy Family.

On reading the horrible insult to God, the Editor immediately despatched messengers to the principal Dublin newsagents, with instructions to buy up all unsold copies.

The messengers returned with a large number of copies, which the Editor caused to be burned in the public thoroughfare.

It is worth noting that the copy which fell into the hands of our correspondent was given him by a schoolboy.

How long are the parents of Irish children going to tolerate such devilish literature coming into this country?

An example of the influence of Catholic morality in the Free State: printed in *Our Boys*, 5 February 1925

There had been more deaths in the Protestant community, but Catholics had suffered most in other respects. The great majority of the wounded were Catholic; over two thousand Catholics and only a handful of Protestants had been driven from their homes; and 95 per cent of the £21,669 compensation for destruction to property was paid out to Catholics. Stanley Baldwin ruled out a Nationalist request for an inquiry 'for fundamental constitutional reasons', saying that 'the matter is entirely within the discretion and responsibility of the government of Northern Ireland'. Leaders of the minority had put the 1920 Government of Ireland Act to the test and found it wanting. Two years later their hope that Dublin would take a more active interest in their plight was dashed by de Valera's constitution.

THE SHADOW OF WAR

'What about the Six Counties?' someone shouted at de Valera when he was speaking at Monaghan on 27 June 1937. 'My reply is get a copy of the new Constitution,' the southern premier responded. 'There is in it an assertion that the national territory is the whole of Ireland not part of it.'

The most controversial sections included: Article 2, which claimed for the

Irish nation jurisdiction over the whole island; Article 3, which accepted that the laws of the state could apply only in the twenty-six counties, 'pending reintegration of the national territory'; Article 4, which described the state as 'Éire, or in English, Ireland'; and articles acknowledging 'the special position of the Holy Catholic Apostolic and Roman Church'. The *Northern Whig* observed that the 1937 constitution proved that 'the South possesses a Catholic Parliament for a Catholic people'. Northern Catholics felt abandoned, for de Valera, in spite of his irredentist claims, had chosen to create a twenty-six-county state that seemed to close off the few remaining routes to reunification – a state verging on the theocratic, with rigid censorship and a constitutional prohibition on divorce and family planning; a state compelling every child to learn Irish and turning its back, like Northern Ireland, on the cultural diversity of its people; and a state with one of the most highly protected economies in the world.

The Westminster government accepted the new constitution philosophically enough and, eager to ensure the friendship of Éire in the event of war, made an agreement with de Valera on 25 April 1938. Britain handed over the 'Treaty ports' of Lough Swilly, Berehaven and Cobh, thus demonstrating that Éire was in practice a sovereign independent state and making neutrality in a European war a practical possibility: 'a more feckless act can hardly be imagined' was Churchill's view of the 'gratuitous surrender'. De Valera, however, was quite unable to move Neville Chamberlain's government on the issue of partition.

In March 1938 Annie Chamberlain, the prime minister's wife, performed the opening ceremony for Sydenham aerodrome alongside the Musgrave yard in east Belfast. By then work was well advanced close by on a new aircraft factory. This had little to do with the Northern Ireland government's meagre financial inducements but was due to the growing threat of a general European war. Short Brothers of Rochester sought a new site well away from the threat of German assault and a business marriage was arranged with Harland and Wolff. By 1938 work was well under way to meet the first orders for Sunderlands, Bristol Bombays and Hereford bombers. Nearby, HMS *Belfast* was launched in March of that year and completed her sea trials in August 1939. Between those dates, profound changes being wrought on the European mainland caused the British government to raise the tempo of the re-armament programme.

While this crisis promised to revitalise Northern Ireland's economy, it put others in peril. During the autumn of 1938 letters from Austria began to land on desks in the Northern Ireland Ministry of Commerce. As Dorothea Both, a maker of artificial flowers in Vienna, explained in her letter of 8 September, an article had appeared on 29 August in the *Zionistische Rundschau* indicating that the Northern Ireland government would welcome emigrants from Austria to 'establish manufactures or trades'. When civil servants opened nearly three hundred letters they were made vividly aware of the tragedy unfolding in

central Europe. Along the margin of Frau Both's letter a government official had written just one word, 'regret': Northern Ireland was not about to become a haven for the persecuted Jews of the Third Reich. Altogether 244 letters seem to have been rejected and those few refugees who did make it to Ulster needed the active assistance of Belfast's Jewish community or of the Society of Friends. Thus Northern Ireland lost the opportunity to help fellow humans and draw on the genius and enterprise of a remarkable people. As it was, industries that had languished for two decades were now called on to make a vital contribution to the United Kingdom's survival.

Hereford bomber production line at Short and Harland, Belfast, on the eve of the Second World War
SHORTS PLC

Lord and Lady Craigavon
relaxing in the Far East
during one of his extended
cruises: as war approached
the prime minister became
incapable of sustained
attention to his duties.
PUBLIC RECORD OFFICE OF
NORTHERN IRELAND

9

WAR AND PEACE

1939–1968

On the last night of peace, 2 September 1939, the blackout came into force all over Northern Ireland and in Pettigo the curtains on the County Fermanagh side of the border were drawn together, while in the County Donegal part of the village, lamps continued to cast their lights into the streets. De Valera's decision to keep Éire neutral ensured that the period of the Second World War was a starkly contrasted experience for people living in the same historic province but divided by a political frontier into citizens of two distinct states.

'Is it credible,' the *Daily Mirror* asked in May 1939, 'that the British government can even dream of repeating in 1939 the hideous blunder of 1918, and of enforcing conscription in any part of Ireland?' Freshly returned from a long Pacific cruise, Craigavon had announced in the spring that he wanted his people to make an equal sacrifice in defence of the realm. De Valera was outraged and declared that as his constitution claimed all Ireland to be part of Éire's territory, conscription in Ulster would be nothing short of 'an act of aggression'. At an interview in London, Chamberlain said to Craigavon: 'If you really want to help us, *don't* press for conscription. It will only be an embarrassment.' The Northern premier complied but Brooke recalled that Craigavon felt 'resentment, anger and hurt pride'. When the war began the prime minister said at Stormont:

> We here today are in a state of war and we are prepared with the rest of the United Kingdom and Empire to face all the responsibilities that imposes on the Ulster people. There is no slackening in our loyalty.

A month later he said: 'We must share and share alike with our fellow citizens across the water'; and later he boasted: 'Ulster is ready when we get the word and always will be.' Already, however, there was mounting evidence that Northern Ireland was not ready.

Sir Wilfrid Spender thought that Craigavon was a premier whom 'true friends would advise to retire now', for he was incapable of doing 'more than one hour's constructive work' in a day. Lady Londonderry confided to Sir

Samuel Hoare that Craigavon had become 'ga-ga'; according to Spender, Dawson Bates was 'incapable of giving his responsible officers coherent directions on policy'; and altogether, Spender concluded, the ministers' 'disregarding of their responsibilities' presented a 'grave danger to the system of democratic government'. In short, the Unionist government seemed utterly unfit to face the challenge of the war. The only exception was Sir Basil Brooke, the minister of agriculture, who threw himself into the task of making the region a major supplier of food to Britain in her time of danger.

In the spring of 1940 the vortex of total war suddenly swung westwards: the Germans overran Denmark and Norway in April; a month later they swept over the Netherlands and Belgium; and then the Wehrmacht forged through the Ardennes, reaching Paris in June. As the shattered remains of the British Army gathered on the Dunkirk beaches Churchill, who had just replaced Chamberlain as prime minister, is said to have remarked gloomily in his map room that the only properly armed and disciplined force left in the United Kingdom was the Ulster Special Constabulary. Then as the Battle of Britain got under way, the Battle of the Atlantic intensified. The fall of France enabled U-boats to operate from Brest and Lorient, and long-range Focke-Wulf Condor bombers flew out from French air bases in search of British shipping off the west coast of Ireland. As Britain's plight became even more desperate Churchill sought drastic political solutions.

'HERE BY THE GRACE OF GOD, ULSTER STOOD A FAITHFUL SENTINEL'

On 24 May 1940 Lord Halifax, the foreign secretary, wrote to Churchill asking him to give

> further thought to the possibilities of securing any improvement in Eire on the political side by any démarche in the direction of Northern Ireland . . . The whole matter would seem to be one of utmost urgency.

Churchill agreed and asked Malcolm MacDonald – though he regarded the former premier's son 'as rat-poison on account of his connection with the Éire ports' – to approach de Valera. In effect, MacDonald, until recently dominions secretary, offered a declaration in favour of the reunification of Ireland in return for British use of the treaty ports. Churchill's cabinet agreed to make this a formal offer on 20 June, the day before France signed an armistice with Germany. Craigavon was not informed until 26 June and he at once fired off this cypher telegram:

> AM PROFOUNDLY SHOCKED AND DISGUSTED BY YOUR LETTER MAKING SUGGESTIONS SO FAR REACHING BEHIND MY BACK AND WITHOUT ANY PRE-CONSULTATION WITH ME FULL STOP TO SUCH TREACHERY TO LOYAL ULSTER I WILL NEVER BE A PARTY.

A cypher riposte made it clear that the Westminster government refused to be deflected and further strongly worded telegrams passed backwards and forwards across the Irish Sea. Then suddenly the crisis was over: on 7 July de Valera rejected the offer of Irish unity, 'which we note is purely tentative and has not been submitted to Lord Craigavon and his colleagues'. The greater crisis of war did not abate, however.

The German occupation of France and Éire's neutrality forced Britain to divert its convoys around the headlands of County Donegal and into the North Channel. Northern Ireland now had a crucial role to play as U-boats continued to wreak havoc on merchant shipping in the Western Approaches. 'All had to come in around Northern Ireland,' Churchill said later. 'Here by the grace of God, Ulster stood a faithful sentinel.' People in Glenties recalled that the walls of their homes shook every night during the autumn of 1940 with the blast of great explosions out in the Atlantic, where Royal Navy convoy escorts were attempting to hold U-boat wolf packs at bay. Obsolete Ansons flew out from Sydenham, Aldergrove and Newtownards in all weathers, but their elusive targets continued to inflict devastating losses. At the same time the Third Reich's western advance brought Northern Ireland well within range of German bombers, now wreaking terrible destruction on British cities.

On a fine Saturday afternoon, 30 November 1940, a single, unobserved German plane flew high across the Ards towards Belfast. The crew brought

The state funeral of Lord Craigavon passing Carson's statue at Stormont, November 1940
NORTHERN IRELAND ASSEMBLY LIBRARY, STORMONT

back photographs of suitable targets, identified by the Luftwaffe's Section 5 photo-reconnaissance unit, including, 'die Werft Harland & Wolff Ltd, die Tankstelle Conns Water, das Flugzeugwerk Short & Harland, das Kraftwerk Belfast, die Grossmühle Rank & Co, das Wasserwerk Belfast, die Kasernenanlagen Victoria Barracks'. The entire city of Belfast, the Germans discovered, was defended by only seven anti-aircraft batteries.

Craigavon had been buried two days before; he had died peacefully in his armchair just after listening to the six o'clock news on the wireless. John Andrews had often deputised for Craigavon and there was no dispute when he was chosen to succeed him as prime minister. The old guard remained in office and under the direction of Andrews it was no more capable than before of coping with the exigencies of war. When Harold Wilson came to Belfast in December 1940 on behalf of the Manpower Requirements Committee, he was appalled by Northern Ireland's poor performance. He reported that 'the province had become a depressed area' which had 'not seen the construction of a single new factory'. Over a period when unemployment in Britain had almost halved, it had risen steadily in Northern Ireland to almost seventy-two thousand by November 1940. Nothing had been done to unite the people of

Harold Wilson (centre front) at Stormont in 1948: when he inspected Northern Ireland on behalf of Churchill's government in December 1940, he was appalled by the region's inadequate industrial performance.
PUBLIC RECORD OFFICE OF NORTHERN IRELAND

the region in common cause against Hitler's Germany. The B Specials formed the nucleus of the Home Guard; opposition MPs condemned this as 'creating a sectarian and political force', making 'political loyalty' a condition of recruitment. 'All sorts of rot going on here,' Lady Londonderry wrote to her husband soon after the outbreak of war. 'Air raid warnings and blackouts! As if anyone cared or wished to bomb Belfast.' After a brief flurry of activity, the regional government's attitude to civil defence soon lapsed back to being as soporific as before.

To fend off criticism, Craigavon had appointed John MacDermott as minister of public security in June 1940. It did not take the new minister long to appreciate the fearfully inadequate defences in the region. On 24 March 1941 MacDermott expressed his anxiety in a letter to Andrews: anti-aircraft cover was less than half the approved strength in Belfast; the city did not possess a single searchlight; and no other town in Northern Ireland had any defence at all. He concluded:

> Up to now we have escaped attack. So had Clydeside until recently. Clydeside got its blitz during the period of the last moon . . . The period of the next moon from, say, the 7th to the 16th of April, may well bring our turn.

On the night of 7–8 April a small squadron of German bombers, led by a pathfinder Heinkel 111 from Kampfgruppe 26, raided Belfast, and completely destroyed the Harland and Wolff fuselage factory, reduced a major timber yard to ashes, and delivered damaging blows to the docks. Sirens had sounded only after the first bombs had fallen and Luftwaffe crews reported that Belfast's defences were 'inferior in quality, scanty and insufficient'. The people of Northern Ireland now knew they were vulnerable after all.

THE BELFAST BLITZ, 1941

Easter Tuesday, 15 April 1941, had been a dull oppressive day but the sky was clearing that evening as 180 German bombers, predominantly Junkers 88s and Heinkels 111s, flew in formation over the Irish Sea. As the raiders approached the Ards they dropped to seven thousand feet. On the Castlereagh Hills ground crews manned anti-aircraft guns; Hawker Hurricane Mark IIs sped down the runway at Aldergrove aerodrome; and at 10.40 p.m. sirens wailed in Belfast.

Casting intense light, hundreds of flares drifted down, then incendiaries, high-explosive bombs and parachute mines rained down. The congested housing north of the city centre received the main force of the attack and there was fearful carnage in the New Lodge, the lower Shankill and the Antrim Road. In Veryan Gardens and Vandyck Gardens 130 homes were destroyed; York Street Spinning Mill was sliced in two; the collapsing 6 storeys obliterated 42 houses; 9 people were killed in a house in Ballynure Street; and 30 died in a shelter in Percy Street. After the raid a Luftwaffe pilot gave this description on German radio:

Above and below: the York Street Spinning Mill before the Easter Tuesday blitz of 1941, and after its destruction. Gallagher's tobacco factory stands in the background.
BELFAST TELEGRAPH

> We were in exceptionally good humour knowing that we were going for a new target, one of England's last hiding places. Wherever Churchill is hiding his war material we will go . . . Belfast is as worthy a target as Coventry, Birmingham, Bristol or Glasgow.

At 1.45 a.m. a bomb fell at the corner of Oxford Street and East Bridge Street, wrecking the city's central telephone exchange. All contact with Britain, the anti-aircraft operations control room and the Hurricane fighters was cut off. For another two hours the Luftwaffe attacked Belfast completely unopposed.

As MacDermott heard the crash of his windows shattering he crawled under his desk and at 4.15 a.m. he telephoned Brooke who was staying nearby. The line was still working. Brooke gave him permission to request fire engines from Éire. At 4.35 a.m. a telegram was sent by railway telegraph and, on being wakened, de Valera agreed without hesitation to send help. Seventy men and thirteen fire engines from Dublin, Dún Laoghaire, Drogheda and Dundalk sped northwards. As they approached the city outskirts the southern firemen saw smoke and flames rising hundreds of feet into the air. John Smith, Belfast's chief fire officer, was found beneath a table in Chichester Street fire station, weeping and refusing to come out. There was little the firemen could do to fight the flames – hoses were cut by falling buildings, fittings were often the incorrect diameter, and the water pressure had fallen too low. Spender felt that the city fire brigade 'made a poor showing' and MacDermott admitted that some civil defence workers had 'sloped off'. An American, seconded to Short and Harland by the Lockheed Aircraft Corporation, wrote to his parents in California:

John MacDermott, minister of Public Security, and afterwards Lord Chief Justice; he was the only member of the government who realised the danger Northern Ireland faced after the fall of France in 1940.
PUBLIC RECORD OFFICE OF NORTHERN IRELAND

> You have heard about how tough the Irish are – well all I can say is that the tough Irish must come from S. Ireland because the boys up in N. Ireland are a bunch of chicken shit yellow bastards – 90% of them left everything and ran like hell.

At dawn on Wednesday 16 April a thick yellow pall covered Belfast. Exhausted air-raid wardens, firemen and ambulance men tore at the smouldering rubble to bring the trapped, dead and injured to the surface. On the Crumlin Road army lorries were piled high with corpses and severed limbs. At the Falls Road Public Baths the pool had to be emptied in order to lay out over 150 corpses. There, the bodies lay for three days as relatives attempted, often in vain, to identify them. Two hundred and fifty-five corpses were laid out in St George's Market. Here, Emma Duffin was one of the nurses on duty: she had seen 'death in many forms, young men dying of ghastly wounds' during the First World War but while Death in hospital beds in France had been 'solemn, tragic, dignified . . . here it was grotesque, repulsive, horrible'. Outside Belfast the Germans had hit at targets that lay within their flight path:

Belfast

Wasserwerk Belfast

Länge (westl. Greenw.): 5° 56′ 55″   Breite: 54° 37′ 20″

Mißweisung: 14° 19 (Mitte 1940)   Zielhöhe über NN 50 m

500   1000 m

Maßstab 1:10 000

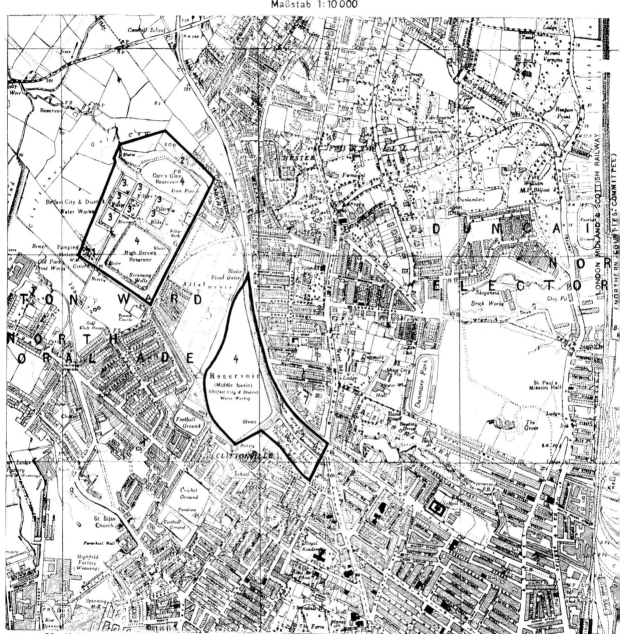

GB 53 75 Wasserwerk Belfast

1) Pumpanlage   etwa   550 qm
2) ansch. Pumpanlagen   etwa   400 qm
3) 7 Filterbecken
4) 4 Rohwasserbecken
                    _____
       bebaute Fläche   etwa   950 qm

Gesamtausdehnung etwa 350 000 qm

in Derry a parachute mine killed 15 people in Messines Park; Newtownards aerodrome was struck by explosives and incendiaries, killing 10 guards; and 14 bombs dropped on Bangor left 5 dead. The official figures for Belfast were 745 people dead and 430 seriously injured. The actual total was at least 900 dead. No other city, except London, had lost so many lives in one air raid.

There was now widespread panic and low civilian morale: some six thousand people arrived in Dublin from Belfast and tens of thousands left the city for the countryside. Of those who remained, forty thousand had to be put up in rest centres and seventy thousand had to be given meals every day in emergency feeding centres. Neither the Government nor the Belfast Corporation were able to do a great deal to improve the protection of citizens, apart from urgently requesting more defence equipment from Britain. One response by the Ministry of Public Security to the desperate situation was to issue this order on 19 April: 'Destroy all dangerous animals at the zoo immediately.' Two RUC marksmen killed thirty-three animals, including, unbelievably, two raccoons. Lord Haw-Haw was threatening another raid and the German bombers returned before Belfast's defences could be significantly strengthened.

At 9.45 p.m. on Sunday 4 May 1941 the first squadrons of German bombers took off from northern France and about an hour after midnight the second major air attack on Belfast began. In the words of one pilot, 'visibility was wonderful. I could make out my targets perfectly.' Until 1.55 a.m. the pathfinders of Kampfgruppe 100 dropped six thousand incendiaries almost exclusively on the harbour, the aircraft factory and the shipyards; then the rest of the bombers were led in by the rapidly spreading conflagration. Ernst von Kuhren, a war correspondent flying with one of the squadron, broadcast his impressions afterwards:

> When we approached the target at half-past two we stared silently into a sea of flames such as none of us had seen before . . . In Belfast there was not a large number of conflagrations, but just one enormous conflagration which spread over the entire harbour and industrial area.

Once again thirteen fire appliances came up from Éire but their efforts were to little avail: the water mains had been cracked in sixty-seven places and when the tide went out the fire hoses could not reach the river water. Much of the densely inhabited area about the Newtownards Road burned fiercely and this time much damage was inflicted on the city centre.

Early on Monday morning a lone German aeroplane flew over Belfast to make a photographic record of the results of the raid. *Der Adler* published aerial views of the city and gave a full page to analysing the successful outcome of the attack. For the first and only time in the war, Northern Ireland made headline news in the German press. *Völkischer Beobachter* began its report

Opposite:
German intelligence map of Belfast, showing the Waterworks on the Cavehill Road: a fearful carnage resulted when this densely inhabited area was blitzed on 15–16 April 1941.
IMPERIAL WAR MUSEUM

Bomb damage to the Belfast Ropeworks after the raid of 4–5 May 1941
PUBLIC RECORD OFFICE OF NORTHERN IRELAND

'Strong Air Fighter Units Bomb Belfast' and 'Back from Belfast: Fires Everywhere.' By now 53.5 per cent of Belfast's housing stock had been destroyed or badly damaged and the death toll for this May raid was 191 – a surprisingly low figure largely explained by two facts: that in this Sabbatarian city the centre was largely deserted when the attack began; and a very large number of people had already fled to the countryside.

The exodus from Belfast during and after the air raids was on a huge scale and MacDermott was right to observe that more were leaving there 'in proportion to population than any other city in the United Kingdom'. On the eve of the May blitz Spender estimated that one hundred thousand people – around one quarter of the population of Belfast – had fled to the Ulster countryside. Yet well over half those killed on 5 May were women and children, and next morning a fresh exodus began.

The mass migration from Belfast brought into the open the extreme deprivation of those now bombed out of congested streets who had endured two decades of unemployment and neglect. Emma Duffin's middle-class sensibilities were offended by 'the incredible dirt of the people, of children crawling with lice, not even house trained'. Moya Woodside recorded that her sister, living thirty miles from Belfast, complained of

> the appalling influx from the slums the day after the raid . . . The whole town
> is horrified by the filth of these evacuees and by their filthy habits and take-it-
> for-granted attitude . . . The smell is awful . . . They don't even use the lavatory,
> they just do it on the floor, grown-ups and children.

In Belfast there remained 150,000 people in target areas without access to
shelters. Radio Paris, under German direction, informed its listeners in the
middle of May: 'Fearing air raids, 20,000 women and children escape every
evening from Belfast to the outskirts of the city.' This was a considerable
underestimate.

Fortunately for the people of Northern Ireland the Germans did not again
return in force. On 26 June 1941 the Wehrmacht crossed the borders of the
Soviet Union, thus ending the isolation of the United Kingdom. By the end
of the year the general European war had become a worldwide conflict and
Hitler sealed his fate, shortly after the Japanese assault on Pearl Harbor, by
casually declaring war on the richest nation on earth – the United States.

THE AMERICANS AND VICTORY

On 26 January 1942 the first American troops stepped ashore at Belfast's
Dufferin Quay. Sir Basil Brooke had been summoned to London a few days
before and told by his uncle, Alan Brooke, chief of imperial general staff, that

*Landing of the first American
troops in Northern Ireland*
by William Conor
ULSTER FOLK AND
TRANSPORT MUSEUM

Churchill wanted him 'to see personally that the hospitality accorded to the Americans was of the very highest order'. It was, and the band of the Royal Ulster Rifles played the 'Star-Spangled Banner' to give what the *Belfast Telegraph* called 'a hearty Ulster welcome'. 'The inevitable dog mascot has made its appearance,' that newspaper continued, 'an American soldier somehow managing to bring along a mongrel known as "Jitterbug".'

In fact several hundred American 'civilian technicians' had been at work over the previous six months, helping to make Derry the most important escort base in the Western Approaches and the premier naval radio station in the European theatre of operations. At one stage 149 vessels were based in the Foyle, together with some 20,000 sailors. By May 1942 the number of Americans in Northern Ireland had reached 37,000; at Langford Lodge on the eastern shores of Lough Neagh a new town sprang up where aircraft were maintained by the Lockheed Overseas Corporation; United States airmen were stationed at airfields across the region; and for a time there were 120,000 Americans based in the North. Some local men resented the competition for the attention of young women. Charlie Gallagher, an air-raid precautions officer in Derry, recollected: 'We were getting our eyes wiped left, right and centre . . .' Most people, however, were flattered by the attention Americans gave to Northern Ireland, particularly when Generals Eisenhower and Patton inspected their troops there and Glenn Miller, Larry Adler and George Formby came to entertain the men.

All the excitement aroused by the American presence could not hide widespread dissatisfaction with the performance of the Government. In December 1941 Harry Midgley, the colourful Northern Ireland Labour Party candidate, won Willowfield in east Belfast in a by-election. The loss of this fervently loyalist seat left Andrews severely shaken and yet he proved incapable of making the cabinet adjustments necessary to silence his critics. He was easily diverted by trivialities and continued to be obsessed by the infiltration of 'Free Staters'. A rebellion of backbenchers and junior ministers slowly matured and on 28 April 1943 Andrews was forced to resign. He seems to have recommended Lord Glentoran as his replacement, but the governor, realising Glentoran was not the party's choice, asked Brooke to form a government on 1 May. Brooke made a clean sweep. Apart from himself, the only member of the previous government to be retained was John MacDermott, now the attorney-general.

By the summer of 1944 the Americans had left Northern Ireland and were advancing from their bridgeheads in northern France; Whitley aircraft flew out from Limavady aerodrome and located U-boats with increasing success; and

escort vessels from Derry co-operated closely with Short Sunderlands, Consolidated Catalinas and Supermarine Stranraers taking off from Lower Lough Erne to close the 'Atlantic gap' and bring the German submarine campaign to an end. As Allied forces rolled back the frontiers of the Third Reich, Northern Ireland was once again becoming an arsenal of victory.

Not until the beginning of 1942 did shipbuilding in Belfast return to normal production; thereafter the Harland and Wolff workforce rose steadily to reach a peak of 30,801 in December 1944. Altogether Queen's Island launched 170 Admiralty and merchant ships between 1939 and 1945, including corvettes, minesweepers, frigates, support vessels, landing craft and three aircraft carriers. In addition the firm repaired around 30,000 vessels at Belfast, Liverpool, London and Derry and manufactured over 13 million aircraft parts, over 500 tanks, thousands of field and anti-aircraft guns, and hundreds of searchlights. Short and Harland dispersed as many of its processes as possible in case of further attacks from the air: fuselages, wings, fins, rudders and components

War effort at Short and Harland
SHORTS PLC

were made at such places as Lambeg, County Antrim, Hawlmark at Newtownards, Altona in Lisburn and the King's Hall in south Belfast. The workforce rose to 23,000 and by the end of the war had completed almost 1,200
Stirling bombers and 125 Sunderland flying boats. Mackie's made 75 million
shells and 65 million parts for bombs; the Sirocco Works in Belfast produced
grenades, radar equipment and gun mountings; and the ropeworks made one
third of the cordage and ropes required by the War Office. The linen industry,
though dislocated when the Germans overran its principal sources of flax,
produced two million parachutes, hundreds of thousands of uniforms, and
great quantities of canvas, machine-gun belts and 'blitz cloth' for reroofing
damaged buildings. The war brought large numbers of women into traditional
male preserves for the first time; in engineering, for example, there were only
250 women employed in 1939 but by 1943 the number had risen to 12,300.

Despite Northern Ireland's impressive wartime output, production levels
were consistently lower in the region than in any other part of the United
Kingdom. There was abundant evidence of incompetent and high-handed
management and low worker morale, resulting in illegal strikes, defective
work, high absenteeism and poor time-keeping.

On the evening of 7 May 1945, news spread that the Germans would
surrender at midnight. People poured into the centre of Belfast to celebrate
and flames leaped up from dozens of bonfires, and, as bunting was hung out,
the beating of drums and the clanging of dustbin lids added to the din of
rejoicing. Next day a huge crowd – the biggest since Covenant Day, 1912 –
gathered in Donegall Square and Donegall Place. 'We must not slack,' Sir
Crawford McCullagh, the lord mayor, told the people. 'Celebrate the victory
and go back to work.' No one seems to have followed the advice of this
discredited leader of a corporation still in commission after being found guilty
of gross corruption in 1941. For the vast majority VE Day was the end of the
war as far as they were concerned.

Anglo-Irish relations were put under severe strain when Churchill's victory
speech not only paid tribute to Northern Ireland but also bitterly referred to
the consequences of Éire's neutrality during the Battle of the Atlantic:

> If it had not been for the loyalty and friendship of Northern Ireland we should
> have been forced to come to close quarters with Mr de Valera or perish for ever
> from the earth.

Four days later de Valera broadcast a dignified response but his even-handed
neutrality had left Éire in a state of diplomatic isolation. MacDermott
expressed his gratitude at Stormont for the aid sent during the blitz and Moya
Woodside wrote that 'an action like this does more for Irish unity than the
words of politicians', while Emma Duffin made this entry in her diary:
'Perhaps, this will draw North and South closer together. I wonder.'

Opposite:
VE Day celebrations,
8 May 1945, in
Donegall Place, Belfast
BELFAST TELEGRAPH

Sir Basil Brooke, prime
minister of Northern
Ireland 1943–63 (front
row, second right), with
Russian officers
NORTHERN IRELAND
ASSEMBLY LIBRARY,
STORMONT

THE WELFARE STATE

Eager to show the loyalty of the majority in Northern Ireland before the
British electorate went to the polls, Brooke called a general election for
15 June 1945. With truth the *Belfast News-Letter* declared that 'the
Constitutional question emerges as the governing issue': 6 Labour candidates
from an assortment of parties won seats in Belfast; the Nationalists held 8; but
with 34 seats the Unionists were still impregnable. In the Westminster elections
in July the only Labour candidate returned from Northern Ireland was the
Independent Jack Beattie. In Britain the Labour Party won the most
overwhelming victory in its history and Clement Attlee's new government
began at once to implement its radical programme which ultimately would do
much to transform the lives of the people of Northern Ireland.

Unionists at Westminster vigorously opposed one welfare measure after
another, yet the same bills were shortly afterwards proposed, often with
enthusiasm, by government ministers in Belfast. The explanation for this
apparent contradiction was that Britain was prepared to pay most of the very
large sums of money needed to finance welfare legislation in Northern
Ireland. The result was a striking advance in the material welfare of the people
of the region.

The most urgent task was to provide dwellings, particularly in Belfast.
William Grant, a former shipyard worker who was now minister of health and
local government, set up the Housing Trust in 1945, with power to borrow
from the Government to build houses and pay back the capital with interest

over sixty years. The trust allocated houses with strict fairness but this could not be said of many local authorities expected to carry the main burden of providing dwellings with the help of government subsidies. Grant's target of one hundred thousand local authority houses was not reached until the early 1960s, but, disappointing though this was, the achievement was vastly more impressive than that of the interwar years. Yet the greatly increased public spending on housing was to set a time bomb ticking which would eventually explode in 1968–9. No steps were taken to ensure the even-handed allocation of council houses. The modernising welfare legislation was allowed to entrench and augment the petty parochialism of the past with grave consequences for the stability of Northern Ireland.

The resentment fuelled by the local administration of public housing expansion was slow in accumulating. By contrast, plans to extend the education system, along the lines of the revolutionising 1944 Butler Act, provoked an immediate storm. Lieutenant-Colonel Samuel Hall-Thompson, the minister of education, published proposals in December 1944 which included an increase in capital grants to Catholic schools from 50 to 65 per cent, to provide books to these schools free of charge and milk and meals to necessitous children. Also, there was to be an end to compulsory Bible instruction in state schools. All the Catholic bishops denounced the plans in their Lenten pastorals, Dr Daniel Mageean, bishop of Down and Connor, observing that 'from bitter experience' he knew 'what had happened in other countries when the state took control of youth'. It was Protestant opposition, however, which caused Hall-Thompson most trouble. 'There are no sacrifices we will not make, in order that our Protestant form of inheritance will be made secure,' declared the dean of Belfast while making an appeal for a £20,000 fighting fund at the Wellington Hall on 8 November 1946. The next day Hall-Thompson was howled down at a meeting of the Ulster Women's Unionist Council when he said that 'in the State schools the religious instruction must be undenominational'. So great was the uproar that Lady Clark asked to be excused from the chair, the minister left early, and members of the audience sang 'Derry's Walls' to mark their triumph. The Reverend Professor Robert Corkey, a former education minister, asserted that state schools would be thrown open to 'Jews, Agnostics, Roman Catholics and Atheists'.

Despite all the opposition, Hall-Thompson had his way and his bill became law in 1947. During the furore very little had been said about the main features of the reform. The principal task was to convert elementary schools into the new primary and secondary schools. Selected by a qualifying examination at eleven, the most able pupils would proceed to grammar school and the remaining 80 per cent were to go on to 'intermediate' or 'technical' secondary

William Grant, the former shipyard worker who became minister of Health and Local Government: he set up the Housing Trust in 1945.
PUBLIC RECORD OFFICE OF NORTHERN IRELAND

Saint Patrick's Girls' Secondary Intermediate School, Downpatrick: education in Northern Ireland was revolutionised by the 1947 Education Act. HMSO (DEPARTMENT OF THE ENVIRONMENT, NORTHERN IRELAND)

school. The traditional grammar schools successfully resisted direct state control and continued to take in some pupils who had not passed the examination but were prepared to pay fees. Thus the 1947 act did less to break down social barriers in the region than might have been expected. In any case the provisions took time to implement: the Ministry of Education estimated that 190 intermediate schools were required, but the counties of Armagh and Tyrone did not have a single one until 1954 and Fermanagh had none until 1955. It is therefore not surprising that the full social and political impact of educational advance was not felt until the mid-1960s.

Schoolchildren were the first to benefit from the region's vastly improved health services. The Belfast Education Committee provided a general school meals service from January 1943 and Stormont did not wait to take a lead from Westminster in combating tuberculosis, responsible for almost half the deaths in the 15–25 age group. With the aid of the drugs BCG and streptomycin, the Tuberculosis Authority's campaign was so effective that by 1954 the death rate was reduced to the same level as that in England and Wales. So well had the authority done its work that it was dissolved in 1959. Then, in July 1948, the National Health Service, totally free and almost completely comprehensive, came into operation in Britain. In the same year an almost identical act passed through Stormont but, because of past neglect, the impact of this new service was more profoundly felt in Northern Ireland than in any other region of the United Kingdom. Deaths of mothers during childbirth fell to the same level as for England and Wales by 1954; and by the 1960s general mortality rates for Northern Ireland were the lowest for any region of the United Kingdom.

ANTI-PARTITION LEAGUE, IRELAND ACT, AND OPERATION HARVEST

Northern Catholics, though they benefited from improved welfare and educational services, did not abandon their aspirations. For a time, indeed, they believed the prospect of reunification was now clearly on the horizon with the advent of a Labour government at Westminster. In November 1945 all the Nationalist MPs and senators, together with many priests and around five hundred other delegates, met in Dungannon to form the Irish Anti-Partition League, 'with the object of uniting all those opposed to partition into a solid block'. De Valera faced a challenge from a new radical republican party, Clann na Poblachta, founded by Seán MacBride, a former IRA chief of staff, and so he did not hesitate to give the league his backing.

De Valera's propaganda drive against partition failed to save him at the polls in February 1948. For the first time in sixteen years Fianna Fáil was out of power and a new coalition government took office with John A. Costello of Fine Gael as taoiseach and MacBride as external affairs minister. It immediately competed stridently with Fianna Fáil for leadership of constitutional republicanism and irredentism. The coalition government announced it was ready to give Unionists 'any reasonable guarantees' if they would accept reunification. 'They may bid as high as they please,' Brooke responded, 'but our answer remains the same – "Ulster is not for sale".'

On 7 September 1948 during a visit to Canada Costello announced that Éire would become a republic. Completely unmoved by the anti-partitionist campaign and keenly aware of Northern Ireland's strategic importance as the Cold War intensified, Attlee gave an assurance that no constitutional change would be made 'without Northern Ireland's free agreement'. As for Brooke, he called a general election for 10 February 1949 to demonstrate once more that Northern Ireland was British. The poll was dubbed 'the chapel gate election' because money was collected outside churches south of the border to help the Anti-Partition League candidates. The Unionist Party could hardly have asked for more favourable circumstances – the evidence of southern interference and clerical manipulation seemed incontrovertible. The election was the most violent since 1921. Candidates were stoned and mobs struggled with each other every evening in the darkness. The Northern Ireland Labour Party was eliminated and for the first time the opposition at Stormont was entirely Catholic, a matter of much satisfaction to Brooke. The most serious casualty in this election was the modest advance in reconciliation made during the war and immediately after. Attlee's Ireland Act of June 1949 included the unequivocal guarantee that

John A. Costello, the Fine Gael taoiseach who took Éire out of the Commonwealth and declared a republic in 1949 PUBLIC RECORD OFFICE OF NORTHERN IRELAND

> in no event will Northern Ireland or any part thereof cease to be part of His Majesty's dominions and of the United Kingdom without the consent of the parliament of Northern Ireland.

Southern politicians on both sides of the Dáil had shown themselves remarkably out of touch with international developments in their genuine conviction that Britain could be persuaded to accede to the demands of the Anti-Partition League. Northern nationalists had tried peaceful constitutional agitation, which had resulted in nothing but humiliation. Brooke – raised to the peerage as Lord Brookeborough in 1949 – was coarsely triumphalist and showed no inclination to foster constitutionalism amongst his opponents. Almost inevitably some northern Catholics decided that the only answer to loyalist intransigence was a new resort to arms.

Towards the end of the war Gerry Boland, Éire's minister for justice, claimed with much justification that the IRA was dead. A campaign in Britain in the first half of 1939, during which the IRA set off 127 explosions, killed 6 people and injured more than 50, had been swiftly brought to an end by special legislation. After another burst of activity in Northern Ireland in 1942–3, the Stormont government had gained the upper hand by curfew and internment. De Valera played his part: his government had consistently interned more IRA suspects than the Northern Ireland authorities, and by hangings, street gunfights and incarceration in bleak camps Fianna Fáil had shattered its former associates north and south.

The IRA fifties campaign: B Specials searching civilians
PUBLIC RECORD OFFICE OF NORTHERN IRELAND

In the early 1950s a new generation of northern republicans, contemptuous of the Anti-Partition League's constitutional campaign, prepared to renew the armed conflict. A carefully planned raid on Gough barracks in County Armagh on 10 June 1954 yielded 250 rifles, 37 Sten guns, 9 Bren guns and

40 training rifles. Other attempts to seize arms failed in the following year and it was not until midnight on 11 December 1956 that Operation Harvest began. Driving sleet gave convenient cover for the initial assault involving around 150 volunteers. Apart from destroying a transmitter in Derry, a Territorial Army building in Enniskillen and a B Special hut in Newry, little was achieved. Brookeborough ordered the cratering or spiking of border roads and a full call-up of B Specials; and large numbers of volunteers were arrested and interned.

Over the next few years the IRA campaign continued fitfully without ever seriously disrupting the life of people in Northern Ireland. The high points of Operation Harvest were usually glorious failures, such as the disastrous attack on Brookeborough RUC barracks on New Year's Eve, 1956, in which Fergal O'Hanlon of Monaghan and Sean South of Garryowen in County Limerick were mortally wounded. When de Valera returned to power in the spring of 1957 he reintroduced internment with devastating effect. Squeezed north and south the IRA army and executive council had no choice but to call off the campaign in February 1962. The final toll was 12 militant republicans and 6 RUC men killed; 32 members of the security forces injured; over 200 convicted for their role in the campaign; and hundreds interned. The *New York Times* observed:

> The original I.R.A.. and Sinn Fein came in like lions . . . and now they go out like lambs . . . the Irish Republican Army belongs to history, and it belongs to better men in times that are gone. So does Sinn Fein. Let us put a wreath of red roses on their grave and move on.

PLANNING CONCILIATION AND ECONOMIC PROGRESS

An expected postwar slump had not materialised, partly due to desperate shortages worldwide and the pump-priming provided by Marshall Plan aid. Harland and Wolff struggled to keep up with orders for liners, oil tankers, refrigerated cargo ships and land engines. In 1951, twenty-one thousand men were fully employed on Queen's Island when the company delivered the aircraft carrier HMS *Eagle*, the largest vessel in the Royal Navy, and *Juan Peron*, the world's biggest whale factory ship, during the building of which 18 men were killed and 59 seriously injured when a gangplank collapsed. At one point sixty-eight vessels were either being built or on order: never before and never again were the yards of Harland and Wolff so occupied. The company outperformed others in the United Kingdom during the 1950s but as a shipbuilding state Britain was suffering relative decline as competition increased from Germany, Japan and Sweden. On 16 March 1960 Dame Pattie Menzies, wife of the Australian prime minister, broke a bottle of red wine on

Linen thread being made ready for export: the post-war boom was followed by near terminal decline in the 1950s.
LISBURN MUSEUM

the bows of the *Canberra* and the 45,270-ton P & O liner entered Belfast Lough. The ship was the largest liner built in Britain since the *Queen Elizabeth*, with a revolutionary design still looking modern more than thirty years later. The launch marked the end of an era, and owing to a lack of orders, by 1962 the workforce in Belfast was reduced to 12,582. The market for large passenger liners was contracting and, in retrospect, the 1950s were years of lost opportunity to adapt and modernise.

For most of the 1940s the only brake on Northern Ireland's linen industry seemed to be shortage of raw material. Trading conditions in 1947, Wallace Clark, owner of Clark's of Upperlands, recalls, 'were in extraordinary contrast to those before the war. In a seller's market, price was of little importance. Yarn was booked on open contract to be invoiced at time of delivery.' By 1951 around seventy-six thousand workers in Northern Ireland were employed in textiles, the great majority in linen. Then in July 1953 the Korean War came to an end and prices all but collapsed. This was no temporary downturn and from now on the industry was in a state of near terminal decline. 'Loving is lovelier on linen' was a slogan used by one Ulster firm in a sales drive in Italy, but the fall in demand could not be stemmed. Technical advance was actually quite rapid; the real problem was that linen, except for certain specialist purposes, was becoming outdated.

Agriculture continued to be Northern Ireland's largest industry and, sustained by guaranteed prices and subsidies, it was well-placed to carve out a good share of Britain's lucrative market. The problem for the Government was that technical progress had the effect of reducing employment opportunities on the land: labour-saving tractors, only numbering 850 in 1939, rose to 16,000 by 1950 and the numbers doubled again by the end of the decade. Not surprisingly, male employment in farming fell by 27 per cent in the 1950s, a decade in which output increased by an average of 2 per cent per annum. In short, Northern Ireland's main economic hope was to attract enough new manufacturing to keep the region's population at work.

Aircraft manufacture in Belfast failed to maintain wartime levels of production. The success of Britain's Vickers Armstrong prevented Short Brothers, as it was renamed in 1948, from becoming a major manufacturer of military aircraft and the numbers employed at Sydenham fell to a plateau of around six thousand. Shorts developed the first tail-less aircraft, the Sherpa, in 1951, and pioneered the vertical take-off SCI in 1955, but much of its highly advanced research and development failed to yield a significant commercial return until the 1960s.

The report by K.S. Isles and Norman Cuthbert, *An Economic Survey of Northern Ireland*, was published in 1957; it was the most penetrating and comprehensive study of its kind so far. The authors detailed the difficulties facing the region; above all, the range of industries that could prosper was restricted by the high cost of fuel and cross-channel transport. Another report, by Sir Robert Hall, published in 1962, recommended that the Government should cease its efforts to support declining industries and concentrate on bringing dynamic outsiders to Northern Ireland.

Brookeborough faced furious criticism when the Hall report was presented at Stormont on 30 October. His government seemed tired and uninspired even to his closest supporters, and in March 1963 Brookeborough was forced

Lord Brookeborough (centre) with his cabinet in the late 1950s: Terence O'Neill, minister of Finance, is seated on the prime minister's right. HMSO (DEPARTMENT OF THE ENVIRONMENT, NORTHERN IRELAND)

by his colleagues to stand down. The parliamentary Unionist Party probably would have chosen Brian Faulkner as his successor but the inner circle chose the finance minister, Captain Terence O'Neill, who, after being handed a whiskey and soda by the governor, was informed of his appointment on 25 March.

The ancient divisions in the region had survived the war intact and were older and more profound than the political frontier weaving its erratic way through the province of Ulster. Any modernisation that ensued after 1945 was due not to Stormont governments but to powerful transformations elsewhere. No advantage was taken of the long period of internal peace and the isolation of the IRA to remedy obvious wrongs and soothe intercommunal resentment still stubbornly alive, especially where pockets of disadvantage were dangerously concentrated. Brookeborough had seen no reason for political reform and the certainty that he would never make a serious attempt to consider a redress of minority grievances was in part responsible for his long-standing popularity with the majority. The appointment of O'Neill, however, seemed to herald a new dawn.

'Our task will be literally to transform Ulster,' O'Neill said to the Ulster Unionist Council a few days after being appointed prime minister. 'To achieve it will demand bold and imaginative measures.' The following year he stated at Stormont that his principal aims were 'to make Northern Ireland economically stronger and prosperous . . . and to build bridges between the two traditions within our community'. Dedicated though he was to the constitutional status quo and continued Unionist rule, O'Neill was the first Northern Ireland prime minister to state clearly that reconciliation was a central part of his programme. He sought to bring the benefits of modernisation to everyone in the region and not just to the Protestant majority, and, aged forty-eight in 1963, O'Neill represented a new liberal Unionist generation prepared to move away from the siege mentality of those involved in the turbulent events surrounding the formation of Northern Ireland.

O'Neill was fortunate in being able to launch his programme at a time when world trading conditions were buoyant and when the Republic of Ireland was not only transforming its economy but also seeking friendlier co-operation with the United Kingdom. In 1959 de Valera was elected president of the republic and was replaced as taoiseach by his pragmatic deputy Sean Lemass. Lemass launched T.K. Whitaker's ambitious programme to dismantle tariffs, encourage foreign investment and remove controls on foreign ownership of manufacturing concerns. O'Neill, too, sought an economic revolution based on comprehensive planning for the whole of Northern Ireland: this had been recommended by Sir Robert Matthew's *Belfast Regional Survey and Plan 1962*, which called for a restriction of further growth in the regional capital and a grandiose scheme to create a new city between Portadown and Lurgan. A detailed plan was prepared by Professor Tom Wilson in 1964 and adopted by the Government the following year.

There is little doubt now that the Wilson plan was seriously flawed, though perhaps no more so than other regional development schemes in the United Kingdom. More ominously for the future, the plan took little heed of political sensitivities, particularly in its implementation. Nationalists were outraged when William Craig, minister of development, announced that the name of the new city was to be Craigavon. They also argued that the predominantly Protestant east was being favoured over the Catholic west; indeed, with the exception of Derry, all the growth centres were in the Protestant heartlands. A further example of insensitivity to minority feeling was the recommendation of the 1965 report of the committee on higher education (which had not a single Catholic member), under the chairmanship of Sir John Lockwood, that Northern Ireland's second university should be sited at Coleraine. Derry had high expectations of being chosen; John Hume, then a teacher at St Columb's, organised an impressive motorcade to Stormont, which included Mayor Albert Anderson, later a Unionist MP, and Eddie McAteer, the Nationalist leader. Nevertheless, the Government endorsed the choice of Coleraine.

For the present, such controversies were but small dark clouds on a far horizon. O'Neill's new economic strategy seemed to be working as multinational firms, including Grundig, British Enkalon, ICI, Michelin and Goodyear, were induced to set up in Northern Ireland. Meanwhile, the economic gap between north and south, which had yawned so wide in the 1950s, was rapidly narrowing, as under the direction of Sean Lemass the republic experienced its first industrial revolution.

Smiling bravely for the cameras: O'Neill meets Taoiseach Sean Lemass in the grounds of Stormont, 14 January 1965
BELFAST TELEGRAPH

'NO MASS, NO LEMASS': 'IRA MURDERER WELCOMED AT STORMONT'

Lemass knew that better relations with Britain were vital to the success of his economic strategy – that must include a rapprochement with Northern Ireland – but Brookeborough flatly refused to touch the hand of friendship Lemass had offered on several occasions. O'Neill was so entirely different from his predecessor that it was he – and probably he alone – who took the initiative and invited Lemass to Stormont. He did not risk informing his colleagues about the taoiseach's visit.

'Welcome to the North,' O'Neill said as Lemass stepped out of his Mercedes shortly after midday on 14 January 1965. There was no reply. Finally breaking his silence in the lavatory of Stormont House, Lemass said: 'I shall get into terrible trouble for this.' He had, after all, fought in the 1916 Easter Rising and had been interned by the British and imprisoned by the first Irish Free State government as a republican die-hard. The taoiseach then relaxed and became more garrulous over a splendid lunch. Summoned only that morning, O'Neill's colleagues smiled bravely for the cameras. After discussions on possible north–south economic co-operation, Lemass then returned to Dublin; that evening on television O'Neill justified the meeting, observing that north and south 'share the same rivers, the same mountains, and some of the same problems'.

The Irish Republican Party's election headquarters in Divis Street: the tricolour on display triggered intense rioting in 1964.
BELFAST TELEGRAPH

No widespread hostile reaction greeted the O'Neill–Lemass meeting, but the following afternoon a car, trailing a very large Ulster flag, drove to Stormont to display placards which read: 'NO MASS, NO LEMASS'; 'DOWN WITH THE LUNDYS'; AND 'IRA MURDERER WELCOMED AT STORMONT'. Two Protestant Unionist councillors and the Reverend Ian Paisley, moderator of the Free Presbyterian Church, then handed in a letter of protest. For the present, Paisley was little more than a gadfly, but as traditional loyalism reawakened, his support would grow with formidable speed. Paisley had been brought into public prominence by his denunciation of ecumenical trends in the principal Christian Churches. He had denounced the Queen Mother and Princess Margaret for 'committing spiritual fornication and adultery with the Anti-Christ' when they had visited Pope John XXIII in 1958; when the pope died in June 1963, and the Union flag was flown at half-mast over Belfast City Hall, Paisley held a rally at the Ulster Hall to excoriate 'the Iscariots of Ulster', assuring his audience that 'this Romish man of sin is now in Hell'; and his demand that a small Irish tricolour be removed from a window in Divis Street helped to precipitate rioting there during the Westminster general election of October 1964. Paisley's pugnacious oratory delivered in a rich mid-Antrim accent ensured gathering support from those Protestant fundamentalists with the liveliest fear of Catholicism; but he was beginning to widen his appeal to greater numbers of loyalists, who were apprehensive that O'Neill's bridge-building gestures to the nationalist minority were weakening the bulwarks of unionism.

O'Neill wrote of Brookeborough that 'in twenty years as Prime Minister he never crossed the border, never visited a Catholic school, and never received or sought a civic reception from a Catholic town'. O'Neill was prepared to lower the Unionist guard: he met Cardinal William Conway, archbishop of Armagh; visited Catholic schools and hospitals, making sure where possible he was photographed in the company of nuns; and was rewarded by a warm response from leaders of the minority. In February 1965 the Nationalist Party for the first time agreed to become the official opposition. At the same time this was an era of rapidly rising expectations and vastly improved international communications.

The Labour Prime Minister Harold Wilson recalled a meeting he had with O'Neill in May 1965: 'Since coming into office he had by Northern Ireland standards carried through a remarkable programme of easement.' The assumption that real progress had been made in ending discriminatory practices was false and, indeed, Wilson made no thorough attempt to see what changes were being made. Though the Electoral Law Amendment Act of 1968 abolished university and business votes, it still denied universal suffrage in local government elections and did nothing to rectify boundary manipulations of earlier decades. If O'Neill was to carry through real reform, he needed the full co-operation of his colleagues and complete domestic calm; in the years following, neither of these conditions were fulfilled.

The year 1966 proved a difficult one for O'Neill. An unseemly row ensued when Belfast Corporation chose 'Carson' as the name for a new bridge across the Lagan and then accepted the alternative 'Queen Elizabeth II' at the prompting of the governor, Lord Erskine. During the Easter Rising commemorations tension rose and 10,500 B Specials were mobilised. Paisley continued to grab the headlines: a march in protest against the Presbyterian Church's 'Romanising tendencies' passed through the Catholic Markets area, leading to intense rioting and his subsequent imprisonment in Crumlin Road gaol. The year was also the fiftieth anniversary of the Somme and for that reason loyalist militants, meeting in the Standard Bar on the Shankill, named the group they formed there the Ulster Volunteer Force. This new terrorist UVF aimed to topple O'Neill and combat the IRA. A press statement on 21 May concluded: 'Known IRA men will be executed mercilessly and without hesitation.' On 27 May the UVF mortally wounded John Scullion, a Catholic but not a known IRA man, in Clonard Street. On 26 June three Catholics were shot in Malvern Street and one, Peter Ward, died of his wounds.

On hearing of the murders, O'Neill returned from his visit to the Somme to proscribe the UVF. He also found men in his own party, led by Brian Faulkner, minister of commerce, plotting to oust him. On his release from

Ian Paisley, Moderator of the Free Presbyterian Church, and wearing a light raincoat, leads a march protesting against ecumenical tendencies in the Presbyterian Church in 1966. Rioting ensued in the Catholic Markets area of Belfast as the demonstrators passed through.
BELFAST TELEGRAPH

prison in October, Paisley told supporters welcoming him home: 'O'Neill must go – O'Neill will go!' Nineteen sixty-seven was the last year of peace but Protestant anger at O'Neill's moderation became ever more evident. The RUC uncovered a UVF plot to assassinate the prime minister, who was dogged at almost every public appearance by Paisley and his followers calling for his resignation. Meanwhile, O'Neill found that he was unable to deliver more than gestures of friendship to the Catholic minority: the result was acute frustration.

THE CIVIL RIGHTS MOVEMENT BEGINS

During the morning of 28 August 1963 seventeen Catholic families occupied prefabricated bungalows due for demolition at Fairmount Park in Dungannon. After television crews arrived the Government promised to speed up the completion of a council housing estate in the Nationalist-held ward of the town. It seemed that a notable victory had been won by the Homeless Citizens' League, formed earlier in the year. Nevertheless, by January 1967 only 34 Catholic families, compared with 264 Protestant ones, had been allocated council houses in Dungannon since 1945. Though Dungannon's population of about seven thousand was evenly divided, the urban district council had been carefully sectioned into three wards, two of them with small but safe Protestant majorities and one with an overwhelming Catholic majority. Thus the town had a perpetual Unionist administration. Local authority housing was intimately connected with political power; no points system operated; and

since only ratepayers – in effect, householders – had a vote in local elections, the ruling Unionists had a strong political motive not to build houses for Catholic families, particularly in the two Unionist wards. Indeed, since 1945 not a single new house had been built in the Nationalist ward when the Homeless Citizens' League was founded. The league's first public protest had been to picket the urban district council offices when Catholic families were refused any of the 142 houses just completed in the Unionist wards.

Dungannon was not unique. The Cameron commission, appointed by O'Neill's government in 1969 to inquire into the disturbances of the previous year, concluded that in certain areas, notably Dungannon, Armagh and Derry, the manipulation of ward boundaries was

> deliberately made and maintained . . . to favour Protestant or Unionist supporters in making public appointments – particularly those of senior officials – and in manipulating housing allocations for political and sectarian ends.

The most striking example of gerrymandering was Londonderry City – Unionist-controlled, though, as the Cameron report pointed out, the adult population was composed of 20,102 Catholics and 10,274 Protestants in 1966. Such gerrymandering was not restricted to the 1920s: boundaries were redrawn to Unionist advantage in Omagh in 1935, Derry in 1936, Armagh in 1946, and County Fermanagh in 1967. The refusal to follow Britain in introducing universal suffrage in local elections also disadvantaged Catholics, being poorer and more overcrowded on average. Reform here might not have

Captain O'Neill (left) attending the Twelfth parade in Portglenone, County Antrim, in 1967 – the last full year of peace.
BELFAST TELEGRAPH

made much difference but Unionist refusal to abolish qualifications laid the party open to the charge of resisting democracy and gave civil rights activists a powerful slogan, 'One Man, One Vote'.

Control of local government automatically conferred power to make appointments. The Cameron Commission, after investigating five Unionist authorities, concluded:

> We are satisfied that all these Unionist controlled councils have used and use their power to make appointments in a way which benefited Protestants . . . In Dungannon Urban District none of the council's administrative, clerical and technical employees was a Catholic.

The most brazen examples of favouritism were to be found west of the Bann but patronage was ubiquitous and had increased since 1945 with the spectacular rise in local government spending. In 1969 the Campaign for Social Justice found that 92.8 per cent of the higher ranks of the civil service down to deputy principal were Protestants. Catholics were also under-represented in other parts of the establishment. As late as 1969 Catholics held only six senior judicial posts out of a total of sixty-eight. There were 22 public boards by 1969, with 332 members in all, but only 49 were Catholics, and only 15.4 per cent of 8,122 employed in the publicly owned water, gas and electricity industries were Catholics. It is much more difficult to assess levels of discrimination in private employment, particularly as hard evidence is available only for the 1970s onwards. Catholics and Protestants discriminated with equal zeal, but for historical reasons Catholics were bound to be at a disadvantage in the game. In the main, traditional employers were Protestant and not all the newly arrived multinational firms were able to resist labour pressure to favour one religion in recruitment. Though the Sirocco Works and Mackie's foundry were sited in largely Catholic districts, the numbers of Catholics employed there were insignificant. On the other hand, because most public houses in the region were owned by Catholics most bar staff were Catholic.

Dungannon's Homeless Citizens' League was significant because it advocated direct action and criticised Nationalist participation in 'gentlemen's agreements' with Unionists to give out local authority houses to their own supporters. It drew inspiration from the black civil rights campaign in the United States: the first picket outside the council offices included people carrying placards that stated: 'IF OUR RELIGION IS AGAINST US, SHIP US TO LITTLE ROCK' and 'RACIAL DISCRIMINATION IN ALABAMA HITS DUNGANNON'. Conn and Patricia McCluskey had taken the lead in Dungannon. In the house of Peter Gormley, a surgeon in the Mater Hospital, they formed the Campaign for Social Justice in Northern Ireland and launched the new organisation on 14 January 1964 in the Wellington Park Hotel, Belfast. Their press release explained that they planned to oppose policies of discrimination, 'collect comprehensive and accurate data on all injustices done against all creeds' and 'seek equality for all'. In effect they had launched the civil rights movement in Northern Ireland.

Only a minority of Protestants seem to have accepted that Catholics had genuine grounds for seeking a redress of their grievances. A handful of Unionist MPs and a key group of senior civil servants urged O'Neill to press forward with reform. Some middle-class Protestants strove through the Northern Ireland Labour Party to see British standards of fair treatment applied in the region but the party was hampered by its inability to win a seat at Westminster. The Nationalist Party did not play a central role: this conservative and clericalist survival of the Irish Parliamentary Party sought, not a reformed administration in Belfast, but an end to partition. Gerry Fitt, the Republican Labour MP for Dock since 1962, got elected for West Belfast in 1966 and the impact he made at Westminster was immediate. This colourful, fast-talking ex-sailor, whose pithy style contrasted with that of the sedate upper-middle-class Unionists, explained Catholic grievances in terms everyone could understand. In particular, he galvanised a group of Labour MPs at Westminster who were concerned about the lack of reform in Northern Ireland and who formed the Campaign for Democracy in Ulster in 1965. It proved impossible, however, to persuade Wilson's government to overturn the convention at Westminster that MPs could not discuss matters relating to Northern Ireland. On 3 July 1966 a much wider audience was alerted to anomalies in Northern Ireland when the *Sunday Times* published journalist Cal McCrystal's article, 'John Bull's Political Slum'. The Labour government, nevertheless, retained its faith that O'Neill could put the region's house in order. The initiative still lay with the people of Northern Ireland themselves.

Nell McCafferty, the journalist and writer, remembered family prayers during her childhood in Derry in the 1950s:

> God send John a job; God send Jackie and Rosaleen a house; Holy Mother of God look down on Peggy in America and Leo in England; Jesus and his Blessed Mother protect Mary that's going with a sailor.

Gerry Fitt, the former sailor elected as Republican Labour MP for West Belfast in 1966: he attempted to draw Westminster's attention to the need for political reform in Northern Ireland. HMSO (DEPARTMENT OF THE ENVIRONMENT, NORTHERN IRELAND)

On the United Kingdom's periphery, the city remained depressed even during years of economic expansion. In March 1966, 5.9 per cent in the region were unemployed but in Derry 23.3 per cent of males and 4.8 per cent of females were out of work. Housing was a central issue here, where local Unionists were resisting an unanswerable case for extending the city boundary, for fear that the electoral balance would be tipped enough to lose them control of the corporation. John Hume, Father Anthony Mulvey and Paddy Doherty (later known as Paddy 'Bogside') applied the principle of self-help to the housing problem in their native city through the Derry Housing Association. Others took their protests to the streets, led by the Derry Unemployed Action Committee and the Derry Housing Action Committee; direct action included resistance to eviction in 1967 and a sit-down protest on Craigavon Bridge in July 1968.

In June 1968 a nineteen-year-old Protestant woman, secretary to a member of the UUP, was allocated a council house in the County Tyrone village of Caledon; as the Cameron Commission reported: 'By no stretch of the imagination could Miss Beattie be regarded as a priority tenant.' Austin Currie, the Nationalist MP for East Tyrone, squatted in the house himself before being removed by a policeman, who happened to be Miss Beattie's brother. The proceedings were fully covered by the region's television stations. Currie telephoned the Northern Ireland Civil Rights Association, formed in Belfast the previous year, to propose a march from Coalisland to Dungannon to draw attention to the misallocation of public housing. On 24 August some 2,500 covered the five miles between the two towns without incident until at the outskirts of Dungannon the marchers found around four hundred police with dogs barring the way. The leaders persuaded the civil rights supporters to content themselves with a public meeting in front of the cordon.

Soon after the march, Eamonn McCann and Eamonn Melaugh of the Derry Housing Action Committee asked that the next civil rights demonstration be held in their city. The date fixed was 5 October 1968: a new phase in the province's history was about to begin.

IO

THE TROUBLES
1968–1996

Only about four hundred demonstrators turned up at Waterside station for the civil rights march to the centre of Derry on 5 October 1968. William Craig, the home affairs minister, had imposed a ban the day before. Fitt arrived with three Westminster MPs, brought directly from the Labour Party Conference then in session. When the march seemed prepared to move off, RUC County Inspector William Meharg warned the demonstrators that he could not allow a march in 'this part of the Maiden City'. In Duke Street, McAteer, Currie and Fitt were struck by batons, Fitt so badly that he was taken, with blood streaming from his head, to an ambulance. Marchers behind sat down and attempted an impromptu meeting only to be assaulted by constables from both ends of the street. As parties of police chased after fleeing demonstrators, water cannon arrived to spray not only marchers but also bystanders and an Ulster Television crew filming from a flat. Later, Catholic youths from the Bogside, almost none of whom had taken part in the march, thrust their way into The Diamond and fought a running battle with the police and more violent disorder erupted the following afternoon and evening.

Derry, 5 October 1968, brought the Northern Ireland problem to the attention of the world.
BELFAST TELEGRAPH

A few hundred feet of film, captured by Radio Telefís Éireann cameraman Gay O'Brien, changed the course of Ulster's history. Images of unrestrained police batoning unarmed demonstrators, including MPs, 'without justification or excuse' as the Cameron Commission judged later, flashed across the world. The British media was convinced that a reactionary regime had been caught in the act of suppressing free speech within the United Kingdom. At a stroke the television coverage of the events of 5 October 1968 destabilised Northern Ireland, and as the sectarian dragon was fully reawakened, the region was plunged into a near-revolutionary crisis, characterised by bitter

The RUC confronts the civil rights marchers in Derry, 5 October 1968
BELFAST TELEGRAPH

intercommunal conflict and protracted violence and destruction.

'WHAT KIND OF ULSTER DO YOU WANT?'

During most of October and November Northern Ireland was in ferment. On Monday 7 October over three thousand students and some academic staff attempted to march from Queen's University to Belfast City Hall only to be redirected by the police when Paisley held a counter-demonstration on their route. The students formed a movement called the People's Democracy to seek 'one man, one vote; fair boundaries; houses on need; jobs on merit; free speech; repeal of the Special Powers Act'. The Civil Rights Association burgeoned as branches sprang up across the region. Excitement was intense in Derry, where a major campaign of civil disobedience was launched and where almost twenty thousand citizens marched on 16 November 1968 in defiance of a ban on all 'non-traditional' parades.

The mounting crisis forced Harold Wilson's administration to confront the region's problems, perhaps for the first time. O'Neill, Craig and Faulkner were summoned to Downing Street and there a package of reforms was insisted on. A five-point programme was announced by O'Neill on 22 November: Londonderry Corporation was to be replaced by an appointed commission; local councils were to adopt a fair points system of housing allocation; sections of the Special Powers Act would be repealed; an ombudsman would investigate grievances; and universal suffrage in local government elections would be considered. In just forty-eight days since 5 October 1968 the Catholic minority had won more political concessions than it had over the previous forty-seven years.

The juggernaut of the mass civil rights movement could not be halted at once by O'Neill's announcement. After ugly scenes in Armagh on 30 November, when Paisley and his followers occupied the city centre to block five thousand civil rights marchers, Captain O'Neill decided to appeal directly to the people by making a television broadcast on 9 December. The prime minister began with the words 'Ulster stands at the crossroads', and asked:

> What kind of Ulster do you want? A happy respected province . . . or a place continually torn apart by riots and demonstrations, and regarded by the rest of Britain as a political outcast?

To the civil rights leaders he said: 'Your voice has been heard, and clearly heard. Your duty now is to take the heat out of the situation.' O'Neill's impassioned appeal was heard and all further street protests were called off. Northern Ireland was at peace, but only a few days into the new year action taken by the People's Democracy and its opponents bleakly demonstrated how ephemeral that peace was to be.

Just before 9 a.m. on New Year's Day, 1969, around forty young people gathered beside Belfast City Hall ready to walk seventy-five miles from there to Derry. Their purpose, Bernadette Devlin explained afterwards, 'was to break the truce, to relaunch the civil rights movement as a mass movement and to show people that O'Neill was, in fact, offering them nothing'. And so the fateful decision was made: much of the route would be through Protestant territory and already, as the marchers set out, about seventy loyalists pulled at their banners and hurled invective. Dangerous confrontation was avoided only by rerouting until on the third day the People's Democracy and their supporters were led into an ambush on the Derry–Claudy road: stones and bottles cascaded down; in and around Burntollet Bridge men swarmed down, armed with crowbars, chair legs, lead piping and other weapons; and police offered little protection, some mingling with attackers in a friendly way. The attack was unrelenting though the marchers did not resist and those still on their feet were subjected to showers of stones and bottles as they entered Derry. Then as darkness fell police discipline collapsed: twenty constables burst into Wellworth's supermarket, smashed glass counters and batoned customers; and a large Reserve RUC force invaded the Bogside, threw bricks through windows, smashed down doors, pelted people with stones and sang sectarian songs into the early hours of Sunday morning.

Northern Ireland had been given a vicious push towards the precipice. The real prospect of peace held out by the truce now vanished. The march had inflamed sectarian passions to a level not seen since 1922. Roads leading into the Catholic districts in Derry were barricaded; the moratorium on street

demonstrations was ended; and on 11 January a civil rights march in Newry quickly went out of control. With increasing desperation, O'Neill attempted to steer a middle course. Craig and Faulkner turned against him and on 3 February twelve Unionist MPs at Portadown called for his resignation. O'Neill called a general election for 24 February; he did rather well in the circumstances but he failed to get an overwhelming mandate for his reform programme and evidence of substantial Catholic support. Militants gained control of the civil rights movement which seemed to seek confrontation, retaliation from the police, and the destabilisation of the region. The final push was given by a series of explosions which, O'Neill wrote later, 'quite literally blew me out of office'. Between 30 March and 25 April water pipelines and electrical installations were damaged by bombs. The RUC announced that the bombings 'were caused by people working to an IRA plan', and believing this to be true, O'Neill mobilised one thousand B Specials and ordered all police officers other than those on traffic duties to carry arms. In fact the bombs had been planted by extreme loyalists intent on implicating militant republicans, as the police proved later in the year. This plot succeeded perfectly: convinced that the civil rights protests were turning into a terrorist campaign, several Unionist MPs threatened to desert O'Neill and join his critics; and on 28 April the prime minister resigned. 'I have tried to break the chains of ancient hatreds,' O'Neill said that evening on television and the *Sunday Times* Insight Team made its own grim assessment:

> The monster of sectarian violence is well out of its cage. The issue now is no
> longer Civil Rights or even houses and jobs. The issue is now whether the state

should exist and who should have the power, and how it should be defended; and this is an issue on which the wild men on both sides have sworn for 40 years, frequently in blood, that they will never back down.

DERRY AND BELFAST, AUGUST 1969

O'Neill was replaced neither by the man who had done most to pull him down, William Craig, nor by Brian Faulkner, the man who could have done most to save him. The Unionist Party chose a safe, compromise candidate, Major James Chichester-Clark. Militant civil rights activists continued to protest on the streets and this led to protracted rioting in Belfast as the summer marching season approached. Intense violence over the Twelfth led to mounting anxiety about the Apprentice Boys parade in Derry in August. John Hume was considered unduly alarmist by the Home Office when he travelled to London to request a ban. With memories of the police invasion after Burntollet still fresh in their minds, the people of the Bogside prepared for a siege and, as arsenals of petrol bombs were made ready, the main roads into the district were barricaded with scaffolding, paving stones, planks and furniture.

Major James Chichester-Clark, prime minister of Northern Ireland, April 1969 to March 1971
HMSO (DEPARTMENT OF THE ENVIRONMENT, NORTHERN IRELAND)

On Tuesday 12 August 1969 fifteen thousand Apprentice Boys came into Derry from all over Northern Ireland for the annual celebration of their ancestors' defiance in 1689. Towards the end of the day as the parade wound past the perimeter of the Bogside loyalist supporters on the walls threw down some pennies on the Catholics below, and Harold Jackson, reporting for the *Guardian*, saw a middle-aged Catholic fire a marble from a catapult. In moments an intense battle developed. Police tried to take down a barricade in Rossville Street: this not only convinced Catholics that their homes were about to be attacked but also created a gap through which Protestants now surged. From the high roof of the Rossville Flats, between fifteen and twenty youths threw down a deadly rain of petrol bombs and the advance was halted. Again and again police vainly attempted to break their way into the Bogside. Radio messages being passed between units registered their frustration:

> Green Two: We are getting it fierce tight here but we'll have to win this war.
> Black Five: We're on fire! . . . They are right on top of us . . .
> Green One: You are on fire! Consolidate. Consolidate what you have there
>   . . . can we get more foot people in there? Over . . . come on armour!
>   Come on armour!

Sometime after midnight the first canisters of CS gas were fired, driving back the rioters for a time; but the wind blew the gas back towards the police. By mid-morning next day the fighting in Derry had become general and intense. Then the taoiseach, Jack Lynch, made a broadcast declaring that 'the Irish

Troops of the 2nd Battalion Grenadier Guards march up Duncreggan Road in Derry on 16 August 1969: forty-eight hours earlier they were on guard duty at Buckingham Palace.
BELFAST TELEGRAPH

Government can no longer stand by and see innocent people injured and perhaps worse', and, as the RUC was 'no longer accepted as an impartial force', he called for a United Nations peacekeeping force. Reunification was, he believed, the only long-term solution. Lynch's broadcast did nothing to calm the violence and the conflict raged on all through a second night. The following day, Home Secretary James Callaghan said at Westminster that troops had been sent into Derry, adding: 'This is a limited operation.' At 4.15 p.m., 14 August, eighty men of the Prince of Wales Own Regiment set out for Derry's Waterloo Place and replaced the RUC. Eddie McAteer spoke to people who had just been in combat with the police and successfully urged them to welcome the troops.

The Battle of the Bogside was over and an uncertain calm settled on the city of Derry. Violence, meanwhile, had spread elsewhere and was about to reach a fearful climax in Belfast.

In response to a Civil Rights Association appeal to take pressure off the Bogside by stretching police resources, Catholics duly rioted in provincial towns across the region. Trouble flared up in Belfast, too, and on Thursday 14 August tension steadily increased in several parts of the city. News came in that a civilian, John Gallagher, had been shot dead when B Specials fired into a crowd in Armagh – the first violent death of the new Troubles. Protestants were angry that whole areas had apparently slipped out of government control, while Catholics were exultant that the regime so many of them loathed was

A man and woman moving some furniture out of Divis Street, Belfast, August 1969; 1,820 families fled their homes in the city during that month, 1,505 of them Catholic.
BELFAST TELEGRAPH

now thrown on the defensive. Fear was at its most intense along the Falls–Shankill divide. Those most in peril lived in one narrow, mixed area – Cupar Street and its vicinity – where the two territories met. That evening as Protestants were gathering under the direction of John McKeague on the Shankill Road, Catholic youths assembled in strength in front of Divis Flats.

As darkness fell police and Special constables on foot attempted to close in from the side streets, and behind them the Protestants mobilised. Suddenly shots rang out, from which side it will never be known for certain. Within minutes gunfire became general. Police armoured cars fired bursts of heavy-calibre bullets from their Browning machine guns, fitted as a desperate measure earlier in the day; many shots hit Divis Flats and a nine-year-old boy was killed as he took refuge in a back room. Protestants surged down the narrow streets interconnecting the Shankill and the Falls, tossing petrol bombs as they went, and as they emerged into Divis Street the mobs clashed repeatedly. There was evidence later that fully armed B Specials had lent their support to the loyalist incursion. Fierce fighting also erupted at Ardoyne. During that night 6 people had been killed in Belfast; at least 12 factories had been destroyed; and over 100 houses had been wrecked and another 300 damaged by petrol bombs. Huge barricades sprang up, particularly in the Falls.

Troops arrived during the afternoon of 15 August. Watching a great pall of smoke rising from a burning mill, one officer thought it all looked like a Second World War newsreel. Residents on the Falls Road, preferring soldiers to armed police, plied them with cups of tea. Not enough troops had been brought in, however, to prevent further violence that night: virtually all the houses in Bombay Street in Clonard were destroyed and a Protestant rioter was killed in Ardoyne. The violence in July and August had resulted in 10 deaths in the region; 154 people suffering gunshot wounds; 745 injured in other ways; 16 factories gutted by fire; 170 homes destroyed; 24 Catholic-owned public houses left in ruins; and in Derry one dairy losing 43,000 milk bottles during the three-day battle in the Bogside. In Belfast alone 1,820 families fled their homes, 1,505 of them Catholic.

Except for the middle-class suburbs, Belfast had become a war zone. By sending troops for active duty in Northern Ireland, the Westminster government had made one of its most crucial military decisions since Suez.

'WHAT A BLOODY AWFUL COUNTRY'

Troops newly arrived in Belfast, August 1969. Divis Tower stands in the background.
BELFAST TELEGRAPH

'The honeymoon period between troops and local people is likely to be short lived. Indeed, it is probably at its height right now.' The GOC, Lieutenant-General Sir Ian Freeland, gave this warning before television cameras soon after his men had moved into Belfast. Martial law, however, had not been declared – it was up to the politicians to decide what to do next. Accustomed to insulating itself from Northern Ireland's domestic problems, London was ill-prepared for the crisis that had broken in the summer of 1969. No serious

thought seems to have been given to invoking the 1920 Government of Ireland Act and restoring the functions of Stormont to Westminster. Callaghan toured the troubled parts of Belfast and Derry towards the end of August and was rapturously received in the Bogside. The home secretary's jaunty, avuncular tone exuded optimism and confidence, but in private he had forebodings about the future, as Richard Crossman, a member of Wilson's government, noted in his diary on 11 September: Callaghan said to him that

> life was very bleak . . . there was no prospect of a solution . . . and the terrible thing was that the only solutions would take ten years, if they would ever work at all.

Callaghan had been more successful in pleasing Catholics than Protestants. The Cameron report, the most authoritative condemnation of discrimination written up to then, was published on 12 September. Loyalist apprehension sharply increased when Lord Hunt's recommendations that the police be disarmed and the Special Constabulary be disbanded and replaced by the Ulster Defence Regiment were made public on Friday 10 October. In a conflict which almost matched 14 August in intensity, Protestants in the Shankill fought the security forces the following night: Constable Victor Arbuckle and two rioters were killed. However, as the year 1969 drew to a close the region was peaceful.

On 29 December 1969 the *Irish Press* reported a split within the IRA, in

A bus continues to burn after rioting on the Crumlin Road, Belfast, 1969

BELFAST TELEGRAPH

which dissidents had broken with the leadership and set up a new command: the Provisional IRA was born. In Belfast fewer than sixty men regarded themselves as IRA members at the beginning of the year and the RUC Special Branch reported that 'the present condition in the streets has caught the IRA largely unprepared in the military sense . . . Reliable sources report a shortage of arms.' In Dublin Cathal Goulding had been steering the movement towards quasi-Marxist political activity and away from violence. Conservative traditionalists, particularly in Belfast, had no liking for this sophisticated radicalism. After the violence of August angry residents in Ardoyne had demanded guns for their defence and castigated the IRA as the 'I Ran Away'. A coup split the movement in December; the breakaway group elected a provisional executive just before Christmas, with the British-born hardliner Seán Mac Stiofáin as chief of staff and the veteran Ruairí Ó Brádaigh as president of Provisional Sinn Féin, its political counterpart.

The Provisionals swiftly established themselves in Catholic housing estates in Belfast, though for the present the old organisation – now known as the Official IRA – kept its hold in the lower Falls and in the Markets. Meanwhile, the Dublin government, though now determined to stay out of the North's imbroglio, had arranged for Irish Army field hospitals and refugee camps to be set up along the border and had established a fund of £100,000, principally to help Catholics driven out of their homes. More than £30,000 vanished to import arms for the Provisional IRA. Dismissed from the government, Neil Blaney and Charles Haughey were charged in May 1970 with conspiracy to smuggle arms. Blaney, the North East Donegal TD who had pressed hard in cabinet to send the Irish Army across the border, was discharged in July and a jury found Haughey not guilty in October. Controversy still rages over the extent to which the Fianna Fáil government was embroiled, but there is no doubt that southern money played a crucial role in putting the Provisionals on their feet. Irish-Americans also supplied cash and arms, including Armalite rifles, capable, when folded, of being carried about in breakfast cereal packets.

During the first few months of 1970 the Provisionals operated with caution, knowing that the great majority of Catholics still welcomed the presence of British troops. If anything, loyalists conflicted more frequently with the soldiers. 'Grown men! Pathetic! Ridiculous!' Freeland once remarked on seeing traditional Orange parades, and as the marching season came round, brushes with troops occurred regularly. His pleas, and those of Sir Arthur Young, to ban all marches were ignored by Stormont. Towards the end of June, however, Provisionals killed four Protestants during an army operation in east Belfast. Then on 3 July, acting on information that there was a cache of arms at 24 Balkan Street, Freeland imposed a thirty-five-hour curfew on the lower Falls, and set his men on a rigorous house-to-house search. The Official IRA now joined the war against the British Army and when its volunteers began shooting, troops fired 1,500 rounds and killed 3 people. Another person was crushed to death by an armoured car. Though over a hundred weapons were found, the curfew was a political blunder, as the *Sunday Times* Insight Team concluded:

> 3–5 July 1970 did convert what was perhaps only an increasingly sullen Catholic acceptance of the Army into outright communal hostility . . . In the months that followed, recruitment to the Provisionals was dizzily fast . . .

That summer the Provisionals launched a bombing campaign and by mid-September there had been a hundred explosions, damaging a telephone exchange, electricity substations and public houses. These were merely a foretaste of what was to come.

The Westminster general election of June 1970 not only gave Paisley a new audience in London but also put the Conservatives in office, with Edward Heath as prime minister and Reginald Maudling as home secretary. Heath's government had no better notion than its Labour predecessor what should be done with Northern Ireland. Maudling was distinctly ill at ease in carrying out his Northern Ireland duties, as a senior army officer recalled:

> Reggie Maudling had no idea. He would never go out. We would get people to meet him and he would wander round and say things like 'Are you going to Ascot?'

He is infamous for the remark he made on his flight back to London after his first visit on 1 July, one version of which runs: 'For God's sake bring me a large Scotch. What a bloody awful country.'

Troops were having little success in curbing the activities of the Official and the Provisional IRA and were failing to win the support of the loyalist militants. As the violence continued to grow the Unionist government demanded more draconian measures, but without success. Chichester-Clark resigned in protest on 20 March 1971 and three days later, Brian Faulkner achieved his long-sought ambition by being elected prime minister. The most articulate of all Northern Ireland premiers, Faulkner had an air of professionalism which seemed to promise that the Government could curb the escalating violence.

That hope was not realised. By 7 May 1971 there had been 136 gelignite explosions since the beginning of the year; in March the Provisional IRA had lured three Royal Highland fusiliers to their deaths; and incidents were steadily becoming more vicious. Once again the approach of the marching season raised political temperatures and, while the tempo of the Provisional IRA bombings increased, rioting broke out all over Northern Ireland in July. On Saturday 7 August, after a van driver had been shot dead and his passenger beaten by soldiers when his vehicle backfired

Brian Faulkner, the last prime minister of Northern Ireland
HMSO (DEPARTMENT OF THE ENVIRONMENT, NORTHERN IRELAND)

outside Springfield Road command post, rioting erupted over much of west
Belfast; and as the fighting spread to Ardoyne on Sunday 8 August, one soldier
was shot dead and six others were injured by gunfire. Next morning
internment was imposed.

INTERNMENT AND DIRECT RULE

Just after 4 a.m. on Monday 9 August 1971 thousands of soldiers across
Northern Ireland set out in arrest squads, each accompanied by an RUC Special
Branch officer to identify suspects. Altogether 342 men were seized and taken
to holding centres; the operation was completed by 7.30 a.m. and, after two
days, 104 men were released and the remainder of the suspects were transferred
either to Crumlin Road gaol or the *Maidstone*, a prison ship moored at Belfast
docks.

Terrible violence followed. Rioting, shooting and burning continued almost
without ceasing. In Belfast, while a pall of smoke hung over the city from
barricades of burning buses, trucks and cars, the Provisional IRA presented
some of their best-known leaders at a secret press conference. Police
intelligence was clearly out of date and the army, which had advised Faulkner
not to take this drastic step, simply lacked the necessary information.
Internment was entirely one-sided. No attempt was made to arrest loyalist
suspects despite the UVF's record of violence. There was not a single person on
the army's list of 452 names who was not an anti-partitionist, and not one of
them was a leading member of the Provisional IRA. Heath had allowed
Faulkner to make his gamble and it had failed.

Tuesday 10 August 1971 was the most violent since August 1969: 11 people
were killed in Belfast alone, including Father Hugh Mullan, shot while
administering the last rites to an injured man in Ballymurphy; about 240
houses in Ardoyne were destroyed by fire; a member of the UDR was shot dead;
and Derry experienced protracted rioting as more than 30 barricades were put
up. As violence intensified, fear spread like a plague. In three weeks more than
one in every hundred families in Belfast were forced by destruction of homes
and intimidation to move: this was the biggest enforced movement of
population in Europe since 1945. Catholic fury, maintained by continuing
arrests, was inflamed further by reports, later authenticated, of the ill-treatment
of suspects.

Angered by the Provisional IRA's ability to wage its bloody and destructive
campaign, loyalists demanded stronger measures and in September the Ulster
Defence Association was formed as a paramilitary organisation in Protestant
working-class districts. The Provisionals lashed out against internment with a
ruthless offensive. Every night the city reverberated to sharp sounds of rifle and
automatic fire, and even in the suburbs windows rattled with the shock wave

of explosions. The violence showed no sign of abating as 1971 drew to a close: over the four months since internment 73 civilians, 30 soldiers and 11 policemen had lost their lives. The explosion in McGurk's public house in Belfast on 4 December killed fifteen people and rescue operations were hampered as nearby the army came under fire and rival crowds fought in the darkness. The bomb had been placed by loyalist paramilitaries. On 11 December an explosion at a Shankill Road furniture store, placed by republican paramilitaries, killed two children and two adults; the surgeon who certified the deaths of the children recalled the scene in the mortuary: 'I remember standing there with two policemen. And we cried our eyes out.' The prospects for 1972 looked bleak indeed.

On Sunday 30 January 1972 at least fifteen thousand people, in defiance of a government ban, marched in protest against internment from the Creggan estate and the Bogside into the centre of Derry. As the army sealed off the approach to the Guildhall, youths pelted the soldiers at the army's barricade with a continuous rain of missiles. Then troops of the 1st Battalion the Parachute Regiment went in and the killing began: the soldiers fired

Bloody Sunday, 30 January 1972: soldiers rounding up suspects after thirteen men and boys had been shot dead by paratroopers
BELFAST TELEGRAPH

108 rounds, injuring thirteen and killing thirteen men, seven of them under nineteen years of age. Lord Widgery, who headed the official inquiry, concluded that some of the shooting 'had bordered on the reckless'. The Derry coroner, Hubert O'Neill, noted that many of the victims were shot in the back and made this condemnation at the close of the official inquest:

> It strikes me that the Army ran amok that day . . . I say it without reservation – it was sheer unadulterated murder.

The Catholics of Derry and people all over Ireland had already come to the same conclusion. On 2 February thirty thousand people in Dublin marched to the British Embassy and burned it down. Militant republican atrocities intensified and Ulster Vanguard, a new loyalist pressure group, assembled some seventy thousand in Belfast's Ormeau Park on 18 March, where its leader, William Craig, declared that 'when the politicians fail us, it may be our job to liquidate the enemy'.

On 24 March Faulkner and his ministers were summoned to London, where Heath bluntly told them of his plans to transfer control of security to Westminster, to appoint a Northern Ireland secretary of state and to end internment. The Unionist ministers were outraged and resigned. The British prime minister thereupon prorogued Stormont for a year and appointed William Whitelaw as secretary of state. For just over fifty years Northern Ireland had been a self-governing part of the United Kingdom but now the British government found Unionist rule wanting. Heath suspended Stormont, but the twelve months of direct rule from Westminster extended to two decades and more as peace eluded Conservative and Labour governments alike.

The parliament of Northern Ireland met for the last time on Tuesday 28 March 1972, as a huge column of loyalists with their bands converged on the majestic drive before Stormont. This was the second day of a protest strike that was interrupting power supplies, closing down businesses and stopping public transport all over the region. Tempestuous cheers greeted Faulkner and Craig when they appeared together on the balcony of the parliament buildings. After Faulkner had urged dignified protest, the immense throng of some one hundred thousand – a tenth of Northern Ireland's Protestant population – dispersed with banners and Ulster flags flying.

Whitelaw had already arrived to face the most intractable problems with energy, great charm and seemingly inexhaustible patience. He planned to restrain the army, phase out internment, stop the violence and end Catholic no-go areas, where republican paramilitaries seemed in control. In addition to this daunting programme, he had to put in place a new government structure and prepare a fresh constitutional arrangement for the region. During that spring the Provisionals' campaign gathered devastating momentum, while loyalist murder gangs roamed the streets with the intention of killing Catholics. The Official IRA did announce a ceasefire on 29 May but a carefully negotiated truce called by the Provisionals on 26 June broke down on 9 July. A new onslaught by the Provisional IRA reached a horrific climax on Friday 21 July 1972: that afternoon twenty bombs were detonated in Belfast in sixty-five minutes. Nine people were killed and at least 130 maimed; only the hard-won experience of the city's hospitals prevented the death toll rising higher than it did. The Dublin newspaper the *Sunday Independent* made this judgement:

> There is a black sin in the face of Irish Republicanism today that will never be erased. Murder now lies at the feet of the Irish nation and there is no gainsaying that fact.

After Bloody Friday the wave of horror and disgust running through Catholic Ireland, north and south, offered Whitelaw the unique opportunity to implement a plan long-prepared by army chiefs: Operation Motorman.

For thirty-six hours during Saturday 29 and Sunday 30 July 1972 huge C130 transport aircraft touched down at Aldergrove every five minutes. From them, seven additional battalions with their support units climbed out to bring

Oxford Street bus station, Belfast, on Bloody Friday, 21 July 1972
BELFAST TELEGRAPH

the army's strength in Northern Ireland to twenty-two thousand, the highest since 1922. The biggest British military operation since the 1956 Suez crisis was about to begin. At first light on Monday 31 July troops in Derry surrounded the Bogside and the Creggan estate and Catholic enclaves in Belfast soon after. The army was careful to tear down barricades in Protestant no-go areas as well. Operation Motorman was an untrammelled success and this time the troops prepared to stay for some time: in Andersonstown and the surrounding area, for example, there were no fewer than sixteen fortified army posts and work began on four large forts, soon given names such as 'Silver City' and 'Fort Apache' by local people – loyalists, in turn, described the occupied enclaves as 'Apache country'. No longer able to store explosives, patrol with firearms or prime bombs with such impunity as before, the Provisionals had suffered a severe military reverse and constitutional politicians were encouraged to move towards a unique compromise experiment: a power-sharing devolutionary government.

The Social Democratic and Labour Party, formed in 1970 to replace the Nationalists as the principal voice of the Catholic minority, for more than a year kept to its position of 'no talks while internment lasts'. Agreeably surprised by a British government discussion paper, however, the party began ne-gotiations in the autumn of 1972. Then in March 1973 new constitutional arrangements were published. Northern Ireland was to have an assembly with legislative powers on two conditions: power had to be shared between Protestant and Catholic representatives; and arrangements had to be made for a Council of Ireland, linking Belfast, London and Dublin on matters of common interest. The bipartisan approach at Westminster, by which government and opposition co-operated to adopt a common policy on Northern Ireland, ensured that this constitutional package rapidly became law.

Whitelaw's hope that the cross-community parties would do well in the assembly elections on 28 June was completely dashed: out of a total of seventy-eight seats the Alliance Party, dedicated to reconciliation, captured eight and the Northern Ireland Labour Party only one. Unionists of various parties opposed to power-sharing numbered twenty-six, leaving Official Unionists under Faulkner's leadership with twenty-four seats. Whitelaw seized on the good performance of the SDLP, which had nineteen members elected, as an opportunity to isolate IRA activists in the minority community. In doing so, the secretary of state gravely underestimated the strength and determination of those assembly deputies who were hostile to his constitutional solution.

When Whitelaw appeared on the steps of Stormont Castle on Wednesday 21 November 1973, journalists saw tears of emotion welling up in his eyes. After ten hours of continuous negotiation, his patient diplomacy had been crowned with success. The eleven members of the government-designate – six Unionist ministers, four SDLP and one Alliance – appeared for a photo call the following day. Faulkner, the man who had introduced internment, was to be chief executive, and his deputy was to be Gerry Fitt, who had started his political career as a republican socialist and was now leader of the SDLP. On 2 December, in an act of startling insensitivity, Heath reassigned Whitelaw and appointed Francis Pym secretary of state. It gave an inauspicious start to the tripartite talks beginning on 6 December at Sunningdale, the civil service staff college in Berkshire.

The Irish government, a Fine Gael–Labour coalition elected earlier in the year, was represented at Sunningdale by the uncharismatic taoiseach Liam Cosgrove; the tireless and articulate foreign affairs minister, Garret FitzGerald; and the most prominent Labour member, Conor Cruise O'Brien, an internationally respected intellectual heavyweight who was to ruffle many a nationalist feather by warning of the dire consequences of ignoring loyalist susceptibilities. The loyalist opposition in the assembly had not been invited to the talks and this strengthened the demand of the SDLP, and of John Hume in particular, that the Council of Ireland be invested with real executive powers to bring north and south closer together. Alone of the republic's representatives, Cruise O'Brien felt that Dublin should be content to settle for the 'miracle' of power-sharing without pressing for a strong Council of Ireland. It took fifty hours' negotiation over four days to reach agreement, announced on Sunday 9 December, but as the Unionist and Alliance delegates flew back to Belfast they were not at all convinced that they could persuade enough Protestants to accept the settlement to make it work. The following day the main loyalist paramilitary groups announced the formation of an Ulster Army Council to resist a Council of Ireland. The Provisional IRA signalled its view by detonating three bombs in London on 18 December, injuring sixty-three people, and another three explosions followed there two days

An arms search in the Markets, Belfast, in April 1974
BELFAST TELEGRAPH

later. The death toll for 1973 in Northern Ireland was 171 civilians, 58 soldiers and 21 police and UDR men, and there were few signs that the Northern Ireland executive, formally installed on New Year's Eve, would be able to ensure that 1974 would be the 'year of reconciliation'.

The hammer blow fell when Heath called a general election for 28 February. Loyalist parties opposed to the December settlement formed a common front named the United Ulster Unionist Council. With the powerful slogan 'Dublin

is just a Sunningdale away', the loyalist pact candidates won 11 of Northern
Ireland's 12 Westminster seats. Unionists who stayed loyal to Faulkner failed to
win a single seat and only Fitt retained his seat for the SDLP. The February
election was in effect a referendum on the Sunningdale Agreement, now
rejected by 51 per cent of the electorate. The same election swept the Conservatives out of office and the new Labour prime minister, Harold Wilson,
appointed Merlyn Rees secretary of state. Constantly required in London
because of Labour's slender majority, Rees had little time to master the
intricacies of the fast-changing political scene in Northern Ireland. Loyalist
politicians could come to no agreement on how best to topple the executive
and in the end their hands were forced by a group of Protestant workers calling
themselves the Ulster Workers' Council.

'WHO DO THESE PEOPLE THINK THEY ARE?': THE UWC STRIKE, MAY 1974

On Tuesday 14 May 1974 the assembly passed an amendment expressing faith
in power-sharing by forty-four votes to twenty-eight. At 6.08 p.m. representatives of the UWC informed journalists at Stormont that a strike would
begin in protest against ratification of the Sunningdale Agreement. At first the
loyalist strike seemed to fail: by 9 a.m. on Wednesday the roads were still open
and most firms reported that 90 per cent of their employees had turned up for
work. That morning at the Vanguard headquarters in Hawthornden Road in
suburban east Belfast the UWC sought the help of the city's UDA, led by Andy
Tyrie. Squads of UDA men and loyalist youths known as Tartans called on
businesses all over Belfast. Robert Fisk, a reporter for *The Times*, recalled that
he 'found that some of the local shopkeepers had closed down so quickly that
they had forgotten to change the 'Open' signs on their front doors . . . by
midday, intimidation was beginning to reach epic proportions'.

At Larne masked UDA men in camouflage jackets prevented the ferry from
sailing and toured the streets carrying wooden clubs to close down shops, and
the town was sealed off with barricades constructed of hijacked vehicles. That
afternoon much of Northern Ireland experienced four-hour power cuts and
three quarters of Derry was without electricity. The strike slowly gained
momentum during the rest of the week. On Friday 17 May car bombs,
probably driven in and planted by the UVF, had exploded without warning in
Monaghan, killing 5, and in central Dublin, where 22 people died and at least
another 100 were injured, the death toll in the city eventually reached 32. 'I
am very happy about the bombings in Dublin,' said Sammy Smyth of the UWC.
'There is a war with the Free State and now we are laughing at them.'

By Saturday 18 May Northern Ireland was experiencing blackouts lasting up
to six hours at a time and dairies and bakeries had been forced to shut down.
On Sunday night the UWC ordered the erection of almost one hundred road

blocks to encircle central Belfast. Lieutenant-General Sir Frank King, GOC Northern Ireland, now had 17,500 soldiers in the region under his command; he was convinced, nevertheless, that the strike was too extensive to be broken by the number of men he had at his disposal. The prime minister, however, was becoming convinced of the need for army intervention of some kind, seemingly signalled by his notorious broadcast on Saturday 25 May which included a denunciation of

> people who spend their lives sponging on Westminster and British democracy and then systematically assault democratic methods. Who do these people think they are?

Nell McCafferty was in Derry with her mother, a Catholic, during the broadcast:

> 'What?' my mother sat up. 'Spongers? Is he calling us "spongers"? In the name of God . . . is he telling us we're spongers?' She made for the radio.

This self-indulgent speech rallied Protestant feeling behind the strikers more than ever. The UDA and UWC fully expected dramatic action on the scale of Operation Motorman. In the event, army intervention was limited to a takeover of fuel supplies and the distribution of petrol from a limited number of stations. In response the UWC ordered a reduction in electricity to 10 per cent of capacity and a withdrawal of workers in essential services. Then at 1.20 p.m. on Monday 27 May Faulkner resigned and a loyalist demonstration at Stormont became a massive victory rally. That night flames leaped up from bonfires in Protestant districts to celebrate the end of one of the most successful general strikes in Europe since 1945.

POLITICAL STALEMATE AND PARAMILITARY VIOLENCE

During fifteen days a self-appointed junta in league with loyalist paramilitaries had made an entire region of the United Kingdom ungovernable. Having wrecked Whitelaw's handiwork, the loyalists concluded that they had the power to destroy any political arrangement made by the British government which did not suit them. Successive Westminster administrations attempted thereafter to square the circle of meeting some nationalist aspirations without completely alienating the unionists at the same time. The failure of these efforts led to a protracted political stalemate.

At Westminster there was all-party backing for legislation to extend direct rule, to wind up the assembly and to have elections for a Constitutional Convention. The elections, held on 1 May 1975, returned 47 Unionists opposed to power-sharing from a total of 78 seats. In November the intransigents endorsed a convention report recommending a return to majority rule. Eventually in the spring of 1976 the Labour government lost

Loyalist celebratory march, headed by Ian Paisley, 1 June 1974: the Ulster Workers' Council strike of May 1974 forced the resignation of chief executive Brian Faulkner and the collapse of the power-sharing administration.
BELFAST TELEGRAPH

patience and wound up the constitutional discussions.

Constitutional initiatives made little impression on the Provisional IRA. The British showed no sign of getting out of Northern Ireland and for this reason the Provisionals took their campaign of violence to Britain – the hope was that public opinion there, already showing growing support for a 'troops out' movement, would become so exasperated that withdrawal would become a major issue. Over the spring and summer of 1973 incendiaries and bombs were detonated in London and the Midlands. On 4 February 1974 the Provisionals denied planting explosives on a coach carrying army families, which blew up on the M62, killing 9 soldiers, a woman and 2 children. Other horrific incidents followed in the autumn: on 5 October 2 soldiers and 3 civilians were killed and 54 people were injured by 'no-warning' bombs in 2 public houses in Guildford, Surrey; a civilian and a soldier were left dead, and 20 people injured, when a public house in Woolwich was bombed on 7 November; and on 21 November bombs detonated in 2 Birmingham public houses killed 21 people and injured more than 180 others. A fresh Provisional

IRA offensive in England was launched during the autumn of 1975 but it fell far short of its objectives. Scotland Yard scored a notable success when, after a siege of 138 hours, 4 Provisional IRA activists cornered in a block of flats in Balcombe Street in London gave themselves up on 12 December.

In Northern Ireland the annual toll of deaths from political violence had been rising since 1974, when 216 had been killed. The death toll for 1975 was 217 civilians, 14 soldiers and 16 RUC and UDR members. That year had been characterised by 'tit-for-tat' sectarian killings and murders arising from paramilitary feuding. Cold-blooded slaughter continued in 1976: violence had become a way of life, particularly in congested working-class districts characterised by poor job opportunities and high levels of deprivation. Large parts of Belfast and Derry remained under the control of paramilitaries and gangs. Extortion and protection racketeering were operating on such a vast scale that the police hardly dared to estimate the annual cost to the community. Those who broke the paramilitary code were brutally beaten, shot in the knee or 'executed'. In such circumstances and with so many weapons of death available, horrific murders were all too possible. In 1976 there were 121 sectarian killings, many of them perpetrated by a gang of UVF murderers known as the Shankill Butchers. Christopher Ewart-Biggs, appointed British ambassador to the Irish Republic in 1976, was killed together with Judith Cooke, a Stormont civil servant, when a land mine placed by the Provisionals exploded under his car on the outskirts of Dublin on 21 July. Jane Ewart-Biggs in her grief did not turn against the Irish but, as Garret FitzGerald observed, 'instead she took to her heart the country that had deprived her of her husband, and has worked ever since for reconciliation'. Very shortly afterwards, indeed, she was deeply involved in a new movement to attempt to end the violence: the Peace People.

On Tuesday 10 August 1976 Anne Maguire and her four children were walking near their home in south Belfast when a wounded gunman's getaway car crashed into them. Mrs Maguire was badly injured, two of her children were killed and a third child died the following day. Next day her sister, Mairead Corrigan, and Betty Williams, who had witnessed the tragedy, founded the Peace People. This new movement captured the imagination of people to an extent that others previously had not. Twenty thousand attended a peace rally in Belfast's Ormeau Park on 21 August; a similar number marched up the Shankill Road a week later; and some twenty-five thousand gathered for a Peace People rally in Derry on 4 September. In the following weeks peace demonstrations were held all over Northern Ireland, in many places south of the border, and in London. However, in such a deeply divided society, embittered by nearly seven years of violence, the Peace People found it difficult to sustain widespread support.

In September 1976 the ever-anxious Rees was replaced by the bombastic

and pugnacious Roy Mason, who theatrically affected the style of a paternalistic colonial governor. In fact the contrast between Rees and Mason was largely one of style. Rees had already abandoned hope of a constitutional arrangement acceptable to London and Dublin, and had authorised more vigorous action by the security forces. During the latter part of 1976 and throughout 1977 there was a dramatic drop in incidents of political violence: at the end of the year Mason told the *Daily Express*: 'We are squeezing the terrorists like rolling up a toothpaste tube.' His triumphalist utterances were premature: the Provisionals launched a new bombing campaign in December, the worst atrocity being the explosion at La Mon House near Belfast on 17 February 1978 when twelve people died and twenty-three were horribly injured.

Mason came under severe criticism in the Bennett report of March 1979 for permitting interrogators at Castlereagh police headquarters to treat suspects in an inhumane way. Fitt withdrew his support in the Commons in protest and a fortnight later James Callaghan, prime minister since April 1976, lost a motion of no confidence by one vote. In the general election of May 1979 the Conservatives were swept to power. For the next eleven years direct rule would continue under the supervision of just one prime minister.

Margaret Thatcher had bought some Galway cut glass in Belfast on one of her celebrated 'shop-abouts' in 1977. It was a small but significant gaffe: she could have chosen a piece made by Tyrone Crystal, a successful firm created by cross-community action in Dungannon. Clearly she had much to learn about the Irish imbroglio. A succession of atrocities was to hasten her political education. Airey Neave, expected to be appointed the next Northern Ireland secretary of state, was murdered by a bomb in his car at Westminster, the day Callaghan had called a general election. Then the south Armagh commando unit of the Provisional IRA carried out two operations on Monday 27 August, making it the bloodiest day of 1979. During that morning at Mullaghmore in County Sligo a radio-triggered

27 August – 'the bloodiest day of 1979': the IRA bomb blasted Lord Mountbatten's boat *Shadow* at Mullaghmore, County Sligo, killing him and three other people on board
BELFAST TELEGRAPH

bomb on board a boat killed Earl Mountbatten, his grandson Nicholas, aged fourteen, Paul Maxwell, aged fifteen, and Dowager Lady Brabourne. Other members of the unit, using a model aircraft radio control device, detonated two explosions near Warrenpoint, leaving eighteen soldiers dead.

Two days later the prime minister flew into Northern Ireland to view the situation for herself. She resisted army demands for more aggressive tactics: while reinforcing her reputation for intransigence in other spheres, she was nevertheless showing greater flexibility than before in her treatment of the

Two IRA bombs killed eighteen soldiers at Warrenpoint, County Down – the biggest death toll in a single incident in ten years of violence
BELFAST TELEGRAPH

Northern Ireland problem. In part this was due to the value she placed on the 'special relationship' between Britain and the United States; for example, in August 1979 the American State Department caused much alarm by suspending the sale of handguns to the RUC. Charles Haughey had become taoiseach in December 1979 and, though he was still tainted with the 1970s arms scandal, Margaret Thatcher went to see him in Dublin on 8 December 1980 – the first visit to the city by a British premier since partition. The conference appeared to be a diplomatic triumph and a joint communiqué announced another meeting to consider 'the totality of relationships within these islands'. A few months later, however, relations between Dublin and London had cooled almost to freezing point as a result of a new grave crisis: the hunger strike in the Maze prison.

THE H–BLOCK HUNGER STRIKE

Whitelaw had granted internees special category status in prison but in 1976 this had been withdrawn for those convicted of terrorist offences and henceforth the new inmates were put into a complex of eight single-storey brick units whose shape led them to be named H-blocks. Mason would not yield to the demand for political status, so prisoners made a 'blanket protest' by refusing to wear prison uniforms and then resorted to a 'dirty protest' – following brawls with warders in 1978 over the emptying of chamber pots, prisoners smeared their excrement over their cell walls. Finally Bobby Sands, former leader of the Provisional IRA active service unit in Twinbrook, began a hunger strike on 1 March 1981 against the advice of the Provisional IRA army council. Sands replied to an army council appeal to hold back in a 'comm' – a secret communication written on toilet paper and generally hidden in the rectum or beneath the foreskin:

> Comrade, find enclosed confirmation of hunger strike. We need that hunger strike statement that fast comrade. The delay is damaging us . . . We accept the tragic consequences that most certainly awaits us . . .

Humphrey Atkins, the secretary of state, refused concessions and admiration for Sands grew rapidly in the Catholic community. There was intense international attention when, on 9 April and the fortieth consecutive day that he had refused food, Sands was returned in a by-election as MP for Fermanagh–South Tyrone. The European Commission of Human Rights condemned 'the inflexible approach of the State authorities'; visits were made to the Maze by members of the Dáil and Monsignor John Magee, Pope John Paul II's secretary; but neither the secretary of state nor the republican prisoners would give way. Then, at 1.17 a.m. on Tuesday 5 May 1981, Sands died on the sixty-sixth day of his hunger strike.

The American government issued a statement expressing deep regret. In

Belgium students invaded the British consulate at Ghent and in Paris thousands marched behind a portrait of Sands, chanting 'The IRA will conquer.' On the day of the funeral at least one hundred thousand people – nearly one fifth of the entire Catholic population of Northern Ireland – crowded the route from St Luke's Church in Twinbrook to Milltown cemetery. The hunger strike went on. Francis Hughes died on 12 May; Raymond McCreesh and Patsy O'Hara on 21 May; Joe McDonnell on 8 July; Martin Hurson on 13 July; Kevin Lynch on 1 August; Kieran Doherty on 2 August; Tom McElwee on 8 August; and Mickey Devine on 20 August. Riots reminiscent of those a decade earlier erupted after every death and meanwhile the Provisionals stepped up their relentless war on the security forces.

Father Denis Faul, the Dungannon priest best known for his documentation of army and police brutality, did more than anyone else to break the deadlock. Towards the end of July he persuaded relatives of some of the hunger strikers to call on Gerry Adams, vice president of Sinn Féin, to end the protest. By 9 September five hunger strikers were being given medical attention at the request of their families. Five days later James Prior, who had acquired a reputation as a patient negotiator, replaced Atkins as secretary of state. On 17 September Prior visited the Maze and Lord Gowrie, the prisons minister, spoke to the hunger strikers for three hours. Concessions were hinted at, and on 3 October 1981 the Provisional IRA called off the hunger strike. During 217 days of protest, 10 prisoners had starved themselves to death and 61 people had been killed, 30 of them members of the security forces. The Foreign

Office privately held the view that the handling of the whole affair had been an unmitigated diplomatic disaster, which was to add to Britain's difficulties during the Falklands War. The concessions granted would have ended the hunger strike in the initial stages, even though formal recognition of political status was not given. Meanwhile, the Provisionals were discovering the new attractions of the ballot box.

BALLOT BOX, ARMALITE, ROLLING DEVOLUTION, NEW IRELAND FORUM

On 1 November 1981 Sinn Féin met for its annual conference, or *ard fheis*, in Dublin's Mansion House. There Danny Morrison, the party's director of publicity, asked rhetorically:

> Who here really believes that we can win the war through the ballot box? But will anyone here object if with a ballot box in this hand and an Armalite in this hand we take power in Ireland?

The delegates did not object and endorsed the movement's new strategy of contesting elections while at the same time continuing its campaign of violence. The standing of the Provisionals in Catholic enclaves had risen spectacularly during and after the hunger strike. In August 1981 Owen Carron, election agent for Sands, won Fermanagh–South Tyrone. Then, in the Westminster general election of June 1983, Fitt was defeated by Gerry Adams in West Belfast and altogether 13.4 per cent of the electorate voted for Sinn Féin candidates. Margaret Thatcher's new government faced the real possibility that the SDLP would be supplanted as the principal representative of Northern Ireland's Catholic minority. It was the electoral success of Sinn Féin that helped to concentrate minds in both London and Dublin. Prior's scheme for 'rolling devolution' and the election of another assembly, which the SDLP refused to attend, solved nothing. The first step in breaking the deadlock was the meeting of a multi-party conference in May 1983: the New Ireland Forum.

Garret FitzGerald described himself as a 'revolving-door Taoiseach' in these years, leading a coalition for short spells and facing Fianna Fáil administrations under Haughey during others. He revolved back into office early in 1983 with a comfortable majority. Now was his opportunity to seek a way out of the impasse: 'I had come to the conclusion,' he wrote later, 'that I must now give priority to heading off the growth of support for the IRA in Northern Ireland by seeking a new understanding with the British government.' He began by implementing Hume's proposal for a forum 'where all constitutional politicians committed to a new Ireland would together define what we really wish this new Ireland to be'. On 30 May the New Ireland Forum held its inaugural meeting in Dublin Castle, where FitzGerald declared:

We represent a powerful collective rejection of murder, bombing and all the other cruelties that are being inflicted . . . the future of this island will be built by the ballot box, and by the ballot box alone.

It was essentially a conference representing 90 per cent of nationalists on the island. After almost a year of discussions, the forum issued a report of its findings at the beginning of May 1984. It offered three options: 'a unitary state, achieved by agreement and consent'; a federal arrangement; and a joint-authority solution under which 'the London and Dublin governments would have equal responsibility for all aspects of the government of Northern Ireland', giving 'equal validity to the two traditions in Northern Ireland'.

The forum discussions were of little more than academic interest unless the British government could be persuaded to listen. FitzGerald had met Margaret Thatcher at Chequers in November 1983; there the taoiseach reminded her that a further rise in support for Sinn Féin would undermine constitutional politics, with grave consequences for both the republic and Britain. The prime minister was clearly moved by his arguments. The Anglo-Irish Inter-governmental Council, set up in November 1981, met regularly from November 1983 onwards and Sir Robert Armstrong, secretary to the cabinet, came to Dublin in March 1984 to begin informal talks with the Irish government, talks which became formal a year later.

Then, at 2.54 a.m. on Friday 12 October 1984, the last day of the Conservative Party annual conference, a bomb planted by the Provisional IRA in the Grand Hotel in Brighton exploded killing five people and horribly wounding many others. The Provisionals regretted their failure to kill the prime minister: 'Today we were unlucky, but remember, we have only to be lucky once.'

The Grand Hotel, Brighton, after the IRA bomb of 1984
PRESS ASSOCIATION

Margaret Thatcher refused to allow this cruel attack to divert her from the developing formal talks between the London and Dublin governments. Both premiers felt compelled to come to agreement because there was not the slightest indication of political compromise in Northern Ireland. Paralysis was ensured by a double veto: the SDLP, looking over its shoulder at Sinn Féin, refused to consider devolved government without the 'Irish Dimension' being given a place of prominence; and the Official Unionists and the Democratic Unionist Party, competing with each other to be the authentic voice of loyalism, refused to accept power-sharing or any concessions to the republic. Of the two standpoints, the Conservative government seemed to find the loyalist one the more exasperating. Unionist complacency was reinforced by Attlee's guarantee and Northern Ireland Protestants were almost completely unprepared for the historic settlement, made without any consultation with them or their representatives, due to be signed by FitzGerald and Thatcher in Hillsborough Castle on 15 November 1985.

THE 1985 ANGLO–IRISH AGREEMENT AND AFTER

An angry loyalist demonstration outside the castle gates the previous evening seemed to justify the massive security operation when helicopters flew in the two premiers and their ministers from Aldergrove to Hillsborough. FitzGerald began with a statement intended to reassure unionists that 'any change in the status of Northern Ireland would only come about with the consent of the majority of the people in Northern Ireland'.

The 1985 Anglo-Irish Agreement's most striking innovation was the Intergovernmental Conference, headed by the secretary of state and the Irish foreign minister, which would meet regularly to promote cross-border co-operation and deal with security, legal and political matters; it was to be serviced by a permanent secretariat of northern and southern civil servants, which had already been set up at Maryfield just outside Holywood. Article 4 stated that both governments supported devolution but only on condition that there was agreement on power-sharing. The agreement won enthusiastic praise from the British press and it was no surprise that Sinn Féin described the agreement as a 'disaster' which copper-fastened partition. With the sole exception of the Alliance Party, the agreement was unacceptable to all sections of unionist opinion. Protestants were appalled that Dublin would have a say in the affairs of a region they regarded as being irretrievably British. In 1912 the loyalists of Ulster could count on the support of a great body of British opinion in their resistance to Home Rule. Now they felt more isolated and friendless than at any time in centuries.

'This is the battle of the loyalist people of the whole of Ulster.' Applause thundered round Belfast City Hall as Paisley spoke these words and seized the

hand of Jim Molyneux, the Official Unionist leader, to symbolise the reunification of Unionist parties making common cause in resistance to the agreement. The number of loyalists who had gathered to make their protest on Saturday 23 November 1985 was immense: two hundred thousand or possibly even more. 'IRON LADY be warned. Your iron WILL MELT from the HEAT OF ULSTER,' one placard proclaimed and thousands of others carried the message 'ULSTER SAYS NO'. Loyalist leaders, however, faced the challenge of sustaining morale and of preventing protest from becoming violent or from dissipating itself in uncoordinated action. The obstacles lying in the path of unionist opposition were formidable: this time no regional institution had been constructed which would have been capable of being torn down by loyalist resistance and the operation of the Intergovernmental Conference could not be wrecked by Unionist non-cooperation. Before the end of the year the accord was formally registered as an international treaty with the United Nations. There was no doubting the historic importance of the agreement: for the first time since the partition of 1920–1 a Westminster government had unequivocally recognised that the republic had a part to play in the governing of Northern Ireland.

Years of loyalist protest failed to dislodge the accord. Days of direct action – notably on 11 December 1985 and 3 March 1986 – risked alienating middle-class support because they brought with them conflict with the police and damage to property. The first anniversary of the Anglo-Irish Agreement was marked by a huge demonstration at Belfast City Hall on Saturday

ULSTER SAYS NO: a massive number of loyalists totally opposed to the Anglo-Irish Agreement, which gave Dublin a say in the affairs of Northern Ireland, campaigned outside Belfast City Hall on 23 November 1985. IRELAND'S SATURDAY NIGHT

Unionists, from both the DUP and the UUP, taking their petition to Buckingham Palace demanding a referendum on the Anglo-Irish Agreement in February 1987: *left to right*: Ken Maginnis, Cecil Walker, Martin Smyth, Ian Paisley, William McCrea, Peter Robinson, James Molyneaux, James Kilfedder, Harold McCusker, William Ross and John Taylor
PACEMAKER

15 November 1986 but the protest was marred by violence and disorder, during which some seventy shops were looted or damaged. In any case, there was growing evidence that the Anglo-Irish accord was producing the beneficial result desired by both Dublin and London: a decline in the support for Sinn Féin and the IRA.

In the republic's general election of 19 February 1987 Sinn Féin put up twenty-seven candidates in twenty-four multi-member constituencies and fought a vigorous campaign. The result was unmitigated humiliation – not one seat was captured and the party received a mere 1.85 per cent of total votes cast. The British general election on 11 June 1987 delivered another hammer blow to the republican movement: the only comfort was the re-election of Adams for West Belfast; the Sinn Féin share of the vote, 13.4 per cent in 1983, dropped to 11.4 per cent; and the SDLP returned three members to Westminster. The Provisionals did not abandon electoral politics but they felt justified in concentrating their energies in the field where they had most experience: the campaign of death and destruction.

Along with many others, Gordon Wilson and his twenty-year-old daughter Marie gathered at the war memorial in Enniskillen on Sunday 8 November 1987 for the annual wreath-laying. Just before 11 a.m., when the ceremony was about to begin, a bomb exploded behind them. The three-storey gable end of St Michael's Reading Rooms crashed down. Buried beneath several feet of rubble, his shoulder dislocated, Gordon Wilson attempted to find his glasses.

His daughter lay buried beside him:

> She held my hand tightly, and gripped me as hard as she could. She said, 'Daddy, I love you very much.' Those were her exact words to me, and those were the last words I ever heard her say.

Altogether eleven people were killed and sixty-three injured, nineteen of them very seriously. Marie Wilson died in hospital and her father that evening gave an interview to Mike Gaston for the BBC. He described in a tone of quiet anguish his last conversation with Marie as they lay beneath the rubble, and he went on to say:

The aftermath of the Remembrance Day bomb at the Cenotaph in Enniskillen, County Fermanagh, November 1987
PACEMAKER

> But I bear no ill will. I bear no grudge. Dirty sort of talk is not going to bring her back to life. She was a great wee lassie. She loved her profession. She was a pet. She's dead. She's in Heaven and we'll meet again. Don't ask me, please, for a purpose. I don't have a purpose. I don't have an answer. But I know there has to be a plan. If I didn't think that, I would commit suicide. It's part of a greater plan, and God is good. And we shall meet again.

No words uttered in more than twenty-five years of violence in Northern Ireland have had such a powerful, emotional impact. In a few sentences he had spoken for all the bereaved and injured, and over the next few days millions across the world were to share his grief.

President Reagan expressed his 'revulsion'; Pope John Paul II told of his 'profound shock'; the Soviet news agency TASS described the bombing as 'barbaric'; and Taoiseach Charles Haughey condemned 'this criminal act of carnage'. In Dublin thousands signed a book of condolences and, on the following Sunday, a minute's silence was observed across the republic and a memorial service in Dublin's St Patrick's Cathedral was televised nationwide. In the Dáil fresh legislation to expedite the extradition of terrorists was pushed through. This, together with closer co-operation north and south of the border in the drive against the Provisionals, seemed to indicate that the Anglo-Irish Agreement was yielding practical results. The accord remained firmly in place, but over the next two years a succession of crises and revelations strained relations between London and Dublin.

On Sunday 6 March 1988 Mairead Farrell, Sean Savage and Daniel McCann were shot dead in Gibraltar. All three were Provisionals intent on car-bombing a parade of the Royal Anglian Regiment due to take place forty-eight hours later. At first public reaction was profound relief that a bloody outrage had been averted by the swift response of an SAS team. Soon after, there was deep disquiet when it emerged that the Provisionals had no bomb in Gibraltar, and that they were unarmed. Clearly the SAS gave them no opportunity to surrender and was determined to kill them outright. To many this incident confirmed the conviction that the Government was pursuing a 'shoot-to-kill' policy against the Provisional IRA, without the sanction of parliament. Then, as a major diplomatic row developed between London and Dublin, the scene swung back dramatically to Northern Ireland.

Michael Stone in the act of killing three men at the funeral of Mairead Farrell, Sean Savage and Daniel McCann, who were shot dead by the SAS in Gibralter on 6 March 1988
PACEMAKER

The bodies of the three Provisionals were flown to Dublin and taken north in a cortège. Great numbers of sympathisers were present at the funerals in Belfast's Milltown cemetery on Wednesday 16 March. Suddenly Michael Stone, a lone loyalist who had infiltrated the crowd, threw three home-made hand grenades and fired shots killing three people and injuring several others

before being overpowered by the police. One of those killed was Kevin Brady, a Provisional IRA activist; his funeral on 19 March in Andersonstown was an occasion when feelings were running high. Two army corporals in civilian clothes strayed into the gathering mourners in a car; a furious crowd closed in and dragged the men away; and later the corporals were stripped, beaten and shot dead.

The Gibraltar killings and the violent episodes ensuing in Belfast came at a time of mounting disquiet in Dublin about the operation of British justice and security policies in Northern Ireland. Southern anxieties arose from incidents long predating the Anglo-Irish Agreement. The first was on 11 November 1982 when three unarmed members of the Provisional IRA were shot dead by police at a checkpoint outside Lurgan. After other incidents which seemed to show that the Government had adopted a shoot-to-kill policy, John Stalker, the deputy chief constable of Greater Manchester, was appointed to conduct an inquiry. From the moment he arrived in Belfast in May 1984 Stalker was sure he was being obstructed by senior officers in the RUC and, following open disagreement with the RUC chief constable, Sir John Hermon, Stalker was removed on 5 June 1986. The Dublin government was appalled, particularly when the attorney-general, Sir Patrick Mayhew, announced in January 1988 that eleven police officers investigated both by Stalker and his successor would not be prosecuted for reasons of 'national security'. Yet signs of strain between Dublin and London actually pointed up the practical value of the Anglo-Irish Agreement. Communications were kept open and co-operation on security measures was both maintained and strengthened.

The weight of responsibility for governing Northern Ireland remained with the Westminster government and this seemed likely to continue for a long time to come. Counter-insurgency measures still were the principal source of anxiety in London, but as a charge on the public purse, they were dwarfed by the costs of propping up the region's ever-weakening economy.

'MORE MONEY FOR THESE PEOPLE?': THE ECONOMY AND THE SUBVENTION

The UWC strike of 1974 succeeded only because the great majority of adult male Protestants were in work and were confident that their jobs were secure. That confidence was misplaced: the region had become more dependent on cheap oil than any other part of the United Kingdom and the blow delivered by the international quadrupling of energy prices, therefore, was acutely felt. The rapid growth of synthetic fibre production had been Northern Ireland's best success story, accounting for one third of the United Kingdom's output by 1973. The industry was concentrated in the Protestant heartland of south County Antrim and, for example, provided nearly three quarters of all manufacturing jobs in Carrickfergus. Now Northern Ireland suffered more than any other part of the United Kingdom: many firms were pushed towards the edge by the sudden rise in transport costs, as well as the leap in the price of electricity, nearly all of it generated in Northern Ireland from imported oil.

Then in 1979 the economy of the western world took a downward plunge and by the second quarter of 1980 this depression was leaving a trail of devastation in Northern Ireland. Between 1979 and the autumn of 1981 no fewer than 110 substantial manufacturing firms in the region closed down. When Grundig finally shut the doors of its prestigious Dunmurry plant in 1980, one of the reasons given by the management for doing so was the existence of 'disturbances of a political nature'. Generous inducements notwithstanding, the continuing violence frightened off overseas investment. It was not violence, however, that was mainly responsible for turning economic decline into a crisis. This depression, the worst since the 1930s, was precipitated by another leap in oil prices and in Northern Ireland this sealed the fate of most of the remaining synthetic fibre plants. The region's fragile economic base was in danger of cracking apart and nothing demonstrated this more than the foundering of the Government's flagship project, the De Lorean sports car factory in Dunmurry in May 1982. In the same year Goodyear closed its Craigavon factory with the loss of 773 jobs. Altogether forty thousand manufacturing jobs disappeared in the decade between 1979 and 1989. This protracted shake-out removed most of the branch factories of British and overseas multinationals, thus leaving the industrial sector once again dominated by the older indigenous firms.

The linen industry's decline had been steep since 1959 when forty-four mills across Northern Ireland had kept forty-five thousand in employment. By 1983 only 6,000 were employed, but thereafter the industry retained a significant, if precarious, niche in a specialised international market. Harland and Wolff, making losses every year since 1964, was saved from closure only when the Stormont government took shares and wrote off losses in 1971. The erection of two great cranes, Goliath and Samson, and the launch of several supertankers gave every indication that all was well but the company's position became desperate with the market collapse in 1974 and it obtained £350 million from the exchequer between 1977 and 1986. In the early 1980s Short Brothers bypassed Harland and Wolff to become Ulster's biggest manufacturing concern. The most profitable division manufactured armaments; most employees, however, were engaged in making small civil aircraft. Official statistics generally placed both Harland and Wolff and Short Brothers in the private sector but both were wholly owned by the Government and utterly dependent on massive subventions from the exchequer. Then in 1989 the Government privatised both companies, which cost the taxpayer £1,486 million.

'More money for these people?' Margaret Thatcher said to Garret FitzGerald when he suggested seeking European contributions for the International Fund for Ireland. 'Why should they have more money? I need that money for my people in England.' In fact she drew back from the consequences of applying undiluted Thatcherism to Northern Ireland, and Ian Aitken, writing in the *Guardian* on 26 July 1989, referred to the region as 'the Independent Keynesian Republic of Northern Ireland, where monetarism remains unknown'. Exceptional efforts to attract new investment brought paltry returns in the harsh economic climate of the 1990s and Northern Ireland had all but ceased to be a manufacturing region. Its economy had in effect become a service economy: the public sector gross domestic product had risen to 44 per cent of the whole by 1986 – a development only made possible by the British subvention, money transferred by Westminster over and above the sum raised in taxation in Northern Ireland, which reached £4 billion by 1993.

The bulk of the subvention was spent neither on direct aid to industry nor on the security forces. The overwhelming share was assigned to the public services and the most visible sign of this expenditure was the transformation of the region's public housing – not only a vital stimulus to the economy but also a major attempt to ease intercommunal tensions.

By the time that republican and loyalist paramilitaries had called their ceasefires in the autumn of 1994 there were thirteen 'peace lines' in Belfast, their location decided on by the security forces and the Northern Ireland Office. The earliest one to be put up was at Cupar Street, a grim and formidable barrier of concrete reminiscent of the Berlin Wall marking the volatile divide between the Protestant Shankill and the Catholic Falls. Later

A Belfast 'peace line': a grim reminder of a divided community
IRISH NEWS

barriers, made of curving brick walls surrounded with shrubs, were almost architecturally pleasing. The peace lines were a visible sign that housing a divided community presented exceptional problems requiring exceptional measures.

In August 1969 the Westminster and Stormont governments agreed to strip all control of public housing away from local councils and transfer it to a regional authority, the Northern Ireland Housing Executive. Then, in 1973, twenty-six district councils replaced the former complex local authority structure, their functions drastically limited by comparison with their predecessors and their counterparts in England, Scotland and Wales. Intimidation, intercommunal violence and enforced population movement ensured that the most urgent task was to attend to the housing needs of the people. By 1976 the total number of houses in Belfast destroyed or damaged in the violence reached 25,000. The Housing Executive began its task, in the words of a government minister, as 'the largest slum landlord in Europe'. A House Condition Survey of 1974 revealed the scale of the problem. In Northern Ireland as a whole 19.6 per cent of the total dwelling stock was statutorily unfit, compared with 7.3 per cent in England and Wales.

Having created a great bureaucratic machine, the governments in Westminster showed a growing reluctance to pay for the new dwellings the region so desperately needed. It was not until 1981, when the political situation seemed especially bleak, that the Government made housing its first social priority. By the mid-1980s the Housing Executive was able to spend around £100 million a year on its capital programme. Between 1982 and 1991 it had spent £2.4 billion on new dwellings, maintenance, grants and renovation. Houses were allocated with scrupulous impartiality, a task made acutely difficult because the continuing Troubles caused both Protestants and Catholics to seek safety in numbers: for example, Catholics clustered in older housing in west and north Belfast, creating intense pressure there.

Nevertheless, the vigorous drive to upgrade Northern Ireland's housing may have contributed significantly to the notable fall in levels of violence in the region in the 1980s by comparison with the 1970s. By the early 1990s it could be said that Northern Ireland's housing crisis was over, though the sale of council houses, the rundown of the Housing Executive and the rise of housing associations meant the partial abandonment of earlier commitments to make dwellings available on the criterion of need.

Better housing, though it did much to banish rioting from the streets, did not encourage Catholics and Protestants to live more closely together; indeed, by the middle 1990s, 90 per cent of people living in 90 per cent of electoral wards were of one religious persuasion. Northern Ireland's society was as polarised as ever, in part a consequence of protracted violence which escalated at the beginning of the century's last decade.

AN UPSURGE IN VIOLENCE, 1988–92

After twenty years of troubles the Provisional IRA had become the most experienced terrorists in Europe, conducting their ruthless campaign on several fronts. Eight soldiers were killed in Tyrone when an unmarked military bus was blown off the road midway between Ballygawley and Omagh on 20 August 1988, bringing the total of soldiers killed so far that year to twenty-one. Locally recruited members of the RUC and UDR were increasingly pushed into the front line and they suffered accordingly. Towards the end of 1990 the Provisionals deployed a new form of attack – the 'human' or 'proxy' bomb. While his family was held hostage in Derry, Patsy Gillespie was forced to drive into the Buncrana Road checkpoint, and there the bomb in his van killed him, together with five soldiers on 24 October 1990. Several members of the security forces stationed in Germany, and two Australians on holiday, were murdered on the European mainland between 1988 and 1990. In Britain eleven young bandsmen were killed on 22 September 1989 by a bomb detonated at the Royal Marines School of Music at Deal in Kent. The Conservative MP for Eastbourne, Ian Gow, was murdered on 30 July 1990. The overturning of the convictions of those imprisoned for the Guildford and Birmingham bombings of 1974, which seriously discredited British justice, was

20 August 1988: eight British soldiers were killed when their bus was bombed at Ballygawley, County Tyrone.
PACEMAKER

a propaganda coup for the Provisionals in their principal killing field: Northern Ireland.

'They really ought to know after all these years that we are not going to be pushed around by terrorist acts,' Prime Minister John Major declared on 22 February 1991 during a visit to Northern Ireland, severely curtailed by the demands of the Gulf War. Both the Provisionals and militant loyalist groups had been increasing the tempo of violence since the beginning of the year. For several years republicans had been responsible for most violent deaths in Northern Ireland, but, particularly in the early 1990s, the UVF and the Ulster Freedom Fighters (a cover name of the UDA) reaped as bloody a harvest, targeting known members of Sinn Féin when possible but continuing also to kill Catholics at random as before. Between January and November 1991 loyalist paramilitaries had murdered thirty-nine people. During the first months of 1992, Northern Ireland seemed to be marking the twentieth anniversary of direct rule by sinking back into the violence and sectarian warfare reminiscent of the worst days of the 1970s.

On Friday 17 January 1992 a minibus was bombed at Teebane Cross near Cookstown, in Country Tyrone. The explosion killed eight men and injured six others: all were Protestants, attacked by the Provisionals because their employer carried out work for the security forces. In direct retaliation two

men of the UFF burst into Sean Graham's betting shop on the Ormeau Road in south Belfast on 5 February and fired indiscriminately, killing five Catholics and wounding seven more. This brought the overall total of victims since 1969 to 2,969. Sectarian 'tit-for-tat' murders throughout 1991 demonstrated how widespread was the threat to ordinary people going about their business. In the same period the Provisionals wreaked much devastation in Belfast, Lurgan and elsewhere with bombs of ever-increasing size. On 10 April 1992, the day after Gerry Adams lost his West Belfast seat in the Westminster general election, a bomb containing 100 pounds of Semtex blew up inside London's financial 'square mile'. Three people, including fifteen-year-old Danielle Carter, were killed; seventy-five others were injured; the Baltic Exchange and the Chamber of Shipping were damaged beyond repair; and the total cost of the destruction was estimated at several hundred million pounds. Sir Patrick Mayhew was appointed secretary of state in the re-elected Conservative government: when he reopened interparty talks on 29 April at

Orangemen passing Sean Graham's betting shop on Belfast's Ormeau Road, where two UFF gunmen killed five Catholics in February 1992
IRISH NEWS

Stormont he said there was a 'strength of feeling' in Northern Ireland that the political impasse must be brought to an end. Few can have doubted, however, that London would still be coping with western Europe's longest-running conflict since 1945 well after the destruction in its financial heart had been fully repaired.

SEARCHING FOR PEACE

There seemed to be grounds for optimism when Ulster Unionist politicians sat willingly round a table at Stormont with representatives of the Dublin government in July 1992, at a time of traditionally heightened tension during the marching season. Then, for the first time since 1922, the Ulster Unionist Party met for talks at Dublin Castle in September. Republicans, now without a parliamentary representative since Gerry Adams had lost his seat to Dr Joe Hendron of the SDLP in the general election, seemed ever more determined, however, to pursue their objectives by violence. For the second time in 1992 Bedford Street in Belfast was severely damaged by bombs on 2 August; on 23 September a 2,000-pound bomb destroyed the Northern Ireland forensic science laboratories at Belvoir in south Belfast, injuring twenty people and damaging seven hundred homes; the main street of Bangor was bombed on 21 October; on 13 November a massive van bomb devastated the commercial heart of Coleraine; and further damage was inflicted on shopping areas of Belfast on 1 December.

Little of value emerged from the talks and the prospects for the future looked ever bleaker as loyalist paramilitaries countered with their own terror. In revenge for the IRA attack on Coleraine, the UFF shot dead three Catholics, including a seventy-two-year-old RAF veteran, in a betting shop in north Belfast on 14 November. 'We again warn Sinn Féin and PIRA that the theatre of war will be full of casualties from the republican community in the coming weeks,' the UFF declared afterwards in a statement made to the BBC. At the end of the year the UFF widened the scope of its threat to include the 'pan-nationalist front' of the IRA, the SDLP and the Irish government, warning that it was 'fully armed and equipped' to intensify its campaign in 1993 'to a ferocity never imagined'.

The year 1993 was indeed marked by ferocity and atrocities perpetrated by both sides. The IRA once more carried its campaign to Britain. Two bombs placed in litter bins in a shopping area of Warrington on 20 March killed Jonathan Ball, aged three, and twelve-year-old Timothy Parry, and injured fifty-six other people. The wave of revulsion and peace demonstrations which ensued failed to deter the militants and on 24 April damage estimated at close to £1 billion was inflicted on London's financial district by an explosion at Bishopsgate. Loyalist paramilitaries killed Sinn Féin activists, launched attacks on the homes of SDLP members and, in reprisal for Warrington, shot dead four Catholic workmen at Castlerock, County Londonderry. Gordon Wilson asked to meet IRA leaders to seek an end to the violence. It was a disheartening experience, as he recalled:

> I couldn't understand how on the one hand they were telling me that they were fighting the British army and the forces of the Crown and yet they were killing two little boys in Warrington.

'As we face into our twenty-fifth year of unbound and unbroken resistance,' the IRA stated in their Easter message, 'we proclaim our determination not to desist from our efforts until our nation's sovereign right to self-determination is finally recognised.' Such efforts included a 1,000-pound bomb in Glengall Street, Belfast, which inflicted damage of some £6.5 million, much of it to the newly refurbished Grand Opera House, on 20 May; widespread destruction two days later caused by explosions in Portadown and Magherafelt; and the detonation of a 1,500-pound bomb in Newtownards on 5 July.

High Street, Portadown after an IRA bombing, May 1993
IRISH NEWS

The Conservative government in London and the Fianna Fáil–Labour coalition in Dublin applied themselves with renewed vigour to working out a common approach to planning Northern Ireland's political future. It was a task frequently set back by mutual distrust and revelations. In the spring journalists revealed that Hume had been having regular discussions with Adams and the

two men issued a joint statement on 24 April signalling that they were not prepared to go back to past political structures at Stormont and that 'an internal settlement is not a solution because it obviously does not deal with all the relationships at the heart of the problem'. Hume told reporters he did not care 'two balls of roasted snow' about criticism coming from within his own party and from MPs and TDs; he was vilified by Unionists and in many newspapers but he was convinced this way of searching for peace was the right one, though it brought him to the point of nervous and physical collapse. Hume and Adams formally submitted a report to the Dublin government in September.

The positive response of the Taoiseach Albert Reynolds to the Hume –Adams talks incensed Unionists and the UFF almost declared war on all northern Catholics: attacks on the nationalist community would intensify 'while their representatives in the pan-nationalist front negotiate over the heads of the loyalist people'. Reports of gun attacks on Catholics came in almost every day and, on 12 October, the UVF ambushed a van in east Belfast, killing one man and wounding several others; three days later the UFF shot a man dead in north Belfast. Then at lunchtime on Saturday 23 October two Provisionals planted a bomb in Frizzell's fish shop on the Shankill Road. Gina Murray's thirteen-year-old daughter Leanne had just gone in to buy some whelks:

> Suddenly there was this huge bang. We ran screaming for Leanne. We couldn't find her. No one had seen her. There were people lying in the street covered in blood. My little girl was underneath all that rubble. We started clawing at it with our bare hands. I was screaming her name but it was no use. My little daughter was dead.

Altogether nine innocent civilians were killed along with Thomas Begley, one of the bombers. The IRA said the room upstairs was the west Belfast UDA head-quarters. The bomb exploded prematurely but civilian casualties could not in any case have been avoided as the timing device could be set only for a maximum of eleven seconds. Adams said the attack could not be excused but at Begley's funeral he was a pallbearer. 'John Hume, Gerry Adams and the nationalist electorate will pay a heavy, heavy price for today's atrocity,' the UDA warned. On 26 October the UFF shot dead two men and wounded five others in a west Belfast refuse yard; two days

Sinn Féin president Gerry Adams carries Thomas Begley's coffin, one of the bombers killed along with nine civilians at Frizzell's fish shop, Shankill Road, Belfast, in October 1993.
PACEMAKER

later, at Bleary in County Down, two brothers were murdered; and on 30 October seven people were killed in the Rising Sun public house in Greysteel, County Londonderry – two men dressed in boiler suits and balaclavas burst into the bar armed with an AK-47 rifle and a Browning pistol and, after shouting 'trick or treat', fired forty-five shots.

In all, twenty-four people had died violently in just one week. Impressively supported peace rallies followed across the region, organised by the Irish Congress of Trade Unions. Obstacles lying in the way of an agreement between London and Dublin were swiftly removed, a process assisted by the revelation towards the end of November that Major's government, like Reynolds's coalition, had been maintaining 'back channel' contacts with Sinn Féin. Finally, on 15 December 1993, a joint declaration was presented to the public by both premiers from Downing Street. It was a substantial and

complex document: both governments stated that Sinn Féin could take part in talks if the IRA ended its campaign, and Dublin offered immediate participation in a Forum for Peace and Reconciliation on the same condition; Britain declared that it had 'no selfish strategic or economic interest in Northern Ireland'; and unionists were assured that their consent would be needed 'to bring about a united Ireland'.

Alliance and the SDLP welcomed the declaration. Paisley condemned the document without hesitation but in time it was, with reservations, accepted by most Unionists. Sinn Féin's dilemma was that it could not embrace the declaration because not a single line could be interpreted as a British intention to leave Northern Ireland and yet the party had been offered a part in

Downing Street Declaration, 15 December 1995: Prime Minister John Major shakes hands with Irish Foreign Minister Dick Spring on his arrival at Downing Street as Taoiseach Albert Reynolds and Secretary of State Patrick Mayhew look on.
PRESS ASSOCIATION

the political process – if the violence continued, it would be difficult to avoid placing the responsibility firmly on the shoulders of the IRA. Sinn Féin did not reject the declaration but asked for 'clarification'. Major, on a visit to Belfast, brusquely dismissed the request: 'There is a gauntlet down on the table. It is marked peace. It is there for Sinn Féin to pick it up. The onus is on them.'

It was to be May 1994 before the British government provided the elucidation demanded and in the interim the relentless cycle of killings and reprisals continued. The public could see no outward signs that behind the scenes real progress was being made to find ways to end the violence. The Combined Loyalist Military Command, incorporating the UVF and UFF, considered the Downing Street Declaration at a conference in east Belfast in January and, meanwhile, Sinn Féin had begun an elaborate process of consultation and debate on the merits of pursuing a 'totally unarmed strategy'. Even when the IRA called a three-day ceasefire over Easter, loyalist paramilitaries had no faith that republicans would consider peace without victory and continued their campaign of assassination. The IRA, in turn, sought with increasing desperation to hunt down Protestant paramilitary activists.

The tit-for-tat slaughter escalated fear throughout the community in May and June 1994. On 16 June INLA gunmen killed three men in the Shankill, two of them members of the UVF. The following day retaliation followed in Newtownards when a Catholic taxi driver and two Protestants (mistaken for Catholics) were murdered. Then at 10.30 p.m. on Saturday 18 June UVF gunmen burst into a small public house in the County Down village of Loughinisland and fired repeatedly at customers watching the World Cup football match between Ireland and Italy. Six people were killed, including Barney Green aged eighty-seven, the oldest victim of the Troubles. One man described the scene immediately afterwards:

> When I arrived there was utter chaos – people screaming, grown men crying, wives, girlfriends, mothers not knowing whether their sons were in the bar. A man was in there with his son and son-in-law. All he could do was cradle their heads and try and comfort them. The son-in-law died at the scene, his son died on the way to hospital.

More murders and the negative response of Sinn Féin to the British

O'Toole's Bar in Loughinisland, where the UVF killed six men as they watched Ireland play Italy in the World Cup on 18 June 1994

BELFAST TELEGRAPH

Copies of the *Belfast Telegraph*'s historic front page were rushed throughout Northern Ireland, announcing the IRA ceasefire from midnight on 31 August 1994
PACEMAKER

government's 'clarification' at conferences held in Letterkenny, County Donegal, helped to maintain an air of gloom over the summer which marked the twenty-fifth anniversary of troops being put on active service in Northern Ireland. Then, at 11 a.m. on Wednesday 31 August, the media received this statement: 'The IRA have decided that as of midnight, 31 August, there will be a complete cessation of military operations. All our units have been instructed accordingly.' The following morning almost all newspapers carried a photograph of a boy in west Belfast hugging a soldier carrying a rifle. 'Give Peace a Chance' the *Daily Mirror* appealed to its readers on its front page and the *Sun* was in a minority in heading its eight-page supplement on the ceasefire, 'Never Forget, Never Forgive'. 'We must make sure,' John Major said, 'the violence is not ended for one week or a month but that it is permanent.'

'ABJECT AND TRUE REMORSE': THE CEASEFIRES AND AFTER

On 1 September 1994 David McKittrick, one of the most respected reporters on the Northern Ireland conflict, wrote in the *Independent*:

> People did not dance in the streets yesterday . . . Because of all the layers of suspicion, and because this is a zero-sum conflict, the immediate reactions were first to establish that it really is over, and second to work out who won. Unionists and the British government want it carved in tablets of stone that the stoppage really is permanent. The government in Dublin, which is a society dedicated to the culture of celebration, is satisfied already.

Three days before the cessation, the UVF and UFF had responded bitterly to a joint statement issued by Hume and Adams which had called for 'fundamental and thorough-going change, based on the right of the Irish people as a whole to national self-determination': the loyalists declared: 'It is not peace that you are after but surrender . . . We care little of your speculative ceasefire talk and will not respond to it.' Actually the Protestant paramilitaries, guided by the Presbyterian minister Roy Magee, had for months been debating the conditions under which they could halt their campaign. When a detailed consultative process was completed the UDA/UFF, the UVF and the Red Hand Commando met in the Shankill under the umbrella of the Combined Loyalist Military Command and the following day, Thursday 13 October, the leaders called a press conference in north Belfast. Gusty Spence, who had been jailed on a murder charge in the 1960s, read out a long statement which included these arresting words:

> In all sincerity we offer to the loved ones of all innocent victims over the past twenty-five years abject and true remorse. No words of ours will compensate for the intolerable suffering they have undergone during the conflict.

The *Belfast Telegraph* front page on 13 October 1994, the day the loyalist ceasefire was announced
BELFAST TELEGRAPH

For the first time in a quarter of a century Ulster was at peace and, as police cast aside their flak jackets and troops pulled back, the easing of tension was palpable and, for the vast majority, the Christmas of 1994 was the happiest for a very long time. The loyalists had declared their ceasefire to be permanent 'dependent upon the continued cessation of all nationalist/republican violence'. The IRA had not used the word 'permanent' and the British government insisted on the 'decommissioning' of arms before Sinn Féin could take full part in political talks. In March 1995, while in America, Mayhew observed of the IRA: 'It is still in being, still maintains its arsenal, is still recruiting, targeting and training, still seeking funds, still carrying out punishment beatings.' He detailed conditions which would have to be met before Sinn Féin could join all-party talks. In the third condition, soon referred to as 'Washington 3', he spelled out the condition that there should be 'the actual decommissioning of some arms as a tangible confidence-building measure'. Republicans were heartened somewhat by the Framework Document, issued by the London and Dublin governments on 22 February 1995: though the paper made it clear that Northern Ireland would remain part of the United Kingdom and again emphasised the need for unionist consent, it highlighted the role of Dublin and cross-border institutions – indeed most Unionists reacted by saying that Major was operating under a nationalist agenda.

A protracted stalemate ensued and by the summer of 1995 Adams was issuing warnings that the peace process was in peril. Sinn Féin was clearly feeling more isolated by Major's dependence on Ulster Unionist support in the Commons; by the formation of a Fine Gael–Labour–Democratic Left coalition in the spring, with John Bruton, an outspoken critic of militant republicanism, as taoiseach; and by the replacement of Molyneaux as leader of the UUP by the notably more hardline David Trimble. It was not until November that London and Dublin agreed to set up an international body, chaired by the former US Senator George Mitchell, to report on paramilitary arms decommissioning. The need to resolve this issue was made more urgent by the imminent visit to Ireland by President Clinton.

Clinton's visit was certainly the most universally joyful occasion the people of Northern Ireland have experienced in modern times. The president did not put a foot wrong in all that he said before ecstatic crowds in Belfast and Derry. Nor he did confine himself to bland generalisations: 'You must be willing,' he declared, 'to say to those who renounce violence that they are entitled to be part of the democratic process.' It is now evident, however, that the IRA had already decided to end its ceasefire. Mitchell reported on 22 January 1996, recommending that decommissioning should take place during, rather than before, political negotiations. That afternoon, Major, speaking in the Commons, passed over Mitchell's core recommendations and said that 'an elective process' was his preferred option. Both the UUP and the DUP welcomed the prime minister's statement, but nationalists were aghast because an election would result in further delays. Hume accused Major of attempting to 'buy votes to keep himself in power'.

On 9 February 1996 the IRA 'with great reluctance' announced an end to their ceasefire from 6 p.m. At 7 p.m. a massive bomb exploded at Canary Wharf

John Hume, leader of the SDLP and a key player in the peace process: in January 1996 he was outraged when John Major, after the launch of the Mitchell Report, called for elections to be held in Northern Ireland.
PACEMAKER

United States president Bill Clinton gets a rapturous reception at Belfast City Hall on 30 November 1995

BELFAST TELEGRAPH

in London killing two people and injuring sixty others, and inflicting damage valued at hundreds of millions of pounds. The loyalist ceasefire held. David Ervine and Gary McMichael, leaders respectively of the Progressive Unionist Party and the Ulster Democratic Party, called for calm: these two men had emerged as highly articulate spokesmen for political parties originating amongst the Protestant paramilitaries. The IRA continued its campaign across the Irish Sea: arms finds dented its impact but the organisation did succeed in bombing Manchester city centre on 15 June. In practice the ceasefire remained intact within Northern Ireland for the time being but a feeling of gloom spread rapidly throughout the region. The results of the elections to the forum on 30 May saw Sinn Féin, with seventeen seats, gain substantial ground primarily at the expense of the SDLP with twenty-one seats. The summer of 1996 was to show how polarised Northern Ireland had become.

In July 1995 the residents of the Catholic Garvaghy Road had made it plain that they would attempt to stop Orangemen marching by this route from Drumcree church to Portadown town centre. After a standoff, a compromise was brokered by the conciliation service Mediation Network and in July 1996 the police hoped that a similar arrangement could be hammered out. No agreement emerged and on 6 July Sir Hugh Annesley, the chief constable, ordered that the Orange lodge return from Drumcree by the way it had come rather than down the Garvaghy Road. Loyalists were outraged: along a barricade of barbed wire half a mile long police fought a running battle with protesters at Drumcree; in Belfast Protestant youths went on the rampage; and Trimble called on Orangemen across the province to 'muster' at Drumcree. By Monday 8 July huge palls of smoke were rising from burning vehicles in north, south and east Belfast; while hundreds of Orangemen made a protest march down the Donegall Road in the city, the police were pelted with bricks and bottles; Coleraine, Newtownards, Lurgan, Portadown and Belfast International Airport were sealed off by barricades and demonstrators and Michael McGoldrick, a part-time taxi driver, was found shot dead near Lurgan, a victim of sectarian assassination. On Tuesday tens of thousands of Orangemen were converging on Drumcree; two more battalions of soldiers arrived to bring the army strength to 18,500 troops, the highest since 1982; trouble flared up in Belfast again when about 2,500 Orangemen marched from Sandy Row and the Shankill to the city centre; the Shore Road was sealed off by a blazing oil tanker; burning cars blocked York Street and the Ligoniel Road; fire crews were attacked at Dundonald; and sectarian gangs drove Catholics from their homes in north Belfast. By Wednesday, as sporadic violence continued, it seemed that the intention of the loyalist protest was to make Northern Ireland ungovernable: more Catholics were intimidated out of the houses in north Belfast; a policeman's home was bombed in Bangor; youths set fire to a hangar at Ards Flying Club; and rioting raged in east Belfast until the early hours of Thursday morning as shops were destroyed on the Cregagh Road.

That Thursday, 11 July, Annesley turned on its head his original decision to ban the procession return route, explaining that otherwise he could not guarantee that lives would not be lost. Just after midday a senior RUC officer told Garvaghy Road residents making a sit-down protest that they must clear the road immediately. Police used their batons freely and by 12.55 the RUC were in position. The barbed wire barricade was pulled aside and around 1,300 Orangemen marched through to the ominous beat of a single drum. Police officers fired off dozens of plastic bullets at residents throwing rocks and petrol bombs. 'This was a disgrace,' Brian Lennon, a local Jesuit priest, declared immediately afterwards. 'This has taken away all the credibility from the police that they won in recent days with their principled stand.' The church representatives felt duped for they had been kept negotiating long after the chief constable had made his decision; Cardinal Cahal Daly did not hide his anger and stated: 'I, with regret, have to say that I feel betrayed – betrayed by the British Government.' Bruton commented that the decision to allow the march to proceed had been 'precipitate' and a 'mistake'.

Nationalist outrage was intensified by the manner in which 500 troops and police imposed a fifteen-hour curfew on some 2,500 people living on the lower Ormeau Road in Belfast to enable lodges to march from Ballynafeigh. 'Ku Klux Klan – Burn Your Crosses On Your Own Lawn,' one placard proclaimed as the Orangemen marched by at 9.30 a.m. on 12 July – a day during which one hundred thousand people, a tenth of the Protestant population, joined parades across Northern Ireland. Now it was the turn of Catholics to take to the streets. Derry experienced the worst night of rioting ever seen in the city, during which twenty vehicles were hijacked and set alight, business premises were destroyed, twenty-two people were treated for serous injuries and a thirty-one-year-old man, Dermot McShane, was killed by an army vehicle in the Strand Road. There was trouble, too, in Dungiven, Strabane, Coalisland, Newry, Keady, Newtownbutler, and in Belfast, where shots were fired at New Barnsley police station. Then, just after midnight on Sunday 14 July, the Killyhevlin Hotel near Enniskillen was wrecked by a 1,200-pound bomb, thought to be the work of a splinter republican group.

Passions continued to run high for the remainder of the 1996 marching season. Mayhew ordered troops to seal off the section of Derry's walls which overlooked the Bogside during the Apprentice Boys' parade on Saturday 10 August, a weekend during which republicans also marked the twenty-fifth anniversary of the introduction of internment. There was some rioting in Derry and a standoff at Bellaghy but most people expressed relief that widespread violence had been averted.

The night sky illuminated by fireworks and arc lights at the confrontation point outside Drumcree church, July 1996
BELFAST TELEGRAPH

'THE WARRE OF IRELAND SHALLE NEVER HAVE ENDE'?

Until the end of the 1980s there was a widespread tendency to regard the Ulster 'problem' as being a curious and unique historical survival. The disintegration of the Soviet bloc at the other end of Europe indicated otherwise. There, the new-found freedom not only cleared the way for an open society and representative democracy but also unleashed long-dormant ethnic antagonisms. As Armenians and Azeris, Moldovans and Transd-niestrians, Serbs, Croats and Muslims, and Russians and Chechens slaughtered each other it was plain they were impelled by atavistic urges remarkably parallel to those fuelling the Troubles in Northern Ireland.

'As in Ulster,' William Millinship of the *Observer* reported from Azerbaijan in March 1992, 'neither side welcomes objective observers, only unqualified sympathy and support.' The physical differences between Azeris and Armenians were apparent to western journalists but the peoples of the former Yugoslavia had intermarried for centuries and share the same language. Separated only by religious affiliation and cultural traditions, the Serbs, Croats and Muslims are divided in ways similar to those tearing Protestants and Catholics asunder in Ulster. Ed Vulliamy made this comparison in the *Guardian* in January 1992:

> The sheer hate is terrifying. The mutually shared venom that divides the Croatians and Serbs is something like that which has inspired the slaughter in Northern Ireland for so long; but it is even more acrid and intense, even more deeply steeped in its bloody past – and much better supported by force of arms.

That hate caused intimidation and bloodshed on a scale which dwarfed the conflict in Ulster. During the first standoff at Drumcree in July 1995 a fearful massacre was taking place at Srebrenica and the following summer, while Northern Ireland was convulsed by a second confrontation at Drumcree, bodies were being unearthed in Bosnia, providing grim evidence that the slaughter at Srebrenica and Bukovar equalled the death toll from political and sectarian violence over more than quarter of a century in Ulster.

Since the Second World War several European governments had been successful in containing or reducing ethnic tensions by fresh constitutional arrangements. Examples include: autonomy for South Tyrol in 1972; devolved governments in Catalonia and the Basque country after Franco's death in 1975; the creation of the canton of Jura in Switzerland in 1978; a measure of self-government for Corsica in 1982; the evolution of Belgium into a federal state by 1988; and the granting of 'special status' to Transdniestria within Moldova in 1992. In Northern Ireland, however, political representatives failed to agree on a mutually acceptable constitutional compromise, partly because of lingering uncertainty about the territorial destiny of the region.

By the autumn of 1996, however, when it was apparent that community relations were as bad as anyone could remember, the paramilitaries on both sides largely stayed their hand, perhaps aware that if they had not done so, the bloodshed could very well have been on a Bosnian scale. Nevertheless, many despair of ever finding a solution capable of restoring calm and mutual respect to Ulster, a despair which brings to mind the words of an adviser to Henry VIII in the sixteenth century:

> It is a proverbe of old date, 'The pryde of Fraunce, the treason of Inglande, and the warre of Ireland, shalle never have ende.' Whiche proverbe, twycheing the warre of Irland, is lyke allwaye to contynue, withoute Godd sett in mennes brestes to fynde some newe remedye, that never was founde before.

Sinn Féin representatives demonstrate in front of Stormont: their exclusion from talks was made more certain by the ending of the IRA ceasefire in February 1996.
IRISH NEWS

SELECT BIBLIOGRAPHY

Adamson, Ian. *The Cruithin*, Bangor, 1974

Akenson, Donald Harman. *Education and Enmity: The Control of Schooling in Northern Ireland 1920–50*, Newton Abbot and New York, 1973

Arthur, Paul. *The People's Democracy 1968–73*, Belfast, 1974

Government and Politics of Northern Ireland, 2nd ed., London and New York, 1987

Arthur, Paul and Keith Jeffery. *Northern Ireland Since 1968*, Oxford, 1988

Aughey, Arthur. *Under Siege: Ulster Unionism and the Anglo-Irish Agreement*, Belfast, 1989

Bagwell, Richard. *Ireland Under the Tudors: With a Succinct Account of the Earlier History*, 3 vols, London, 1885–90

Ireland Under the Stuarts and During the Interregnum, 3 vols, London, 1909–16

Bardon, Jonathan. *The Struggle for Ireland 400–1450 AD*, Dublin, 1970

Belfast: An Illustrated History, Belfast, 1982

A History of Ulster, Belfast, 1992

Bardon, Jonathan and Stephen Conlin. *Belfast: 1000 Years*, Belfast, 1985

Barritt, Denis P. and Charles F. Carter. *The Northern Ireland Problem: A Study in Group Relations*, 2nd ed., Oxford, 1972 (1st ed. 1962)

Bartlett, Thomas and D.W. Hayton (eds). *Penal Era and Golden Age: Essays in Irish History, 1690–1800,* Belfast, 1979

Bartlett, Thomas and Keith Jeffery (eds). *A Military History of Ireland*, Cambridge, 1996

Barton, Brian. *Brookeborough: The Making of a Prime Minister*, Belfast, 1988

The Blitz: Belfast in the War Years, Belfast, 1989

Barzilay, David. *The British Army in Ulster*, 4 vols, Belfast, 1973–81

Beckett, J.C. *Protestant Dissent in Ireland, 1687–1780*, London, 1948

The Making of Modern Ireland 1603–1923, London, 1966

Bell, Jonathan and Mervyn Watson. *Irish Farming 1750–1900*, Edinburgh, 1986

Bell, Robert. *The Book of Ulster Surnames*, Belfast, 1988

Bell, Robert, Robert Johnstone and Robin Wilson (eds). *Troubled Times: Fortnight Magazine and the Troubles in Northern Ireland 1970–91*, Belfast, 1991

Benn, George. *A History of the Town of Belfast from the Earliest Times to the Close of the Eighteenth Century,* Belfast, 1877

Beresford, David. *Ten Men Dead: The Story of the 1981 Irish Hunger Strike*, London, 1987

Bew, Paul, Peter Gibbon and Henry Patterson. *Northern Ireland 1921–1994: Political Forces and Social Classes*, London, 1995

Bishop, Patrick and Eamonn Mallie. *The Provisional IRA*, London, 1989

Bolton, G.C. *The Passing of the Irish Act of Union: A Study in Parliamentary Politics*, Oxford, 1966

Bowman, John. *De Valera and the Ulster Question 1917–1973*, Oxford, 1982

Bowyer Bell, J. *The Secret Army: A History of the IRA*, Dublin, 1970

　The Irish Troubles: A Generation of Violence 1967–1992, Dublin, 1993

Boyce, D. George. *The Irish Question and British Politics 1868–1986*, London, 1988

　Nineteenth-Century Ireland: The Search for Stability, Dublin, 1990

Boyle, Kevin and Tom Hadden. *Ireland: A Positive Proposal*, Harmondsworth, 1985

Brady, Ciaran and Raymond Gillespie (eds). *Natives and Newcomers: Essays on the Making of Irish Colonial Society 1534–1641*, Dublin, 1986

Brady, Ciaran, Mary O'Dowd and Brian Walker (eds). *Ulster: An Illustrated History*, London, 1989

Brett, Charles E.B. *Buildings of Belfast 1700–1914*, London, 1967

　Housing a Divided Community, Dublin and Belfast, 1986

Bryson, Lucy and Clem McCartney. *Clashing Symbols: A Report on the Use of Flags, Anthems and Other National Symbols in Northern Ireland*, Belfast, 1994

Buckland, Patrick. *Irish Unionism: Two: Ulster Unionism and the Origins of Northern Ireland, 1886–1922*, Dublin and New York, 1973

　The Factory of Grievances: Devolved Government in Northern Ireland 1921–39, Dublin and New York, 1979

　James Craig, Lord Craigavon, Dublin, 1980

　A History of Northern Ireland, Dublin, 1981

Byrne, F.J. *Irish Kings and High-Kings*, London, 1973

Camblin, G. *The Town in Ulster*, Belfast, 1951

Cameron Report. *Disturbances in Northern Ireland: Report of the Commission Appointed by the Governor of Northern Ireland*, Belfast, Cmd 532, 1969

Campbell, Flann. *The Dissenting Voice: Protestant Democracy in Ulster from Plantation to Partition*, Belfast, 1991

Canavan, Tony. *Frontier Town: An Illustrated History of Newry*, Belfast, 1989

Carson, Douglas. *Ulster Castles and Defensive Buildings*, London, 1977

Carson, John T. *God's River in Spate: The Story of the Religious Awakening of Ulster in 1859*, Belfast, 1958

Churchill, W.S. *The World Crisis: The Aftermath*, London, 1929

Clark, Samuel and James S. Donnelly, Jr (eds). *Irish Peasants: Violence and Political Unrest 1780–1914*, Manchester, 1983

Clark, Wallace. *Rathlin – Disputed Island*, Belfast, 1971

　Linen on the Green: An Irish Mill Village 1730–1982, Belfast, 1982

Clarkson, L.A. and E.M. Crawford. *Ways to Wealth: The Cust Family of Eighteenth-Century Armagh*, Belfast, 1985

Connolly, Sean J. *Priests and People in Pre-Famine Ireland 1780–1845*, Dublin, 1982

　Religion and Society in Nineteenth-Century Ireland, Dundalk, 1985

Coote, Charles. *Statistical Survey of the County of Armagh*, Dublin, 1804

Corlett, John. *Aviation in Ulster*, Belfast, 1981

Crawford, W.H. *Domestic Industry in Ireland: The Experience of the Linen Industry*, Dublin, 1972

Curl, James Steven. *The Londonderry Plantation 1609–1914*, Chichester, 1986

Daly, Mary E. *The Famine in Ireland*, Dundalk, 1986

Darby, John. *Conflict in Northern Ireland: The Development of a Polarised Community*, Dublin and New York, 1976

Intimidation and the Control of Conflict in Northern Ireland, Dublin, 1986

Darby, John (ed.). *Northern Ireland: The Background to the Conflict*, Belfast and New York, 1983

Day, Angelique and Patrick Williams (eds). *The Ordnance Survey Memoirs of Ireland*, 13 vols, Belfast, 1990–2

de Latocnaye, Le Chevalier. *A Frenchman's Walk Through Ireland 1796–7*, translated from the French by John Stevenson, 1917; reprinted, with an introduction by John A. Gamble, Belfast, 1984

de Paor, Liam. *Divided Ulster*, Harmondsworth, 1970

Deutsch, Richard and Vivien Magowan. *Northern Ireland: A Chronology of Events 1968–74*, 3 vols, Belfast, 1973–5

Devlin, Bernadette. *The Price of My Soul*, London, 1969

Devlin, Paddy. *Yes, We Have No Bananas: Outdoor Relief in Belfast, 1920–39*, Belfast, 1981

Dickson, Charles. *Revolt in the North: Antrim and Down in 1798*, Dublin and London, 1960

Dickson, R.J. *Ulster Emigration to Colonial America 1718–1775*, London, 1966

Dillon, Martin. *The Shankill Butchers: A Case Study of Mass Murder*, London, 1989

Dolan, Liam. *The Third Earl of Leitrim*, Fanad, 1978

Land War and Eviction in Derryveagh 1840–65, Dundalk, 1980

Donnelly, James S. *Landlord and Tenant in Nineteenth-Century Ireland*, Dublin, 1973

Egan, Bowes and Vincent McCormack. *Burntollet*, London, 1969

Elliott, Marianne. *Partners in Revolution: The United Irishmen and France*, London and New Haven, 1982

Wolfe Tone: Prophet of Irish Independence, London and New Haven, 1989

Ellis, Peter Berresford. *The Boyne Water: The Battle of the Boyne, 1690*, London, 1976; reprinted Belfast, 1989

Ellis, S.G. *Tudor Ireland: Crown, Community and the Conflict of Cultures, 1470–1603*, London and New York, 1985

Evans, E. Estyn. *Mourne Country*, 3rd ed., Dundalk, 1978

The Personality of Ireland: Habitat, Heritage and History, Belfast, 1981

Fallon, Niall. *The Armada in Ireland*, London, 1978

Farrell, Michael. *Northern Ireland: The Orange State*, London, 1976

The Poor Law and the Workhouse in Belfast 1838–1948, Belfast, 1978

Arming the Protestants: The Formation of the Ulster Special Constabulary 1920–27,
    Dingle and London, 1983

Fisk, Robert. *The Point of No Return: The Strike Which Broke the British in Ulster*,
    London, 1975

In Time of War: Ireland, Ulster and the Price of Neutrality 1939–45, London, 1983

FitzGerald, Garret. *All in a Life: An Autobiography*, Dublin, 1991

Fitzpatrick, Rory. *God's Frontiersmen: The Scots-Irish Epic*, London, 1989

Flackes, W.D. *Northern Ireland: A Political Directory, 1968–79*, Dublin and
    New York, 1980

Flackes, W.D. and Sydney Elliott. *Northern Ireland: A Political Directory 1968–93*,
    Belfast, 1994

Foster, R.F. 'History and the Irish Question', *Journal of the Royal Historical Society*,
    vol. 20 (1983)

Modern Ireland 1600–1972, London, 1988

Gaffikin, Frank and Mike Morrissey. *Northern Ireland: The Thatcher Years*, London and
    New Jersey, 1990

Gillespie, Raymond. *Colonial Ulster: The Settlement of East Ulster*, Cork, 1985

Giraldus Cambrensis. *Expugnatio Hibernica: The Conquest of Ireland*, edited by
    A.B. Scott and F.X. Martin, Dublin, 1978

Glassie, Henry. *Passing the Time: Folklore and History of an Ulster Community*,
    Dublin and Philadelphia, 1982

Gray, John. *City in Revolt: James Larkin and the Belfast Dock Strike of 1907*,
    Belfast, 1985

Gribbon, Sybil. *Edwardian Belfast: A Social Profile*, Belfast, 1982

Hall, Michael. *20 Years: A Concise Chronology of Events in Ireland from 1968–1988*,
    Belfast, 1988

Hamill, Desmond. *Pig in the Middle: The Army in Northern Ireland 1969–1984*,
    London, 1985

Hand, Geoffrey J. *see Report of the Irish Boundary Commission*

Harbison, Peter. *Pre-Christian Ireland*, London, 1988

Haren, Michael and Yolande de Pontfarcy. *The Medieval Pilgrimage to St Patrick's
    Purgatory*, Enniskillen/Monaghan, 1988

Harkness, David. *Northern Ireland Since 1920*, Dublin, 1983

Harkness, David and Mary O'Dowd (eds). *The Town in Ireland*, Belfast, 1981

Harris, R.I.D., C.W. Jefferson and J.E. Spencer (eds). *The Northern Ireland Economy:
    A Comparative Study in the Economic Development of a Peripheral Region*, London
    and New York, 1990

Harris, Rosemary. *Prejudice and Tolerance in Ulster: A Study of Neighbours and 'Strangers'
    in a Border Community*, Manchester, 1972

Hayes, Maurice. *Whither Cultural Diversity?*, Community Relations Council pamphlet
    no. 2, Belfast, 1990

Minority Verdict: Experiences of a Catholic Public Servant, Belfast, 1995

Hayes-McCoy, G.A. *Scots Mercenary Forces in Ireland, 1565–1603*, Dublin and
      London, 1937
   Ulster and Other Irish Maps, c. 1600, Dublin, 1964
   Irish Battles: A Military History of Ireland, London, 1969
Heatley, Fred. *Henry Joy McCracken and His Times*, Belfast, 1967
Hill, Lord George. *Facts from Gweedore*, London, 1845
Hill, George. *An Historical Account of the MacDonnells of Antrim*, Belfast, 1873
   An Historical Account of the Plantation in Ulster 1608–20, Belfast, 1877
Holmes, R.F. *Henry Cooke*, Belfast, 1981
Jackson, Alvin. *The Ulster Party: Irish Unionists in the House of Commons, 1884–1911*,
      Oxford, 1989
   Sir Edward Carson, Dundalk, 1993
Jalland, Patricia. *The Liberals and Ireland: The Ulster Question in British Politics to 1914*,
      Brighton, 1980
Jeffery, Keith (ed.). *The Divided Province: The Troubles in Northern Ireland 1969–1985*,
      London, 1985
Johnson, David. *The Interwar Economy in Ireland*, Dundalk, 1985
Kee, Robert. *The Green Flag*, London, 1972; later published as three separate
      volumes: *The Most Distressful Country* (vol. 1), *The Bold Fenian Men* (vol. 2), and
      Ourselves Alone (vol. 3), London, 1989
Kennedy, Dennis. *The Widening Gulf: Northern Attitudes to the Independent Irish State
      1919–49*, Belfast, 1988
Kennedy, Liam. *The Modern Industrialisation of Ireland 1940–1988*, Dundalk, 1989
Kennedy, Liam and Philip Ollerenshaw (eds). *An Economic History of Ulster
      1820–1939*, Manchester, 1985
Kenny, Anthony. *The Road to Hillsborough: The Shaping of the Anglo-Irish Agreement*,
      Oxford, 1986
Kinealy, Christine. *This Great Calamity: The Irish Famine 1845–52*, Dublin, 1994
Kinsella, Thomas (trans.). *The Táin: Translated from the Irish Epic 'Táin Bó Cuailnge'*,
      Oxford, 1970
Lacy, Brian. *Archaeological Survey of County Donegal*, Lifford, 1983
   Siege City: The Story of Derry and Londonderry, Belfast, 1990
Laffan, Michael. *The Partition of Ireland 1911–1925*, Dundalk, 1983
Lee, Joseph J. *The Modernisation of Irish Society 1848–1918*, Dublin, 1973
   Ireland 1912–1985: Politics and Society, Cambridge, 1989
Livingstone, Peadar. *The Fermanagh Story*, Enniskillen, 1969
   The Monaghan Story, Enniskillen, 1980
Longford, Frank Pakenham, Earl of, and Anne McHardy. *Ulster*, London, 1981
Loughlin, James. *Gladstone: Home Rule and the Ulster Question 1882–93*,
      Dublin, 1986
Loughrey, Patrick (ed.). *The People of Ireland*, Belfast, 1988
Lydon, James (ed.). *England and Ireland in the Later Middle Ages*, Dublin, 1981

Lyons, F.S.L. *John Dillon: A Biography*, London, 1968
  Ireland Since the Famine, London, 1971
Mac Cuarta, Brian (ed.). *Ulster 1641: Aspects of the Rising*, Belfast, 1993
Mac Niocaill, Gearóid. *Ireland Before the Vikings*, Dublin, 1972
Macaulay, Revd Ambrose. *Patrick Dorrian, Bishop of Down and Connor, 1865–85*,
  Dublin, 1987
McCann, Eamonn. *War and an Irish Town*, Harmondsworth, 1974
McClean, Dr Raymond. *The Road to Bloody Sunday*, Swords, 1983
McCluskey, Conn. *Up Off Their Knees: A Commentary on the Civil Rights Movement in
  Northern Ireland*, Galway, 1989
McCutcheon, W.A. *The Industrial Archaeology of Northern Ireland*, Belfast, 1980
McEvoy, James. *Statistical Survey of the County of Tyrone*, Dublin, 1802
McGarry, John and Brendan O'Leary. *Explaining Northern Ireland: Broken Images*,
  Oxford, 1995
McGuffin, John. *Internment*, Tralee, 1973
McKittrick, David. *Despatches from Belfast*, Belfast, 1989
  Endgame: The Search for Peace in Northern Ireland, Belfast, 1994
  The Nervous Peace, Belfast, 1996
MacKnight, Thomas. *Ulster As It Is*, 2 vols, London, 1896
McMinn, J.R.B. *Against the Tide: J.B. Armour, Irish Presbyterian Minister and Home
  Ruler*, Belfast, 1985
McNeill, Mary. *The Life and Times of Mary Ann McCracken 1770–1866: A Belfast
  Panorama*, Dublin, 1960; reprinted Belfast, 1988
McNeill, T.E. *Anglo-Norman Ulster: The History and Archaeology of an Irish Barony
  1177–1400*, Edinburgh, 1980
McParlan, James. *Statistical Survey of the County of Donegal*, Dublin, 1802
Maguire, W.A. *The Downshire Estates in Ireland, 1801–45*, Oxford, 1972
  Living Like a Lord: The Second Marquis of Donegall, 1769–1844, Belfast, 1984
Maguire, W.A. (ed.). *Kings in Conflict: The Revolutionary War in Ireland and its Aftermath
  1689–1750*, Belfast, 1990
Mallie, Eamonn and David McKittrick. *The Fight for Peace: The Secret Story Behind the
  Irish Peace Process*, London, 1996
Mallory, J.P. and T.E. McNeill. *The Archaeology of Ulster: From Colonisation to
  Plantation*, Belfast, 1991
Maloney, Ed and Andy Pollak. *Paisley*, Dublin, 1986
Messenger, Betty. *Picking Up the Linen Threads: A Study in Industrial Folklore*,
  Belfast, 1980
Middlemas, Keith (ed.). *Thomas Jones: Whitehall Diary, vol. 3: Ireland 1918–1925*,
  Oxford, 1971
Miller, David W. (ed.). *Peep O' Day Boys and Defenders: Selected Documents on the
  County Armagh Disturbances*, Belfast, 1990

Moody, T.W. *The Londonderry Plantation, 1609–41: The City of London and the Plantation of Ulster*, Belfast, 1939

Morgan, Hiram. *Tyrone's Rebellion: The Outbreak of the Nine Years War in Tudor Ireland*, Dublin, 1993

Moss, Michael and John R. Hume. *Shipbuilders to the World: 125 Years of Harland and Wolff, Belfast, 1861–1986*, Belfast, 1986

Munck, Ronnie and Bill Rolston. *Belfast in the Thirties: An Oral History*, Belfast, 1987

Murphy, Desmond. *Derry, Donegal and Modern Ulster 1790–1921*, Derry, 1981

Nelson, Sarah. *Ulster's Uncertain Defenders: Protestant Political, Paramilitary and Community Groups and the Northern Ireland Conflict*, Belfast, 1984

A New History of Ireland

Vol. 2: Cosgrove, Art (ed.). *Medieval Ireland 1169–1534*, Oxford, 1987

Vol. 3: Moody, T.W., F.X. Martin and F.J. Byrne (eds). *Early Modern Ireland 1534–1691*, 2nd ed., Oxford, 1978

Vol. 4: Vaughan, W.E. and T.W. Moody (eds). *Eighteenth-Century Ireland 1691–1800*, Oxford, 1986

Vol. 5: Vaughan, W.E. (ed.). *Ireland Under the Union, 1: 1801–70*, Oxford, 1989

Vol. 9: Moody, T.W., F.X. Martin and F.J. Byrne (eds). *Maps, Genealogies, Lists: A Companion to Irish History, Part 2*, Oxford, 1984

Nicholls, Kenneth. *Gaelic and Gaelicised Ireland in the Middle Ages*, Dublin, 1972

Ó Corráin, Donncha. *Ireland Before the Normans*, Dublin, 1972

O'Connell, Maurice R. *Irish Politics and Social Conflict in the Age of the American Revolution*, Philadelphia, 1965

O'Dowd, Liam, Bill Rolston and Mike Tomlinson (eds). *Northern Ireland: Between Civil Rights and Civil War*, London, 1980

O'Farrell, P. *Ireland's English Question: Anglo-Irish Relations 1534–1970*, London, 1971

O'Malley, Padraig. *The Uncivil Wars: Ireland Today*, Belfast, 1983

Northern Ireland: Questions of Nuance, Belfast, 1990

O'Neill, K. *Family and Farm in Pre-Famine Ireland: The Parish of Killashandra*, Wisconsin, 1984

O'Neill, Terence. *Ulster at the Crossroads*, with an introduction by John Cole, London, 1969

The Autobiography of Terence O'Neill, Prime Minister of Northern Ireland 1963–1969, London, 1972

Orpen, Goddard H. *Ireland Under the Normans, 1169–1333*, 4 vols, Oxford, 1911–20; reprinted Dublin, 1968

Orr, Philip. *The Road to the Somme: Men of the Ulster Division Tell Their Story*, Belfast, 1987

Parkhill, Trevor and Sheela Speers (eds). *Kings in Conflict: Ireland in the 1690s*, Educational Resource Pack, documentary research by Patricia Hill, Donald McBride and Patricia Pauley, Belfast, 1990

Patterson, Henry. *Class Conflict and Sectarianism: The Protestant Working Class and the Belfast Labour Movement 1868–1920*, Belfast, 1980

Perceval-Maxwell, Michael. *The Scottish Migration to Ulster in the Reign of James I*, London and New York, 1973

'The Ulster rising of 1641 and the depositions', *Irish Historical Studies*, vol. 21 (1978–9)

Phoenix, Eamon. *Northern Nationalism: Nationalist Politics, Partition and the Catholic Minority in Northern Ireland, 1890–1940*, Belfast, 1994

Public Record Office of Northern Ireland. *The Act of Union; Eighteenth-Century Ulster: Emigration to North America; The Great Famine; The Penal Laws; The '98 Rebellion; The United Irishmen; The Volunteers, 1778–84*, all in the Education Facsimile Series, Belfast, n.d.

Purdie, Bob. *Politics in the Streets: The Origins of the Civil Rights Movement in Northern Ireland*, Belfast, 1990

Quinn, D.B. *The Elizabethans and the Irish*, New York, 1966

Report of the Irish Boundary Commission, with an introduction by Geoffrey J. Hand, Dublin, 1969

Robinson, Philip S. *The Plantation of Ulster: British Settlement in an Irish Landscape, 1600–1670*, Dublin and New York, 1984

Roebuck, Peter (ed.). *Plantation to Partition: Essays in Ulster History in Honour of J.L. McCracken*, Belfast, 1981

Rose, Richard. *Governing Without Consensus: An Irish Perspective*, London, 1971

Rowthorn, Bob and Naomi Wayne. *Northern Ireland: The Political Economy of Conflict*, Oxford, 1988

Ryder, Chris. *The RUC: A Force Under Fire*, London, 1989

    The Ulster Defence Regiment: An Instrument of Peace?, London, 1991

Sampson, G. Vaughan. *Statistical Survey of the County of Londonderry*, Derry, 1814

Senior, H. *Orangeism in Ireland and Britain 1795–1836*, London, 1966

Silke, John J. *Kinsale: The Spanish Intervention in Ireland at the End of the Elizabethan Wars*, Liverpool, 1970

Simms, Katharine. 'The medieval kingdom of Lough Erne', *Clogher Record*, vol. 9 (1977)

    From Kings to Warlords: The Changing Political Structure of Gaelic Ireland in the Later Middle Ages, Woodbridge and Wolfboro, 1987

Stalker, John. *Stalker*, London, 1988

Stevenson, David. *Scottish Covenanters and Irish Confederates: Scottish-Irish Relations in the Mid-Seventeenth Century*, Belfast, 1981

Stewart, A.T.Q. *The Ulster Crisis*, London, 1967

    The Narrow Ground: Aspects of Ulster, 1609–1969, London, 1977

    Edward Carson, Dublin, 1981

    The Summer Soldiers: The 1798 Rebellion in Antrim and Down, Belfast, 1995

Sunday Times Insight Team. *Ulster*, Harmondsworth, 1972

Vaughan, W.E. *Sin, Sheep and Scotsmen: John George Adair and the Derryveagh Evictions, 1861*, Belfast, 1983

  Landlords and Tenants in Ireland 1848–1904, Dundalk, 1984

Walker, Brian. *Faces of the Past*, Belfast, 1974

  Sentry Hill: An Ulster Farm and Family, Belfast, 1981

  Ulster Politics: The Formative Years 1868–86, Belfast, 1989

Walker, Graham. *The Politics of Frustration: Harry Midgley and the Failure of Labour in Northern Ireland*, Manchester, 1985

Walsh, Micheline Kerney. *Destruction by Peace: Hugh O'Neill After Kinsale*: *Glanconcadhain 1602–Rome 1616*, Armagh, 1986

Whyte, John H. *Interpreting Northern Ireland*, Oxford, 1990

Wichert, Sabine. *Northern Ireland Since 1945*, Harlow, 1991

Wilson, Gordon with Alf McCreary. *Marie: A Story From Enniskillen*, London, 1990

Wilson, Tom. *Ulster: Conflict and Consent*, Oxford, 1989

Woodham-Smith, Cecil. *The Great Hunger: Ireland 1845–1849*, London, 1989

Woodman, P.C. *Excavations at Mount Sandel 1973–77, County Londonderry*, Belfast, 1985

Wright, Frank. *Northern Ireland: A Comparative Analysis*, Dublin, 1987

INDEX

NOTE: page numbers in bold refer to illustrations.